Docker Networking Cookbook

60 practical recipes that help you gain expertise with
Docker networking and understand the underlying
constructs that make it all work

Jon Langemak

BIRMINGHAM - MUMBAI

Docker Networking Cookbook

First published: November 2016

Production reference: 1231116

Published by Packt Publishing Ltd.
Livery Place
35 Livery Street
Birmingham B3 2PB, UK.

ISBN 978-1-78646-114-8

www.packtpub.com

Credits

Author
Jon Langemak

Reviewer
Francisco Souza

Commissioning Editor
Priya Singh

Acquisition Editor
Rahul Nair

Content Development Editor
Rashmi Suvarna

Technical Editor
Mohd Riyan Khan

Copy Editor
Dipti Mankame

Project Coordinator
Judie Jose

Proofreader
Safis Editing

Indexer
Pratik Shirodkar

Graphics
Kirk D'Penha

Production Coordinator
Deepika Naik

Cover Work
Deepika Naik

About the Author

Jon Langemak has over 10 years of experience in designing, building, and maintaining high-performance networks. He is passionate about network operations, automation, and open source tooling. His current focus is on disruptive technologies and the impact they have on network operations. Outside of work, Jon blogs at `dasblinkenlichten.com` and enjoys collaborating with others in the network community on new ideas and concepts.

I would like to thank my wife for her encouragement and for tolerating the countless days of late night writing. I would also like to thank all of the amazing people in the networking community I've had the privilege to meet over the past few years. I consider myself lucky to call many of you friends and appreciate all the support and inspiration you continue to provide me. And finally, I'd like to thank my parents, who piqued my interest in computing by giving me my first computer in elementary school. Thank you for supporting my interests and ambitions; you have always been there for me.

About the Reviewer

Francisco Souza is a senior software engineer working with video publishing platforms at The New York Times. Prior to that, he worked with the open source PaaS Tsuru, created back in 2012 and later adapted to leverage Docker for container management. Francisco is also a Docker Captain, and he likes to explore topics such as concurrency, parallelism, and distributed systems.

He has also worked as a reviewer in the book *Extending Docker, Russ McKendrick, Packt publishing*.

www.PacktPub.com

eBooks, discount offers, and more

Did you know that Packt offers eBook versions of every book published, with PDF and ePub files available? You can upgrade to the eBook version at www.PacktPub.com and as a print book customer, you are entitled to a discount on the eBook copy. Get in touch with us at customercare@packtpub.com for more details.

At www.PacktPub.com, you can also read a collection of free technical articles, sign up for a range of free newsletters and receive exclusive discounts and offers on Packt books and eBooks.

https://www.packtpub.com/mapt

Get the most in-demand software skills with Mapt. Mapt gives you full access to all Packt books and video courses, as well as industry-leading tools to help you plan your personal development and advance your career.

Why Subscribe?

- ▸ Fully searchable across every book published by Packt
- ▸ Copy and paste, print, and bookmark content
- ▸ On demand and accessible via a web browser

Table of Contents

Preface

The aim of this book is to provide you with in-depth knowledge of how Docker implements container networking. Whether you use Docker every day or are just getting started, this book will introduce you to how Docker uses Linux networking primitives to network containers. Through numerous examples, we'll cover everything from the fundamentals of Linux networking to the latest Docker networking drivers. Along the way, we'll also look at integrating existing networking constructs and third-party plugins into Docker. The end goal is for you to be comfortable with the process Docker uses to provide networking capabilities to containers.

Like many open source projects, Docker is a fast-moving piece of software. At the time of publication, the most recent version of Docker was 1.12. I've done my best to ensure that the content in this book reflects the most up-to-date features and configurations based on this version. Regardless of the version, many of these features have existed in one form or another since the very early versions of Docker. So while there have been significant changes in Docker networking over the last couple of years, much of the network functionality is still implemented in the same manner. It is for this reason that I believe the majority of the content in this book will remain relevant for a long time to come.

What this book covers

Chapter 1, Linux Networking Constructs, will focus on introducing you to Linux networking primitives. Topics such as interface creation, addressing, and general connectivity will be discussed in detail. You will also be introduced to common Linux command-line syntax and tooling as it relates to Linux host network configuration. Understanding these basic constructs will greatly increase your ability to understand how Docker handles container networking.

Chapter 2, Configuring and Monitoring Docker Networks, explains the default means in which Docker handles container networking. These include bridge, host, and mapped container modes of Docker network operation. We'll also begin our exploration of how Docker handles mapping container-based services to the outside or external network. There will also be discussion around Linux host requirements for Docker networking and some of the possible Docker service-level parameters that can be modified.

Chapter 3, *User-Defined Networks*, begins our discussion on Docker user-defined networks. The advent of user-defined networks has greatly increased the flexibility of Docker networking providing the end user far more possibilities in regard to container connectivity. We'll discuss the syntax required to create user-defined networks as well as show examples of how to create user-defined bridge and overlay-based networks. Finally, we'll cover some options to isolate network segments within Docker.

Chapter 4, *Building Docker Networks*, begins with a deep dive into how Docker provides container connectivity. Starting with a container that was provisioned without a network interface, we'll cover all the steps required in order to get the container communicating on the network. We'll then move on to discuss other options to use custom bridges with Docker and cover multiple use cases related to using OVS in conjunction with Docker.

Chapter 5, *Container Linking and Docker DNS*, discusses the available options for container name resolution. This includes both the default name resolution behavior as well as the new embedded DNS server functionality that exists with user-defined networks. You will become comfortable with the process used to determine name server assignment in each of these scenarios.

Chapter 6, *Securing Container Networks*, shows a variety of features and strategies that are related to container security. You will be exposed to several options to limit the scope of container exposure and connectivity. We'll also discuss options to implement a container-based load balancer that utilizes a user-defined overlay network.

Chapter 7, *Working with Weave Net*, will be our first look at a third-party networking solution that integrates with Docker. Weave provides multiple methods to integrate with Docker including its own CLI tool as well as a full-blown Docker driver. An example of using Weave to provide network isolation will also be demonstrated.

Chapter 8, *Working with Flannel*, examines the third-party network plugin built by the team at CoreOS. Flannel is an interesting example of how a networking plugin can be integrated into Docker just by changing Docker service-level parameters. In addition to providing overlay type networking, Flannel also offers a host gateway backend that allows the hosts to route directly to each other so long as they meet certain requirements.

Chapter 9, *Exploring Network Features*, focuses on how newer networking features are integrated into Docker. We'll examine how you can gain access to and test these new features by evaluating different versions of Docker engine. Through the course of the chapter, we'll also examine the now integrated MacVLAN network driver as well as the IPVLAN network driver, which is still in testing.

Chapter 10, *Leveraging IPv6*, covers IPv6 and Docker's support of it. IPv6 is a big topic and one that deserves a great amount of attention considering the current state of IPv4. In this chapter, we'll review some of the basics of working with IPv6 on a Linux system. We'll then spend some time reviewing how Docker supports IPv6 and discuss some of the options you have around deployment.

Chapter 11, Troubleshooting Docker Networks, examines some of the common steps you might take when troubleshooting Docker networking. The focus will be on validating the configuration, but you'll also learn some steps you can take to prove that the configuration is working as intended.

What you need for this book

All of the labs shown in this book were performed on Ubuntu Linux hosts running version 16.04 and Docker engine version 1.12.

 You'll note that the network interface names used on the hosts in this book use the familiar eth (eth0, eth1, and so on) naming convention. While this is still the standard on many versions of Linux, newer versions that run systemd (such as Ubuntu 16.04) now use something called Predictable Network Interface Names (PNIN). With PNIN, the network interface uses more predictable names based on the information about the interface itself. In these cases, the interface names will show up using different names, such as ens1 or ens32. For the sake of making the content in this book easier to understand, I chose to disable PNIN on all of the hosts. If you're interested in doing the same instructions can be found by doing a web search for 'Ubuntu disable predictable interface names'. If you chose not to, just know that your interface names will show up differently than mine do in the examples.

The requirements for labs shown in this book are included at the beginning of each recipe. Later recipes may build on configurations shown in earlier recipes.

Who this book is for

This book is for people who are interested in learning more about how Docker implements container networking. While the recipes cover many of the basics required to get you up and running, it is assumed that you have a working knowledge of Linux and Docker. It is also assumed that you have a basic understanding of networking.

Conventions

In this book, you will find a number of text styles that distinguish between different kinds of information. Here are some examples of these styles and an explanation of their meaning.

Code words in text, file paths, and executables are shown as follows:

"Interfaces on the host can be seen by using the `ip link show` command".

Any command-line input or output is written as follows:

```
user@net1:~$ sudo ifdown eth1 && sudo ifup eth1
```

When possible any multiline command-line input will be written using the Linux line continuation method of including a trailing \ at the end of the line to be continued:

```
user@net1:~$ sudo ip netns exec ns_1 ip link set \
dev edge_veth1 master edge_bridge1
```

In some cases command-line output will also be multiline. In those cases, formatting was done in an effort to make the output easily readable.

When we wish to draw your attention to a particular part of command-line output, the relevant lines or items are set in bold:

```
user@net2:~$ ip addr show eth0
2: eth0: <BROADCAST,MULTICAST,UP,LOWER_UP> mtu 1500 qdisc pfifo_fast
state UP group default qlen 1000
    link/ether 00:0c:29:59:ca:ca brd ff:ff:ff:ff:ff:ff
    inet 172.16.10.2/26 brd 172.16.10.63 scope global eth0
       valid_lft forever preferred_lft forever
    inet6 fe80::20c:29ff:fe59:caca/64 scope link
       valid_lft forever preferred_lft forever
user@net2:~$
```

 Warnings or important notes appear in a box like this.

Reader feedback

Feedback from our readers is always welcome. Let us know what you think about this book— what you liked or disliked. Reader feedback is important for us as it helps us develop titles that you will really get the most out of.

To send us general feedback, simply e-mail feedback@packtpub.com, and mention the book's title in the subject of your message.

If there is a topic that you have expertise in and you are interested in either writing or contributing to a book, see our author guide at www.packtpub.com/authors.

Customer support

Now that you are the proud owner of a Packt book, we have a number of things to help you to get the most from your purchase.

Errata

Although we have taken every care to ensure the accuracy of our content, mistakes do happen. If you find a mistake in one of our books—maybe a mistake in the text or the code—we would be grateful if you could report this to us. By doing so, you can save other readers from frustration and help us improve subsequent versions of this book. If you find any errata, please report them by visiting `http://www.packtpub.com/submit-errata`, selecting your book, clicking on the **Errata Submission Form** link, and entering the details of your errata. Once your errata are verified, your submission will be accepted and the errata will be uploaded to our website or added to any list of existing errata under the Errata section of that title.

To view the previously submitted errata, go to `https://www.packtpub.com/books/content/support` and enter the name of the book in the search field. The required information will appear under the **Errata** section.

Piracy

Piracy of copyrighted material on the Internet is an ongoing problem across all media. At Packt, we take the protection of our copyright and licenses very seriously. If you come across any illegal copies of our works in any form on the Internet, please provide us with the location address or website name immediately so that we can pursue a remedy.

Please contact us at `copyright@packtpub.com` with a link to the suspected pirated material.

We appreciate your help in protecting our authors and our ability to bring you valuable content.

Questions

If you have a problem with any aspect of this book, you can contact us at `questions@packtpub.com`, and we will do our best to address the problem.

1
Linux Networking Constructs

In this chapter, we will cover the following recipes:

- ► Working with interfaces and addresses
- ► Configuring Linux host routing
- ► Exploring bridges
- ► Making connections
- ► Exploring network namespaces

Introduction

Linux is a powerful operating system with many robust networking constructs. Much like any networking technology, they are powerful individually but become much more powerful when combined in creative ways. Docker is a great example of a tool that combines many of the individual components of the Linux network stack into a complete solution. While Docker manages most of this for you, it's still helpful to know your way around when looking at the Linux networking components that Docker uses.

In this chapter, we'll spend some time looking at these constructs individually outside of Docker. We'll learn how to make network configuration changes on Linux hosts and validate the current state of the network configuration. While this chapter is not dedicated to Docker itself, it is important to understand the primitives for later chapters, where we discuss how Docker uses these constructs to network containers.

Working with interfaces and addresses

Understanding how Linux handles networking is an integral part of understanding how Docker handles networking. In this recipe, we'll focus on Linux networking basics by learning how to define and manipulate interfaces and IP addresses on a Linux host. To demonstrate the configuration, we'll start building a lab topology in this recipe and continue it through the other recipes in this chapter.

Getting ready

In order to view and manipulate networking settings, you'll want to ensure that you have the `iproute2` toolset installed. If it's not present on the system, it can be installed using the following command:

```
sudo apt-get install iproute2
```

In order to make network changes to the host, you'll also need root-level access.

For the purpose of demonstration in this chapter, we'll be using a simple lab topology. The initial network layout of the host looks like this:

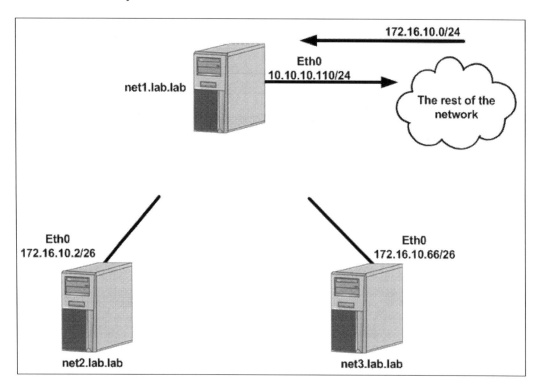

In this case, we have three hosts, each with a single eth0 interface already defined:

- ▶ net1: 10.10.10.110/24 with a default gateway of 10.10.10.1
- ▶ net2: 172.16.10.2/26
- ▶ net3: 172.16.10.66/26

How to do it...

The network configuration on most end hosts is generally limited to the IP address, the subnet mask, and the default gateway of a single interface. This is because most hosts are network endpoints offering a discrete set of services on a single IP interface. But what happens if we want to define more interfaces or manipulate the existing one? To answer that question, let's first look at simple single-homed server such as net2 or net3 in the preceding example.

On Ubuntu hosts, all of the interface configuration is done in the /etc/network/ interfaces file. Let's examine that file on the host net2:

```
# The loopback network interface
auto lo
iface lo inet loopback


# The primary network interface
auto eth0
iface eth0 inet static
        address 172.16.10.2
        netmask 255.255.255.192
```

We can see that this file defines two interfaces—the local loopback interface and the interface eth0. The eth0 interface defines the following information:

- ▶ address: The IP address of the hosts interface
- ▶ netmask : The subnet mask associated with the IP interface

The information in this file will be processed each time the interface attempts to come into the up or operational state. We can validate that this configuration file was processed at system boot by checking the current IP address of the interface eth0 with the ip addr show <interface name> command:

```
user@net2:~$ ip addr show eth0
2: eth0: <BROADCAST,MULTICAST,UP,LOWER_UP> mtu 1500 qdisc pfifo_fast
state UP group default qlen 1000
    link/ether 00:0c:29:59:ca:ca brd ff:ff:ff:ff:ff:ff
    inet 172.16.10.2/26 brd 172.16.10.63 scope global eth0
```

```
        valid_lft forever preferred_lft forever
    inet6 fe80::20c:29ff:fe59:caca/64 scope link
        valid_lft forever preferred_lft forever
user@net2:~$
```

Now that we've reviewed a single-homed configuration, let's take a look and see what it would take to configure multiple interfaces on a single host. As things stand, the net1 host is the only host that has any sort of reachability off its local subnet. This is because it has a defined default gateway pointing back to the rest of the network. In order to make net2 and net3 reachable we need to find a way to connect them back to the rest of the network as well. To do this, let's assume that the host net1 has two additional network interfaces that we can connect directly to hosts net2 and net3:

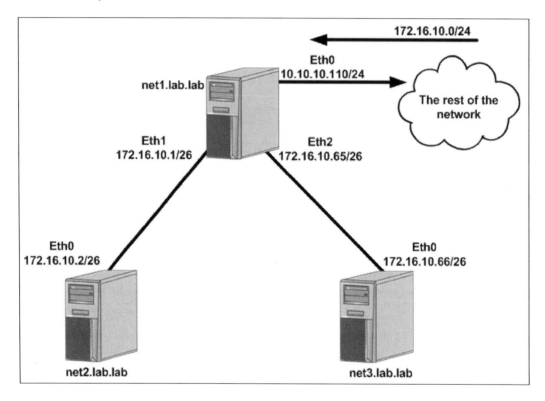

Let's walk through how to configure additional interfaces and IP addresses on the net1 to complete the topology.

The first thing we want to do is verify that we have additional interfaces available to work with on `net1`. To do this, we would use the `ip link show` command:

```
user@net1:~$ ip link show
1: lo: <LOOPBACK,UP,LOWER_UP> mtu 65536 qdisc noqueue state UNKNOWN mode
DEFAULT group default
    link/loopback 00:00:00:00:00:00 brd 00:00:00:00:00:00
2: eth0: <BROADCAST,MULTICAST,UP,LOWER_UP> mtu 1500 qdisc pfifo_fast
state UP mode DEFAULT group default qlen 1000
    link/ether 00:0c:29:2d:dd:79 brd ff:ff:ff:ff:ff:ff
3: eth1: <BROADCAST,MULTICAST> mtu 1500 qdisc noop state DOWN mode
DEFAULT group default qlen 1000
    link/ether 00:0c:29:2d:dd:83 brd ff:ff:ff:ff:ff:ff
4: eth2: <BROADCAST,MULTICAST> mtu 1500 qdisc noop state DOWN mode
DEFAULT group default qlen 1000
    link/ether 00:0c:29:2d:dd:8d brd ff:ff:ff:ff:ff:ff
user@net1:~$
```

We can see from the output that in addition to the `eth0` interface, we also have interfaces `eth1` and `eth2` available to us. To see which interfaces have IP addresses associated with them, we can use the `ip address show` command:

```
user@net1:~$ ip address show
1: lo: <LOOPBACK,UP,LOWER_UP> mtu 65536 qdisc noqueue state UNKNOWN group
default
    link/loopback 00:00:00:00:00:00 brd 00:00:00:00:00:00
    inet 127.0.0.1/8 scope host lo
       valid_lft forever preferred_lft forever
    inet6 ::1/128 scope host
       valid_lft forever preferred_lft forever
2: eth0: <BROADCAST,MULTICAST,UP,LOWER_UP> mtu 1500 qdisc pfifo_fast
state UP group default qlen 1000
    link/ether 00:0c:29:2d:dd:79 brd ff:ff:ff:ff:ff:ff
    inet 10.10.10.110/24 brd 10.10.10.255 scope global eth0
       valid_lft forever preferred_lft forever
    inet6 fe80::20c:29ff:fe2d:dd79/64 scope link
       valid_lft forever preferred_lft forever
3: eth1: <BROADCAST,MULTICAST> mtu 1500 qdisc noop state DOWN group
default qlen 1000
```

```
    link/ether 00:0c:29:2d:dd:83 brd ff:ff:ff:ff:ff:ff
4: eth2: <BROADCAST,MULTICAST> mtu 1500 qdisc noop state DOWN group
default qlen 1000
    link/ether 00:0c:29:2d:dd:8d brd ff:ff:ff:ff:ff:ff
user@net1:~$
```

The preceding output proves that we currently only have a single IP address allocated on the interface eth0. This means that we can use the interface eth1 for connectivity to server net2 and eth2 for connectivity to the server net3.

There are two ways we can configure these new interfaces. The first is to update the network configuration file on net1 with the relevant IP address information. Let's do that for the link facing the host net2. To configure this connectivity, simply edit the file /etc/network/interfaces and add the relevant configuration for both interfaces. The finished configuration should look like this:

```
# The primary network interface
auto eth0
iface eth0 inet static
        address 10.10.10.110
        netmask 255.255.255.0
        gateway 10.10.10.1
auto eth1
iface eth1 inet static
        address 172.16.10.1
        netmask 255.255.255.192
```

Once the file is saved, you need to find a way to tell the system to reload the configuration file. One way to do this would be to reload the system. A simpler method would be to reload the interfaces. For instance, we could execute the following commands to reload interface eth1:

```
user@net1:~$ sudo ifdown eth1 && sudo ifup eth1
ifdown: interface eth1 not configured
user@net1:~$
```

> While not required in this case, bringing the interface down and up at the same time is a good habit to get into. This ensures that you don't cut yourself off if you take down the interface you're managing the host from.

In some cases, you may find that this method of updating the interface configuration doesn't work as expected. Depending on your version of Linux, you may experience a condition where the previous IP address is not removed from the interface causing the interface to have multiple IP addresses. To resolve this, you can manually delete the old IP address or alternatively reboot the host, which will prevent legacy configurations from persisting.

After the commands are executed, we should be able to see that the interface `eth1` is now properly addressed:

```
user@net1:~$ ip addr show dev eth1
3: eth1: <BROADCAST,MULTICAST,UP,LOWER_UP> mtu 1500 qdisc pfifo_fast
state UP group default qlen 1000
    link/ether 00:0c:29:2d:dd:83 brd ff:ff:ff:ff:ff:ff
    inet 172.16.10.1/26 brd 172.16.10.63 scope global eth1
        valid_lft forever preferred_lft forever
    inet6 fe80::20c:29ff:fe2d:dd83/64 scope link
        valid_lft forever preferred_lft forever
user@net1:~$
```

To configure the interface `eth2` on host `net1`, we'll use a different approach. Rather than relying on configuration files, we'll use the `iproute2` command-line to update the configuration of the interface. To do this, we simply execute the following commands:

```
user@net1:~$ sudo ip address add 172.16.10.65/26 dev eth2
user@net1:~$ sudo ip link set eth2 up
```

It should be noted here that this configuration is not persistent. That is, since it's not part of a configuration file that's loaded at system initialization, this configuration will be lost on reboot. This is the same case for any network-related configuration done manually with the `iproute2` or other command-line toolsets.

It is the best practice to configure interface information and addressing in the network configuration file. Altering interface configuration outside of the configuration file is done in these recipes for the purpose of example only.

Up to this point, we've only modified existing interfaces by adding IP information to them. We have not actually added a new interface to any of the systems. Adding interfaces is a fairly common task, and, as later recipes will show, there are a variety of interface types that can be added. For now, let's focus on adding what Linux refers to as dummy interfaces. Dummy interfaces act like loopback interfaces in networking and describe an interface type that is always up and online. Interfaces are defined or created by using the `ip link add` syntax. You then specify a name and define what type of interface it is you are defining. For instance, let's define a dummy interface on the hosts `net2` and `net3`:

```
user@net2:~$ sudo ip link add dummy0 type dummy
user@net2:~$ sudo ip address add 172.16.10.129/26 dev dummy0
user@net2:~$ sudo ip link set dummy0 up

user@net3:~$ sudo ip link add dummy0 type dummy
user@net3:~$ sudo ip address add 172.16.10.193/26 dev dummy0
user@net3:~$ sudo ip link set dummy0 up
```

After defining the interface, each host should be able to ping their own `dummy0` interface:

```
user@net2:~$ ping 172.16.10.129 -c 2
PING 172.16.10.129 (172.16.10.129) 56(84) bytes of data.
64 bytes from 172.16.10.129: icmp_seq=1 ttl=64 time=0.030 ms
64 bytes from 172.16.10.129: icmp_seq=2 ttl=64 time=0.031 ms
--- 172.16.10.129 ping statistics ---
2 packets transmitted, 2 received, 0% packet loss, time 999ms
rtt min/avg/max/mdev = 0.030/0.030/0.031/0.005 ms
user@net2:~$

user@net3:~$ ping 172.16.10.193 -c 2
PING 172.16.10.193 (172.16.10.193) 56(84) bytes of data.
64 bytes from 172.16.10.193: icmp_seq=1 ttl=64 time=0.035 ms
```

```
64 bytes from 172.16.10.193: icmp_seq=2 ttl=64 time=0.032 ms
--- 172.16.10.193 ping statistics ---
2 packets transmitted, 2 received, 0% packet loss, time 999ms
rtt min/avg/max/mdev = 0.032/0.033/0.035/0.006 ms
user@net3:~$
```

 You might be wondering why we had to turn up the dummy0 interface if they're considered to be always up. In reality, the interface is reachable without turning up the interface. However, the local route for the interface will not appear in the systems routing table without turning the interface up.

Configuring Linux host routing

Once you've defined new IP interfaces, the next step is to configure routing. In most cases, Linux host routing configuration is limited solely to specifying a host's default gateway. While that's typically as far as most need to go, a Linux host is capable of being a full-fledged router. In this recipe, we'll learn how to interrogate a Linux hosts routing table as well as manually configure routes.

Getting ready

In order to view and manipulate networking settings, you'll want to ensure that you have the iproute2 toolset installed. If not present on the system, it can be installed by using the following command:

```
sudo apt-get install iproute2
```

In order to make network changes to the host, you'll also need root-level access. This recipe will continue the lab topology from the previous recipe. We left the topology looking like this after the previous recipe:

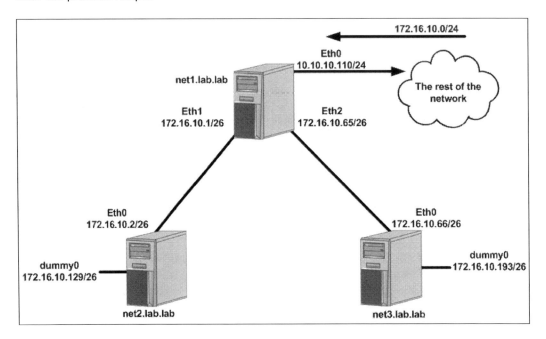

How to do it...

Despite Linux hosts being capable of routing, they do not do so by default. In order for routing to occur, we need to modify a kernel-level parameter to enable IP forwarding. We can check the current state of the setting a couple of different ways:

▶ By using the `sysctl` command:

```
sysctl net.ipv4.ip_forward
```

▶ By querying the `/proc/` filesystem directly:

```
more /proc/sys/net/ipv4/ip_forward
```

In either case, if the returned value is 1, IP forwarding is enabled. If you do not receive a 1, you'll need to enable IP forwarding in order for the Linux host to route packets through the system. You can manually enable IP forwarding by using the `sysctl` command or again by directly interacting with the `/proc/` filesystem:

```
sudo sysctl -w net.ipv4.ip_forward=1
echo 1 | sudo tee /proc/sys/net/ipv4/ip_forward
```

While this enables IP forwarding on the fly, this setting does not persist through a reboot. To make the setting persistent, you need to modify `/etc/sysctl.conf`, uncomment the line for IP forwarding, and ensure it's set to `1`:

```
…<Additional output removed for brevity>…
# Uncomment the next line to enable packet forwarding for IPv4
net.ipv4.ip_forward=1
…<Additional output removed for brevity>…
```

> You may note that we're only modifying settings related to IPv4 at this time. Don't worry; we'll cover IPv6 and Docker networking later on in *Chapter 10, Leveraging IPv6*.

Once we've verified forwarding is configured, let's look at the routing table on all three lab hosts by using the `ip route show` command:

```
user@net1:~$ ip route show
default via 10.10.10.1 dev eth0
10.10.10.0/24 dev eth0   proto kernel   scope link   src 10.10.10.110
172.16.10.0/26 dev eth1   proto kernel   scope link   src 172.16.10.1
172.16.10.64/26 dev eth2   proto kernel   scope link   src 172.16.10.65


user@net2:~$ ip route show
172.16.10.0/26 dev eth0   proto kernel   scope link   src 172.16.10.2
172.16.10.128/26 dev dummy0   proto kernel   scope link   src 172.16.10.129


user@net3:~$ ip route show
172.16.10.64/26 dev eth0   proto kernel   scope link   src 172.16.10.66
172.16.10.192/26 dev dummy0   proto kernel   scope link   src 172.16.10.193
```

There are a couple of interesting items to note here. First off, we notice that the hosts have routes listed that are associated with each of their IP interfaces. Based on the subnet mask associated with the interface, the host can determine the network the interface is associated with. This route is inherent and would be said to be directly connected. Directly connected routes are how the system knows what IP destinations are directly connected versus which ones need to be forwarded to a next hop to reach a remote destination.

Second, in the last recipe, we added two additional interfaces to the host net1 to provide connectivity to hosts net2 and net3. However, this alone only allows net1 to talk to net2 and net3. If we want net2 and net3 to be reachable via the rest of the network, they'll need a default route pointing at their respective interfaces on net1. Once again, let's do this in two separate manners. On net2, we'll update the network configuration file and reload the interface, and on net3, we'll add the default route directly through the command line.

On host net2, update the file /etc/network/interfaces and add a gateway on the eth0 interface pointing at the connected interface on the host net1:

```
# The primary network interface
auto eth0
iface eth0 inet static
        address 172.16.10.2
        netmask 255.255.255.192
        gateway 172.16.10.1
```

To activate the new configuration, we'll reload the interface:

```
user@net2:~$ sudo ifdown eth0 && sudo ifup eth0
```

Now we should be able to see the default route in the net2 host's routing table pointing out of eth0 at the net1 host's directly connected interface (172.16.10.1):

```
user@net2:~$ ip route show
default via 172.16.10.1 dev eth0
172.16.10.0/26 dev eth0   proto kernel   scope link   src 172.16.10.2
172.16.10.128/26 dev dummy0   proto kernel   scope link   src 172.16.10.129
user@net2:~$
```

On the host net3, we'll use the iproute2 toolset to modify the hosts routing table dynamically. To do this, we'll execute the following command:

```
user@net3:~$ sudo ip route add default via 172.16.10.65
```

 Note that we use the keyword default. This represents the default gateway or the destination of 0.0.0.0/0 in **Classless Inter-domain Routing (CIDR)** notation. We could have executed the command using the 0.0.0.0/0 syntax as well.

After executing the command, we'll check the routing table to make sure that we now have a default route pointing at net1 (`172.16.10.65`):

```
user@net3:~$ ip route show
default via 172.16.10.65 dev eth0
172.16.10.64/26 dev eth0   proto kernel   scope link   src 172.16.10.66
172.16.10.192/26 dev dummy0   proto kernel   scope link   src 172.16.10.193
user@net3:~$
```

At this point, the hosts and the rest of the network should have full network reachability to all of their physical interfaces. However, the dummy interfaces created in the previous recipe are not reachable by any other hosts than the ones they are defined on. In order to make those reachable, we're going to need to add some static routes.

The dummy interface networks are `172.16.10.128/26` and `172.16.10.192/26`. Because these networks are part of the larger `172.16.10.0/24` summary, the rest of the network already knows to route to the net1 host's `10.10.10.110` interface to get to these prefixes. However, net1 currently doesn't know where those prefixes live and will, in turn, loop the traffic right back to where it came from following its default route. To solve this, we need to add two static routes on net1:

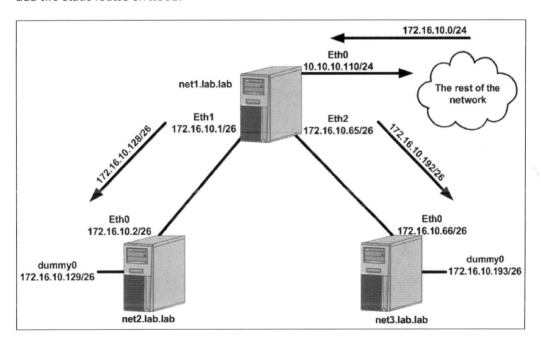

We can add these routes ad hoc through the `iproute2` command-line tools or we can add them in a more persistent fashion as part of the host's network script. Let's do one of each:

To add the `172.16.10.128/26` route pointing at `net2`, we'll use the command-line tool:

```
user@net1:~$ sudo ip route add 172.16.10.128/26 via 172.16.10.2
```

As you can see, adding manual routes is done through the `ip route add` command syntax. The subnet that needs to be reached is specified along with the associated next hop address. The command takes effect immediately as the host populates the routing table instantly to reflect the change:

```
user@net1:~$ ip route
default via 10.10.10.1 dev eth0
10.10.10.0/24 dev eth0   proto kernel   scope link   src 10.10.10.110
172.16.10.0/26 dev eth1   proto kernel   scope link   src 172.16.10.1
172.16.10.64/26 dev eth2   proto kernel   scope link   src 172.16.10.65
172.16.10.128/26 via 172.16.10.2 dev eth1
user@net1:~$
```

If we wish to make a route persistent, we can allocate it as a `post-up` interface configuration. The `post-up` interface configurations take place directly after an interface is loaded. If we want the route `172.16.10.192/26` to be added to the hosts routing table the instant `eth2` comes online, we can edit the `/etc/network/interfaces` configuration script as follows:

```
auto eth2
iface eth2 inet static
        address 172.16.10.65
        netmask 255.255.255.192
        post-up ip route add 172.16.10.192/26 via 172.16.10.66
```

After adding the configuration, we can reload the interface to force the configuration file to reprocess:

```
user@net1:~$ sudo ifdown eth2 && sudo ifup eth2
```

In some cases, the host may not process the `post-up` command because we defined the address on the interface manually in an earlier recipe. Deleting the IP address before reloading the interface would resolve this issue; however, in these cases, rebooting the host is the easiest (and cleanest) course of action.

And our routing table will now show both routes:

```
user@net1:~$ ip route
default via 10.10.10.1 dev eth0
10.10.10.0/24 dev eth0  proto kernel  scope link  src 10.10.10.110
172.16.10.0/26 dev eth1  proto kernel  scope link  src 172.16.10.1
172.16.10.64/26 dev eth2  proto kernel  scope link  src 172.16.10.65
172.16.10.128/26 via 172.16.10.2 dev eth1
172.16.10.192/26 via 172.16.10.66 dev eth2
user@net1:~$
```

To verify this is working as expected, let's do some testing from a remote workstation that's attempting to ping the dummy interface on the host net2 (172.16.10.129). Assuming the workstation is connected to an interface that's not on the external network, the flow might look like this:

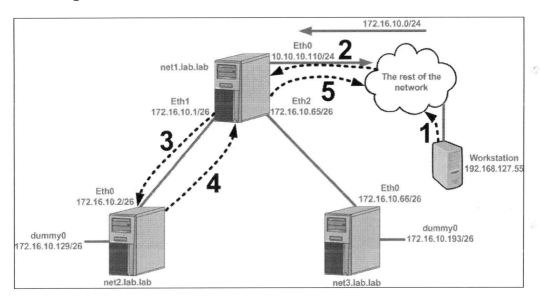

1. A workstation with an IP address of 192.168.127.55 is attempting to reach the dummy interface connected to net2 at its IP address of 172.16.10.129. The workstation sends the traffic towards its default gateway since the destination it's looking for is not directly connected.

2. The network has a route for 172.16.10.0/24 pointing at net1's eth0 interface (10.10.10.110). The destination IP address (172.16.10.129) is a member of that larger prefix, so the network forwards the workstation's traffic on to the host net1.

3. The net1 host examines the traffic, interrogates its routing table, and determines that it has a route for that prefix pointing towards the net2 with a next hop of 172.16.10.2.

4. The net2 receives the request, realizes that the dummy interface is directly connected, and attempts to send a reply back to the workstation. Not having a specific route for the destination of 192.168.127.55, the host net2 sends its reply to its default gateway, which is net1 (172.16.10.1).

5. Similarly, net1 does not have a specific route for the destination of 192.168.127.55, so it forwards the traffic back to the network via its default gateway. It is assumed that the network has reachability to return the traffic to the workstation.

In the case that we'd like to remove statically defined routes, we can do so with the ip route delete subcommand. For instance, here's an example of adding a route and then deleting it:

```
user@net1:~$ sudo ip route add 172.16.10.128/26 via 172.16.10.2
user@net1:~$ sudo ip route delete 172.16.10.128/26
```

Notice how we only need to specify the destination prefix when deleting the route, not the next hop.

Exploring bridges

Bridges in Linux are a key building block for network connectivity. Docker uses them extensively in many of its own network drivers that are included with docker-engine. Bridges have been around for a long time and are, in most cases, very similar to a physical network switch. Bridges in Linux can act like layer 2 or layer 3 bridges.

Layer 2 versus layer 3

The nomenclature refers to different layers of the OSI network model. Layer 2 represents the **data link layer** and is associated with switching frames between hosts. Layer 3 represents the **network layer** and is associated with routing packets across the network. The major difference between the two is switching versus routing. A layer 2 switch is capable of sending frames between hosts on the same network but is not capable of routing them based on IP information. If you wish to route between two hosts on different networks or subnets, you'll need a layer 3 capable device that can route between the two subnets. Another way to look at this is that layer 2 switches can only deal with MAC addresses and layer 3 devices can deal with IP addresses.

By default, Linux bridges are layer 2 constructs. In this manner, they are often referred to as protocol independent. That is, any number of higher level (layer 3) protocols can run on the same bridge implementation. However, you can also assign an IP address to a bridge that turns it into a layer 3 capable networking construct. In this recipe, we'll show you how to create, manage, and inspect Linux bridges by walking through a couple of examples.

Getting ready

In order to view and manipulate networking settings, you'll want to ensure that you have the `iproute2` toolset installed. If not present on the system, it can be installed by using the following command:

```
sudo apt-get install iproute2
```

In order to make network changes to the host, you'll also need root-level access. This recipe will continue the lab topology from the previous recipe. All of the prerequisites mentioned earlier still apply.

How to do it...

To demonstrate how bridges work, let's consider making a slight change to the lab topology we've been working with:

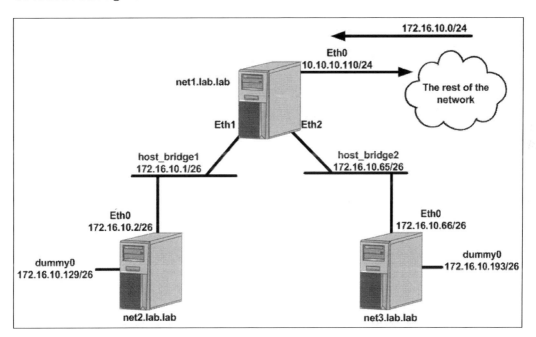

Rather than having the servers directly connect to each other via physical interfaces, we'll instead leverage bridges on the host net1 for connectivity to downstream hosts. Previously, we relied on a one-to-one mapping for connections between net1 and any other hosts. This meant that we'd need a unique subnet and IP address configuration for each physical interface. While that's certainly doable, it's not very practical. Leveraging bridge interfaces rather than standard interfaces affords us some flexibility we didn't have in the earlier configurations. We can assign a single IP address to a bridge interface and then plumb many physical connections into the same bridge. For example, a net4 host could be added to the topology and its interface on net1 could simply be added to host_bridge2. That would allow it to use the same gateway (172.16.10.65) as net3. So while the physical cabling requirement for adding hosts won't change, this does prevent us from having to define one-to-one IP address mappings for each host.

 From the perspective of the hosts net2 and net3, nothing will change when we reconfigure to use bridges.

Since we're changing how we define the net1 host's eth1 and eth2 interface, we'll start by flushing their configuration:

```
user@net1:~$ sudo ip address flush dev eth1
user@net1:~$ sudo ip address flush dev eth2
```

Flushing the interface simply clears any IP-related configuration off of the interface. The next thing we have to do is to create the bridges themselves. The syntax we use is much like we saw in the previous recipe when we created the dummy interfaces. We use the ip link add command and specify a type of bridge:

```
user@net1:~$ sudo ip link add host_bridge1 type bridge
user@net1:~$ sudo ip link add host_bridge2 type bridge
```

After creating the bridges, we can verify that they exist by examining the available interfaces with the ip link show <interface> command:

```
user@net1:~$ ip link show host_bridge1
5: host_bridge1: <BROADCAST,MULTICAST> mtu 1500 qdisc noop state DOWN
mode DEFAULT group default
    link/ether f6:f1:57:72:28:a7 brd ff:ff:ff:ff:ff:ff
user@net1:~$ ip link show host_bridge2
6: host_bridge2: <BROADCAST,MULTICAST> mtu 1500 qdisc noop state DOWN
mode DEFAULT group default
    link/ether be:5e:0b:ea:4c:52 brd ff:ff:ff:ff:ff:ff
user@net1:~$
```

Next, we want to make them layer 3 aware, so we assign an IP address to the bridge interface. This is very similar to how we assigned IP addressing to physical interfaces in previous recipes:

```
user@net1:~$ sudo ip address add 172.16.10.1/26 dev host_bridge1
user@net1:~$ sudo ip address add 172.16.10.65/26 dev host_bridge2
```

We can verify that the IP addresses were assigned by using the `ip addr show dev <interface>` command:

```
user@net1:~$ ip addr show dev host_bridge1
5: host_bridge1: <BROADCAST,MULTICAST> mtu 1500 qdisc noop state DOWN
group default
    link/ether f6:f1:57:72:28:a7 brd ff:ff:ff:ff:ff:ff
    inet 172.16.10.1/26 scope global host_bridge1
       valid_lft forever preferred_lft forever
user@net1:~$ ip addr show dev host_bridge2
6: host_bridge2: <BROADCAST,MULTICAST> mtu 1500 qdisc noop state DOWN
group default
    link/ether be:5e:0b:ea:4c:52 brd ff:ff:ff:ff:ff:ff
    inet 172.16.10.65/26 scope global host_bridge2
       valid_lft forever preferred_lft forever
user@net1:~$
```

The next step is to bind the physical interfaces associated with each downstream host to the correct bridge. In our case, we want the host net2, which is connected to net1's eth1 interface to be part of the bridge host_bridge1. Similarly, we want the host net3, which is connected to net1's eth2 interface, to be part of the bridge host_bridge2. Using the `ip link set` subcommand, we can define the bridges to be the masters of the physical interfaces:

```
user@net1:~$ sudo ip link set dev eth1 master host_bridge1
user@net1:~$ sudo ip link set dev eth2 master host_bridge2
```

We can verify that the interfaces were successfully bound to the bridge by using the `bridge link show` command.

 The `bridge` command is part of the `iproute2` package and is used to validate bridge configuration.

```
user@net1:~$ bridge link show
3: eth1 state UP : <BROADCAST,MULTICAST,UP,LOWER_UP> mtu 1500 master
host_bridge1 state forwarding priority 32 cost 4
```

```
4: eth2 state UP : <BROADCAST,MULTICAST,UP,LOWER_UP> mtu 1500 master
host_bridge2 state forwarding priority 32 cost 4
user@net1:~$
```

Finally, we need to turn up the bridge interfaces as they are, by default, created in a down state:

```
user@net1:~$ sudo ip link set host_bridge1 up
user@net1:~$ sudo ip link set host_bridge2 up
```

Once again, we can now check the link status of the bridges to verify that they came up successfully:

```
user@net1:~$ ip link show host_bridge1
5: host_bridge1: <BROADCAST,MULTICAST,UP,LOWER_UP> mtu 1500 qdisc noqueue
state UP mode DEFAULT group default
    link/ether 00:0c:29:2d:dd:83 brd ff:ff:ff:ff:ff:ff
user@net1:~$ ip link show host_bridge2
6: host_bridge2: <BROADCAST,MULTICAST,UP,LOWER_UP> mtu 1500 qdisc noqueue
state UP mode DEFAULT group default
    link/ether 00:0c:29:2d:dd:8d brd ff:ff:ff:ff:ff:ff
user@net1:~$
```

At this point, you should once again be able to reach the hosts net2 and net3. However, the dummy interfaces are now unreachable. This is because the routes for the dummy interfaces were automatically withdrawn after we flushed interface eth1 and eth2. Removing the IP addresses from those interfaces made the next hops used to reach the dummy interfaces unreachable. It is common for a device to withdraw a route from its routing table when the next hop becomes unreachable. We can add them again rather easily:

```
user@net1:~$ sudo ip route add 172.16.10.128/26 via 172.16.10.2
user@net1:~$ sudo ip route add 172.16.10.192/26 via 172.16.10.66
```

Now that everything is working again, we can perform some extra steps to validate the configuration. Linux bridges, much like real layer 2 switches, can also keep track of the MAC addresses they receive. We can view the MAC addresses the system is aware of by using the bridge fdb show command:

```
user@net1:~$ bridge fdb show
...<Additional output removed for brevity>...
00:0c:29:59:ca:ca dev eth1
00:0c:29:17:f4:03 dev eth2
user@net1:~$
```

The two MAC addresses we see in the preceding output reference the directly connected interfaces that `net1` talks to in order to get to hosts `net2` and `net3` as well as the subnets defined on their associated `dummy0` interfaces. We can verify this by looking at the hosts ARP table:

```
user@net1:~$ arp -a
? (10.10.10.1) at 00:21:d7:c5:f2:46 [ether] on eth0
? (172.16.10.2) at 00:0c:29:59:ca:ca [ether] on host_bridge1
? (172.16.10.66) at 00:0c:29:17:f4:03 [ether] on host_bridge2
user@net1:~$
```

 There aren't many scenarios where the old tool is better, but in the case of the `bridge` command-line tool, some might argue that the older `brctl` tool has some advantages. For one, the output is a little easier to read. In the case of learned MAC addresses, it will give you a better view into the mappings with the `brctl showmacs <bridge name>` command. If you want to use the older tool, you can install the `bridge-utils` package.

Removing interfaces from bridges can be accomplished through the `ip link set` subcommand. For instance, if we wanted to remove `eth1` from the bridge `host_bridge1` we would run this command:

```
sudo ip link set dev eth1 nomaster
```

This removes the master slave binding between `eth1` and the bridge `host_bridge1`. Interfaces can also be reassigned to new bridges (masters) without removing them from the bridge they are currently associated with. If we wanted to delete the bridge entirely, we could do so with this command:

```
sudo ip link delete dev host_bridge2
```

It should be noted that you do not need to remove all of the interfaces from the bridge before you delete it. Deleting the bridge will automatically remove all master bindings.

Making connections

Up until this point, we've focused on physical cables to make connections between interfaces. But how would we connect two interfaces that didn't have physical interfaces? For this purpose, Linux networking has an internal interface type called **Virtual Ethernet (VETH)** pairs. VETH interfaces are always created in pairs making them act like a sort of virtual patch cable. VETH interfaces can also have IP addresses assigned to them, which allow them to participate in a layer 3 routing path. In this recipe, we'll examine how to define and implement VETH pairs by building off the lab topology we've used in previous recipes.

Getting ready

In order to view and manipulate networking settings, you'll want to ensure that you have the `iproute2` toolset installed. If not present on the system, it can be installed by using the command:

```
sudo apt-get install iproute2
```

In order to make network changes to the host, you'll also need root-level access. This recipe will continue the lab topology from the previous recipe. All of the prerequisites mentioned earlier still apply.

How to do it...

Let's once again modify the lab topology, so we can make use of VETH pairs:

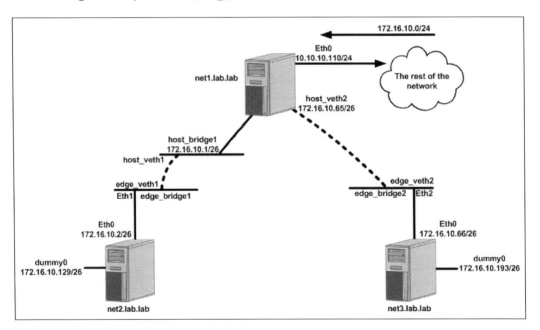

Once again, the configuration on hosts `net2` and `net3` will remain unchanged. On the host `net1`, we're going to implement VETH pairs in two different manners.

On the connection between `net1` and `net2`, we're going to use two different bridges and connect them together with a VETH pair. The bridge `host_bridge1` will remain on `net1` and maintain its IP address of `172.16.10.1`. We're also going to add a new bridge named `edge_bridge1`. This bridge will not have an IP address assigned to it but will have `net1`'s interface facing `net2` (`eth1`) as a member of it. At that point, we'll use a VETH pair to connect the two bridges allowing traffic to flow from `net1` across both bridges to `net2`. In this case, the VETH pair will be used as a layer 2 construct.

On the connection between `net1` and `net3` we're going to use a VETH pair but in a slightly different fashion. We'll add a new bridge called `edge_bridge2` and put `net1` host's interface facing the host `net3` (`eth2`) on that bridge. Then we will provision a VETH pair and place one end on the bridge `edge_bridge2`. We'll then assign the IP address previously assigned to the `host_bridge2` to the host side of the VETH pair. In this case, the VETH pair will be used as a layer 3 construct.

Let's start on the connection between `net1` and `net2` by adding the new edge bridge:

```
user@net1:~$ sudo ip link add edge_bridge1 type bridge
```

Then, we'll add the interface facing `net2` to `edge_bridge1`:

```
user@net1:~$ sudo ip link set dev eth1 master edge_bridge1
```

Next, we'll configure the VETH pair that we'll use to connect `host_bridge1` and `edge_bridge1`. VETH pairs are always defined in a pair. Creating the interface will spawn two new objects, but they are reliant on each other. That is, if you delete one end of the VETH pair, the other end will get deleted right along with it. To define the VETH pair, we use the `ip link add` subcommand:

```
user@net1:~$ sudo ip link add host_veth1 type veth peer name edge_veth1
```

 Note that the command defines the name for both sides of the VETH connection.

We can see their configuration using the `ip link show` subcommand:

```
user@net1:~$ ip link show
...<Additional output removed for brevity>...
13: edge_veth1@host_veth1: <BROADCAST,MULTICAST,M-DOWN> mtu 1500 qdisc
noop state DOWN mode DEFAULT group default qlen 1000
    link/ether 0a:27:83:6e:9a:c3 brd ff:ff:ff:ff:ff:ff
14: host_veth1@edge_veth1: <BROADCAST,MULTICAST,M-DOWN> mtu 1500 qdisc
noop state DOWN mode DEFAULT group default qlen 1000
    link/ether c2:35:9c:f9:49:3e brd ff:ff:ff:ff:ff:ff
user@net1:~$
```

Note that we have two entries showing an interface for each side of the defined VETH pair. The next step is to place the ends of the VETH pair in the correct place. In the case of the connection between `net1` and `net2`, we want one end on `host_bridge1` and the other on `edge_bridge1`. To do this, we use the same syntax we used for assigning interfaces to bridges:

```
user@net1:~$ sudo ip link set host_veth1 master host_bridge1
user@net1:~$ sudo ip link set edge_veth1 master edge_bridge1
```

We can verify the mappings using the `ip link show` command:

```
user@net1:~$ ip link show
...<Additional output removed for brevity>...
9: edge_veth1@host_veth1: <BROADCAST,MULTICAST,M-DOWN> mtu 1500 qdisc
noop master edge_bridge1 state DOWN mode DEFAULT group default qlen 1000
    link/ether f2:90:99:7d:7b:e6 brd ff:ff:ff:ff:ff:ff
10: host_veth1@edge_veth1: <BROADCAST,MULTICAST,M-DOWN> mtu 1500 qdisc
noop master host_bridge1 state DOWN mode DEFAULT group default qlen 1000
    link/ether da:f4:b7:b3:8d:dd brd ff:ff:ff:ff:ff:ff
```

The last thing we need to do is bring up the interfaces associated with the connection:

```
user@net1:~$ sudo ip link set host_bridge1 up
user@net1:~$ sudo ip link set edge_bridge1 up
user@net1:~$ sudo ip link set host_veth1 up
user@net1:~$ sudo ip link set edge_veth1 up
```

To reach the dummy interface off of `net2`, you'll need to add the route back since it was once again lost during the reconfiguration:

```
user@net1:~$ sudo ip route add 172.16.10.128/26 via 172.16.10.2
```

At this point, we should have full reachability to `net2` and its `dummy0` interface through `net1`.

On the connection between host `net1` and `net3`, the first thing we need to do is clean up any unused interfaces. In this case, that would be `host_bridge2`:

```
user@net1:~$ sudo ip link delete dev host_bridge2
```

Then, we need to add the new edge bridge (`edge_bridge2`) and associate `net1`'s interface facing `net3` to the bridge:

```
user@net1:~$ sudo ip link add edge_bridge2 type bridge
user@net1:~$ sudo ip link set dev eth2 master edge_bridge2
```

We'll then define the VETH pair for this connection:

```
user@net1:~$ sudo ip link add host_veth2 type veth peer name edge_veth2
```

In this case, we're going to leave the host side VETH pair unassociated from the bridges and instead assign an IP address directly to it:

```
user@net1:~$ sudo ip address add 172.16.10.65/25 dev host_veth2
```

Just like any other interface, we can see the assigned IP address by using the `ip address show dev` command:

```
user@net1:~$ ip addr show dev host_veth2
12: host_veth2@edge_veth2: <BROADCAST,MULTICAST,UP,LOWER_UP> mtu 1500
qdisc pfifo_fast state UP group default qlen 1000
    link/ether 56:92:14:83:98:e0 brd ff:ff:ff:ff:ff:ff
    inet 172.16.10.65/25 scope global host_veth2
       valid_lft forever preferred_lft forever
    inet6 fe80::5492:14ff:fe83:98e0/64 scope link
       valid_lft forever preferred_lft forever
user@net1:~$
```

We will then place the other end of the VETH pair into `edge_bridge2` connecting `net1` to the edge bridge:

```
user@net1:~$ sudo ip link set edge_veth2 master edge_bridge2
```

And once again, we turn up all the associated interfaces:

```
user@net1:~$ sudo ip link set edge_bridge2 up
user@net1:~$ sudo ip link set host_veth2 up
user@net1:~$ sudo ip link set edge_veth2 up
```

Finally, we read our route to get to `net3`'s dummy interface:

```
user@net1:~$ sudo ip route add 172.16.10.192/26 via 172.16.10.66
```

After the configuration is completed, we should once again have full reachability into the environment and all the interfaces. If there are any issues with your configuration, you should be able to diagnose them through the use of the `ip link show` and `ip addr show` commands.

If you're ever questioning what the other end of a VETH pair is, you can use the `ethtool` command-line tool to return the other side of the pair. For instance, assume that we create a non-named VETH pair as follows:

```
user@docker1:/$ sudo ip link add type veth
user@docker1:/$ ip link show
...<output removed for brevity>,,,
16: veth1@veth2: <BROADCAST,MULTICAST,M-DOWN> mtu 1500 qdisc noop state
DOWN mode DEFAULT group default qlen 1000
    link/ether 12:3f:7b:8d:33:90 brd ff:ff:ff:ff:ff:ff
17: veth2@veth1: <BROADCAST,MULTICAST,M-DOWN> mtu 1500 qdisc noop state
DOWN mode DEFAULT group default qlen 1000
    link/ether 9e:9f:34:bc:49:73 brd ff:ff:ff:ff:ff:ff
```

While obvious in this example, we could use `ethtool` to determine the interface index or ID of one or the other side of this VETH pair:

```
user@docker1:/$ ethtool -S veth1
NIC statistics:
     peer_ifindex: 17
user@docker1:/$ ethtool -S veth2
NIC statistics:
     peer_ifindex: 16
user@docker1:/$
```

This can be a handy troubleshooting tool later on when determining the ends of a VETH pair is not as obvious as it is in these examples.

Exploring network namespaces

Network namespaces allow you to create isolated views of the network. A namespace has a unique routing table that can differ entirely from the default routing table on the host. In addition, you can map interfaces from the physical host into namespaces for use within the namespace. The behavior of network namespaces closely mimics that of **Virtual Routing and Forwarding** (**VRF**) instances, which are available in most modern networking hardware. In this recipe, we'll learn the basics of network namespaces. We'll walk through the process of creating the namespace and discuss how to use different types of interfaces within a network namespace. Finally, we'll show how to connect multiple namespaces together.

Getting ready

In order to view and manipulate networking settings, you'll want to ensure that you have the `iproute2` toolset installed. If not present on the system, it can be installed using the following command:

```
sudo apt-get install iproute2
```

In order to make network changes to the host, you'll also need root-level access. This recipe will continue the lab topology from the previous recipe. All of the prerequisites mentioned earlier still apply.

How to do it...

The concept of network namespaces is best demonstrated through an example, so let's jump right back to the lab topology from the previous recipes:

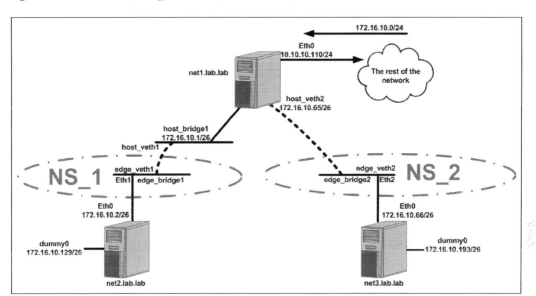

This diagram is the same topology we used in the last recipe, with one significant difference. We have the addition of two namespaces, **NS_1** and **NS_2**. Each namespace encompasses certain interfaces on the host `net1`:

- ▶ NS_1:
    - ❑ edge_bridge1
    - ❑ eth1
    - ❑ edge_veth1

- ► NS_2:

  - ❑ edge_bridge2
  - ❑ eth2
  - ❑ edge_veth2

Take note of where the boundary for the namespaces falls. In either case, the boundary falls on a physical interface (the net1 host's eth1 and eth2) or directly in the middle of a VETH pair. As we'll see shortly, VETH pairs can bridge between namespaces making them an ideal tool for connecting network namespaces together.

To begin the reconfiguration, let's start by defining the namespaces, and then adding interfaces to the namespace. Defining a namespace is rather straightforward. We use the ip netns add subcommand:

```
user@net1:~$ sudo ip netns add ns_1
user@net1:~$ sudo ip netns add ns_2
```

Namespaces can then be viewed by using the ip netns list command:

```
user@net1:~$ ip netns list
ns_2
ns_1
user@net1:~$
```

Once the namespaces are created, we can allocate the specific interfaces we identified as being part of each namespace. In most cases, this means telling an existing interface which namespace it belongs to. However, not all interfaces can be moved into a network namespace. Bridges for instances can live in network namespaces but need to be instantiated from within the name space. To do this, we can use the ip netns exec subcommand to run the command from within the namespace. For instance, to create the edge bridges in each namespace, we would run these two commands:

```
user@net1:~$ sudo ip netns exec ns_1 ip link add \
edge_bridge1 type bridge
user@net1:~$ sudo ip netns exec ns_2 ip link add \
edge_bridge2 type bridge
```

Let's break that command into two pieces:

- ► sudo ip nent exec ns_1: This tells the host you want to run a command inside a specific namespace, in this case ns_1

- ► ip link add edge_bridge1 type bridge: As we saw in earlier recipes, we execute the command to build a bridge and give it a name, in this case, edge_bridge1.

Using this same syntax, we can now examine the network configuration of a specific namespace. For instance, we could look at the interfaces with `sudo ip netns exec ns_1 ip link show`:

```
user@net1:~$ sudo ip netns exec ns_1 ip link show
1: lo: <LOOPBACK> mtu 65536 qdisc noop state DOWN mode DEFAULT group
default
    link/loopback 00:00:00:00:00:00 brd 00:00:00:00:00:00
2: edge_bridge1: <BROADCAST,MULTICAST> mtu 1500 qdisc noop state DOWN
mode DEFAULT group default
    link/ether 26:43:4e:a6:30:91 brd ff:ff:ff:ff:ff:ff
user@net1:~$
```

As we expected, we see the bridge we instantiated inside the namespace. The other two interface types that the diagram shows in the namespace are of types that can be dynamically allocated into the namespace. To do that, we use the `ip link set` command:

```
user@net1:~$ sudo ip link set dev eth1 netns ns_1
user@net1:~$ sudo ip link set dev edge_veth1 netns ns_1
user@net1:~$ sudo ip link set dev eth2 netns ns_2
user@net1:~$ sudo ip link set dev edge_veth2 netns ns_2
```

Now if we look at the available host interfaces, we should note that the interfaces we moved no longer exist in the default namespace:

```
user@net1:~$ ip link show
1: lo: <LOOPBACK,UP,LOWER_UP> mtu 65536 qdisc noqueue state UNKNOWN mode
DEFAULT group default
    link/loopback 00:00:00:00:00:00 brd 00:00:00:00:00:00
2: eth0: <BROADCAST,MULTICAST,UP,LOWER_UP> mtu 1500 qdisc pfifo_fast
state UP mode DEFAULT group default qlen 1000
    link/ether 00:0c:29:2d:dd:79 brd ff:ff:ff:ff:ff:ff
5: host_bridge1: <NO-CARRIER,BROADCAST,MULTICAST,UP> mtu 1500 qdisc
noqueue state DOWN mode DEFAULT group default
    link/ether 56:cc:26:4c:76:f6 brd ff:ff:ff:ff:ff:ff
7: edge_bridge1: <NO-CARRIER,BROADCAST,MULTICAST,UP> mtu 1500 qdisc
noqueue state DOWN mode DEFAULT group default
    link/ether 00:00:00:00:00:00 brd ff:ff:ff:ff:ff:ff
8: edge_bridge2: <NO-CARRIER,BROADCAST,MULTICAST,UP> mtu 1500 qdisc
noqueue state DOWN mode DEFAULT group default
    link/ether 00:00:00:00:00:00 brd ff:ff:ff:ff:ff:ff
```

```
10: host_veth1@if9: <NO-CARRIER,BROADCAST,MULTICAST,UP> mtu 1500 qdisc
pfifo_fast master host_bridge1 state LOWERLAYERDOWN mode DEFAULT group
default qlen 1000
    link/ether 56:cc:26:4c:76:f6 brd ff:ff:ff:ff:ff:ff
12: host_veth2@if11: <NO-CARRIER,BROADCAST,MULTICAST,UP> mtu 1500 qdisc
pfifo_fast state LOWERLAYERDOWN mode DEFAULT group default qlen 1000
    link/ether 2a:8b:54:81:36:31 brd ff:ff:ff:ff:ff:ff
user@net1:~$
```

You likely noticed that edge_bridge1 and edge_bridge2 still exist in this output since we never deleted them. This is interesting because they now also exist inside the namespaces ns_1 and ns_2. It's important to point out that since the namespaces are totally isolated even the interface names can overlap.

Now that all of the interfaces are in the right namespace, all that's left to do is to apply standard bridge mapping and turn up the interfaces. Since we had to recreate the bridge interfaces in each namespace, we'll need to reattach the interfaces to each bridge. This is done just like you would normally; we just run the command within the namespace:

```
user@net1:~$ sudo ip netns exec ns_1 ip link set \
dev edge_veth1 master edge_bridge1
user@net1:~$ sudo ip netns exec ns_1 ip link set \
dev eth1 master edge_bridge1
user@net1:~$ sudo ip netns exec ns_2 ip link set \
dev edge_veth2 master edge_bridge2
user@net1:~$ sudo ip netns exec ns_2 ip link set \
dev eth2 master edge_bridge2
```

Once we have all of the interfaces in the right namespace and attached to the right bridges, all that's left is to bring them all up:

```
user@net1:~$ sudo ip netns exec ns_1 ip link set edge_bridge1 up
user@net1:~$ sudo ip netns exec ns_1 ip link set edge_veth1 up
user@net1:~$ sudo ip netns exec ns_1 ip link set eth1 up
user@net1:~$ sudo ip netns exec ns_2 ip link set edge_bridge2 up
user@net1:~$ sudo ip netns exec ns_2 ip link set edge_veth2 up
user@net1:~$ sudo ip netns exec ns_2 ip link set eth2 up
```

After the interfaces come up, we should once again have connectivity to all of the networks attached to all three hosts.

While this example of namespaces only moved layer 2 type constructs into a namespace, they also support layer 3 routing with unique routing table instances per namespace. For instance, if we look at the routing table of one of the namespaces we'll see that it's completely empty:

```
user@net1:~$ sudo ip netns exec ns_1 ip route
user@net1:~$
```

This is because we don't have any interfaces with IP addresses defined in the namespace. This demonstrates that both layer 2 and layer 3 constructs are isolated within a namespace. That's one major area where network namespaces and VRF instances differ. VRF instances only account for layer 3 configuration, whereas network namespaces isolate both layer 2 and layer 3 constructs. We'll see an example of layer 3 isolation with network namespaces in *Chapter 3*, *User-Defined Networks*, when we discuss the process Docker uses for networking containers.

2

Configuring and Monitoring Docker Networks

In this chapter, we will cover the following recipes:

- ► Verifying host-level settings that impact Docker networking
- ► Connecting containers in bridge mode
- ► Exposing and publishing ports
- ► Connecting containers to existing containers
- ► Connecting containers in host mode
- ► Configuring service-level settings

Introduction

Docker makes consuming container technology easier than it's ever been before. Known for its ease of use, Docker offers many advanced features but installs with a sane set of defaults that make it easy to quickly start building containers. And while network configuration is typically the one area that requires additional attention before use, Docker makes it easy to get your containers up and on the network.

Verifying host-level settings that impact Docker networking

Docker relies on the host being capable of performing certain functions to make Docker networking work. Namely, your Linux host must be configured to allow IP forwarding. In addition, since the release of Docker 1.7, you may now choose to use hairpin **Network Address Translation (NAT)** rather than the default Docker user land proxy. In this recipe, we'll review the requirement for the host to have IP forwarding enabled. We'll also talk about NAT hairpin and discuss the host-level requirements for that option as well. In both cases, we'll show Docker's default behavior with regard to its settings as well as how you can alter them.

Getting ready

You'll need access to a Linux host running Docker and the ability to stop and restart the service. Since we'll be modifying system-level kernel parameters, you'll also need root-level access to the system.

How to do it...

As we saw in *Chapter 1, Linux Networking Constructs*, a Linux host must have IP forwarding enabled to be able to route traffic between interfaces. Since Docker does just that, IP forwarding must be enabled for Docker networking to function as desired. If Docker detects that IP forwarding is disabled, it will warn you of the issue when you attempt to run a container:

```
user@docker1:~$ docker run --name web1 -it \
jonlangemak/web_server_1 /bin/bash
WARNING: IPv4 forwarding is disabled. Networking will not work.
root@071d673821b8:/#
```

Most Linux distributions default the IP forward value to `disabled` or `0`. Fortunately for us, in a default configuration, Docker takes care of updating this setting to the correct value when the Docker service starts. For instance, let's take a look at a freshly rebooted host that doesn't have the Docker service enabled at boot time. If we check the value of the setting before starting Docker, we can see that it's disabled. Starting the Docker engine automatically enables the setting for us:

```
user@docker1:~$ more /proc/sys/net/ipv4/ip_forward
0
user@docker1:~$
user@docker1:~$ sudo systemctl start docker
user@docker1:~$ sysctl net.ipv4.ip_forward
```

```
net.ipv4.ip_forward = 1
user@docker1:~$
```

This default behavior in Docker can be changed by passing `--ip-forward=false` as a runtime option to the Docker service.

 The configuration of Docker-specific parameters varies widely based on the **init system** used. At the time of writing, many newer Linux operating systems use `systemd` as their init system. Always consult the Docker documentation to see its recommendation for service configuration based on the operating system you are using. Docker service configuration and options are talked about in greater detail as part of an upcoming recipe in this chapter. In this recipe, just focus on the impact changing these settings has on both Docker and the host itself.

Further discussion on the kernel IP forward parameter can be found in the recipe *Configuring Linux host routing* in *Chapter 1, Linux Networking Constructs*. There you'll find how to update the parameter yourself as well as how to make the setting persistent through reboots.

Another recent feature of Docker that relies on a kernel-level parameter is the hairpin NAT functionality. Earlier versions of Docker implemented, and relied on, what's known as the Docker **userland proxy** to facilitate intercontainer and published port communication. By default, any containers exposing ports did so through the userland proxy process. For instance, if we start an example container we can see that in addition to the Docker process itself, we also now have a `docker-proxy` process:

```
user@docker1:~$ docker run --name web1 -d -P jonlangemak/web_server_1
bf3cb30e826ce53e6e7db4e72af71f15b2b8f83bd6892e4838ec0a59b17ac33f
user@docker1:~$
user@docker1:~$ ps aux | grep docker
root       771  0.0  0.1 509676 41656 ?          Ssl  19:30   0:00 /usr/
bin/docker daemon
root      1861  0.2  0.0 117532 28024 ?          Sl   19:41   0:00 docker-
proxy -proto tcp -host-ip 0.0.0.0 -host-port 32769 -container-ip
172.17.0.2 -container-port 80
...<Additional output removed for brevity>...
user@docker1:~$
```

Every published port will start a new `docker-proxy` process on the Docker host. As an alternative to the userland proxy, you have the option to have Docker use hairpin NAT rather than userland proxies. Hairpin NAT relies on the host system being configured to enable routing on the host's local loopback interfaces. Again, the Docker service takes care of updating the correct host parameter to enable this functionality when the Docker service starts if it's told to do so.

Hairpin NAT relies on the kernel parameter `net.ipv4.conf.docker0.route_localnet` being enabled (set to 1) in order for the host machine to access container services through the hosts loopback interface. This can be achieved in the same way as we described with the IP forward parameter:

Using the `sysctl` command:

```
sysctl net.ipv4.conf.docker0.route_localnet
```

By querying the `/proc/` filesystem directly:

```
more /proc/sys/net/ipv4/conf/docker0/route_localnet
```

If the returned value is 0, it's likely that Docker is in its default configuration and is relying on the userland proxy. Since you have the option to run Docker in either mode, we need to do more than change the kernel parameters in order to make the change to hairpin NAT. We also need to tell Docker to change the way it publishes ports by passing the option `--userland-proxy=false` as a runtime option to the Docker service. Doing so will enable hairpin NAT and also tell Docker to update the kernel parameter to the correct setting for hairpin NAT to work. Let's enable hairpin NAT to validate that Docker is doing what it should be doing.

First, let's check the value of the kernel parameter:

```
user@docker1:~$ sysctl net.ipv4.conf.docker0.route_localnet
net.ipv4.conf.docker0.route_localnet = 0
user@docker1:~$
```

It's currently disabled. Now we can tell Docker to disable the userland proxy by passing the `--userland-proxy=false` as a parameter to the Docker service. Once the Docker service is told to disable the userland proxy, and the service is restarted, we should see that the parameter is enabled on the host:

```
user@docker1:~$ sysctl net.ipv4.conf.docker0.route_localnet
net.ipv4.conf.docker0.route_localnet = 1
user@docker1:~$
```

Running a container with a mapped port at this point will not create additional `docker-proxy` process instances:

```
user@docker1:~$ docker run --name web1 -d -P jonlangemak/web_server_1
5743fac364fadb3d86f66cb65532691fe926af545639da18f82a94fd35683c54
user@docker1:~$ ps aux | grep docker
root      2159  0.1  0.1 310696 34880 ?        Ssl  14:26   0:00 /usr/
bin/docker daemon --userland-proxy=false
user@docker1:~$
```

In addition, we are still able to access the container through the host's local interface:

```
user@docker1:~$ curl 127.0.0.1:32768
<body>
   <html>
      <h1><span style="color:#FF0000;font-size:72px;">Web Server #1 -
Running on port 80</span>
      </h1>
</body>
   </html>
user@docker1:~$
```

Disabling the parameter once again causes this connection to fail:

```
user@docker1:~$ sudo sysctl -w net.ipv4.conf.docker0.route_localnet=0
net.ipv4.conf.docker0.route_localnet = 0
user@docker1:~$ curl 127.0.0.1:32768
curl: (7) Failed to connect to 127.0.0.1 port 32768: Connection timed out
user@docker1:~$
```

Connecting containers in bridge mode

As we mentioned earlier, Docker comes with a set of sensible defaults to get your containers communicating on the network. From a network perspective, the Docker default is to attach any spawned container to the docker0 bridge. In this recipe, we'll show how to connect containers in the default bridge mode and explain how network traffic leaving and destined for the container is handled.

Getting ready

You'll need access to a Docker host and an understanding of how your Docker host is connected to the network. In our example, we'll be using a Docker host that has two physical network interfaces, like the one shown in the following diagram:

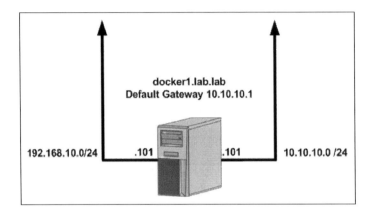

You'll want to make sure that you have access to view `iptables` rules to verify **netfilter** policies. If you wish to download and run example containers, your Docker host will also need access to the Internet. In some cases, the changes we make may require you to have root-level access to the system.

How to do it...

After installing and starting Docker, you should notice the addition of a new Linux bridge named `docker0`. By default, the `docker0` bridge has an IP address of `172.17.0.1/16`:

```
user@docker1:~$ ip addr show docker0
5: docker0: <NO-CARRIER,BROADCAST,MULTICAST,UP> mtu 1500 qdisc noqueue
state DOWN group default
    link/ether 02:42:54:87:8b:ea brd ff:ff:ff:ff:ff:ff
    inet 172.17.0.1/16 scope global docker0
       valid_lft forever preferred_lft forever
user@docker1:~$
```

Docker will place any containers that are started without specifying a network on the `docker0` bridge. Now, let's look at an example container running on this host:

```
user@docker1:~$ docker run -it jonlangemak/web_server_1 /bin/bash
root@abe6eae2e0b3:/# ip addr
```

```
1: lo: <LOOPBACK,UP,LOWER_UP> mtu 65536 qdisc noqueue state UNKNOWN qlen
1
    link/loopback 00:00:00:00:00:00 brd 00:00:00:00:00:00
    inet 127.0.0.1/8 scope host lo
        valid_lft forever preferred_lft forever
    inet6 ::1/128 scope host
        valid_lft forever preferred_lft forever
6: eth0@if7: <BROADCAST,MULTICAST,UP,LOWER_UP> mtu 1500 qdisc noqueue
state UP
    link/ether 02:42:ac:11:00:02 brd ff:ff:ff:ff:ff:ff
    inet 172.17.0.2/16 scope global eth0
        valid_lft forever preferred_lft forever
    inet6 fe80::42:acff:fe11:2/64 scope link
        valid_lft forever preferred_lft forever
root@abe6eae2e0b3:/#
```

By running the container in interactive mode, we can examine what the container believes its network configuration to be. In this case, we can see that the container has a single non-loopback network adapter (eth0) with an IP address of 172.17.0.2/16.

In addition, we can see that the container believes its default gateway is the docker0 bridge interface on the Docker host:

```
root@abe6eae2e0b3:/# ip route
default via 172.17.0.1 dev eth0
172.17.0.0/16 dev eth0   proto kernel   scope link   src 172.17.0.2
root@abe6eae2e0b3:/#
```

By running some basic tests, we can see that the container has access to physical interface of the Docker host as well as Internet-based resources.

 Internet-based access for the container itself is predicated on the fact that the Docker host has access to the Internet.

```
root@abe6eae2e0b3:/# ping 10.10.10.101 -c 2
PING 10.10.10.101 (10.10.10.101): 48 data bytes
56 bytes from 10.10.10.101: icmp_seq=0 ttl=64 time=0.084 ms
56 bytes from 10.10.10.101: icmp_seq=1 ttl=64 time=0.072 ms
--- 10.10.10.101 ping statistics ---
2 packets transmitted, 2 packets received, 0% packet loss
```

```
round-trip min/avg/max/stddev = 0.072/0.078/0.084/0.000 ms
root@abe6eae2e0b3:/#
root@abe6eae2e0b3:/# ping 4.2.2.2 -c 2
PING 4.2.2.2 (4.2.2.2): 48 data bytes
56 bytes from 4.2.2.2: icmp_seq=0 ttl=50 time=29.388 ms
56 bytes from 4.2.2.2: icmp_seq=1 ttl=50 time=26.766 ms
--- 4.2.2.2 ping statistics ---
2 packets transmitted, 2 packets received, 0% packet loss
round-trip min/avg/max/stddev = 26.766/28.077/29.388/1.311 ms
root@abe6eae2e0b3:/#
```

Given that the network the container lives on was created by Docker, we can safely assume that the rest of network is not aware of it. That is, the outside network has no knowledge of the 172.17.0.0/16 network since it's local to the Docker host. That being said, it seems curious that the container is able to reach resources that live beyond the docker0 bridge. Docker makes this work by hiding container's IP addresses behind the Docker host's IP interfaces. The traffic flow is shown in the following image:

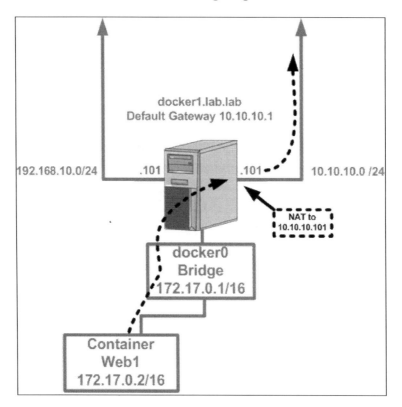

Since the containers' traffic is seen on the physical network as the Docker host's IP address, other network resources know how to return the traffic to the container. To perform this outbound NAT, Docker uses the Linux netfilter framework. We can see these rules using the netfilter command-line tool `iptables`:

```
user@docker1:~$ sudo iptables -t nat -L
Chain PREROUTING (policy ACCEPT)
target      prot opt source              destination
DOCKER      all  --  anywhere            anywhere           ADDRTYPE
match dst-type LOCAL


Chain INPUT (policy ACCEPT)
target      prot opt source              destination


Chain OUTPUT (policy ACCEPT)
target      prot opt source              destination
DOCKER      all  --  anywhere            !127.0.0.0/8        ADDRTYPE
match dst-type LOCAL


Chain POSTROUTING (policy ACCEPT)
target      prot opt source              destination
MASQUERADE  all  --  172.17.0.0/16         anywhere


Chain DOCKER (2 references)
target      prot opt source              destination
RETURN      all  --  anywhere            anywhere
user@docker1:~$
```

As you can see, we have a rule in the POSTROUTING chain that masquerades or hides, anything sourced from our docker0 bridge (172.17.0.0/16) behind the host's interface.

Although outbound connectivity is configured and allowed by default, Docker does not by default provide a means to access services in the containers from outside the Docker host. In order to do this, we must pass Docker additional flags at container runtime. Specifically, we can pass the -P flag when we run the container. To examine this behavior, let's look at a container image that exposes a port:

```
docker run --name web1 -d -P jonlangemak/web_server_1
```

This tells Docker to map a random port to any ports that the container image exposes. In the case of this demo container, the image exposes port 80. After running the container, we can see the host port mapped to the container:

```
user@docker1:~$ docker run --name web1 -P -d jonlangemak/web_server_1
556dc8cefd79ed1d9957cc52827bb23b7d80c4b887ee173c2e3b8478340de948
user@docker1:~$
user@docker1:~$ docker port web1
80/tcp -> 0.0.0.0:32768
user@docker1:~$
```

As we can see, the containers port 80 has been mapped to host port 32768. This means that we can access the service running on port 80 of the container through the host's interfaces at port 32768. Much like the outbound container access, inbound connectivity also uses netfilter to create the port mapping. We can see this by checking the NAT and filter table:

```
user@docker1:~$ sudo iptables -t nat -L
Chain PREROUTING (policy ACCEPT)
target       prot opt source               destination
DOCKER       all  --  anywhere             anywhere             ADDRTYPE
match dst-type LOCAL


Chain INPUT (policy ACCEPT)
target       prot opt source               destination


Chain OUTPUT (policy ACCEPT)
target       prot opt source               destination
DOCKER       all  --  anywhere             !127.0.0.0/8          ADDRTYPE
match dst-type LOCAL


Chain POSTROUTING (policy ACCEPT)
target       prot opt source          destination
MASQUERADE   all  --  172.17.0.0/16   anywhere
MASQUERADE   tcp  --  172.17.0.2      172.17.0.2          tcp dpt:http


Chain DOCKER (2 references)
target       prot opt source               destination
```

```
RETURN      all  --  anywhere            anywhere
DNAT        tcp  --  anywhere            anywhere               tcp
dpt:32768 to:172.17.0.2:80
user@docker1:~$ sudo iptables -t filter -L
Chain INPUT (policy ACCEPT)
target      prot opt source             destination


Chain FORWARD (policy ACCEPT)
target      prot opt source             destination
DOCKER-ISOLATION  all  --  anywhere             anywhere
DOCKER      all  --  anywhere            anywhere
ACCEPT      all  --  anywhere            anywhere               ctstate
RELATED,ESTABLISHED
ACCEPT      all  --  anywhere            anywhere
ACCEPT      all  --  anywhere            anywhere


Chain OUTPUT (policy ACCEPT)
target      prot opt source             destination


Chain DOCKER (1 references)
target      prot opt source             destination
ACCEPT      tcp  --  anywhere            172.17.0.2             tcp
dpt:http


Chain DOCKER-ISOLATION (1 references)
target      prot opt source             destination
RETURN      all  --  anywhere            anywhere
user@docker1:~$
```

Since the connectivity is being exposed on all interfaces (0.0.0.0), our inbound diagram will look like this:

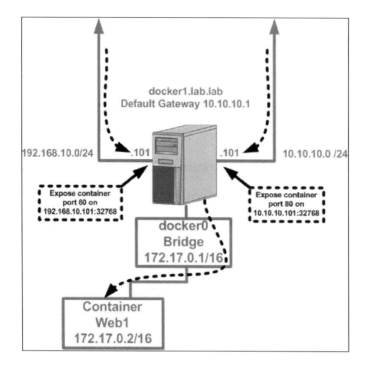

If not defined otherwise containers that live on the same host, and hence the same docker0 bridge, can inherently communicate with each other by their assigned IP address on any port, which is bound to a service. Allowing this communication is the default behavior and can be changed as we'll see in a later chapters when we discuss **Inter-Container Communication** (**ICC**) configuration.

> It should be noted that this is the default behavior for containers that are run without specifying any additional network parameters, that is, containers that use the Docker default bridge network. Later chapters will introduce other options that allow you to place containers living on the same host on different networks.

Communication between containers that live on different hosts requires using a combination of both the previously discussed flows. To test this out, let's expand our lab by adding a second host named docker2. Let's assume container web2 on the host docker2 wishes to access the container web1 living on host docker1, which is hosting a service on port 80. The flow will look like this:

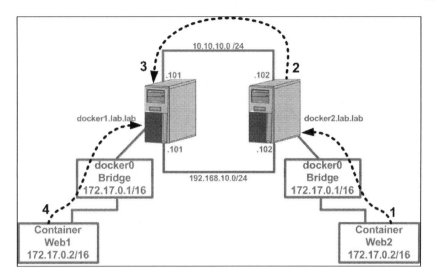

Let's walk through the flow at each step and show what the packets look like as they hit the wire in each step. In this case, the container `web1` is exposing port `80`, which has been published to port `32771` on the host `docker1`.

1. Traffic leaves the container `web2` destined for the exposed port (`32771`) on the `10.10.10.101` interface of host `docker1`:

```
▷ Frame 3: 236 bytes on wire (1888 bits), 236 bytes captured (1888 bits)
▷ Ethernet II, Src: 02:42:ac:11:00:02 (02:42:ac:11:00:02), Dst: 02:42:14:4e:f2:e1 (02:42:14:4e:f2:e1)
▷ Internet Protocol Version 4, Src: 172.17.0.2, Dst: 10.10.10.101
▷ Transmission Control Protocol, Src Port: 35138 (35138), Dst Port: filenet-rmi (32771), Seq: 1, Ack: 1, Len: 170
◢ Hypertext Transfer Protocol
   ◢ GET / HTTP/1.1\r\n
      ▷ [Expert Info (Chat/Sequence): GET / HTTP/1.1\r\n]
        Request Method: GET
        Request URI: /
        Request Version: HTTP/1.1
```

2. Traffic arrives at the container's default gateway, which is the IP interface of the `docker0` bridge (`172.17.0.1`). The host does a route lookup and determines that the destination lives out of its `10.10.10.102` interface, so it hides the container's real source IP behind that interface's IP address:

```
▷ Frame 3: 236 bytes on wire (1888 bits), 236 bytes captured (1888 bits)
▷ Ethernet II, Src: Vmware_7f:3d:64 (00:0c:29:7f:3d:64), Dst: Vmware_50:b8:cc (00:0c:29:50:b8:cc)
▷ Internet Protocol Version 4, Src: 10.10.10.102, Dst: 10.10.10.101
▷ Transmission Control Protocol, Src Port: 35140 (35140), Dst Port: filenet-rmi (32771), Seq: 1, Ack: 1, Len: 170
◢ Hypertext Transfer Protocol
   ◢ GET / HTTP/1.1\r\n
      ▷ [Expert Info (Chat/Sequence): GET / HTTP/1.1\r\n]
        Request Method: GET
        Request URI: /
        Request Version: HTTP/1.1
```

3. Traffic arrives at the `docker1` host and is examined by the netfilter rules. `docker1` has a rule that exposes the service port of container 1 (`80`) on port `32271` of the host:

```
Frame 4: 236 bytes on wire (1888 bits), 236 bytes captured (1888 bits)
Ethernet II, Src: Vmware_7f:3d:64 (00:0c:29:7f:3d:64), Dst: Vmware_50:b8:cc (00:0c:29:50:b8:cc)
Internet Protocol Version 4, Src: 10.10.10.102, Dst: 10.10.10.101
Transmission Control Protocol, Src Port: 35146 (35146), Dst Port: filenet-rmi (32771), Seq: 1, Ack: 1, Len: 170
Hypertext Transfer Protocol
   GET / HTTP/1.1\r\n
      [Expert Info (Chat/Sequence): GET / HTTP/1.1\r\n]
      Request Method: GET
      Request URI: /
      Request Version: HTTP/1.1
```

4. The destination port is changed from `32771` to `80` and passed along to the `web1` container, which receives the traffic on the correct port `80`:

```
Frame 3: 236 bytes on wire (1888 bits), 236 bytes captured (1888 bits)
Ethernet II, Src: 02:42:3c:30:06:ce (02:42:3c:30:06:ce), Dst: 02:42:ac:11:00:02 (02:42:ac:11:00:02)
Internet Protocol Version 4, Src: 10.10.10.102, Dst: 172.17.0.2
Transmission Control Protocol, Src Port: 35150 (35150), Dst Port: http (80), Seq: 1, Ack: 1, Len: 170
Hypertext Transfer Protocol
   GET / HTTP/1.1\r\n
      [Expert Info (Chat/Sequence): GET / HTTP/1.1\r\n]
      Request Method: GET
      Request URI: /
      Request Version: HTTP/1.1
```

To try this out for ourselves, let's first run the `web1` container and check what port the service is exposed on:

```
user@docker1:~/apache$ docker run --name web1 -P \
-d jonlangemak/web_server_1
974e6eba1948ce5e4c9ada393b1196482d81f510de 12337868ad8ef65b8bf723
user@docker1:~/apache$
user@docker1:~/apache$ docker port web1
80/tcp -> 0.0.0.0:32771
user@docker1:~/apache$
```

Now let's run a second container called web2 on the host docker2 and attempt to access web1's service on port 32771...

```
user@docker2:~$ docker run --name web2 -it \
jonlangemak/web_server_2 /bin/bash
root@a97fea6fb0c9:/#
root@a97fea6fb0c9:/# curl http://10.10.10.101:32771
<body>
  <html>
    <h1><span style="color:#FF0000;font-size:72px;">Web Server #1 -
Running on port 80</span>
    </h1>
</body>
  </html>
```

Exposing and publishing ports

As we've seen in the previous examples, exposing services living in containers to the outside world is a critical component of Docker. Up until this point, we've let the images and the Docker engine do the heavy lifting for us in terms of the actual port mapping. To do this, Docker uses a combination of metadata from container images as well as a built-in system for tracking port allocations. In this recipe, we'll walk through the process for defining ports to be exposed as well as options for publishing ports.

Getting ready

You'll need access to a Docker host and an understanding of how your Docker host is connected to the network. In this recipe, we'll be using the `docker1` host that we used in previous recipes. You'll want to make sure that you have access to view `iptables` rules to verify netfilter policies. If you wish to download and run example containers, your Docker host will also need access to the Internet. In some cases, the changes we make may require you to have root-level access to the system.

How to do it...

While often confused, exposing ports and publishing ports are two totally different actions. Exposing ports is really just a way of documenting what ports a container might offer services on. These definitions are stored in the container metadata as part of the image and can be read by the Docker engine. Publishing ports is the actual process of mapping a container port to a host port. This can either be done automatically using the exposed port definitions, or it can be done manually without the use of exposed ports.

Let's first discuss how ports are exposed. The most common mechanism for exposing ports is to define them in an image's **Dockerfile**. When you build a container image, you're given the opportunity to define ports to be exposed. Consider this Dockerfile definition that I used to build some of the demo containers for this book:

```
FROM ubuntu:12.04
MAINTAINER Jon Langemak jon@interubernet.com
RUN apt-get update && apt-get install -y apache2 net-tools inetutils-ping curl
ADD index.html /var/www/index.html
ENV APACHE_RUN_USER www-data
ENV APACHE_RUN_GROUP www-data
ENV APACHE_LOG_DIR /var/log/apache2
EXPOSE 80
CMD ["/usr/sbin/apache2", "-D", "FOREGROUND"]
```

As part of the Dockerfile, I can define ports I wish to expose. In this case, I know that Apache will, by default, offer its web server on port 80 so that's the port I wish to expose.

 Note that, by default, Docker always assumes the ports you're referring to are TCP. If you wish to expose UDP ports, you can do so by including the /udp flag at the end of the port definition. For instance, EXPOSE 80/udp.

Now, let's run a container built with this Dockerfile to see what happens:

```
user@docker1:~$ docker run --name web1 -d jonlangemak/web_server_1
b0177ed2d38afe4f4d8c26531d00407efc0fee6517ba5a0f49955910a5dbd426
user@docker1:~$
user@docker1:~$ docker port web1
user@docker1:~$
```

As we can see, despite having a defined port to expose, Docker has not actually mapped any ports between the host and the container. If you recall from earlier recipe where a container provided a service, we included the -P flag in the docker run command syntax. The -P flag tells Docker to publish all exposed ports. Let's try running this container with the -P flag set:

```
user@docker1:~$ docker run --name web1 -d -P jonlangemak/web_server_1
d87d36d7cbcfb5040f78ff730d079d353ee81fde36ecbb5ff932ff9b9bef5502
user@docker1:~$
user@docker1:~$ docker port web1
80/tcp -> 0.0.0.0:32775
user@docker1:~$
```

Here, we can see that Docker has now automatically mapped the exposed port to a random high port on the host. Port 80 will now be considered published.

In addition to exposing ports through the image Dockerfile, we can also expose them at container runtime. Any ports that are exposed in this manner are combined with the ports exposed in the Dockerfile. For example, let's run the same container again and expose port 80 UDP as part of the docker run command:

```
user@docker1:~$ docker run --name web1 --expose=80/udp \
-d -P jonlangemak/web_server_1
f756deafed26f9635a3b9c738089495efeae86a393f94f17b2c4fece9f71a704
user@docker1:~$
user@docker1:~$ docker port web1
80/udp -> 0.0.0.0:32768
```

```
80/tcp -> 0.0.0.0:32776
user@docker1:~$
```

As you can see, we have published not only the port from the Dockerfile (80/tcp) but also the port from the docker run command (80/udp).

 Exposing ports at container runtime allows you some extra flexibility as you can define port ranges to be exposed. This is not currently possible during image creation with the Dockerfile expose syntax. When exposing a wide range of ports, you can filter the output of the docker port command by adding the container port you are looking for to the end of the command.

While the expose method is certainly handy, it doesn't solve all of our needs. For cases where you want more control over ports and interfaces used, you can bypass expose and directly publish ports when starting a container. While passing the -P flag publishes all exposed ports, passing the -p flag allows you to specify specific ports and interfaces to use when mapping ports. The -p flag can take several different forms with the syntax looking like this:

```
-p <host IP interface>:<host port>:<container port>
```

Any of the options may be omitted with the only required field being the container port. For example, here are a couple of different ways you could use this syntax:

▶ Specify the host port and container port:

```
-p <host port>:<container port>
```

▶ Specify the host interface, host port, and container port:

```
-p <host IP interface>:<host port>:<container port>
```

▶ Specify the host interface, have Docker choose a random host port, and specify the container port:

```
-p <host IP interface>::<container port>
```

▶ Specify only a container port and have Docker use a random host port:

```
-p <container port>
```

All the published ports we've seen up until this point have used a destination IP address of (0.0.0.0), which means that they are bound to all IP interfaces of the Docker host. By default, the Docker service always binds published ports to all host interfaces. However, as we'll see in the following recipe of this chapter, we can tell Docker to use a specific interface by passing the Docker service the --ip parameter.

Given that we can also define which interface to bind published ports to as part of the docker run command, we need to know which option takes priority. The general rule is that any option defined at container runtime wins. For instance, let's look at an example where we tell the Docker service to bind to the 192.168.10.101 IP address of the docker1 host by passing the following option to the service:

```
--ip=10.10.10.101
```

Now, let's run a container in a couple of different ways and see the outcome:

```
user@docker1:~$ docker run --name web1 -P -d jonlangemak/web_server_1
629129ccaebaa15720399c1ac31c1f2631fb4caedc7b3b114a92c5a8f797221d
user@docker1:~$ docker port web1
80/tcp -> 10.10.10.101:32768
user@docker1:~$
```

In the preceding example, we see the expected behavior. Ports that are published are bound to the IP address specified in the service level --ip option (10.10.10.101). However, if we specify an IP address at container runtime, we can override the service-level settings:

```
user@docker1:~$ docker run --name web2 -p 0.0.0.0::80 \
-d jonlangemak/web_server_2
7feb252d7bd9541fe7110b2aabcd6a50522531f8d6ac5422f1486205fad1f666
user@docker1:~$ docker port web2
80/tcp -> 0.0.0.0:32769
user@docker1:~$
```

We can see that we specified a host IP address of 0.0.0.0, which will match all the IP addresses on the Docker host. When we check the port mapping, we see that the 0.0.0.0 specified in the command overrode the service-level default.

It's possible that you won't find a use for exposed ports and instead rely solely on manually publishing them. The EXPOSE command is not a requirement of the Dockerfile for image creation. Container images that don't define an exposed port can be directly published as shown in the following commands:

```
user@docker1:~$ docker run --name noexpose -p 0.0.0.0:80:80 \
-d jonlangemak/web_server_noexpose
2bf21219b45ba05ef7169fc30d5eac73674857573e54fd1a0499b73557fdfd45
user@docker1:~$ docker port noexpose
80/tcp -> 0.0.0.0:80
user@docker1:~$
```

In the preceding example, the container image `jonlangemak/web_server_noexpose` is a container that does not expose any ports as part of its definition.

Connecting containers to existing containers

Docker network connectivity up until this point has relied on exposing individual services hosted in a container to the physical network. However, what if you want to expose a service from one container to another without exposing it to the Docker host? In this recipe we'll walk through how to map services between two containers running on the same Docker host.

Getting ready

You'll need access to a Docker host and an understanding of how your Docker host is connected to the network. In this recipe, we'll be using the `docker1` host that we used in previous recipes. You'll want to make sure that you have access to view `iptables` rules to verify netfilter policies. If you wish to download and run example containers, your Docker host will also need access to the Internet. In some cases, the changes we make may require you to have root-level access to the system.

How to do it...

Mapping services from one container to another is sometimes referred to as mapped container mode. Mapped container mode allows you to start a container that utilizes an existing, or primary, container's network configuration. That is, a mapped container will use the same IP and port configuration as the primary container. For the sake of example, let's consider running the following container:

```
user@docker1:~$ docker run --name web4 -d -P \
jonlangemak/web_server_4_redirect
```

Running this container starts the container in bridge mode and attaches it to the `docker0` bridge as we would expect.

The topology will look pretty standard at this point, something like what is shown in the following topology:

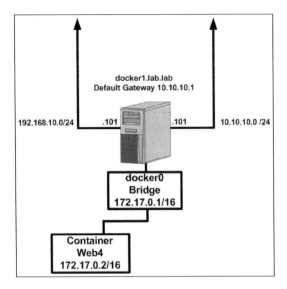

Now run a second container on the same host, but this time specify that the network should be that of the primary container web4:

```
user@docker1:~$ docker run --name web3 -d --net=container:web4 \
jonlangemak/web_server_3_8080
```

Our topology now looks as follows:

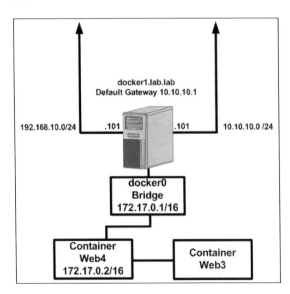

Note how the container `web3` is now depicted as being attached directly to `web4` rather than to the `docker0` bridge. By looking at the networking configuration of each container, we can validate that this is actually the case:

```
user@docker1:~$ docker exec web4 ip addr show
1: lo: <LOOPBACK,UP,LOWER_UP> mtu 65536 qdisc noqueue state UNKNOWN qlen
1
    link/loopback 00:00:00:00:00:00 brd 00:00:00:00:00:00
    inet 127.0.0.1/8 scope host lo
       valid_lft forever preferred_lft forever
    inet6 ::1/128 scope host
       valid_lft forever preferred_lft forever
16: eth0@if17: <BROADCAST,MULTICAST,UP,LOWER_UP> mtu 1500 qdisc noqueue
state UP
    link/ether 02:42:ac:11:00:02 brd ff:ff:ff:ff:ff:ff
    inet 172.17.0.2/16 scope global eth0
       valid_lft forever preferred_lft forever
    inet6 fe80::42:acff:fe11:2/64 scope link
       valid_lft forever preferred_lft forever
user@docker1:~$
user@docker1:~$ docker exec web3 ip addr show
1: lo: <LOOPBACK,UP,LOWER_UP> mtu 65536 qdisc noqueue state UNKNOWN qlen
1
    link/loopback 00:00:00:00:00:00 brd 00:00:00:00:00:00
    inet 127.0.0.1/8 scope host lo
       valid_lft forever preferred_lft forever
    inet6 ::1/128 scope host
       valid_lft forever preferred_lft forever
16: eth0@if17: <BROADCAST,MULTICAST,UP,LOWER_UP> mtu 1500 qdisc noqueue
state UP
    link/ether 02:42:ac:11:00:02 brd ff:ff:ff:ff:ff:ff
    inet 172.17.0.2/16 scope global eth0
       valid_lft forever preferred_lft forever
    inet6 fe80::42:acff:fe11:2/64 scope link
       valid_lft forever preferred_lft forever
user@docker1:~$
```

As we can see, the interfaces are identical both in IP configuration as well as MAC addresses. Using the syntax of `--net:container<container name/ID>` in the `docker run` command joins the new container to the same network construct that the referenced container is in. This means that the mapped container has the same network configuration as the primary container.

There is a limitation to this configuration that is worth noting. A container that joins another container's network cannot publish any of its own ports. So while this means that we can't publish ports of mapped containers to the host, we can consume them locally. Going back to our example, this means that we can't publish port `8080` of container web3 to the host. However, container web4 can consume nonpublished services of the container web3 locally. For instance, each of the containers in this example hosts a web service:

- web3 hosts a web server running on port `8080`
- web4 hosts a web server running on port `80`

From an external host perspective, there is no way to access the web service of the container web3. We can however, access these services through the container web4. The container web4 is hosting a PHP script named `test.php` that pulls the index pages of its own web server as well as that of a web server running on port `8080`. The script is as follows:

```
<?
$page = file_get_contents('http://localhost:80/');
echo $page;
$page1 = file_get_contents('http://localhost:8080/');
echo $page1;
?>
```

The script lives in the web server's root hosting directory (`/var/www/`), so we can access the port by browsing to the web4 container's published port followed by `test.php`:

```
user@docker1:~$ docker port web4
80/tcp -> 0.0.0.0:32768
user@docker1:~$
user@docker1:~$ curl http://localhost:32768/test.php
<body>
   <html>
      <h1><span style="color:#FF0000;font-size:72px;">Web Server #4 -
Running on port 80</span>
      </h1>
```

```
</body>
  </html>
<body>
  <html>
      <h1><span style="color:#FF0000;font-size:72px;">Web Server #3 -
Running on port 8080</span>
      </h1>
</body>
  </html>
user@docker1:~$
```

As you can see, the script is able to pull the index page from both containers. Let's stop the container `web3` and run this test again to prove that it's really the one providing this index page response:

```
user@docker1:~$ docker stop web3
web3
user@docker1:~$ curl http://localhost:32768/test.php
<body>
  <html>              ˙
      <h1><span style="color:#FF0000;font-size:72px;">Web Server #4 -
Running on port 80</span>
      </h1>
</body>
  </html>
user@docker1:~$
```

As you can see, we no longer get the response from the mapped container. Mapped container mode is useful for scenarios where you need to provide a service to an existing container, but don't need to publish any of the mapped container's ports directly to the Docker host or outside network. Although there is a limitation that mapped containers cannot publish any of their own ports, this does not mean we can't publish them ahead of time.

For instance, we could expose port `8080` when we run the primary container:

```
user@docker1:~$ docker run --name web4 -d --expose 8080 \
-P jonlangemak/web_server_4_redirect
user@docker1:~$ docker run --name web3 -d --net=container:web4 \
jonlangemak/web_server_3_8080
```

Because we published the port for the mapped container when we ran the primary container (web4), we don't need to publish it when we run our mapped container (web3). We should now be able to access each service directly through its published port:

```
user@docker1:~$ docker port web4
80/tcp -> 0.0.0.0:32771
8080/tcp -> 0.0.0.0:32770
user@docker1:~$
user@docker1:~$ curl localhost:32771
<body>
   <html>
      <h1><span style="color:#FF0000;font-size:72px;">Web Server #4 -
Running on port 80</span>
      </h1>
</body>
   </html>
user@docker1:~$ curl localhost:32770
<body>
   <html>
      <h1><span style="color:#FF0000;font-size:72px;">Web Server #3 -
Running on port 8080</span>
      </h1>
</body>
   </html>
user@docker1:~$
```

Care should be taken in mapped container mode to not attempt to expose or publish the same port on different containers. Since the mapped containers share the same network construct as the primary container, this would cause a port conflict.

Connecting containers in host mode

All the configurations we have done up until this point have relied on using the docker0 bridge to facilitate connectivity between containers. We've had to consider port mappings, NATing, and container connection points. These considerations had to be made because of the nature of how we connect and address containers and to ensure a flexible deployment model. Host mode takes a different approach and binds containers directly to the Docker host's interfaces. This not only removes the need for inbound and outbound NAT but also restricts how we can deploy containers. Since the containers will be in the same network construct as the physical host, we cannot overlap service ports as this would cause a conflict. In this recipe, we'll walk through deploying a container in host mode and describe the pros and cons of this approach.

Getting ready

You'll need access to a Docker host and an understanding of how your Docker host is connected to the network. In this recipe, we'll be using the `docker1` and `docker2` hosts that we used in previous recipes. You'll want to make sure that you have access to view `iptables` rules to verify netfilter policies. If you wish to download and run example containers, your Docker host will also need access to the Internet. In some cases, the changes we make may require you to have root-level access to the system.

How to do it...

Deploying containers in this mode is rather easy from a Docker point of view. Much like mapped container mode where we put one container into another's network construct; host mode puts a container directly into the Docker host's network construct. Ports no longer need to be published and exposed since you're mapping the container directly onto the host's network interfaces. This means that container processes can do certain privileged actions such as open lower level ports on the host. For this reason, this option should be used with caution as the container will have more access to the system in this configuration.

This also means that Docker is not aware of what port your container is using and is unable to prevent you from deploying containers that have overlapping ports. Let's deploy a test container in host mode, so you can see what I mean:

```
user@docker1:~$ docker run --name web1 -d --net=host \
jonlangemak/web_server_1
64dc47af71fade3cde02f7fed8edf7477e3cc4c8fc7f0f3df53afd129331e736
user@docker1:~$
user@docker1:~$ curl localhost
<body>
  <html>
    <h1><span style="color:#FF0000;font-size:72px;">Web Server #1 -
Running on port 80</span>
    </h1>
</body>
  </html>
user@docker1:~$
```

To achieve host mode, we pass the `--net=host` flag at container runtime. In this case, you can see that without any port mapping, we can still access the service living in the container. Docker is simply binding the container to the Docker host, which means that any services the container offers are automatically mapped to the Docker host's interfaces.

If we try to run another container offering services on port `80`, we'll see that Docker doesn't try and stop us:

```
user@docker1:~$ docker run --name web2 -d --net=host \
jonlangemak/web_server_2
c1c00aa387111e1bb09e3daacc2a2820c92f6a91ce73694c1e88691c3955d815
user@docker1:~$
```

While that looks like a successful container start from a Docker perspective, the container actually died right after being spawned. If we check the logs for container `web2`, we'll see that it ran into a conflict and was unable to start:

```
user@docker1:~$ docker logs web2
apache2: Could not reliably determine the server's fully qualified domain
name, using 127.0.1.1 for ServerName
(98)Address already in use: make_sock: could not bind to address
0.0.0.0:80
no listening sockets available, shutting down
Unable to open logs
user@docker1:~$
```

Deploying containers in host mode limits the number of services you can run unless your containers are built to offer the same service on different ports.

Since the configuration of the service and what ports it consumes are the responsibility of the container, there is a means by which we can deploy multiple containers each using the same service port. Take for example our earlier example of two Docker hosts, each with two network interfaces:

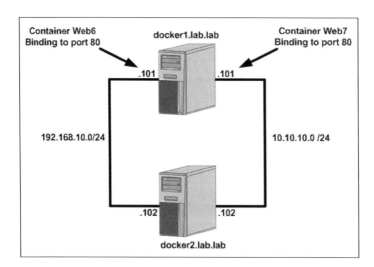

In a scenario where your Docker host has multiple network interfaces, you can have containers binding to the same port but on different interfaces. Again, since this is the responsibility of the container, Docker doesn't have any visibility into how you achieve this as long as you don't try to bind the same port to multiple interfaces.

The solution is to change how services bind to the interfaces. Most services bind to all interfaces (0.0.0.0) when the service starts. For instance, we can see that our container web1 is bound to 0.0.0.0:80 on the Docker host:

```
user@docker1:~$ sudo netstat -plnt
Active Internet connections (only servers)
Proto Recv-Q Send-Q Local Address          Foreign Address         State
PID/Program name
tcp        0      0 0.0.0.0:80              0.0.0.0:*
LISTEN      3724/apache2
tcp        0      0 0.0.0.0:22              0.0.0.0:*
LISTEN      1056/sshd
tcp6       0      0 :::22                   :::*
LISTEN      1056/sshd
user@docker1:~$
```

Rather than having the service bind to all interfaces, we can limit the scope of the service by having it bind to a specific interface. If we can bind a container service to only one interface, we can bind the same port to a different interface without causing conflict. For the purpose of this example, I've created two container images that allow you to pass them an environmental variable ($APACHE_IPADDRESS). The variable is referenced in the Apache configuration and specifies which interface the service should bind to. We can test this by deploying two containers in host mode to the same host:

```
user@docker1:~$ docker run --name web6 -d --net=host \
-e APACHE_IPADDRESS=10.10.10.101 jonlangemak/web_server_6_pickip
user@docker1:~$ docker run --name web7 -d --net=host \
-e APACHE_IPADDRESS=192.168.10.101 jonlangemak/web_server_7_pickip
```

Note that in each case, I pass the container a different IP address for it to bind to. A quick look at port bindings on the host should confirm the containers are no longer binding to all interfaces:

```
user@docker1:~$ sudo netstat -plnt
[sudo] password for user:
Active Internet connections (only servers)
Proto Recv-Q Send-Q Local Address          Foreign Address         State
PID/Program name
```

```
tcp         0         0 192.168.10.101:80        0.0.0.0:*
LISTEN         1518/apache2
tcp         0         0 10.10.10.101:80          0.0.0.0:*
LISTEN         1482/apache2
tcp         0         0 0.0.0.0:22               0.0.0.0:*
LISTEN         1096/sshd
tcp6        0         0 :::22                     :::*
LISTEN         1096/sshd
user@docker1:~$
```

Note that Apache is no longer binding to all interfaces and that we have two Apache processes, one bound to each interface of the Docker host. A test from the other Docker host will prove that each container is serving Apache on its respective interface:

```
user@docker2:~$ curl http://10.10.10.101
<body>
   <html>
      <h1><span style="color:#FF0000;font-size:72px;">Web Server #6 -
Running on port 80</span>
      </h1>
</body>
   </html>
user@docker2:~$
user@docker2:~$ curl http://192.168.10.101
<body>
   <html>
      <h1><span style="color:#FF0000;font-size:72px;">Web Server #7 -
Running on port 80</span>
      </h1>
</body>
   </html>
user@docker2:~$
```

While there are some limitations to host mode, it is also less complicated and likely offers higher performance because of the lack of NAT and the use of the `docker0` bridge.

> Keep in mind that since Docker isn't involved in host mode that you may need to manually open firewall ports if you have a host-based firewall that is enforcing policy in order for the containers to be reachable.

Configuring service-level settings

While many settings can be configured at container runtime, there are some settings that must be configured as part of starting the Docker service. That is, they need to be defined as a Docker option in the service configuration. In earlier recipes, we were exposed to some of these service-level options, such as `--ip-forward`, `--userland-proxy`, and `--ip`. In this recipe, we'll cover how you can pass service-level parameters to the Docker service as well as discuss the functionality of a few key parameters.

Getting ready

You'll need access to a Docker host and an understanding of how your Docker host is connected to the network. In this recipe, we'll be using the `docker1` and `docker2` hosts that we used in previous recipes. You'll want to make sure that you have access to view `iptables` rules to verify netfilter policies. If you wish to download and run example containers, your Docker host will also need access to the Internet.

How to do it...

In order to pass runtime options or parameters to the Docker, we need to modify the service configuration. In our case, we're using Ubuntu version 16.04, which uses `systemd` to manage services running on the Linux host. The recommended approach to passing parameters to Docker is to use a `systemd` drop in file. To create the drop in file we can follow these steps to create a service directory and a Docker configuration file:

```
sudo mkdir /etc/systemd/system/docker.service.d
sudo vi /etc/systemd/system/docker.service.d/docker.conf
```

Insert the following lines into the `docker.conf` configuration file:

```
[Service]
ExecStart=
ExecStart=/usr/bin/dockerd
```

If you wish to pass any parameters to Docker service, you can do so by appending them to the third line. For instance, if I wanted to disable Docker automatically enabling IP forwarding on the host when the service starts, my file would look like:

```
[Service]
ExecStart=
ExecStart=/usr/bin/dockerd --ip-forward=false
```

After making changes to system-related files, you need to ask `systemd` to reload the configuration. This is done with the following command:

```
sudo systemctl daemon-reload
```

And finally, you can restart the service for the settings to take effect:

```
systemctl restart docker
```

Each time you change the configuration, you will need to reload the `systemd` configuration as well as restart the service.

docker0 bridge addressing

As we saw earlier, the IP address of the `docker0` bridge is by default `172.17.0.1/16`. However, if you wish, you can change this IP address using the `--bip` configuration flag. For example, you might wish to change the `docker0` bridge subnet to be `192.168.127.1/24`. This can be done by passing the following option to the Docker service:

```
ExecStart=/usr/bin/dockerd --bip=192.168.127.1/24
```

When changing this setting make sure that you configure the IP address (`192.168.127.1/24`) rather than the subnet (`192.168.127.0/24`) you wish to define. Previous versions of Docker required the host to be rebooted or the existing bridge be manually deleted before a new bridge IP could be assigned. In newer versions, you simply reload the `systemd` configuration and restart the service for the new bridge IP to be assigned:

```
user@docker1:~$ sudo systemctl daemon-reload
user@docker1:~$ sudo systemctl restart docker
user@docker1:~$
user@docker1:~$ ip addr show docker0
5: docker0: <NO-CARRIER,BROADCAST,MULTICAST,UP> mtu 1500 qdisc noqueue
state DOWN group default
    link/ether 02:42:a6:d1:b3:37 brd ff:ff:ff:ff:ff:ff
    inet 192.168.127.1/24 scope global docker0
       valid_lft forever preferred_lft forever
user@docker1:~$
```

In addition to changing the IP address of the `docker0` bridge, you may also define which IP addresses Docker can assign to containers. This is done by using the `--fixed-cidr` configuration flag. For instance, assume the following configuration:

```
ExecStart=/usr/bin/dockerd --bip=192.168.127.1/24
--fixed-cidr=192.168.127.128/25
```

In this scenario, the `docker0` bridge interface itself lives in the `192.168.127.0/24` subnet, but we are telling Docker to only assign container IP addresses out of the subnet `192.168.127.128/25`. If we add this configuration and once again reload `systemd` and restart the service, we can see that Docker will assign the first container an IP address of `192.168.127.128`:

```
user@docker1:~$ docker run --name web1 -it \
jonlangemak/web_server_1 /bin/bash
root@ff8872212cb4:/# ip addr show eth0
6: eth0@if7: <BROADCAST,MULTICAST,UP,LOWER_UP> mtu 1500 qdisc noqueue
state UP
    link/ether 02:42:c0:a8:7f:80 brd ff:ff:ff:ff:ff:ff
    inet 192.168.127.128/24 scope global eth0
       valid_lft forever preferred_lft forever
    inet6 fe80::42:c0ff:fea8:7f80/64 scope link
       valid_lft forever preferred_lft forever
root@ff8872212cb4:/#
```

Since the containers use the defined `docker0` bridge IP address as their default gateway, the fixed CIDR range must be a smaller subnet of the one defined on the `docker0` bridge itself.

Docker interface binding for published ports

In some scenarios, you may have a Docker host that has multiple network interfaces that live in different network segments. For instance, consider the example where you have two hosts that both have two network interfaces:

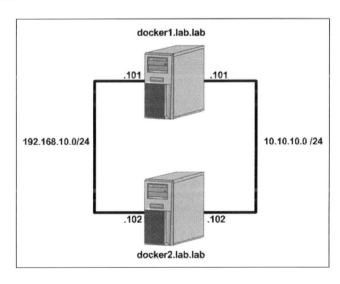

Consider the case where we start a container providing a web service on the host `docker1` using this syntax:

```
docker run -d --name web1 -P jonlangemak/web_server_1
```

As you can see, we've passed the `-P` flag telling Docker to publish any exposed ports present in the image to the Docker host on a random port. If we examine the port mapping, we note that while there's a dynamic port assignment, there is not a host IP address assignment:

```
user@docker1:~$ docker run -d --name web1 -P jonlangemak/web_server_1
d96b4dd005edb2218257a7701b674f51f4318b92baf4be686400d77912c75e58
user@docker1:~$ docker port web1
80/tcp -> 0.0.0.0:32768
user@docker1:~$
```

Rather than specifying a specific IP address, Docker specifies all interfaces with `0.0.0.0`. This means that the service in the container can be accessed on port `32768` on any of the Docker host's IP interfaces. We can prove this by testing from the `docker2` host:

```
user@docker2:~$ curl http://10.10.10.101:32768
<body>
   <html>
      <h1><span style="color:#FF0000;font-size:72px;">Web Server #1 -
Running on port 80</span>
      </h1>
</body>
   </html>
user@docker2:~$ curl http://192.168.10.101:32768
<body>
   <html>
      <h1><span style="color:#FF0000;font-size:72px;">Web Server #1 -
Running on port 80</span>
      </h1>
</body>
   </html>
user@docker2:~$
```

If we wish to limit the interface Docker publishes ports on by default, we can pass the `--ip` option to the Docker service. To continue the example, my options could now look like this:

```
ExecStart=/usr/bin/dockerd --bip=192.168.127.1/24
--fixed-cidr=192.168.127.128/25 --ip=192.168.10.101
```

Passing these options to the Docker service, and rerunning our container, will cause ports to only be mapped to the defined IP address:

```
user@docker1:~$ docker port web1
80/tcp -> 192.168.10.101:32768
user@docker1:~$
```

And if we run our test from the `docker2` host a second time, we should see that the service is only exposed on the `192.168.10.101` interface and not on the `10.10.10.101` interface:

```
user@docker2:~$ curl http://10.10.10.101:32768
curl: (7) Failed to connect to 10.10.10.101 port 32768: Connection
refused
user@docker2:~$
user@docker2:~$ curl http://192.168.10.101:32768
<body>
  <html>
     <h1><span style="color:#FF0000;font-size:72px;">Web Server #1 -
Running on port 80</span>
     </h1>
</body>
  </html>
user@docker2:~$
```

Keep in mind that this setting only applies to published ports. This does not impact the interface a container might use for outbound connectivity. That is dictated by the host's routing table.

Container interface MTU

In some cases, it may be necessary to change the MTU of the container's network interface. This can be done by passing the `--mtu` option to the Docker service. For instance, we may wish to lower the MTU of the container's interface to `1450` to account for some type of encapsulation. To do this, you could pass the following flag:

```
ExecStart=/usr/bin/dockerd  --mtu=1450
```

After adding this option, you might examine the `docker0` bridge MTU and find it unchanged as shown in the following code:

```
user@docker1:~$ ip addr show docker0
5: docker0: <NO-CARRIER,BROADCAST,MULTICAST,UP> mtu 1500 qdisc noqueue
state DOWN group default
    link/ether 02:42:a6:d1:b3:37 brd ff:ff:ff:ff:ff:ff
    inet 192.168.127.1/24 scope global docker0
       valid_lft forever preferred_lft forever
    inet6 fe80::42:a6ff:fed1:b337/64 scope link
       valid_lft forever preferred_lft forever
user@docker1:~$
```

This is actually expected behavior. Linux bridges, by default, automatically use the lowest MTU of any slave interface associated with it. When we told Docker to use a MTU of `1450`, we were really telling it to start any containers with a MTU of `1450`. Since we have no containers running at this point, the MTU of the bridge is unchanged. Let's start a container to validate this:

```
user@docker1:~$ docker run --name web1 -d jonlangemak/web_server_1
18f4c038eadba924a23bd0d2841ac52d90b5df6dd2d07e0433eb5315124ce427
user@docker1:~$
user@docker1:~$ docker exec web1 ip addr show
1: lo: <LOOPBACK,UP,LOWER_UP> mtu 65536 qdisc noqueue state UNKNOWN qlen
1
    link/loopback 00:00:00:00:00:00 brd 00:00:00:00:00:00
    inet 127.0.0.1/8 scope host lo
       valid_lft forever preferred_lft forever
    inet6 ::1/128 scope host
       valid_lft forever preferred_lft forever
10: eth0@if11: <BROADCAST,MULTICAST,UP,LOWER_UP> mtu 1450 qdisc noqueue
state UP
    link/ether 02:42:c0:a8:7f:02 brd ff:ff:ff:ff:ff:ff
    inet 192.168.127.2/24 scope global eth0
       valid_lft forever preferred_lft forever
    inet6 fe80::42:c0ff:fea8:7f02/64 scope link
       valid_lft forever preferred_lft forever
user@docker1:~$
```

We can see that the container has the correct MTU of 1450. Checking the Docker host we should see that the MTU of the bridge is now also lower:

```
user@docker1:~$ ip addr show docker0
5: docker0: <BROADCAST,MULTICAST,UP,LOWER_UP> mtu 1450 qdisc noqueue
state UP group default
    link/ether 02:42:a6:d1:b3:37 brd ff:ff:ff:ff:ff:ff
    inet 192.168.127.1/24 scope global docker0
       valid_lft forever preferred_lft forever
    inet6 fe80::42:a6ff:fed1:b337/64 scope link
       valid_lft forever preferred_lft forever
user@docker1:~$
```

Starting the container with a lower MTU automatically impacted the bridge MTU as we expected.

Container default gateway

By default, Docker sets the default gateway of any containers to that of the docker0 bridge IP address. This makes sense because the containers need to route through the docker0 bridge to reach the outside network. It is, however, possible to override this setting and have Docker set the default gateway to another IP address on the docker0 bridge network.

For instance, we can change the default gateway to 192.168.127.50 by passing the Docker service these configuration options.

```
ExecStart=/usr/bin/dockerd --bip=192.168.127.1/24 --fixed-
cidr=192.168.127.128/25 --default-gateway=192.168.127.50
```

If we add these settings, restart the service, and spawn a container, we can see that the new container has a default gateway of 192.168.127.50 as configured:

```
user@docker1:~$ docker run --name web1 -it \
jonlangemak/web_server_1 /bin/bash
root@b36baa4d0950:/# ip addr show eth0
12: eth0@if13: <BROADCAST,MULTICAST,UP,LOWER_UP> mtu 1500 qdisc noqueue
state UP
    link/ether 02:42:c0:a8:7f:80 brd ff:ff:ff:ff:ff:ff
    inet 192.168.127.128/24 scope global eth0
       valid_lft forever preferred_lft forever
    inet6 fe80::42:c0ff:fea8:7f80/64 scope link
       valid_lft forever preferred_lft forever
root@b36baa4d0950:/#
```

```
root@b36baa4d0950:/# ip route show
default via 192.168.127.50 dev eth0
192.168.127.0/24 dev eth0   proto kernel   scope link   src 192.168.127.128
root@b36baa4d0950:/#
```

Keep in mind that at this point, this container has no connectivity off it's current subnet because that gateway does not currently exist. In order for the container to have connectivity off its local subnet `192.168.127.50` would need to be reachable from the containers and have connectivity to the outside network.

There are other options configured at the service level such as `--iptables` and `--icc`. Those will be discussed in later chapters as we discuss their relevant use cases.

3

User-Defined Networks

In this chapter, we will cover the following recipes:

- ▸ Viewing the Docker network configuration
- ▸ Creating user-defined networks
- ▸ Connecting containers to networks
- ▸ Defining a user-defined bridge network
- ▸ Creating a user-defined overlay network
- ▸ Isolating networks

Introduction

Earlier versions of Docker relied on a mostly static network model, which worked relatively well for most container networking needs. However, if you wanted to do something different, you weren't left with many options. For instance, you could tell Docker to deploy containers to a different bridge, but there wasn't a strong integration point between Docker and that network. With the introduction of user-defined networking in Docker 1.9, the game has changed. You can now create and manage bridge and multi-host networks directly through the Docker engine. In addition, the door has also been opened for third-party network plugins to integrate with Docker through libnetwork and its **Container Network Model** (**CNM**) model.

 CNM is Docker's model for defining a container network model. In *Chapter 7, Working with Weave Net*, we'll examine a third-party plugin (Weave) that can integrate as a Docker driver. The focus in this chapter will be on the default network drivers natively included with a Docker engine.

The move to a driver-based model symbolizes a great change in Docker networking. In addition to defining new networks, you're now also given the ability to connect and disconnect container interfaces dynamically. This inherent flexibility opens the door to many new possibilities to connect containers.

Viewing the Docker network configuration

As mentioned, defining and managing networks can now be done directly through Docker with the addition of the `network` subcommand. The `network` command provides you with all the options you need to build networks and connect containers to them:

```
user@docker1:~$ docker network --help


docker network --help


Usage:   docker network COMMAND


Manage Docker networks


Options:
        --help    Print usage


Commands:
   connect      Connect a container to a network
   create       Create a network
   disconnect   Disconnect a container from a network
   inspect      Display detailed information on one or more networks
   ls           List networks
   rm           Remove one or more networks


Run 'docker network COMMAND --help' for more information on a command.
user@docker1:~$
```

In this recipe, we'll learn how to view defined Docker networks as well as inspect them for specific details.

Getting ready

The `docker network` subcommand was introduced in Docker 1.9, so you'll need a Docker host running at least that version. In our examples, we'll be using Docker version 1.12. You'll also want to have a good understanding of your current network layout, so you can follow along as we inspect the current configuration. It is assumed that each Docker host is in its native configuration.

How to do it...

The first thing we want to do is figure out what networks Docker thinks are already defined. This can be done using the `network ls` subcommand:

```
user@docker1:~$ docker network ls
NETWORK ID          NAME                DRIVER              SCOPE
200d5292d5db        bridge              bridge              local
12e399864b79        host                host                local
cb6922b8b84f        none                null                local
user@docker1:~$
```

As we can see, Docker shows that we have three different networks already defined. To view more information about a network, we can use the `network inspect` subcommand to retrieve specifics about the network definition as well as its current state. Let's take a close look at each defined network.

Bridge

The bridge network represents the `docker0` bridge that the Docker engine creates by default:

```
user@docker1:~$ docker network inspect bridge
[
    {
        "Name": "bridge",
        "Id":
"62fcda0787f2be01e65992e2a5a636f095970ea83c59fdf0980da3f3f555c24e",
        "Scope": "local",
        "Driver": "bridge",
        "EnableIPv6": false,
        "IPAM": {
            "Driver": "default",
```

```
            "Options": null,
            "Config": [
                {
                    "Subnet": "172.17.0.0/16"
                }
            ]
        },
        "Internal": false,
        "Containers": {},
        "Options": {
            "com.docker.network.bridge.default_bridge": "true",
            "com.docker.network.bridge.enable_icc": "true",
            "com.docker.network.bridge.enable_ip_masquerade": "true",
            "com.docker.network.bridge.host_binding_ipv4": "0.0.0.0",
            "com.docker.network.bridge.name": "docker0",
            "com.docker.network.driver.mtu": "1500"
        },
        "Labels": {}
    }
]
user@docker1:~$
```

The output from the `inspect` command shows us a wealth of information about the defined network:

- `Driver`: In this case, we can see that the network bridge implements the `Driver` bridge. Although this may seem obvious, it's important to call out that all network functionality, including native functionality, is implemented through drivers.

- `Subnet`: In this case, the `subnet` is the default we expect from the `docker0` bridge, `172.17.0.1/16`.

- `bridge.default_bridge`: A value of `true` implies that Docker will provision all containers to this bridge unless told otherwise. That is, if you start a container without specifying a network (`--net`), the container will end up on this bridge.

- `bridge.host_binding_ipv4`: By default, this will be set to `0.0.0.0` or all interfaces. As we saw in *Chapter 2, Configuring and Monitoring Docker Networks*, we can tell Docker at a service level to limit this by passing the `--ip` flag as a Docker option to the service.

- `bridge.name`: As we suspected, this network represents the `docker0` bridge.

▶ `driver.mtu`: By default, this will be set to `1500`. As we saw in *Chapter 2, Configuring and Monitoring Docker Networks*, we can tell Docker at a service level to change **MTU (Maximum Transmission Unit)** by passing the `--mtu` flag as a Docker option to the service.

None

The `none` network represents just what it says, nothing. The `none` mode is used when you wish to define a container with absolutely no network definition. After inspecting the network, we can see that there isn't much there as far as a network definition is concerned:

```
user@docker1:~$ docker network inspect none
[
    {
        "Name": "none",
        "Id":
"a191c26b7dad643ca77fe6548c2480b1644a86dcc95cde0c09c6033d4eaff7f2",
        "Scope": "local",
        "Driver": "null",
        "EnableIPv6": false,
        "IPAM": {
            "Driver": "default",
            "Options": null,
            "Config": []
        },
        "Internal": false,
        "Containers": {},
        "Options": {},
        "Labels": {}
    }
]
user@docker1:~$
```

As you can see, `Driver` is represented by `null`, implying that this isn't a `Driver` for this network at all. There are a few use cases for the `none` network mode and we'll cover those later on when we talk about connecting and disconnecting containers to defined networks.

Host

The *host* network represents the host mode we saw in *Chapter 2, Configuring and Monitoring Docker Networks*, where a container was bound directly to the Docker host's own network interfaces. By taking a closer look, we can see that much like the `none` network, there isn't much defined for this network:

```
user@docker1:~$ docker network inspect host
[
    {
        "Name": "host",
        "Id":
"4b94353d158cef25b9c9244ca9b03b148406a608b4fd85f3421c93af3be6fe4b",
        "Scope": "local",
        "Driver": "host",
        "EnableIPv6": false,
        "IPAM": {
            "Driver": "default",
            "Options": null,
            "Config": []
        },
        "Internal": false,
        "Containers": {},
        "Options": {},
        "Labels": {}
    }
]
user@docker1:~$
```

Although the host network certainly does more than the `none` mode, it wouldn't appear so from inspecting its definition. The key difference here is that this network uses the host `Driver`. As this network type uses the existing host's network interfaces, we don't need to define any of that as part of the network.

When using the `network ls` command, you can pass additional parameters to further filter or alter the output:

- ▶ `--quiet` (`-q`): This only shows the numeric network IDs
- ▶ `--no-trunc`: This prevents the command from automatically truncating the network ID in the output that allows you to see the full network ID
- ▶ `--filter` (`-f`): This filters the output based on either network ID, network name, or by network definition (built-in or user-defined)

For example, we can show all user-defined networks with this filter:

```
user@docker1:~$ docker network ls -f type=custom
NETWORK ID          NAME                DRIVER              SCOPE
a09b7617c550        mynetwork           bridge              local
user@docker1:~$
```

Or we can show all networks with a network ID that contains `158`:

```
user@docker1:~$ docker network ls -f id=158
NETWORK ID          NAME                DRIVER              SCOPE
4b94353d158c        host                host                local
user@docker1:~$
```

Creating user-defined networks

As we've seen so far, there are at least two different network drivers that are inherently part of every Docker installation, bridge, and host. In addition to those two, while not defined initially because of prerequisites, there is another `Driver` overlay that is available out-of-the-box as well. Later recipes in this chapter will cover specifics regarding the bridge and overlay drivers.

Because it wouldn't make sense to create another iteration of the host network using the host `Driver`, the built-in user-defined networks are limited to the bridge and overlay drivers. In this recipe, we'll show you the basics of creating a user-defined network as well as options that are relevant to the `network create` and `network rm` Docker subcommands.

Getting ready

The `docker network` subcommand was introduced in Docker 1.9, so you'll need a Docker host running at least that version. In our examples, we'll be using Docker version 1.12. You'll also want to have a good understanding of your current network layout, so you can follow along as we inspect the current configuration. It is assumed that each Docker host is in its native configuration.

 Warning: Creating network interfaces on a Linux host must be done with caution. Docker will do its best to prevent you from shooting yourself in the foot, but you must have a good idea of your network topology before defining new networks on a Docker host. A common mistake to avoid is to define a new network that overlaps with other subnets in your network. In the case of remote administration, this can cause host and container connectivity issues.

How to do it...

Networks are defined by using the `network create` subcommand, which has the following options:

```
user@docker1:~$ docker network create --help


Usage:  docker network create [OPTIONS] NETWORK


Create a network


Options:
  --aux-address value      Auxiliary IPv4 or IPv6 addresses used by Network
  driver (default map[])
  -d, --driver string      Driver to manage the Network (default "bridge")
  --gateway value          IPv4 or IPv6 Gateway for the master subnet
  (default [])
  --help                   Print usage
  --internal               Restrict external access to the network
  --ip-range value         Allocate container ip from a sub-range (default
  [])
  --ipam-driver string     IP Address Management Driver (default "default")
  --ipam-opt value         Set IPAM driver specific options (default map[])
  --ipv6                   Enable IPv6 networking
  --label value            Set metadata on a network (default [])
  -o, --opt value          Set driver specific options (default map[])
  --subnet value           Subnet in CIDR format that represents a network
  segment (default [])
user@docker1:~$
```

Let's spend a little time discussing what each of these options means:

- ▸ `aux-address`: This allows you to define IP addresses that Docker should not assign to containers when they are spawned. These are the equivalent of IP reservations in a DHCP scope.

- ▸ `Driver`: Which `Driver` the network implements. The built-in options include bridge and overlay, but you can also use third-party drivers as well.

- ▸ `gateway`: The Gateway for the network. If not specified, Docker will assume that it is the first available IP address in the subnet.

- ▸ `internal`: This option allows you to isolate networks and is covered in greater detail later in this chapter.

- ▸ `ip-range`: This allows you to specify a smaller subnet of the defined network subnet to use for container addressing.

- ▸ `ipam-driver`: In addition to consuming third-party network drivers, you can also leverage third-party IPAM drivers. For the purposes of this book, we'll be focusing mostly on the default or built-in IPAM `Driver`.

- ▸ `ipv6`: This enables IPv6 networking on the network.

- ▸ `label`: This allows you to specify additional information about the network that will be stored as metadata.

- ▸ `ipam-opt`: This allows you to specify options to pass to the IPAM `Driver`.

- ▸ `opt`: This allows you to specify options that can be passed to the network `Driver`. Specific options for each built-in `Driver` will be discussed in the relevant recipes.

- ▸ `subnet`: This defines the subnet associated with the network type you are creating.

You might notice some overlap here between some of the settings we can define at a service level for Docker networking and the user-defined options listed in the preceding term list. Examining the options, you may be tempted to compare the following configuration flags:

Service (docker0)	User Defined
--fixed-cidr	--ip-range
--bip	--subnet
--default-gateway	--gateway

While these settings are largely equivalent, they are not all identical. The only two that act in the exact same fashion are `--fixed-cidr` and `ip-range`. Both of those options, define a smaller subnetwork of the larger master network to be used for container IP addressing. The other two options are similar, but not identical.

In the case of the service options, `--bip` applies to the `docker0` bridge and `--default-gateway` applies to the containers themselves. On the user-defined side, the `--subnet` and the `--gateway` option, apply directly to the network construct being defined (in this comparison, a bridge). Recall that the `--bip` option expects to receive an IP address in a network, not the network itself. Having the bridge IP defined in this manner covers both the subnet as well as the gateway, which are defined separately when defining a user-defined network. That being said, the service definition is a little more flexible in that it allows you to define both the interface of the bridge as well as the gateway assigned to containers.

Keeping with the theme of having sane defaults, none of these options are actually required to create a user-defined network. You can create your first user-defined network by just giving it a name:

```
user@docker1:~$ docker network create mynetwork
3fea20c313e8880538ab50fd591398bdfdac2378abac29aacb1be131cbfab40f
user@docker1:~$
```

Upon inspection, we can see what Docker uses for defaults:

```
user@docker1:~$ docker network inspect mynetwork
[
    {
        "Name": "mynetwork",
        "Id":
"a09b7617c5504d4afd80c26b82587000c64046f1483de604c51fa4ba53463b50",
        "Scope": "local",
        "Driver": "bridge",
        "EnableIPv6": false,
        "IPAM": {
            "Driver": "default",
            "Options": {},
            "Config": [
                {
                    "Subnet": "172.18.0.0/16",
                    "Gateway": "172.18.0.1/16"
                }
            ]
        },
        "Internal": false,
        "Containers": {},
```

```
        "Options": {},
        "Labels": {}
    }
]
user@docker1:~$
```

Docker assumes that if you don't specify a `Driver` that you'd like to create a network using the bridge `Driver`. It also automatically chooses and assigns a subnet for this bridge if you don't define one when you create the network.

 It is always advisable that you specify subnets for network, you create. As we'll see later on, not all network topologies rely on hiding the container networks behind the host interfaces. In those cases, defining a routable non-overlapping subnet will be a necessity.

It also automatically selects the first useable IP address for the Subnet as the gateway. Because we didn't define any options specific to the `Driver`, the network has none but again, there are defaults that are used in this case. Those will be discussed in the recipes related to each specific `Driver`.

Networks that are empty, that is, they have no active endpoints, may be deleted using the `network rm` command:

```
user@docker1:~$ docker network rm mynetwork
user@docker1:~$
```

One other item that's worth noting here is that Docker makes user-defined networks persistent. In most cases, any Linux network constructs that are manually defined are lost when the system reboots. Docker records the network configuration and takes care of replaying it back when the Docker service restarts. This is a huge advantage to building the networks through Docker rather than on your own.

Connecting containers to networks

While having the ability to create your own networks is a huge leap forward, it means nothing without a means to connect containers to it. In previous versions of Docker, this was traditionally done during container runtime by passing the `--net` flag specifying which network the container should use. While this is certainly still the case, the `docker network` subcommand also allows you to connect and disconnect running containers to existing networks.

Getting ready

The `docker network` subcommand was introduced in Docker 1.9, so you'll need a Docker host running at least that version. In our examples, we'll be using Docker version 1.12. You'll also want to have a good understanding of your current network layout, so you can follow along as we inspect the current configuration. It is assumed that each Docker host is in its native configuration.

How to do it...

Connecting and disconnecting containers is done via the `network connect` and `network disconnect` subcommands:

```
user@docker1:~$ docker network connect --help

Usage:  docker network connect [OPTIONS] NETWORK CONTAINER

Connects a container to a network
  --alias=[]          Add network-scoped alias for the container
  --help              Print usage
  --ip                IP Address
  --ip6               IPv6 Address
  --link=[]           Add link to another container
user@docker1:~$
```

Let's review what our options are for connecting containers to networks:

> ► **Alias**: This allows you to define an alias for container name resolution in the network you are connecting the container to. We'll talk more about this in *Chapter 5, Container Linking and Docker DNS*, where we discuss DNS and linking.

> ► **IP**: This defines an IP address to be used for the container. This will work so long as the IP address is not currently in use. Once allocated, it will remain reserved as long as the container is running or paused. Stopping the container will remove the reservation.

> ► **IP6**: This defines an IPv6 address to be used for the container. The same allocation and reservation requirements that applied to the IPv4 address also apply to the IPv6 address.

> ► **Link**: This allows you to specify a link to another container. We'll talk more about this in *Chapter 5, Container Linking and Docker DNS*, where we discuss DNS and linking.

Once a `network connect` request is sent, Docker handles all the configuration required in order for the container to start using the new interface. Let's take a look at a quick example:

```
user@docker1:~$ docker run --name web1 -d jonlangemak/web_server_1
```

```
e112a2ab8197ec70c5ee49161613f2244f4353359b27643f28a18be47698bf59
user@docker1:~$
user@docker1:~$ docker exec web1 ip addr
1: lo: <LOOPBACK,UP,LOWER_UP> mtu 65536 qdisc noqueue state UNKNOWN qlen
1
    link/loopback 00:00:00:00:00:00 brd 00:00:00:00:00:00
    inet 127.0.0.1/8 scope host lo
        valid_lft forever preferred_lft forever
    inet6 ::1/128 scope host
        valid_lft forever preferred_lft forever
8: eth0@if9: <BROADCAST,MULTICAST,UP,LOWER_UP> mtu 1500 qdisc noqueue
state UP
    link/ether 02:42:ac:11:00:02 brd ff:ff:ff:ff:ff:ff
    inet 172.17.0.2/16 scope global eth0
        valid_lft forever preferred_lft forever
    inet6 fe80::42:acff:fe11:2/64 scope link
        valid_lft forever preferred_lft forever
user@docker1:~$
```

In the above output we started a simple container without specifying any network-related configuration. The result is the container being mapped to the docker0 bridge. Now let's try connecting this container to the network we created in the previous recipe, mynetwork:

```
user@docker1:~$ docker network connect mynetwork web1
user@docker1:~$
user@docker1:~$ docker exec web1 ip addr
1: lo: <LOOPBACK,UP,LOWER_UP> mtu 65536 qdisc noqueue state UNKNOWN qlen
1
    link/loopback 00:00:00:00:00:00 brd 00:00:00:00:00:00
    inet 127.0.0.1/8 scope host lo
        valid_lft forever preferred_lft forever
    inet6 ::1/128 scope host
        valid_lft forever preferred_lft forever
8: eth0@if9: <BROADCAST,MULTICAST,UP,LOWER_UP> mtu 1500 qdisc noqueue
state UP
    link/ether 02:42:ac:11:00:02 brd ff:ff:ff:ff:ff:ff
    inet 172.17.0.2/16 scope global eth0
        valid_lft forever preferred_lft forever
```

```
    inet6 fe80::42:acff:fe11:2/64 scope link
        valid_lft forever preferred_lft forever
10: eth1@if11: <BROADCAST,MULTICAST,UP,LOWER_UP> mtu 1500 qdisc noqueue
state UP
    link/ether 02:42:ac:12:00:02 brd ff:ff:ff:ff:ff:ff
    inet 172.18.0.2/16 scope global eth1
        valid_lft forever preferred_lft forever
    inet6 fe80::42:acff:fe12:2/64 scope link
        valid_lft forever preferred_lft forever
user@docker1:~$
```

As you can see, the container now has an IP interface on the network `mynetwork`. If we now once again inspect the network, we should see a container association:

```
user@docker1:~$ docker network inspect mynetwork
[
    {
        "Name": "mynetwork",
        "Id":
"a09b7617c5504d4afd80c26b82587000c64046f1483de604c51fa4ba53463b50",
        "Scope": "local",
        "Driver": "bridge",
        "EnableIPv6": false,
        "IPAM": {
            "Driver": "default",
            "Options": {},
            "Config": [
                {
                    "Subnet": "172.18.0.0/16",
                    "Gateway": "172.18.0.1/16"
                }
            ]
        },
        "Internal": false,
        "Containers": {
"e112a2ab8197ec70c5ee49161613f2244f4353359b27643f28a18be47698bf59": {
            "Name": "web1",
```

```
        "EndpointID":
"678b07162dc958599bf7d463da81a4c031229028ebcecb1af37ee7d448b54e3d",

            "MacAddress": "02:42:ac:12:00:02",

            "IPv4Address": "172.18.0.2/16",

            "IPv6Address": ""
        }
    },
    "Options": {},
    "Labels": {}
    }
]
user@docker1:~$
```

Networks can be disconnected just as easily. For instance, we can now remove the container from the `docker0` bridge by removing it from the bridge network:

```
user@docker1:~$ docker network disconnect bridge web1
user@docker1:~$
user@docker1:~$ docker exec web1 ip addr
1: lo: <LOOPBACK,UP,LOWER_UP> mtu 65536 qdisc noqueue state UNKNOWN qlen
1
    link/loopback 00:00:00:00:00:00 brd 00:00:00:00:00:00
    inet 127.0.0.1/8 scope host lo
       valid_lft forever preferred_lft forever
    inet6 ::1/128 scope host
       valid_lft forever preferred_lft forever
10: eth1@if11: <BROADCAST,MULTICAST,UP,LOWER_UP> mtu 1500 qdisc noqueue
state UP
    link/ether 02:42:ac:12:00:02 brd ff:ff:ff:ff:ff:ff
    inet 172.18.0.2/16 scope global eth1
       valid_lft forever preferred_lft forever
    inet6 fe80::42:acff:fe12:2/64 scope link
       valid_lft forever preferred_lft forever
user@docker1:~$
```

It's interesting to point out that Docker also takes care of ensuring container connectivity when you connect and disconnect networks from the containers. For instance, before disconnecting the container from the bridge network, the default Gateway of the container was still out of the `docker0` bridge:

```
user@docker1:~$ docker exec web1 ip route
```

```
default via 172.17.0.1 dev eth0
172.17.0.0/16 dev eth2   proto kernel   scope link   src 172.17.0.2
172.18.0.0/16 dev eth1   proto kernel   scope link   src 172.18.0.2
user@docker1:~$
```

This makes sense as we wouldn't want to interrupt container connectivity while connecting the container to a new network. However, once we remove the network hosting the default gateway by disconnecting the interface to the bridge network, we see that Docker updates the default gateway to the remaining interface out of the `mynetwork` bridge:

```
user@docker1:~$ docker exec web1 ip route
default via 172.18.0.1 dev eth1
172.18.0.0/16 dev eth1   proto kernel   scope link   src 172.18.0.2
user@docker1:~$
```

This ensures that the container has connectivity regardless of which network it's connected to.

Finally, I want to point out an interesting aspect of the `none` network type when you are connecting and disconnecting containers to networks. As I mentioned earlier, the `none` network type tells Docker to not assign the container to any networks. This however, does not mean just initially, it's a configuration state telling Docker that the container should not have any networks associated with it. For instance, assume we start the following container with a network of `none`:

```
user@docker1:~$ docker run --net=none --name web1 -d jonlangemak/web_
server_1
9f5d73c55ee859335cd2449b058b68354f5b71cf37e57b72f5c984afcafb4b21
user@docker1:~$ docker exec web1 ip addr
1: lo: <LOOPBACK,UP,LOWER_UP> mtu 65536 qdisc noqueue state UNKNOWN qlen
1
    link/loopback 00:00:00:00:00:00 brd 00:00:00:00:00:00
    inet 127.0.0.1/8 scope host lo
       valid_lft forever preferred_lft forever
    inet6 ::1/128 scope host
       valid_lft forever preferred_lft forever
user@docker1:~$
```

As you can see, the container doesn't have any network interfaces besides its loopback. Now, let's try and connect this container to a new network:

```
user@docker1:~$ docker network connect mynetwork web1
```

```
Error response from daemon: Container cannot be connected to multiple
networks with one of the networks in private (none) mode
user@docker1:~$
```

Docker is telling us that this container was defined to have no networks and is preventing us from connecting the container to any network. If we inspect the none network, we can see that this container is in fact attached to it:

```
user@docker1:~$ docker network inspect none
[
    {
        "Name": "none",
        "Id":
"a191c26b7dad643ca77fe6548c2480b1644a86dcc95cde0c09c6033d4eaff7f2",
        "Scope": "local",
        "Driver": "null",
        "EnableIPv6": false,
        "IPAM": {
            "Driver": "default",
            "Options": null,
            "Config": []
        },
        "Internal": false,
        "Containers": {
"931a0d7ad9244c135a19de6e23de314698112ccd00bc3856f4fab9b8cb241e60": {
                "Name": "web1",
                "EndpointID":
"6a046449576e0e0a1e8fd828daa7028bacba8de335954bff2c6b21e01c78baf8",
                "MacAddress": "",
                "IPv4Address": "",
                "IPv6Address": ""
            }
        },
        "Options": {},
        "Labels": {}
    }
]
user@docker1:~$
```

In order to connect this container to a new network, we first have to disconnect it from the `none` network:

```
user@docker1:~$ docker network disconnect none web1
user@docker1:~$ docker network connect mynetwork web1
user@docker1:~$ docker exec web1 ip addr
1: lo: <LOOPBACK,UP,LOWER_UP> mtu 65536 qdisc noqueue state UNKNOWN qlen
1
    link/loopback 00:00:00:00:00:00 brd 00:00:00:00:00:00
    inet 127.0.0.1/8 scope host lo
       valid_lft forever preferred_lft forever
    inet6 ::1/128 scope host
       valid_lft forever preferred_lft forever
18: eth0@if19: <BROADCAST,MULTICAST,UP,LOWER_UP> mtu 1500 qdisc noqueue
state UP
    link/ether 02:42:ac:12:00:02 brd ff:ff:ff:ff:ff:ff
    inet 172.18.0.2/16 scope global eth0
       valid_lft forever preferred_lft forever
    inet6 fe80::42:acff:fe12:2/64 scope link
       valid_lft forever preferred_lft forever
user@docker1:~$
```

Once you disconnect it from the `none` network, you are free to connect it to any other defined network.

Defining a user-defined bridge network

Through the use of the bridge `Driver`, users can provision custom bridges to connect to containers. You can create as many as you like with the only real limitation being that you must use unique IP addressing on each bridge. That is, you can't overlap with existing subnets that are already defined on other network interfaces.

In this recipe, we'll learn how to define a user-defined bridge as well as some of the unique options available to you during its creation.

Getting ready

The `docker network` subcommand was introduced in Docker 1.9, so you'll need a Docker host running at least that version. In our examples, we'll be using Docker version 1.12. You'll also want to have a good understanding of your current network layout, so you can follow along as we inspect the current configuration. It is assumed that each Docker host is in its native configuration.

How to do it...

In the previous recipe, we talked about the process for defining a user-defined network. While the options discussed there are relevant to all network types, we can pass other options to the `Driver` our network implements by passing the `--opt` flag. Let's quickly review the options that are available with the bridge `Driver`:

- ▶ `com.docker.network.bridge.name`: This is the name you wish to give to the bridge.

- ▶ `com.docker.network.bridge.enable_ip_masquerade`: This instructs the Docker host to hide or masquerade all containers in this network behind the Docker host's interfaces if the container attempts to route off the local host .

- ▶ `com.docker.network.bridge.enable_icc`: This turns on or off **Inter-Container Connectivity (ICC)** mode for the bridge. This feature is covered in greater detail in *Chapter 6, Securing Container Networks*.

- ▶ `com.docker.network.bridge.host_binding_ipv4`: This defines the host interface that should be used for port binding.

- ▶ `com.docker.network.driver.mtu`: This sets MTU for containers attached to this bridge.

These options can be directly compared with the options we define under the Docker service to make changes to the default `docker0` bridge.

User Defined Bridge (com.docker.network.)	Service Options	Default Setting
bridge.name	N/A	N/A
bridge.enable_ip_masquerade	--ip-masq	true
bridge.enable_icc	--icc	false
bridge.host_binding_ipv4	--ip	0.0.0.0
driver.mtu	--mtu	1500

The preceding table compares the service-level settings that impact the `docker0` bridge to the settings available to you as part of defining a user-defined bridge network. It also lists the default setting used if the setting is not specified in either case.

Between the Driver-specific options and the generic options that are part of the `network create` subcommand, we have quite a bit of flexibility when defining container networks. Let's walk through a couple of quick examples of building user-defined bridges:

Example 1

```
docker network create --driver bridge \
--subnet=10.15.20.0/24 \
--gateway=10.15.20.1 \
--aux-address 1=10.15.20.2 --aux-address 2=10.15.20.3 \
--opt com.docker.network.bridge.host_binding_ipv4=10.10.10.101 \
--opt com.docker.network.bridge.name=linuxbridge1 \
testbridge1
```

The preceding `network create` statement defines a network with the following characteristics:

- A user-defined network of type `bridge`
- A subnet of `10.15.20.0/24`
- A `gateway` or bridge IP interface of `10.15.20.1`
- Two reserved addresses: `10.15.20.2` and `10.15.20.3`
- A port binding interface of `10.10.10.101` on the host
- A Linux interface name of `linuxbridge1`
- A Docker network name of `testbridge1`

Keep in mind that some of these options are included for example purpose only. Practically, we don't need to define the `Gateway` for the network `Driver` in the preceding example since the defaults will cover us.

If we create the earlier-mentioned network upon inspection, we should see the attributes we defined:

```
user@docker1:~$ docker network inspect testbridge1
[
    {
        "Name": "testbridge1",
        "Id":
"97e38457e68b9311113bc327e042445d49ff26f85ac7854106172c8884d08a9f",
```

```
        "Scope": "local",
        "Driver": "bridge",
        "EnableIPv6": false,
        "IPAM": {
            "Driver": "default",
            "Options": {},
            "Config": [
                {
                    "Subnet": "10.15.20.0/24",
                    "Gateway": "10.15.20.1",
                    "AuxiliaryAddresses": {
                        "1": "10.15.20.2",
                        "2": "10.15.20.3"
                    }
                }
            ]
        },
        "Internal": false,
        "Containers": {},
        "Options": {
            "com.docker.network.bridge.host_binding_ipv4":
"10.10.10.101",
            "com.docker.network.bridge.name": "linuxbridge1"
        },
        "Labels": {}
    }
]
user@docker1:~$
```

> The options you pass to the network are not validated. That is, if you misspell
> host_binding as host_bniding, Docker will still let you create the
> network, and the option will get defined; however, it won't work.

Example 2

```
docker network create \
--subnet=192.168.50.0/24 \
--ip-range=192.168.50.128/25 \
--opt com.docker.network.bridge.enable_ip_masquearde=false \
testbridge2
```

The preceding `network create` statement defines a network with the following characteristics:

- A user-defined network of type `bridge`
- A subnet of `192.168.50.0/24`
- A `gateway` or bridge IP interface of `192.168.50.1`
- A container network range of `192.168.50.128/25`
- IP masquerade on the host turned off
- A Docker network named `testbridge2`

As stated in Example 1, we don't need to define the driver type if we're creating a bridge network. In addition, if we're OK with the gateway being the first available IP in the container defined subnet, we can exclude that from the definition as well. Inspecting this network after creation should show us results similar to this:

```
user@docker1:~$ docker network inspect testbridge2
[
    {
        "Name": "testbridge2",
        "Id":
"2c8270425b14dab74300d8769f84813363a9ff15e6ed700fa55d7d2c3b3c1504",
        "Scope": "local",
        "Driver": "bridge",
        "EnableIPv6": false,
        "IPAM": {
            "Driver": "default",
            "Options": {},
            "Config": [
                {
                    "Subnet": "192.168.50.0/24",
                    "IPRange": "192.168.50.128/25"
                }
```

```
            ]
        },
        "Internal": false,
        "Containers": {},
        "Options": {
            "com.docker.network.bridge.enable_ip_masquearde": "false"
        },
        "Labels": {}
    }
]
user@docker1:~$
```

Creating a user-defined overlay network

While the ability to create your own bridge is certainly appealing, your scope is still limited to that of a single Docker host. The overlay network `Driver` aims to solve that by allowing you to extend one or more subnets across multiple Docker hosts using an overlay network. Overlay networks are a means to build isolated networks on top of existing networks. In this case, the existing network provides transport for the overlay and is often named the **underlay network**. The overlay `Driver` implements what Docker refers to as multi-host networking.

In this recipe, we'll learn how to configure the prerequisites for the overlay `Driver` as well as deploy and validate overlay-based networks.

Getting ready

Throughout the following examples, we'll be using this lab topology:

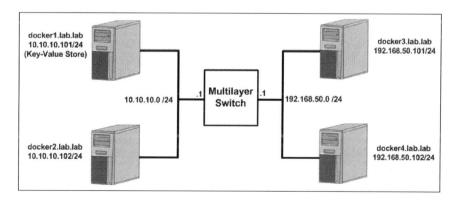

The topology consists of a total of four Docker host's two of which are in the `10.10.10.0/24` subnet and the other two are in the `192.168.50.0/24` subnet. As we walk through this recipe, the hosts shown in the diagram will play the following roles:

- ▸ docker1: Docker host serving a Consul **key-value store**
- ▸ docker2: Docker host participating in overlay networks
- ▸ docker3: Docker host participating in overlay networks
- ▸ docker4: Docker host participating in overlay networks

As mentioned earlier, the overlay `Driver` isn't instantiated by default. This is because there are several prerequisites required for the overlay `Driver` to work.

A key-value store

Since we're now dealing with a distributed system, Docker needs a place to store information about the overlay network. To do this, Docker uses a key-value store and supports Consul, etcd, and ZooKeeper for this purpose. It will store information that requires consistency across all the nodes such as IP address allocations, network IDs, and container endpoints. In our examples, we'll be deploying Consul.

As luck would have it, Consul can be deployed as a Docker container itself:

```
user@docker1:~$ docker run -d -p 8500:8500 -h consul \
--name consul progrium/consul -server  bootstrap
```

Running this image will start a single instance of the Consul key-value store. A single instance is all we need for basic lab testing. In our case, we'll start this image on the host `docker1`. All the Docker hosts that participate in the overlay must have reachability to the key-value store across the network.

> Running Consul with a single cluster member should only be done for demonstration purposes. You need at least three cluster members to have any sort of failure tolerance. Make sure that you research the key-value store you decide to deploy and understand its configuration and failure tolerances.

Linux kernel version of 3.16

Your Linux kernel version needs to be 3.16 or greater. You can check your current kernel version with the following command:

```
user@docker1:~$ uname -r
4.2.0-34-generic
user@docker1:~$
```

Open ports

Docker hosts must be able to talk to each other using the following ports:

- ▸ TCP and UDP 7946 (Serf)
- ▸ UDP 4789 (VXLAN)
- ▸ TCP 8500 (Consul key-value store)

Docker service configuration options

All the hosts that are participating in the overlay need access to the key-value store. To tell them where it is, we define a couple of service-level options:

```
ExecStart=/usr/bin/dockerd --cluster-store=consul://10.10.10.101:8500/
network --cluster-advertise=eth0:0
```

The cluster-store variable defines where the key-value store is. In our case, it's a container running on the host docker1 (10.10.10.101). We also need to enable the cluster-advertise feature and pass it an interface and port. This configuration relates more to using a Swarm cluster, but the flag is also used as part of enabling multi-host networking. That being said, you need to pass it a valid interface and a port. In this case, we use the host physical interface and port 0. In our example, we'll add these options to hosts docker2, docker3, and docker4 as those are the hosts we'll have participating in the overlay network.

After adding the option, reload the systemd configuration and restart the Docker service. You can verify that Docker has accepted the command by checking the output of the docker info command:

```
user@docker2:~$ docker info
...<Additional output removed for brevity>...
Cluster store: consul://10.10.10.101:8500/network
Cluster advertise: 10.10.10.102:0
...<Additional output removed for brevity>...
```

How to do it...

Now that we've met the prerequisites for using the overlay Driver, we can deploy our first user-defined overlay network. Defining a user-defined overlay network follows much the same process as that of defining a user-defined bridge network. For instance, let's configure our first overlay network using this command:

```
user@docker2:~$ docker network create -d overlay myoverlay
e4bdaa0d6f3afe1ae007a07fe6a1f49f1f963a5ddc8247e716b2bd218352b90e
user@docker2:~$
```

Much like with user-defined bridges, we don't have to enter much information to create our first overlay network. In fact, the only difference here is that we have to specify the `Driver` as type overlay because the default `Driver` type is bridge. Once we enter the command, we should be able to see the network defined on any node participating in overlay networking.

```
user@docker3:~$ docker network ls
NETWORK ID          NAME                DRIVER              SCOPE
55f86ddf18d5        bridge              bridge              local
8facf9d2a7cc        host                host                local
3ad850433ed9        myoverlay           overlay             global
453ad78e11fe        none                null                local
user@docker3:~$
```

```
user@docker4:~$ docker network ls
NETWORK ID          NAME                DRIVER              SCOPE
3afd680b6ce1        bridge              bridge              local
a92fe912af1d        host                host                local
3ad850433ed9        myoverlay           overlay             global
7dbc77e5f782        none                null                local
user@docker4:~$
```

The host `docker2` pushes the network configuration into the store when it creates the network. Now all the hosts can see the new network since they're all reading and writing data to and from the same key-value store. Once the network is created, any node participating in the overlay (configured with the correct service-level options) can view, connect containers to, and delete the overlay network.

For instance, if we go to host `docker4`, we can delete the network that we created on host `docker2` initially:

```
user@docker4:~$ docker network rm myoverlay
myoverlay
user@docker4:~$ docker network ls
NETWORK ID          NAME                DRIVER              SCOPE
3afd680b6ce1        bridge              bridge              local
a92fe912af1d        host                host                local
7dbc77e5f782        none                null                local
user@docker4:~$
```

Let's now define a new overlay with a little more configuration. Unlike the user-defined bridge, the overlay `Driver` does not currently support any additional options being passed to it during creation with the `--opt` flag. That being said, the only options that we can configure on overlay type networks are those that are part of the `network create` subcommand.

- ▶ `aux-address`: As with the user-defined bridge, this command allows you to define IP addresses that Docker should not assign to containers when they are spawned.

- ▶ `gateway`: Although you can define a gateway for the network, and if you don't, Docker will do it for you, this isn't actually used in overlay networks. That is, there is no interface that this IP address gets assigned to.

- ▶ `internal`: This option allows you to isolate networks and is covered in greater detail later in this chapter.

- ▶ `ip-range`: Allows you to specify a smaller subnet of the defined network subnet to use for container addressing.

- ▶ `ipam-driver`: In addition to consuming third-party network drivers, you can also leverage third-party IPAM drivers. For the purposes of this book we'll be focusing mostly on the default or built-in IPAM driver.

- ▶ `ipam-opt`: This allows you to specify options to pass to the IPAM driver.

- ▶ `subnet`: This defines the subnet associated with the network type you are creating.

Let's redefine the network `myoverlay` on the host `docker4`:

```
user@docker4:~$ docker network create -d overlay \
--subnet 172.16.16.0/24   --aux-address ip2=172.16.16.2 \
--ip-range=172.16.16.128/25 myoverlay
```

In this example, we define the network with the following attributes:

- ▶ A subnet of `172.16.16.0/24`

- ▶ A reserved or auxiliary address of `172.16.16.2` (Recall that Docker will allocate a Gateway IP to be the first IP in the subnet despite the fact that it's not actually being used. In this case, this means that `.1` and `.2` are technically reserved at this point.)

- ▶ A container assignable IP range of `172.16.16.128/25`

- ▶ A name of `myoverlay`

As before, this network is now available for consumption on all three hosts participating in the overlay configuration. Let's now define our first container on the overlay network from host `docker2`:

```
user@docker2:~$ docker run --net=myoverlay --name web1 \
-d -P jonlangemak/web_server_1
3d767d2d2bda91300827f444aa6c4a0762a95ce36a26537aac7770395b5ff673
user@docker2:~$
```

Here, we ask the host to start a container named `web1` and attach it to the network `myoverlay`. Let's now inspect the container's IP interface configuration:

```
user@docker2:~$ docker exec web1 ip addr
1: lo: <LOOPBACK,UP,LOWER_UP> mtu 65536 qdisc noqueue state UNKNOWN
    link/loopback 00:00:00:00:00:00 brd 00:00:00:00:00:00
    inet 127.0.0.1/8 scope host lo
       valid_lft forever preferred_lft forever
    inet6 ::1/128 scope host
       valid_lft forever preferred_lft forever
7: eth0@if8: <BROADCAST,MULTICAST,UP,LOWER_UP> mtu 1450 qdisc noqueue
state UP
    link/ether 02:42:ac:10:10:81 brd ff:ff:ff:ff:ff:ff
    inet 172.16.16.129/24 scope global eth0
       valid_lft forever preferred_lft forever
    inet6 fe80::42:acff:fe10:1081/64 scope link
       valid_lft forever preferred_lft forever
10: eth1@if11: <BROADCAST,MULTICAST,UP,LOWER_UP> mtu 1500 qdisc noqueue
state UP
    link/ether 02:42:ac:12:00:02 brd ff:ff:ff:ff:ff:ff
    inet 172.18.0.2/16 scope global eth1
       valid_lft forever preferred_lft forever
    inet6 fe80::42:acff:fe12:2/64 scope link
       valid_lft forever preferred_lft forever
user@docker2:~$
```

Surprisingly, the container has two interfaces. The `eth0` interface is attached to the network associated with the overlay network `myoverlay`, but `eth1` is associated with a new network `172.18.0.0/16`.

You've likely noticed by this point that the name of the interfaces within the container use VETH pair naming syntax. Docker uses VETH pairs to connect containers to bridges and configures the container IP address directly on the container side interface. This will be covered extensively in *Chapter 4, Building Docker Networks*, where we walk through the details of how Docker attaches containers to the network.

To figure out where it's attached, let's try and find the other end of the VETH pair that the container's `eth1` interface attaches to. As shown in *Chapter 1, Linux Networking Constructs*, we could use `ethtool` to look up the `interface ID` for a VETH pairs peer. However, there's an easier way to do this when looking at user-defined networks. Notice in the preceding output that the VETH pair name has a syntax of:

```
<interface name>@if<peers interface ID>
```

As luck would have it, the number shown after `if` is the `interface ID` of the other side of the VETH pair. So, in the preceding output, we see that the `eth1` interface's matching interface has an `interface ID` of 11. Looking at the local Docker host, we can see that we have an interface 11 defined and that its `peer interface ID` is 10, which matches `interface ID` in the container:

```
user@docker2:~$ ip addr show
...<Additional output removed for brevity>...
9: docker_gwbridge: <BROADCAST,MULTICAST,UP,LOWER_UP> mtu 1500 qdisc
noqueue state UP group default
    link/ether 02:42:af:5e:26:cc brd ff:ff:ff:ff:ff:ff
    inet 172.18.0.1/16 scope global docker_gwbridge
       valid_lft forever preferred_lft forever
    inet6 fe80::42:afff:fe5e:26cc/64 scope link
       valid_lft forever preferred_lft forever
11: veth02e6ea5@if10: <BROADCAST,MULTICAST,UP,LOWER_UP> mtu 1500 qdisc
noqueue master docker_gwbridge state UP group default
    link/ether ba:c7:df:7c:f4:48 brd ff:ff:ff:ff:ff:ff
    inet6 fe80::b8c7:dfff:fe7c:f448/64 scope link
       valid_lft forever preferred_lft forever
user@docker2:~$
```

Notice that this end of the VETH pair (`interface ID 11`) has a master named `docker_gwbridge`. That is, this end of the VETH pair is part of the bridge `docker_gwbridge`. Let's look at the networks defined on the Docker host again:

```
user@docker2:~$ docker network ls
NETWORK ID          NAME                DRIVER
9c91f85550b3        myoverlay           overlay
b3143542e9ed        none                null
323e5e3be7e4        host                host
6f60ea0df1ba        bridge              bridge
e637f106f633        docker_gwbridge     bridge
user@docker2:~$
```

In addition to our overlay network, there's also a new user-defined bridge of the same name. If we inspect this bridge, we see our container is connected to it as expected and the network has some options defined:

```
user@docker2:~$ docker network inspect docker_gwbridge
[
    {
        "Name": "docker_gwbridge",
        "Id":
"10a75e3638b999d7180e1c8310bf3a26b7d3ec7b4e0a7657d9f69d3b5d515389",
        "Scope": "local",
        "Driver": "bridge",
        "EnableIPv6": false,
        "IPAM": {
            "Driver": "default",
            "Options": null,
            "Config": [
                {
                    "Subnet": "172.18.0.0/16",
                    "Gateway": "172.18.0.1/16"
                }
            ]
        },
        "Internal": false,
        "Containers": {

"e3ae95368057f24fefe1a0358b570848d8798ddfd1c98472ca7ea250087df452": {
                "Name": "gateway_e3ae95368057",
                "EndpointID":
"4cdfc1fb130de499eefe350b78f4f2f92797df9fe7392aeadb94d136abc7f7cd",
                "MacAddress": "02:42:ac:12:00:02",
                "IPv4Address": "172.18.0.2/16",
                "IPv6Address": ""
            }
        },
        "Options": {
            "com.docker.network.bridge.enable_icc": "false",
            "com.docker.network.bridge.enable_ip_masquerade": "true",
```

```
        "com.docker.network.bridge.name": "docker_gwbridge"
    },
    "Labels": {}
  }
]
user@docker2:~$
```

As we can see, ICC mode for this bridge is disabled. ICC prevents containers on the same network bridge from communicating directly with each other. But what is the purpose of this bridge and why are containers spawned on the `myoverlay` network being attached to it?

The `docker_gwbridge` network is the solution to external container connectivity for overlay connected containers. Overlay networks can be thought of as layer 2 network segments. You can attach multiple containers to them and anything on that network can talk across the local network segment. However, this doesn't allow the container to talk to resources off the network. This limits Docker's ability to access container resources through published ports as well as the container's ability to talk to the outside network. If we examine the container's routing configuration, we can see that its default gateway points to the interface of the `docker_gwbridge`:

```
user@docker2:~$ docker exec web1 ip route
default via 172.18.0.1 dev eth1
172.16.16.0/24 dev eth0  proto kernel  scope link  src 172.16.16.129
172.18.0.0/16 dev eth1  proto kernel  scope link  src 172.18.0.2
user@docker2:~$
```

This coupled with the fact that the `docker_gwbridge` has IP masquerading enabled means that the container can still talk to the outside network:

```
user@docker2:~$ docker exec -it web1 ping 4.2.2.2
PING 4.2.2.2 (4.2.2.2): 48 data bytes
56 bytes from 4.2.2.2: icmp_seq=0 ttl=50 time=27.473 ms
56 bytes from 4.2.2.2: icmp_seq=1 ttl=50 time=37.736 ms
--- 4.2.2.2 ping statistics ---
2 packets transmitted, 2 packets received, 0% packet loss
round-trip min/avg/max/stddev = 27.473/32.605/37.736/5.132 ms
user@docker2:~$
```

As with the default bridge network, containers will hide behind their Docker host IP interface if they attempt to route through to reach the outside network.

It also means that since I published ports on this container using the `-P` flag that Docker has published those ports using `docker_gwbridge`. We can verify the ports were published by using the `docker port` subcommand:

```
user@docker2:~$ docker port web1
80/tcp -> 0.0.0.0:32768
user@docker2:~$
```

And verify that port is published on the `docker_gwbridge` by checking the netfilter rules with `iptables`:

```
user@docker2:~$ sudo iptables -t nat -L
...<Additional output removed for brevity>...
Chain DOCKER (2 references)
target      prot opt source        destination
RETURN      all  --  anywhere      anywhere
RETURN      all  --  anywhere      anywhere
DNAT        tcp  --  anywhere      anywhere      tcp dpt:32768 to:172.18.0.2:80
user@docker2:~$
```

As you can see in the preceding output, Docker is using the container's interface on the `docker_gwbridge` to provide port publishing to the Docker host's interfaces.

At this point, our container topology looks like this:

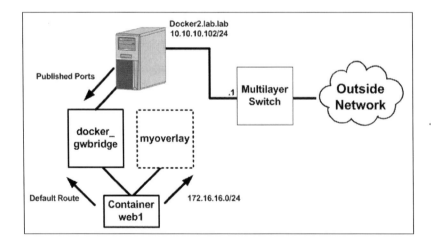

Adding a container to an overlay network automatically created the bridge
`docker_gwbridge`, which is used for container connectivity onto and off the host.
The `myoverlay` overlay network is used only for connectivity related to the defined
subnet, `172.16.16.0/24`.

Let's now start two more containers, one on the host `docker3` and another on the
host `docker4`:

```
user@docker3:~$ docker run --net=myoverlay --name web2 -d jonlangemak/
web_server_2
da14844598d5a6623de089674367d31c8e721c05d3454119ca8b4e8984b91957
user@docker3:~$
user@docker4:~$  docker run --net=myoverlay --name web2 -d jonlangemak/
web_server_2
be67548994d7865ea69151f4797e9f2abc28a39a737eef48337f1db9f72e380c
docker: Error response from daemon: service endpoint with name web2
already exists.
user@docker4:~$
```

Notice that, when I attempt to run the same container on both hosts, Docker tells me that
the container `web2` already exists. Docker won't allow you to run a container with the same
name on the same overlay network. Recall that Docker is storing information related to each
container on the overlay in the key-value store. Using unique names becomes important when
we start talking about Docker name resolution.

> You may notice at this point that the containers can resolve each other by
> name. This is one of the really powerful features that come along with user-
> defined networks. We'll talk about this in much more detail in *Chapter 5,*
> *Container Linking and Docker DNS*, where we discuss DNS and linking.

Restart the container on `docker4` with a unique name:

```
user@docker4:~$ docker run --net=myoverlay --name web2-2 -d jonlangemak/
web_server_2
e64d00093da3f20c52fca52be2c7393f541935da0a9c86752a2f517254496e26
user@docker4:~$
```

Now we have three containers running, one on each host participating in the overlay. Let's take a brief moment to visualize what's going on here:

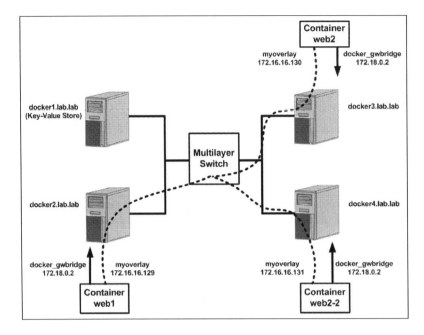

I've removed the host and underlay networking on the diagram to make this easier to read. As described, each container has two IP network interfaces. One IP address is on the shared overlay network and is in the `172.16.16.128/25` network. The other is on the bridge `docker_gwbridge` and is the same on each host. Since the `docker_gwbridge` lives on each host independently, there is no need to have unique addressing for this interface. The container interface on that bridge serves only as a means for the container to talk to the outside network. That is, every container on the same host, which has a network interface on an overlay type network, will receive an IP address on this same bridge.

You might be wondering if this raises a security concern since all containers with overlay networks, regardless of which they are connected to, will also have an interface on a shared bridge (`docker_gwbridge`). Recall earlier that I pointed out that the `docker_gwbridge` had ICC mode disabled. This means that, while many containers can be deployed to the bridge, none of them can actually communicate directly with each other through their IP interfaces on that bridge. We'll talk much more about this in *Chapter 6, Securing Container Networks*, where we discuss container security, but for now know that ICC prevents ICC from occurring on the shared bridge.

Containers on the overlay network believe that they are on the same network segment, or are layer 2 adjacent to each other. Let's prove this by connecting to the web service on container `web2` from container `web1`. Recall that when we provisioned the container `web2`, we did not ask it to publish any ports.

As with other Docker network constructs, containers connected to the same overlay network can talk directly to each other on any port in which they have a service bound to without the need to publish the port:

 It's important to remember that the Docker host has no direct means to connect to the overlay connected containers. With the bridge network type this was feasible because the host had an interface on the bridge, in the case of overlay type networks, this interface does not exist.

```
user@docker2:~$ docker exec web1 curl -s http://172.16.16.130
<body>
   <html>
      <h1><span style="color:#FF0000;font-size:72px;">Web Server #2 -
Running on port 80</span></h1>
</body>
   </html>
user@docker2:~$
```

As you can see, we can successfully access the web server running in container `web2` from container `web1`. Not only are these containers on totally different hosts, but the hosts themselves are on totally different subnets. This type of communication was only available previously when both containers sat on the same host, and were connected to the same bridge. We can prove that the containers believe themselves to be layer 2 adjacent by checking the ARP and MAC entries on each respective container:

```
user@docker2:~$ docker exec web1 arp -n
Address          HWtype   HWaddress          Flags Mask          Iface
172.16.16.130    ether    02:42:ac:10:10:82 C                    eth0
172.18.0.1       ether    02:42:07:3d:f3:2c C                    eth1
user@docker2:~$


user@docker3:~$ docker exec web2 ip link show dev eth0
6: eth0@if7: <BROADCAST,MULTICAST,UP,LOWER_UP> mtu 1450 qdisc noqueue
state UP
    link/ether 02:42:ac:10:10:82 brd ff:ff:ff:ff:ff:ff
user@docker3:~$
```

We can see that the container has an ARP entry from the remote container specifying its IP address as well as its MAC address. If the containers were not on the same network, the container `web1` would not have an ARP entry for `web2`.

We can verify that we have local connectivity between all three containers from container web2-2 on host docker4:

```
user@docker4:~$ docker exec -it web2-2 ping 172.16.16.129 -c 2
PING 172.16.16.129 (172.16.16.129): 48 data bytes
56 bytes from 172.16.16.129: icmp_seq=0 ttl=64 time=0.642 ms
56 bytes from 172.16.16.129: icmp_seq=1 ttl=64 time=0.777 ms
--- 172.16.16.129 ping statistics ---
2 packets transmitted, 2 packets received, 0% packet loss
round-trip min/avg/max/stddev = 0.642/0.710/0.777/0.068 ms

user@docker4:~$ docker exec -it web2-2 ping 172.16.16.130 -c 2
PING 172.16.16.130 (172.16.16.130): 48 data bytes
56 bytes from 172.16.16.130: icmp_seq=0 ttl=64 time=0.477 ms
56 bytes from 172.16.16.130: icmp_seq=1 ttl=64 time=0.605 ms
--- 172.16.16.130 ping statistics ---
2 packets transmitted, 2 packets received, 0% packet loss
round-trip min/avg/max/stddev = 0.477/0.541/0.605/0.064 ms

user@docker4:~$ docker exec -it web2-2 arp -n
Address          HWtype  HWaddress           Flags Mask        Iface
172.16.16.129    ether   02:42:ac:10:10:81 C               eth0
172.16.16.130    ether   02:42:ac:10:10:82 C               eth0
user@docker4:~$
```

Now that we know the overlay works, let's talk about how it's implemented. The mechanism used for overlay transport is VXLAN. We can see the container-generated packets as they traverse the underlay network by looking at a packet capture taken on the physical network:

```
▷ Internet Protocol Version 4, Src: 10.10.10.102, Dst: 192.168.50.101
▷ User Datagram Protocol, Src Port: 34492 (34492), Dst Port: vxlan (4789)
◢ Virtual eXtensible Local Area Network
    ▷ Flags: 0x0800, VXLAN Network ID (VNI)
      Group Policy ID: 0
      VXLAN Network Identifier (VNI): 260
      Reserved: 0
▷ Ethernet II, Src: 02:42:ac:10:10:81 (02:42:ac:10:10:81), Dst: 02:42:ac:10:10:82 (02:42:ac:10:10:82)
▷ Internet Protocol Version 4, Src: 172.16.16.129, Dst: 172.16.16.130
▷ Transmission Control Protocol, Src Port: 50606 (50606), Dst Port: http (80), Seq: 1, Ack: 1, Len: 165
◢ Hypertext Transfer Protocol
    ◢ GET / HTTP/1.1\r\n
        ▷ [Expert Info (Chat/Sequence): GET / HTTP/1.1\r\n]
          Request Method: GET
          Request URI: /
          Request Version: HTTP/1.1
```

In the preceding screenshot of a packet taken from the capture, I want to call out a couple
of items:

▶ The outer IP packet is sourced from the `docker2` host (`10.10.10.102`) and
   destined to the `docker3` host (`192.168.50.101`).

▶ We can see that outer IP packet is UDP and is detected as being VXLAN
   encapsulation.

▶ The **VNI** (**VXLAN Network Identifier**) or segment ID is `260`. VNI is unique per subnet.

▶ The inner frame has a layer 2 and layer 3 header. The layer 2 header has a
   destination MAC addresses of container `web2` as shown earlier. The IP packet shows
   a source of container `web1` and a destination of container `web2`.

The Docker hosts encapsulate the overlay traffic using their own IP interface and send
it across the underlay network to the destination Docker host. Information from the key-
value store is used to determine what host a given container is on in order for the VXLAN
encapsulation to send the traffic to the right host.

You might now be wondering where all the configuration for this VXLAN overlay is. At this
point, we haven't seen any configuration that actually talks about VXLAN or tunneling. To
provide VXLAN encapsulation, Docker creates what I refer to as an *overlay namespace* for
each user-defined overlay network. As we saw in *Chapter 1, Linux Networking Constructs*, you
can use the `ip netns` tool to interact with the network namespace. However, since Docker
stores their network namespaces in a nondefault location, we won't be able to see any of the
namespaces using the `ip netns` tool. By default, namespaces are stored in `/var/run/`
`netns`. The problem is that Docker stores its network namespaces in `/var/run/docker/`
`netns`, which means the `ip netns` tool is looking in the wrong place to see network
namespaces created by Docker. As a work around to this issue, we can create a
`symlink` that links `/var/run/docker/netns/` to `/var/run/nents` as follows:

```
user@docker4:~$ cd /var/run
user@docker4:/var/run$ sudo ln -s /var/run/docker/netns netns
```

```
user@docker4:/var/run$ sudo ip netns list
eb40d6527d17 (id: 2)
2-4695c5484e (id: 1)
user@docker4:/var/run$
```

Notice that there are two network namespace defined. The overlay namespace will be identified with the following syntax x-<id> where x is a random number.

 The other namespace we see displayed in the output is associated with the container running on the host. In the next chapter, we'll be doing a deep dive on how these namespaces are created and used by Docker.

So in our case, the overlay namespace is 2-4695c5484e, but where did it come from? If we inspect the network configuration of this namespace, we'll see that it has some unusual interfaces defined:

```
user@docker4:/var/run$ sudo ip netns exec 2-4695c5484e ip link show
1: lo: <LOOPBACK,UP,LOWER_UP> mtu 65536 qdisc noqueue state UNKNOWN mode
DEFAULT group default qlen 1
    link/loopback 00:00:00:00:00:00 brd 00:00:00:00:00:00
2: br0: <BROADCAST,MULTICAST,UP,LOWER_UP> mtu 1450 qdisc noqueue state UP
mode DEFAULT group default
    link/ether a6:1e:2a:c4:cb:14 brd ff:ff:ff:ff:ff:ff
11: vxlan1: <BROADCAST,MULTICAST,UP,LOWER_UP> mtu 1450 qdisc noqueue
master br0 state UNKNOWN mode DEFAULT group default
    link/ether a6:1e:2a:c4:cb:14 brd ff:ff:ff:ff:ff:ff link-netnsid 0
13: veth2@if12: <BROADCAST,MULTICAST,UP,LOWER_UP> mtu 1450 qdisc noqueue
master br0 state UP mode DEFAULT group default
    link/ether b2:fa:2d:cc:8b:51 brd ff:ff:ff:ff:ff:ff link-netnsid 1
user@docker4:/var/run$
```

These interfaces define the overlay network namespace I mentioned earlier. Earlier we saw that the container web2-2 has two interfaces. The eth1 interface was one end of a VETH pair with the other end placed on the docker_gwbridge. The VETH pair shown in the preceding overlay network namespace represents one side of the pair for the container's eth0 interface. We can prove this by matching up the sides of the VETH pair by interface ID. Notice that this end of the VETH pair shows the other end to have an interface ID of 12. If we look at the container web2-2, we'll see that its eth0 interface has an ID of 12. In turn, the container's interface shows a pair ID of 13, which matches the output we saw in the overlay namespace:

```
user@docker4:/var/run$ docker exec web2-2 ip link show
```

```
1: lo: <LOOPBACK,UP,LOWER_UP> mtu 65536 qdisc noqueue state UNKNOWN qlen
1
    link/loopback 00:00:00:00:00:00 brd 00:00:00:00:00:00
```

12: eth0@if13: `<BROADCAST,MULTICAST,UP,LOWER_UP>` mtu 1450 qdisc noqueue
state UP

```
    link/ether 02:42:ac:10:10:83 brd ff:ff:ff:ff:ff:ff
14: eth1@if15: <BROADCAST,MULTICAST,UP,LOWER_UP> mtu 1500 qdisc noqueue
state UP
    link/ether 02:42:ac:12:00:02 brd ff:ff:ff:ff:ff:ff
user@docker4:/var/run$
```

Now that we know how the container's overlay interface (eth0) is connected, we need to know how traffic headed into the overlay namespace gets encapsulated and sent to the other Docker hosts. This is done through the overlay namespace's vxlan1 interface. This interface has specific forwarding entries that describe all of the other endpoints on the overlay:

```
user@docker4:/var/run$ sudo ip netns exec 2-4695c5484e \
bridge fdb show dev vxlan1
a6:1e:2a:c4:cb:14 master br0 permanent
a6:1e:2a:c4:cb:14 vlan 1 master br0 permanent
```
02:42:ac:10:10:82 dst 192.168.50.101 link-netnsid 0 self permanent
02:42:ac:10:10:81 dst 10.10.10.102 link-netnsid 0 self permanent
```
user@docker4:/var/run$
```

Notice that we have two entries referencing a MAC address and a destination. The MAC address represents the MAC address of another container on the overlay, and the IP address is the Docker host in which the container lives. We can verify that by checking one of the other hosts:

```
user@docker2:~$ ip addr show dev eth0
2: eth0: <BROADCAST,MULTICAST,UP,LOWER_UP> mtu 1500 qdisc pfifo_fast
state UP group default qlen 1000
    link/ether f2:e8:00:24:e2:de brd ff:ff:ff:ff:ff:ff
```
    inet **10.10.10.102/24** brd 10.10.10.255 scope global eth0
```
        valid_lft forever preferred_lft forever
    inet6 fe80::f0e8:ff:fe24:e2de/64 scope link
        valid_lft forever preferred_lft forever
user@docker2:~$
```
user@docker2:~$ **docker exec web1 ip link show dev eth0**
```
7: eth0@if8: <BROADCAST,MULTICAST,UP,LOWER_UP> mtu 1450 qdisc noqueue
state UP
```

```
     link/ether 02:42:ac:10:10:81 brd ff:ff:ff:ff:ff:ff
user@docker2:~$
```

With this information, the overlay namespace knows that in order to reach that destination MAC address, it needs to encapsulate traffic in VXLAN and send it towards `10.10.10.102` (`docker2`).

Isolating networks

User-defined networks can support what's referred to as internal mode. We saw this option in the earlier recipe about creating user-defined networks, but didn't spend much time discussing it. Using the `--internal` flag when creating a network prevents containers connected to the network from talking to any outside networks.

Getting ready

The `docker network` subcommand was introduced in Docker 1.9, so you'll need a Docker host running at least that version. In our examples, we'll be using Docker version 1.12. You'll also want to have a good understanding of your current network layout so that you can follow along as we inspect the current configuration. It is assumed that each Docker host is in its native configuration.

How to do it...

Making a user-defined network internal is pretty straightforward, you just add the option `--internal` to the `network create` subcommand. Since a user-defined network can be of type bridge or type overlay, we should understand how Docker implements isolation in either case.

Creating internal user-defined bridges

Define a user-defined bridge and pass it the `internal` flag, as well as the flag to give the bridge a custom name on the host. We can do this with this command:

```
user@docker2:~$ docker network create --internal \
-o com.docker.network.bridge.name=mybridge1 myinternalbridge
aa990a5436fb2b01f92ffc4d47c5f76c94f3c239f6e9005081ff5c5ecdc4059a
user@docker2:~$
```

Now, let's take a look at the IP information that Docker assigned to the bridge:

```
user@docker2:~$ ip addr show dev mybridge1
13: mybridge1: <NO-CARRIER,BROADCAST,MULTICAST,UP> mtu 1500 qdisc noqueue
state DOWN group default
```

```
link/ether 02:42:b5:c7:0e:63 brd ff:ff:ff:ff:ff:ff
inet 172.19.0.1/16 scope global mybridge1
   valid_lft forever preferred_lft forever
user@docker2:~$
```

Taking this information, we now check and see what Docker has programmed in netfilter for this bridge. Let's check the filter table and see:

> In this case, I'm using the `iptables-save` syntax to query the current rules. Sometimes, this can be more readable than looking at individual tables.

```
user@docker2:~$ sudo iptables-save
# Generated by iptables-save v1.4.21
…<Additional output removed for brevity>…
-A DOCKER-ISOLATION ! -s 172.19.0.0/16 -o mybridge1 -j DROP
-A DOCKER-ISOLATION ! -d 172.19.0.0/16 -i mybridge1 -j DROP
-A DOCKER-ISOLATION -j RETURN
COMMIT
# Completed on Tue Oct  4 23:45:24 2016
user@docker2:~$
```

Here, we can see that Docker has added two rules. The first says that any traffic that is not sourced from the bridge subnet and is leaving the bridge interface should be dropped. This can be hard to comprehend, so it's easiest to think of this in terms of an example. Say that a host on your network `192.168.127.57` was trying to access something on this bridge. That flows source IP address would not be in the bridge subnet, which fulfills the first part of the rule. It would also be attempting to go out of (or onto) `mybridge1` meeting the second part of the rule. This rule effectively prevents all inbound communication.

The second rule looks for traffic that does not have a destination in the bridge subnet, and that has an ingress interface of the bridge `mybridge1`. In this case, a container might have an IP address of 172.19.0.5/16. If it were attempting to talk off of it's local network, the destination would not be in the `172.19.0.0/16` which would match the first part of the rule. As it attempted to leave the bridge towards an external network, it would match the second part of the rule as it's coming into the `mybridge1` interface. This rule effectively prevents all outbound communication.

Between these two rules, no traffic is allowed in or out of the bridge. This does not, however, prevent container-to-container connectivity between containers on the same bridge.

It should be noted that Docker will allow you to specify the publish (-P) flag when running containers against an internal bridge. However, no ports will ever get mapped:

```
user@docker2:~$ docker run --net=myinternalbridge --name web1 -d -P
jonlangemak/web_server_1
b5f069a40a527813184c7156633c1e28342e0b3f1d1dbb567f94072bc27a5934
user@docker2:~$ docker port web1
user@docker2:~$
```

Creating internal user-defined overlays

Creating internal overlays follows the same process. We just pass the --internal flag to the network create subcommand. However, in the case of overlay networks, the isolation model is much simpler. We can create an internal overlay network as follows:

```
user@docker2:~$ docker network create -d overlay \
--subnet 192.10.10.0/24 --internal myinternaloverlay
1677f2c313f21e58de256d9686fd2d872699601898fd5f2a3391b94c5c4cd2ec
user@docker2:~$
```

Once created, it's really no different than a non-internal overlay. The difference comes when we run containers on the internal overlay:

```
user@docker2:~$ docker run --net=myinternaloverlay --name web1 -d -P
jonlangemak/web_server_1
c5b05a3c829dfc04ecc91dd7091ad7145cbce96fc7aa0e5ad1f1cf3fd34bb02b
user@docker2:~$
```

Checking the container interface configuration, we can see that the container only has one interface, which is a member of the overlay network (192.10.10.0/24). The interface that would normally connect the container to the docker_gwbridge (172.18.0.0/16) network for external connectivity is missing:

```
user@docker2:~$ docker exec -it web1 ip addr
1: lo: <LOOPBACK,UP,LOWER_UP> mtu 65536 qdisc noqueue state UNKNOWN qlen
1
    link/loopback 00:00:00:00:00:00 brd 00:00:00:00:00:00
    inet 127.0.0.1/8 scope host lo
       valid_lft forever preferred_lft forever
    inet6 ::1/128 scope host
       valid_lft forever preferred_lft forever
11: eth0@if12: <BROADCAST,MULTICAST,UP,LOWER_UP> mtu 1450 qdisc noqueue
state UP
```

```
link/ether 02:42:c0:0a:0a:02 brd ff:ff:ff:ff:ff:ff
inet 192.10.10.2/24 scope global eth0
   valid_lft forever preferred_lft forever
inet6 fe80::42:c0ff:fe0a:a02/64 scope link
   valid_lft forever preferred_lft forever
user@docker2:~$
```

Overlay networks are inherently isolated, hence, need for the `docker_gwbridge`. Not mapping a container interface to `docker_gwbridge` means that there's no way to talk in or out of the overlay network that provides the isolation.

4
Building Docker Networks

In this chapter, we will cover the following recipes:

- ▸ Manually networking containers
- ▸ Specifying your own bridge
- ▸ Using an OVS bridge
- ▸ Using an OVS bridge to connect Docker hosts
- ▸ OVS and Docker together

Introduction

As we've seen in earlier chapters, Docker does a great job of handling many container networking needs. However, this does not limit you to using only Docker-provided network elements to connect containers. So while Docker can facilitate the networking for you, you can also connect containers manually. The drawback to this approach is that Docker becomes unaware of the network state of the container because it wasn't involved in network provisioning. As we'll see in *Chapter 7, Working with Weave Net,* Docker now also supports custom or third-party network drivers that help bridge the gap between native Docker and third-party or custom container network configurations.

Manually networking containers

In *Chapter 1, Linux Networking Constructs* and *Chapter 2, Configuring and Monitoring Docker Networks*, we reviewed common Linux network constructs as well as covered the Docker native options for container networking. In this recipe, we'll walk through how to manually network a container the same way that Docker does in the default bridge network mode. Understanding how Docker handles networking provisioning for containers is a key building block in understanding non-native options for container networking.

Getting ready

In this recipe, we'll be demonstrating the configuration on a single Docker host. It is assumed that this host has Docker installed and that Docker is in its default configuration. In order to view and manipulate networking settings, you'll want to ensure that you have the `iproute2` toolset installed. If not present on the system, it can be installed by using the command:

```
sudo apt-get install iproute2
```

In order to make network changes to the host, you'll also need root-level access.

How to do it...

In order to manually provision a container's network, we need to explicitly tell Docker not to provision a container's network at runtime. To do this, we run a container using a network mode of `none`. For instance, we can start one of the web server containers without any network configuration by using this syntax:

```
user@docker1:~$ docker run --name web1 --net=none -d \
jonlangemak/web_server_1
c108ca80db8a02089cb7ab95936eaa52ef03d26a82b1e95ce91ddf6eef942938
user@docker1:~$
```

After the container starts, we can check its network configuration using the `docker exec` subcommand:

```
user@docker1:~$ docker exec web1 ip addr
1: lo: <LOOPBACK,UP,LOWER_UP> mtu 65536 qdisc noqueue state UNKNOWN qlen 1
    link/loopback 00:00:00:00:00:00 brd 00:00:00:00:00:00
    inet 127.0.0.1/8 scope host lo
       valid_lft forever preferred_lft forever
    inet6 ::1/128 scope host
       valid_lft forever preferred_lft forever
user@docker1:~$
```

As you can see, the container doesn't have any interfaces defined besides its local loopback interface. At this point, there is no means to connect to the container. What we've done is essentially created a container in a bubble:

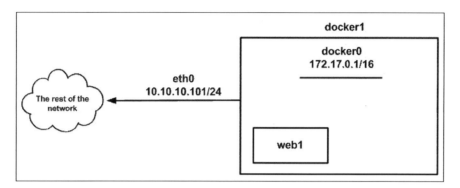

Because we're aiming to mimic the default network configuration, we now need to find a way to connect the container web1 to the docker0 bridge and assign it an IP address from within the bridges IP allocation (172.17.0.0/16).

That being said, the first thing we need to do is create the interfaces that we'll use to connect the container to the docker0 bridge. As we saw in *Chapter 1, Linux Networking Constructs*, Linux has a networking component named **Virtual Ethernet** (**VETH**) pairs, which will work well for this purpose. One end of the interface will connect to the docker0 bridge and the other end will connect to the container.

Let's start by creating our VETH pair:

```
user@docker1:~$ sudo ip link add bridge_end type veth \
peer name container_end
user@docker1:~$ ip link show
…<Additional output removed for brevity>…
5: container_end@bridge_end: <BROADCAST,MULTICAST,M-DOWN> mtu 1500 qdisc
noop state DOWN mode DEFAULT group default qlen 1000
    link/ether ce:43:d8:59:ac:c1 brd ff:ff:ff:ff:ff:ff
6: bridge_end@container_end: <BROADCAST,MULTICAST,M-DOWN> mtu 1500 qdisc
noop state DOWN mode DEFAULT group default qlen 1000
    link/ether 72:8b:e7:f8:66:45 brd ff:ff:ff:ff:ff:ff
user@docker1:~$
```

As expected, we now have two interfaces that are directly associated with each other. Let's now bind one end to the docker0 bridge and turn up the interface:

```
user@docker1:~$ sudo ip link set dev bridge_end master docker0
```

```
user@docker1:~$ sudo ip link set bridge_end up
user@docker1:~$ ip link show bridge_end
6: bridge_end@container_end: <NO-CARRIER,BROADCAST,MULTICAST,UP,M-
DOWN> mtu 1500 qdisc pfifo_fast master docker0 state LOWERLAYERDOWN mode
DEFAULT group default qlen 1000
    link/ether 72:8b:e7:f8:66:45 brd ff:ff:ff:ff:ff:ff
user@docker1:~$
```

 The state of the interface at this point will show as LOWERLAYERDOWN. This is because the other end of the interface is unbound and still in a down state.

The next step is to connect the other end of the VETH pair to the container. This is where things get interesting. Docker creates each container in its own network namespace. This means the other end of the VETH pair needs to land in the container's network namespace. The trick is determining what the container's network namespace is. The namespace for a given container can be located in two different ways.

The first way relies on correlating the container's **process ID** (**PID**) to a defined network namespace. It's more involved than the second method but gives you some good background as to some of the internals of network namespaces. As you might recall from *Chapter 3, User-Defined Networks*, by default we can't use the command-line tool ip netns to view Docker-created namespaces. In order to view them, we need to create a symlink that ties the location of where Docker stores its network namespaces (/var/run/docker/netns), to the location that ip netns is looking (/var/run/netns):

```
user@docker1:~$ cd /var/run
user@docker1:/var/run$ sudo ln -s /var/run/docker/netns netns
```

Now if we attempt to list the namespaces, we should see at least one listed in the return:

```
user@docker1:/var/run$ sudo ip netns list
712f8a477cce
default
user@docker1:/var/run$
```

But how do we know that this is the namespace associated with this container? To make that determination, we first need to find the PID of the container in question. We can retrieve this information by inspecting the container:

```
user@docker1:~$ docker inspect web1
…<Additional output removed for brevity>…
        "State": {
            "Status": "running",
```

```
                "Running": true,
                "Paused": false,
                "Restarting": false,
                "OOMKilled": false,
                "Dead": false,
                "Pid": 3156,
                "ExitCode": 0,
                "Error": "",
                "StartedAt": "2016-10-05T21:32:00.163445345Z",
                "FinishedAt": "0001-01-01T00:00:00Z"
            },
…<Additional output removed for brevity>…
user@docker1:~$
```

Now that we have PID, we can use the `ip netns identify` subcommand to find the network namespace name from the PID:

```
user@docker1:/var/run$ sudo ip netns identify 3156
712f8a477cce
user@docker1:/var/run$
```

> Even if you choose to use the second method, make sure that you create the symlink so that `ip netns` works for later steps.

The second way to find a container network namespace is much easier. We can simply inspect and reference the container's network configuration:

```
user@docker1:~$ docker inspect web1
…<Additional output removed for brevity>…
"NetworkSettings": {
            "Bridge": "",
            "SandboxID":
"712f8a477cceefc7121b2400a22261ec70d6a2d9ab2726cdbd3279f1e87dae22",
            "HairpinMode": false,
            "LinkLocalIPv6Address": "",
            "LinkLocalIPv6PrefixLen": 0,
            "Ports": {},
            "SandboxKey": "/var/run/docker/netns/712f8a477cce",
```

```
            "SecondaryIPAddresses": null,
            "SecondaryIPv6Addresses": null,
            "EndpointID": "",
...<Additional output removed for brevity>...
user@docker1:~$
```

Notice the field named SandboxKey. You'll notice the file path references the location where we said that Docker stores its network namespaces. The filename referenced in this path is the name of the container's network namespace. Docker refers to network namespaces as sandboxes, hence the naming convention used.

Now that we have the network namespace name we can build the connectivity between the container and the docker0 bridge. Recall that VETH pairs can be used to connect network namespaces together. In this example, we'll be placing the container end of the VETH pair in the container's network namespace. This will bridge the container into the default network namespace on the docker0 bridge. To do this, we'll first move the container end of the VETH pair into the namespace we discovered earlier:

```
user@docker1:~$ sudo ip link set container_end netns 712f8a477cce
```

We can validate the VETH pair is in the namespace using the docker exec subcommand:

```
user@docker1:~$ docker exec web1 ip link show
1: lo: <LOOPBACK,UP,LOWER_UP> mtu 65536 qdisc noqueue state UNKNOWN
    link/loopback 00:00:00:00:00:00 brd 00:00:00:00:00:00
5: container_end@if6: <BROADCAST,MULTICAST> mtu 1500 qdisc noop state
DOWN qlen 1000
    link/ether 86:15:2a:f7:0e:f9 brd ff:ff:ff:ff:ff:ff
user@docker1:~$
```

At this point, we've successfully bridged the container and the default namespace together using a VETH pair, so our connectivity now looks something like this:

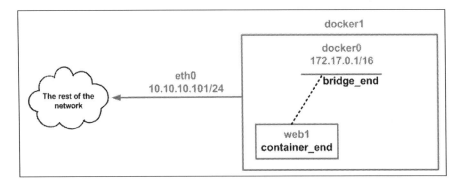

However, the container `web1` is still lacking any kind of IP connectivity since it has not yet been allocated a routable IP address. Recall in *Chapter 1, Linux Networking Constructs*, we saw that a VETH pair interface can be assigned an IP address directly. To give the container a routable IP address, Docker simply allocates an unused IP address from the `docker0` bridge subnet to the container end of the VETH pair.

> IPAM is a huge advantage of allowing Docker to manage your container networking for you. Without IPAM, you'll need to track allocations on your own and make sure that you don't assign any overlapping IP addresses.

```
user@docker1:~$ sudo ip netns exec 712f8a477cce ip \
addr add 172.17.0.99/16 dev container_end
```

At this point, we could turn up the interface and we should have reachability to the container from the host. But before we do that let's make things a little cleaner by renaming the `container_end` VETH pair to just `eth0`:

```
user@docker1:~$ sudo ip netns exec 712f8a477cce ip link \
set dev container_end name eth0
```

Now we can turn up the newly named `eth0` interface, which is the container side of the VETH pair:

```
user@docker1:~$ sudo ip netns exec 712f8a477cce ip link \
set eth0 up
user@docker1:~$ ip link show bridge_end
6: bridge_end@if5: <BROADCAST,MULTICAST,UP,LOWER_UP> mtu 1500 qdisc
pfifo_fast master docker0 state UP mode DEFAULT group default qlen 1000
    link/ether 86:04:ed:1b:2a:04 brd ff:ff:ff:ff:ff:ff
user@docker1:~$ sudo ip netns exec 4093b3b4e672 ip link show eth0
5: eth0@if6: <BROADCAST,MULTICAST,UP,LOWER_UP> mtu 1500 qdisc pfifo_fast
state UP mode DEFAULT group default qlen 1000
    link/ether 86:15:2a:f7:0e:f9 brd ff:ff:ff:ff:ff:ff
user@docker1:~$ sudo ip netns exec 4093b3b4e672 ip addr show eth0
5: eth0@if6: <BROADCAST,MULTICAST,UP,LOWER_UP> mtu 1500 qdisc pfifo_fast
state UP group default qlen 1000
    link/ether 86:15:2a:f7:0e:f9 brd ff:ff:ff:ff:ff:ff
    inet 172.17.0.99/16 scope global eth0
       valid_lft forever preferred_lft forever
    inet6 fe80::8415:2aff:fef7:ef9/64 scope link
       valid_lft forever preferred_lft forever
user@docker1:~$
```

If we check from the host, we should now have reachability to the container:

```
user@docker1:~$ ping 172.17.0.99 -c 2
PING 172.17.0.99 (172.17.0.99) 56(84) bytes of data.
64 bytes from 172.17.0.99: icmp_seq=1 ttl=64 time=0.104 ms
64 bytes from 172.17.0.99: icmp_seq=2 ttl=64 time=0.045 ms
--- 172.17.0.99 ping statistics ---
2 packets transmitted, 2 received, 0% packet loss, time 999ms
rtt min/avg/max/mdev = 0.045/0.074/0.104/0.030 ms
user@docker1:~$
user@docker1:~$ curl http://172.17.0.99
<body>
   <html>
      <h1><span style="color:#FF0000;font-size:72px;">Web Server #1 -
Running on port 80</span></h1>
</body>
   </html>
user@docker1:~$
```

With the connectivity in place, our topology now looks like this:

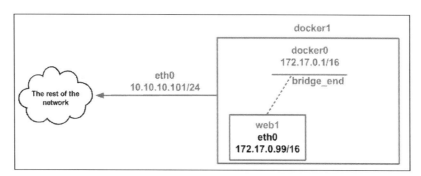

So, while we have IP connectivity, it's only for hosts on the same subnet. The last remaining piece would be to solve for container connectivity at the host level. For outbound connectivity the host hides the container's IP address behind the host's interface IP addresses. For inbound connectivity, in the default network mode, Docker uses port mappings to map a random high port on the Docker host's NIC to the container's exposed port.

Solving for outbound in this case is as simple as giving the container a default route pointing at the `docker0` bridge and ensuring that you have a netfilter masquerade rule that will cover this:

```
user@docker1:~$ sudo ip netns exec 712f8a477cce ip route \
add default via 172.17.0.1
user@docker1:~$ docker exec -it web1 ping 4.2.2.2 -c 2
PING 4.2.2.2 (4.2.2.2): 48 data bytes
56 bytes from 4.2.2.2: icmp_seq=0 ttl=50 time=39.764 ms
56 bytes from 4.2.2.2: icmp_seq=1 ttl=50 time=40.210 ms
--- 4.2.2.2 ping statistics ---
2 packets transmitted, 2 packets received, 0% packet loss
round-trip min/avg/max/stddev = 39.764/39.987/40.210/0.223 ms
user@docker1:~$
```

If you're using the `docker0` bridge as we did in this example, you won't need to add a custom netfilter masquerade rule. This is because the default masquerade rule already covers the entire subnet of the `docker0` bridge:

```
user@docker1:~$ sudo iptables -t nat -L
...<Additional output removed for brevity>...
Chain POSTROUTING (policy ACCEPT)
target     prot opt source               destination
MASQUERADE  all  --  172.17.0.0/16        anywhere
...<Additional output removed for brevity>...
user@docker1:~$
```

For inbound services, we'll need to create a custom rule that uses **Network Address Translation** (**NAT**) to map a random high port on the host to the exposed service port in the container. We could do that with a rule like this:

```
user@docker1:~$ sudo iptables -t nat -A DOCKER ! -i docker0 -p tcp -m tcp \
--dport 32799 -j DNAT --to-destination 172.17.0.99:80
```

In this case, we NAT the port `32799` on the host interface to port `80` on the container. This will allow systems on the outside network to access the web server running in `web1` via the Docker host's interface on port `32799`.

In the end, we have successfully replicated what Docker provides in the default network mode:

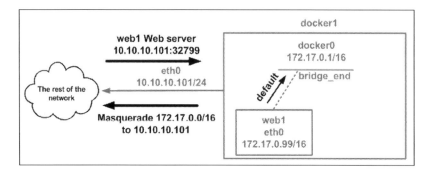

This should give you some appreciation for what Docker does behind the scenes. Keeping track of container IP addressing, port allocations for published ports, and the `iptables` rule set are three of the major things that Docker tracks on your behalf. Given the ephemeral nature of containers, this would be almost impossible to do manually.

Specifying your own bridge

In the majority of network scenarios, Docker relies heavily on the `docker0` bridge. The `docker0` bridge is created automatically when the Docker engine service is started and is the default connection point for any containers spawned by the Docker service. We also saw in earlier recipes that it was possible to modify some of this bridge's attributes at a service level. In this recipe, we'll show you how to tell Docker to use a different bridge entirely.

Getting ready

In this recipe, we'll be demonstrating the configuration on a single Docker host. It is assumed that this host has Docker installed and that Docker is in its default configuration. In order to view and manipulate networking settings, you'll want to ensure that you have the `iproute2` toolset installed. If not present on the system, it can be installed using the command:

```
sudo apt-get install iproute2
```

In order to make network changes to the host, you'll also need root-level access.

How to do it...

Much like any of the other service level parameters, specifying a different bridge for Docker to use is done through updating the systemd drop-in file we showed you how to create in *Chapter 2, Configuring and Monitoring Docker Networks*.

Before we specify the new bridge, let's first make sure that there are no containers running, stop the Docker service, and delete the `docker0` bridge:

```
user@docker1:~$ docker ps -a
CONTAINER ID        IMAGE               COMMAND             CREATED
STATUS              PORTS               NAMES
user@docker1:~$
user@docker1:~$ sudo systemctl stop docker
user@docker1:~$
user@docker1:~$ sudo ip link delete dev docker0
user@docker1:~$
user@docker1:~$ ip link show dev docker0
Device "docker0" does not exist.
user@docker1:~$
```

At this point, the default `docker0` bridge has been deleted. Now, let's create a new bridge for Docker to use.

 If you aren't familiar with the `iproute2` command-line tool please refer to the examples in *Chapter 1, Linux Networking Constructs*.

```
user@docker1:~$ sudo ip link add mybridge1 type bridge
user@docker1:~$ sudo ip address add 10.11.12.1/24 dev mybridge1
user@docker1:~$ sudo ip link set dev mybridge1 up
user@docker1:~$ ip addr show dev mybridge1
7: mybridge1: <BROADCAST,MULTICAST,UP,LOWER_UP> mtu 1500 qdisc noqueue
state UNKNOWN group default
    link/ether 9e:87:b4:7b:a3:c0 brd ff:ff:ff:ff:ff:ff
    inet 10.11.12.1/24 scope global mybridge1
       valid_lft forever preferred_lft forever
    inet6 fe80::9c87:b4ff:fe7b:a3c0/64 scope link
       valid_lft forever preferred_lft forever
user@docker1:~$
```

We first created a bridge named `mybridge1`, then gave it an IP address of `10.11.12.1/24`, and finally turned up the interface. At this point, the interface is up and reachable. We can now tell Docker to use this bridge as its default bridge. To do this, edit the systemd drop-in file for Docker and make sure that the last line reads as follows:

```
ExecStart=/usr/bin/dockerd --bridge=mybridge1
```

Now save the file, reload the systemd configuration, and start the Docker service:

```
user@docker1:~$ sudo systemctl daemon-reload
user@docker1:~$ sudo systemctl start docker
```

Now if we start a container, we should see it assigned to the bridge `mybridge1`:

```
user@docker1:~$ docker run --name web1 -d -P jonlangemak/web_server_1
e8a05afba6235c6d8012639aa79e1732ed5ff741753a8c6b8d9c35a171f6211e
user@docker1:~$ ip link show
1: lo: <LOOPBACK,UP,LOWER_UP> mtu 65536 qdisc noqueue state UNKNOWN mode
DEFAULT group default qlen 1
    link/loopback 00:00:00:00:00:00 brd 00:00:00:00:00:00
2: eth0: <BROADCAST,MULTICAST,UP,LOWER_UP> mtu 1500 qdisc pfifo_fast
state UP mode DEFAULT group default qlen 1000
    link/ether 62:31:35:63:65:63 brd ff:ff:ff:ff:ff:ff
3: eth1: <BROADCAST,MULTICAST> mtu 1500 qdisc noop state DOWN mode
DEFAULT group default qlen 1000
    link/ether 36:b3:5c:94:c0:a6 brd ff:ff:ff:ff:ff:ff
17: mybridge1: <BROADCAST,MULTICAST,UP,LOWER_UP> mtu 1500 qdisc noqueue
state UP mode DEFAULT group default qlen 1000
    link/ether 7a:1b:30:e6:94:b7 brd ff:ff:ff:ff:ff:ff
22: veth68fb58a@if21: <BROADCAST,MULTICAST,UP,LOWER_UP> mtu 1500 qdisc
noqueue master mybridge1 state UP mode DEFAULT group default
    link/ether 7a:1b:30:e6:94:b7 brd ff:ff:ff:ff:ff:ff link-netnsid 0
user@docker1:~$
```

Notice that the `docker0` bridge was not created when the service was started. Also, notice that we see one side of a VETH pair in the default namespace whose master interface is `mybridge1`.

Using what we learned from the first recipe in this chapter, we can also confirm that the other end of the VETH pair is in the container's network namespace:

```
user@docker1:~$ docker inspect web1 | grep SandboxKey
            "SandboxKey": "/var/run/docker/netns/926ddab911ae",
user@docker1:~$
user@docker1:~$ sudo ip netns exec 926ddab911ae ip link show
1: lo: <LOOPBACK,UP,LOWER_UP> mtu 65536 qdisc noqueue state UNKNOWN mode
DEFAULT group default qlen 1
    link/loopback 00:00:00:00:00:00 brd 00:00:00:00:00:00
21: eth0@if22: <BROADCAST,MULTICAST,UP,LOWER_UP> mtu 1500 qdisc noqueue
state UP mode DEFAULT group default
    link/ether 02:42:0a:0b:0c:02 brd ff:ff:ff:ff:ff:ff link-netnsid 0
user@docker1:~$
```

We can tell this is a VETH pair because it uses the `<interface>@<interface>` naming syntax. And if we compare the VETH pair interface numbers, we can see that these two are a match with the host side of the VETH pair, having an index of `22` connecting to the container side of the VETH pair with an index of `21`.

 You'll probably notice that I flip between using the `ip netns exec` and `docker exec` commands to execute commands inside a container. The point of that is not to be confusing but rather to show what Docker is doing on your behalf. It should be noted that, in order to use the `ip netns exec` syntax, you need the symlink in place that we demonstrated in an earlier recipe. Using the `ip netns exec` is only required when you're manually configuring namespaces.

If we look at the network configuration of the container, we can see that Docker has assigned it an IP address within the range of the `mybridge1` subnet:

```
user@docker1:~$ docker exec web1 ip addr show dev eth0
8: eth0@if9: <BROADCAST,MULTICAST,UP,LOWER_UP> mtu 1500 qdisc noqueue
state UP
    link/ether 02:42:0a:0b:0c:02 brd ff:ff:ff:ff:ff:ff
    inet 10.11.12.2/24 scope global eth0
       valid_lft forever preferred_lft forever
    inet6 fe80::42:aff:fe0b:c02/64 scope link
       valid_lft forever preferred_lft forever
user@docker1:~$
```

Docker is now also keeping track of IP allocations for the bridge as it allocates container IP addresses. IP address management is a large understated value that Docker provides in the container network space. Mapping IP addresses to containers and managing that on your own would be a significant undertaking.

The last piece of this would be handling the NAT configuration for the container. Since the `10.11.12.0/24` space is not routable, we'll need to hide or masquerade the container's IP address behind a physical interface on the Docker host. Luckily, so long as Docker is managing the bridge for you, Docker still takes care of making the appropriate netfilter rules. We can make sure that this is in place by inspecting the netfilter ruleset:

```
user@docker1:~$ sudo iptables -t nat -L -n
...<Additional output removed for brevity>...
Chain POSTROUTING (policy ACCEPT)
```

```
target       prot opt source              destination
MASQUERADE   all  --   10.11.12.0/24        0.0.0.0/0
...<Additional output removed for brevity>...
Chain DOCKER (2 references)
target       prot opt source              destination
RETURN       all  --   0.0.0.0/0            0.0.0.0/0
DNAT         tcp  --   0.0.0.0/0            0.0.0.0/0               tcp
dpt:32768 to:10.11.12.2:80
```

In addition, since we exposed ports on the container with the -P flag, the inbound NAT has also been allocated. We can see this NAT translation as well in the DOCKER chain of the same preceding output. In summary, as long as you're using a Linux bridge, Docker will handle the entire configuration for you just as it did with the docker0 bridge.

Using an OVS bridge

For users that are looking for additional features, **OpenVSwitch** (**OVS**) is becoming a popular replacement for the native Linux bridge. OVS offers a dramatic enhancement to the Linux bridge at the cost of a slightly higher level of complexity. For instance, an OVS bridge cannot be managed directly by the iproute2 toolset we have been using up to this point and requires its own command-line management tools. However, if you're looking for features that don't exist on the Linux bridge, OVS is likely your best choice. Docker cannot natively manage an OVS bridge, so using one requires that you build the connectivity between the bridge and the container manually. That is, we can't just tell the Docker service to use an OVS bridge rather than the default docker0 bridge. In this recipe, we'll show how to install, configure, and connect containers directly to an OVS bridge in place of the standard docker0 bridge.

Getting ready

In this recipe, we'll be demonstrating the configuration on a single Docker host. It is assumed that this host has Docker installed and that Docker is in its default configuration. In order to view and manipulate networking settings you'll want to ensure that you have the iproute2 toolset installed. If not present on the system, it can be installed using the command:

```
sudo apt-get install iproute2
```

In order to make network changes to the host, you'll also need root-level access.

How to do it...

The first step we'll need to perform is to install OVS on our Docker host. To do this, we can pull down the OVS package directly:

```
user@docker1:~$ sudo apt-get install openvswitch-switch
```

As mentioned earlier, OVS has its own command-line toolset and one of the tools is named `ovs-vsctl`, which is used to directly manage OVS bridges. More specifically, `ovs-vsctl` is used to view and manipulate the OVS configuration database. To ensure that OVS gets installed correctly, we can run the following command:

```
user@docker1:~$ sudo ovs-vsctl -V
ovs-vsctl (Open vSwitch) 2.5.0
Compiled Mar 10 2016 14:16:49
DB Schema 7.12.1
user@docker1:~$
```

This returns the OVS version number and verifies that we have communication to OVS. The next thing we want to do is to create an OVS bridge. To do it, we'll once again use the `ovs-vsctl` command-line tool:

```
user@docker1:~$ sudo ovs-vsctl add-br ovs_bridge
```

This command will add an OVS bridge named `ovs_bridge`. Once created, we can view the bridge interface just like we did any other network interface:

```
user@docker1:~$ ip link show dev ovs_bridge
6: ovs_bridge: <BROADCAST,MULTICAST> mtu 1500 qdisc noop state DOWN mode
DEFAULT group default qlen 1
    link/ether b6:45:81:aa:7c:47 brd ff:ff:ff:ff:ff:ff
user@docker1:~$
```

However, to view any bridge-specific information, we'll once again need to rely on the `ocs-vsctl` command-line tool. We can see information about the bridge using the `show` subcommand:

```
user@docker1:~$ sudo ovs-vsctl show
0f2ced94-aca2-4e61-a844-fd6da6b2ce38
    Bridge ovs_bridge
        Port ovs_bridge
            Interface ovs_bridge
                type: internal
    ovs_version: "2.5.0"
user@docker1:~$
```

Assigning the OVS bridge an IP address and changing its state can once again be done using the more familiar `iproute2` tools:

```
user@docker1:~$ sudo ip addr add dev ovs_bridge 10.11.12.1/24
user@docker1:~$ sudo ip link set dev ovs_bridge up
```

Once up, the interface acts much like any other bridge interface. We can see the IP interface is up and the local host can access it directly:

```
user@docker1:~$ ip addr show dev ovs_bridge
6: ovs_bridge: <BROADCAST,MULTICAST,UP,LOWER_UP> mtu 1500 qdisc noqueue
state UNKNOWN group default qlen 1
    link/ether b6:45:81:aa:7c:47 brd ff:ff:ff:ff:ff:ff
    inet 10.11.12.1/24 scope global ovs_bridge
       valid_lft forever preferred_lft forever
    inet6 fe80::b445:81ff:feaa:7c47/64 scope link
       valid_lft forever preferred_lft forever
user@docker1:~$
user@docker1:~$ ping 10.11.12.1 -c 2
PING 10.11.12.1 (10.11.12.1) 56(84) bytes of data.
64 bytes from 10.11.12.1: icmp_seq=1 ttl=64 time=0.036 ms
64 bytes from 10.11.12.1: icmp_seq=2 ttl=64 time=0.025 ms
--- 10.11.12.1 ping statistics ---
2 packets transmitted, 2 received, 0% packet loss, time 999ms
rtt min/avg/max/mdev = 0.025/0.030/0.036/0.007 ms
user@docker1:~$
```

The next thing we want to do is to create our VETH pair that we'll use to connect a container to the OVS bridge:

```
user@docker1:~$ sudo ip link add ovs_end1 type veth \
peer name container_end1
```

Once created, we need to add the OVS end of the VETH pair to the OVS bridge. This is one of the big areas where OVS differs from a standard Linux bridge. Each connection to OVS is in the form of a port. This is a much stronger imitation of a physical switch than what the Linux bridge provides. Once again, because we're interacting directly with the OVS bridge, we'll need to use the `ovs-vsctl` command-line tool:

```
user@docker1:~$ sudo ovs-vsctl add-port ovs_bridge ovs_end1
```

Once added, we can query the OVS to see all the bridge's ports:

```
user@docker1:~$ sudo ovs-vsctl list-ports ovs_bridge
ovs_end1
user@docker1:~$
```

If you examine the defined interfaces, you'll see that the OVS end of the VETH pair lists `ovs-system` as its master:

```
user@docker1:~$ ip link show dev ovs_end1
8: ovs_end1@container_end1: <BROADCAST,MULTICAST> mtu 1500 qdisc noop
master ovs-system state DOWN mode DEFAULT group default qlen 1000
    link/ether 56:e0:12:94:c5:43 brd ff:ff:ff:ff:ff:ff
user@docker1:~$
```

Without getting into too much detail, this is expected. The `ovs-system` interface represents the OVS data path. For now, just know that this is the expected behavior.

Now that the OVS end is completed, we need to focus on the container end. The first step here will be to start a container without any network configuration. Next, we'll follow the same steps we did earlier to manually connect a container namespace to the other end of a VETH pair:

- Start the container:

  ```
  docker run --name web1 --net=none -d jonlangemak/web_server_1
  ```

- Find the containers network namespace:

  ```
  docker inspect web1 | grep SandboxKey
  "SandboxKey": "/var/run/docker/netns/54b7dfc2e422"
  ```

- Move the container end of the VETH pair into that namespace:

  ```
  sudo ip link set container_end1 netns 54b7dfc2e422
  ```

- Rename the VETH interface to `eth0`:

  ```
  sudo ip netns exec 54b7dfc2e422 ip link set dev \
  container_end1 name eth0
  ```

- Set `eth0` interface's IP address to a valid IP in that subnet:

  ```
  sudo ip netns exec 54b7dfc2e422 ip addr add \
  10.11.12.99/24 dev eth0
  ```

- Bring the container-side interface up:

  ```
  sudo ip netns exec 54b7dfc2e422 ip link set dev eth0 up
  ```

- Bring the OVS side of the VETH pair up:

  ```
  sudo ip link set dev ovs_end1 up
  ```

At this point, the container is successfully connected to the OVS and reachable through the host:

```
user@docker1:~$ ping 10.11.12.99 -c 2
```

```
PING 10.11.12.99 (10.11.12.99) 56(84) bytes of data.
```

64 bytes from 10.11.12.99: icmp_seq=1 ttl=64 time=0.469 ms

64 bytes from 10.11.12.99: icmp_seq=2 ttl=64 time=0.028 ms

```
--- 10.11.12.99 ping statistics ---
2 packets transmitted, 2 received, 0% packet loss, time 999ms
rtt min/avg/max/mdev = 0.028/0.248/0.469/0.221 ms
user@docker1:~$
```

If we want to dig a little deeper into OVS, we can examine the switches' MAC address table by using the following command:

```
user@docker1:~$ sudo ovs-appctl fdb/show ovs_bridge
port   VLAN   MAC                    Age
LOCAL       0   b6:45:81:aa:7c:47     7
    1       0   b2:7e:e8:42:58:39     7
user@docker1:~$
```

Notice the MAC address that it learned on port 1. But what is port 1? To look at all of the ports for a given OVS you can use this command:

```
user@docker1:~$ sudo ovs-dpctl show
system@ovs-system:
        lookups: hit:13 missed:11 lost:0
        flows: 0
        masks: hit:49 total:1 hit/pkt:2.04
        port 0: ovs-system (internal)
        port 1: ovs_bridge (internal)
        port 2: ovs_end1
user@docker1:~$
```

Here, we can see that port 1 is the OVS bridge that we provisioned and what we attached the OVS end of the VETH pair to.

As we can see, the amount of work required to make the connection to OVS can be extensive. Luckily, there are some great tools out there that can help make this a lot easier. One of the more notable tools was built by Jérôme Petazzoni and is named **Pipework**. It's available on GitHub at the following URL:

```
https://github.com/jpetazzo/pipework
```

If we use Pipework to plumb the connections to OVS, and assume that the bridge is already created, we can take the number of steps required to connect the container to the bridge from 6 to 1.

To use Pipework, you must first download it from GitHub. This can be done by using the Git client:

```
user@docker1:~$ git clone https://github.com/jpetazzo/pipework
...<Additional output removed for brevity>...
user@docker1:~$ cd pipework/
user@docker1:~/pipework$ ls
docker-compose.yml  doctoc  LICENSE  pipework  pipework.spec  README.md
user@docker1:~/pipework$
```

To demonstrate using Pipework, let's start a new container named web2 without any network configuration:

```
user@docker1:~$ docker run --name web2 --net=none -d \
jonlangemak/web_server_2
985384d0b0cd1a48cb04de1a31b84f402197b2faade87d073e6acdc62cf29151
user@docker1:~$
```

Now, all we have to do to connect this container to our existing OVS bridge is to run the following command, which specifies the name of the OVS bridge , the container name, and the IP address we wish to assign to the container:

```
user@docker1:~/pipework$ sudo ./pipework ovs_bridge \
web2 10.11.12.100/24
Warning: arping not found; interface may not be immediately reachable
user@docker1:~/pipework$
```

Pipework takes care of all the leg work for us including resolving the container name to a network namespace, creating a unique VETH pair, properly placing the ends of the VETH pair in the container and on the specified bridge, and assigning the container an IP address.

Pipework can also help us add additional interfaces to a container on the fly. Considering that we started this container with a network mode of none, the container currently only has a connection to the OVS based on the first Pipework configuration. However, we can add the connection to the docker0 bridge back by using Pipework as well:

```
user@docker1:~/pipework$ sudo ./pipework docker0 -i eth0 web2 \
172.17.0.100/16@172.17.0.1
```

The   syntax is similar, but in this case we specify the interface name we wanted to use (eth0) and also add a gateway for the interface of 172.17.0.1. This will allow the container to use the docker0 bridge as a default gateway and, in turn, allow it outbound access using the default Docker masquerade rule. We can verify the configuration is present in the container with a couple, docker exec commands:

```
user@docker1:~/pipework$ docker exec web2 ip addr
```

```
1: lo: <LOOPBACK,UP,LOWER_UP> mtu 65536 qdisc noqueue state UNKNOWN qlen
1
    link/loopback 00:00:00:00:00:00 brd 00:00:00:00:00:00
    inet 127.0.0.1/8 scope host lo
        valid_lft forever preferred_lft forever
    inet6 ::1/128 scope host
        valid_lft forever preferred_lft forever
9: eth1@if10: <BROADCAST,MULTICAST,UP,LOWER_UP> mtu 1500 qdisc noqueue
state UP qlen 1000
    link/ether da:40:35:ec:c2:45 brd ff:ff:ff:ff:ff:ff
    inet 10.11.12.100/24 scope global eth1
        valid_lft forever preferred_lft forever
    inet6 fe80::d840:35ff:feec:c245/64 scope link
        valid_lft forever preferred_lft forever
11: eth0@if12: <BROADCAST,MULTICAST,UP,LOWER_UP> mtu 1500 qdisc noqueue
state UP qlen 1000
    link/ether 2a:d0:32:ef:e1:07 brd ff:ff:ff:ff:ff:ff
    inet 172.17.0.100/16 scope global eth0
        valid_lft forever preferred_lft forever
    inet6 fe80::28d0:32ff:feef:e107/64 scope link
        valid_lft forever preferred_lft forever
user@docker1:~/pipework$ docker exec web2 ip route
default via 172.17.0.1 dev eth0
10.11.12.0/24 dev eth1  proto kernel  scope link  src 10.11.12.100
172.17.0.0/16 dev eth0  proto kernel  scope link  src 172.17.0.100
user@docker1:~/pipework$
```

So while Pipework can make a lot of this manual work easier, you should always look to see if Docker has a native means to provide the network connectivity you're looking for. Having Docker manage your container network connectivity has lots of benefits including automatic IPAM allocations and netfilter configuration for inbound and outbound connectivity to your containers. Many of these non-native configurations already have third-party Docker network plugins in the works that will allow you to leverage them seamlessly from Docker.

Using an OVS bridge to connect Docker hosts

The previous recipe showed how we can use OVS in place of a standard Linux bridge. This, by itself, isn't very interesting since it doesn't do a lot more than a standard Linux bridge can. What may be interesting is using some of the more advanced features of OVS in conjunction with your Docker containers. For instance, once the OVS bridges are created, it's rather trivial to provision GRE tunnels between two distinct Docker hosts. This would allow any containers connected to either Docker host to talk directly to each other. In this recipe, we'll discuss the configuration required to connect two Docker hosts using an OVS provided GRE tunnel.

> Again, this recipe is for the purpose of example only. This behavior is already supported by Docker's user-defined overlay network type. If for some reason you need to use GRE rather than VXLAN, this might be a suitable alternative. As always, make sure that you use any Docker native networking constructs before you start customizing your own. It will save you a lot of headache down the road!

Getting ready

In this recipe, we'll be demonstrating the configuration on two Docker hosts. The hosts need to be able to talk to each other across the network. It is assumed that hosts have Docker installed and that Docker is in its default configuration. In order to view and manipulate networking settings, you'll want to ensure that you have the `iproute2` toolset installed. If not present on the system, it can be installed by using the command:

```
sudo apt-get install iproute2
```

In order to make network changes to the host, you'll also need root-level access.

How to do it...

For the purpose of this recipe, we'll start by assuming a base configuration on both hosts used in this example. That is, each host only has Docker installed, and its configuration is unchanged from the default.

The topology we'll use will look like what's shown in the following image. Two Docker hosts on two distinct subnets:

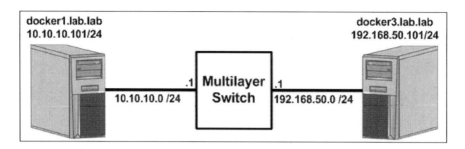

The goal of this configuration will be to provision OVS on each host, connect the containers to the OVS, and then connect the two OVS switches together to allow OVS-to-OVS direct communication over GRE. We'll follow these steps on each host to accomplish this:

1. Install OVS.

2. Add an OVS bridge named `ovs_bridge`.

3. Assign that bridge an IP address.

4. Run a container with its network mode set to `none`.

5. Use Pipework to connect that container to the OVS bridge (it is assumed that you have Pipework installed on each host. If you do not, please refer to the previous recipe for installation steps).

6. Build a GRE tunnel to the other host using OVS.

Let's start the configuration on the first host `docker1`:

```
user@docker1:~$ sudo apt-get install openvswitch-switch
...<Additional output removed for brevity>...
Setting up openvswitch-switch (2.0.2-0ubuntu0.14.04.3) ...
openvswitch-switch start/running
user@docker1:~$
user@docker1:~$ sudo ovs-vsctl add-br ovs_bridge
user@docker1:~$ sudo ip addr add dev ovs_bridge 10.11.12.1/24
user@docker1:~$ sudo ip link set dev ovs_bridge up
user@docker1:~$
user@docker1:~$ docker run --name web1 --net=none -dP \
jonlangemak/web_server_1
5e6b335b12638a7efecae650bc8e001233842bb97ab07b32a9e45d99bdffe468
user@docker1:~$
```

```
user@docker1:~$ cd pipework
user@docker1:~/pipework$ sudo ./pipework ovs_bridge \
web1 10.11.12.100/24
Warning: arping not found; interface may not be immediately reachable
user@docker1:~/pipework$
```

At this point, you should have a container up and running. You should be able to reach the container from the local Docker host:

```
user@docker1:~$ curl http://10.11.12.100
<body>
  <html>
    <h1><span style="color:#FF0000;font-size:72px;">Web Server #1 -
Running on port 80</span>
    </h1>
</body>
  </html>
user@docker1:~$
```

Now, let's perform a similar configuration on the second host `docker3`:

```
user@docker3:~$ sudo apt-get install openvswitch-switch
…<Additional output removed for brevity>…
Setting up openvswitch-switch (2.0.2-0ubuntu0.14.04.3) ...
openvswitch-switch start/running
user@docker3:~$
user@docker3:~$ sudo ovs-vsctl add-br ovs_bridge
user@docker3:~$ sudo ip addr add dev ovs_bridge 10.11.12.2/24
user@docker3:~$ sudo ip link set dev ovs_bridge up
user@docker3:~$
user@docker3:~$ docker run --name web2 --net=none -dP \
jonlangemak/web_server_2
155aff2847e27c534203b1ae01894b0b159d09573baf9844cc6f5c5820803278
user@docker3:~$
user@docker3:~$ cd pipework
user@docker3:~/pipework$ sudo ./pipework ovs_bridge web2 10.11.12.200/24
Warning: arping not found; interface may not be immediately reachable
user@docker3:~/pipework$
```

This completes the configuration of the second host. Ensure that you have connectivity to the `web2` container running on the local host:

```
user@docker3:~$ curl http://10.11.12.200
<body>
  <html>
    <h1><span style="color:#FF0000;font-size:72px;">Web Server #2 -
Running on port 80</span>
    </h1>
</body>
  </html>
user@docker3:~$
```

At this point, our topology looks like this:

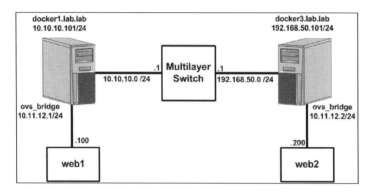

If our goal is to allow the container `web1` to talk directly to the container `web2`, we would have two options. First, since Docker is unaware of the OVS switch, it is not attempting to apply netfilter rules based on containers connected to it. That being said, with the correct routing configuration, the two containers could natively route to each other. However, even in this trivial example, that would be a lot of configuration. Since we're sharing a common subnet between the two hosts (as Docker does even in its default mode), the configuration becomes less than trivial. To make this work, you would need to do the following things:

- ► Add routes into each container telling them that the specific /32 route for the other container lived off subnet. This is because each container believes that the entire 10.11.12.0/24 network is local since they both have an interface on that network. You would need a prefix more specific (smaller) than /24 to force the container to route to reach the destination.

- ► Add routes on each Docker host telling them that the specific /32 route for the other containers lived off subnet. Again, this is because each host believes that the entire 10.11.12.0/24 network is local since they both have an interface on that network. You would need a prefix more specific (smaller) than /24 to force the host to route to reach the destination.

▶ Add routes on the multilayer switch, so it knows that `10.11.12.100` is reachable via `10.10.10.101` (docker1) and `10.11.12.200` is reachable via `192.168.50.101` (docker3).

Now imagine if you were working with a real network and had to add those routes on every device in the path. The second, and better, option is to create a tunnel between the two OVS bridges. This would prevent the network from ever seeing the `10.11.12.0/24` traffic, which means it doesn't need to know how to route it:

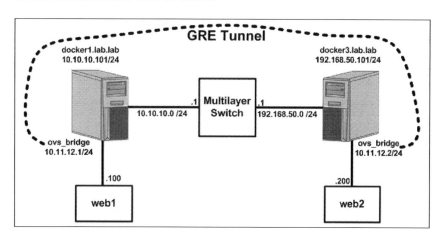

Fortunately for us, this configuration is easy to do with OVS. We simply add another OVS port of type GRE and specify the other Docker host as the remote tunnel destination.

On the host `docker1`, build the GRE tunnel as follows:

```
user@docker1:~$ sudo ovs-vsctl add-port ovs_bridge ovs_gre \
-- set interface ovs_gre type=gre options:remote_ip=192.168.50.101
```

On the host `docker3`, build the GRE tunnel as follows:

```
user@docker3:~$ sudo ovs-vsctl add-port ovs_bridge ovs_gre \
-- set interface ovs_gre type=gre options:remote_ip=10.10.10.101
```

At this point, the two containers should be able to communicate with one another directly:

```
user@docker1:~$ docker exec -it web1 curl http://10.11.12.200
<body>
  <html>
    <h1><span style="color:#FF0000;font-size:72px;">Web Server #2 -
Running on port 80</span>
    </h1>
</body>
```

```
    </html>
user@docker1:~$


user@docker3:~$ docker exec -it web2 curl http://10.11.12.100
<body>
    <html>
        <h1><span style="color:#FF0000;font-size:72px;">Web Server #1 -
Running on port 80</span>
        </h1>
</body>
    </html>
user@docker3:~$
```

As a final proof that this is traversing the GRE tunnel, we can run `tcpdump` on one of the host's physical interfaces while doing a ping test between the containers:

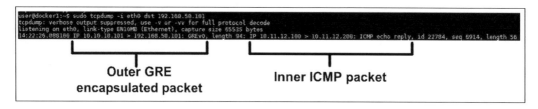

As a final proof that this is traversing the GRE tunnel, we can run `tcpdump` on one of the host's physical interfaces while doing a ping test between the containers:

OVS and Docker together

The recipes until this point have shown several possibilities for what's possible when manually configuring Docker networks. Although these are all possible solutions, they all require a fair amount of manual intervention and configuration and are not easily consumable in their current form. If we use the previous recipe as an example, there are a few notable drawbacks:

▸ You are responsible for keeping track of IP allocations on the containers increasing your risk of assigning conflicting IP addresses to different containers

▸ There is no dynamic port mapping or inherent outbound masquerading to facilitate communication between a container and the rest of the network

▸ While we used Pipework to lessen the configuration burden, there was still a fair amount of manual configuration that needed to be done to connect a container to the OVS bridge

▸ The majority of the configuration would not persist through a host reboot by default

This being said, using what we've learned so far, there is a different way that we can leverage the GRE capability of OVS while still using Docker to manage container networking. In this recipe, we'll review that solution as well as describe how to make it a more persistent solution that will survive a host reboot.

Again, this recipe is for the purpose of example only. This behavior is already supported by Docker's user-defined overlay network type. If for some reason, you need to use GRE rather than VXLAN, this might be a suitable alternative. As always, make sure that you use any Docker native networking constructs before you start customizing your own. It will save you a lot of headache down the road!

Getting ready

In this recipe, we'll be demonstrating the configuration on two Docker hosts. The hosts need to be able to talk to each other across the network. It is assumed that hosts have Docker installed and that Docker is in its default configuration. In order to view and manipulate networking settings, you'll want to ensure that you have the `iproute2` toolset installed. If not present on the system, it can be installed using the command:

```
sudo apt-get install iproute2
```

In order to make network changes to the host, you'll also need root-level access.

How to do it...

Using the previous recipe for inspiration, our new topology will look similar, but will have one significant difference:

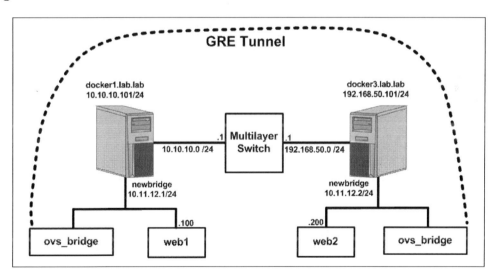

You'll notice that each host now has a Linux bridge named `newbridge`. We're going to tell Docker to use this bridge rather than the `docker0` bridge for default container connectivity. This means that we're only using OVS for its GRE capabilities turning it into a slave to `newbridge`. Using a Linux bridge for container connectivity means that Docker is able to do IPAM for us as well as handle inbound and outbound netfilter rules. Using a bridge other than `docker0` has more to do with configuration than usability, as we'll see shortly.

We're going to once again start the configuration from scratch assuming that each host only has Docker installed in its default configuration. The first thing we want to do is to configure the two bridges we'll be using on each host. We'll start with the host `docker1`:

```
user@docker1:~$ sudo apt-get install openvswitch-switch
...<Additional output removed for brevity>...
Setting up openvswitch-switch (2.0.2-0ubuntu0.14.04.3) ...
openvswitch-switch start/running
user@docker1:~$
user@docker1:~$ sudo ovs-vsctl add-br ovs_bridge
user@docker1:~$ sudo ip link set dev ovs_bridge up
user@docker1:~$
user@docker1:~$ sudo ip link add newbridge type bridge
user@docker1:~$ sudo ip link set newbridge up
user@docker1:~$ sudo ip address add 10.11.12.1/24 dev newbridge
user@docker1:~$ sudo ip link set newbridge up
```

At this point, we have both an OVS bridge as well as a standard Linux bridge configured on the host. To finish up the bridge configuration, we need to create the GRE interface on the OVS bridge and then bind the OVS bridge to the Linux bridge:

```
user@docker1:~$ sudo ovs-vsctl add-port ovs_bridge ovs_gre \
-- set interface ovs_gre type=gre options:remote_ip=192.168.50.101
user@docker1:~$
user@docker1:~$ sudo ip link set ovs_bridge master newbridge
```

Now that the bridge configuration is complete, we can tell Docker to use `newbridge` as its default bridge. We do that by editing the systemd drop-in file and adding the following options:

```
ExecStart=/usr/bin/dockerd --bridge=newbridge --fixed-
cidr=10.11.12.128/26
```

Notice that, in addition to telling Docker to use a different bridge, I'm also telling Docker to only allocate container IP addressing from `10.11.12.128/26`. When we configure the second Docker host (`docker3`), we'll tell Docker to only assign container IP addressing from `10.11.12.192/26`. This is a hack, but it prevents the two Docker hosts from issues overlapping IP addresses without having to be aware of what the other host has already allocated.

Chapter 3, User-Defined Networks, demonstrated that the native overlay network gets around this by tracking IP allocations between all hosts that participate in the overlay network.

To make Docker use the new options, we need to reload the system configuration and restart the Docker service:

```
user@docker1:~$ sudo systemctl daemon-reload
user@docker1:~$ sudo systemctl restart docker
```

And finally, start a container without specifying a network mode:

```
user@docker1:~$ docker run --name web1 -d -P jonlangemak/web_server_1
82c75625f8e5436164e40cf4c453ed787eab102d3d12cf23c86d46be48673f66
user@docker1:~$
user@docker1:~$ docker exec web1 ip addr
...<Additional output removed for brevity>...
8: eth0@if9: <BROADCAST,MULTICAST,UP,LOWER_UP> mtu 1500 qdisc noqueue
state UP
    link/ether 02:42:0a:0b:0c:80 brd ff:ff:ff:ff:ff:ff
    inet 10.11.12.128/24 scope global eth0
       valid_lft forever preferred_lft forever
    inet6 fe80::42:aff:fe0b:c80/64 scope link
       valid_lft forever preferred_lft forever
user@docker1:~$
```

As expected, the first container we ran gets the first available IP address in the `10.11.12.128/26` network. Now, let's move on to configuring the second host `docker3`:

```
user@docker3:~$ sudo apt-get install openvswitch-switch
...<Additional output removed for brevity>...
Setting up openvswitch-switch (2.0.2-0ubuntu0.14.04.3) ...
openvswitch-switch start/running
user@docker3:~$
user@docker3:~$ sudo ovs-vsctl add-br ovs_bridge
user@docker3:~$ sudo ip link set dev ovs_bridge up
user@docker3:~$
user@docker3:~$ sudo ip link add newbridge type bridge
user@docker3:~$ sudo ip link set newbridge up
user@docker3:~$ sudo ip address add 10.11.12.2/24 dev newbridge
```

```
user@docker3:~$ sudo ip link set newbridge up
user@docker3:~$
user@docker3:~$ sudo ip link set ovs_bridge master newbridge
user@docker3:~$ sudo ovs-vsctl add-port ovs_bridge ovs_gre \
-- set interface ovs_gre type=gre options:remote_ip=10.10.10.101
user@docker3:~$
```

On this host, tell Docker to use the following options by editing the systemd drop-in file:

```
ExecStart=/usr/bin/dockerd --bridge=newbridge --fixed-
cidr=10.11.12.192/26
```

Reload the system configuration and restart the Docker service:

```
user@docker3:~$ sudo systemctl daemon-reload
user@docker3:~$ sudo systemctl restart docker
```

Now spin up a container on this host:

```
user@docker3:~$ docker run --name web2 -d -P jonlangemak/web_server_2
eb2b26ee95580a42568051505d4706556f6c230240a9c6108ddb29b6faed9949
user@docker3:~$
user@docker3:~$ docker exec web2 ip addr
...<Additional output removed for brevity>...
9: eth0@if10: <BROADCAST,MULTICAST,UP,LOWER_UP> mtu 1500 qdisc noqueue
state UP
    link/ether 02:42:0a:0b:0c:c0 brd ff:ff:ff:ff:ff:ff
    inet 10.11.12.192/24 scope global eth0
       valid_lft forever preferred_lft forever
    inet6 fe80::42:aff:fe0b:cc0/64 scope link
       valid_lft forever preferred_lft forever
user@docker3:~$
```

At this point, each container should be able to talk to the other across the GRE tunnel:

```
user@docker3:~$ docker exec -it web2 curl http://10.11.12.128
<body>
  <html>
    <h1><span style="color:#FF0000;font-size:72px;">Web Server #1 -
Running on port 80</span>
    </h1>
</body>
```

```
    </html>
user@docker3:~$
```

In addition, each host still has all the benefits Docker provides through IPAM, publishing ports, and container masquerading for outbound access.

We can verify port publication:

```
user@docker1:~$ docker port web1
80/tcp -> 0.0.0.0:32768
user@docker1:~$ curl http://localhost:32768
<body>
  <html>
    <h1><span style="color:#FF0000;font-size:72px;">Web Server #1 -
Running on port 80</span>
    </h1>
</body>
  </html>
user@docker1:~$
```

And we can verify outbound access through the default Docker masquerade rule:

```
user@docker1:~$ docker exec -it web1 ping 4.2.2.2 -c 2
PING 4.2.2.2 (4.2.2.2): 48 data bytes
56 bytes from 4.2.2.2: icmp_seq=0 ttl=50 time=30.797 ms
56 bytes from 4.2.2.2: icmp_seq=1 ttl=50 time=31.399 ms
--- 4.2.2.2 ping statistics ---
2 packets transmitted, 2 packets received, 0% packet loss
round-trip min/avg/max/stddev = 30.797/31.098/31.399/0.301 ms
user@docker1:~$
```

The last advantage to this setup is that we can easily make it persist through host reboots. The only configuration that will need to be recreated will be the configuration for the Linux bridge `newbridge` and the connection between `newbridge` and the OVS bridge. To make this persistent, we can add the following configuration in each host's network configuration file (`/etc/network/interfaces`).

> Ubuntu will not process bridge-related configuration in the interface's file unless you have the bridge utilities package installed on the host.
> ```
> sudo apt-get install bridge-utils
> ```

▶ Host `docker1`:

```
auto newbridge
iface newbridge inet static
    address 10.11.12.1
    netmask 255.255.255.0
    bridge_ports ovs_bridge
```

▶ Host `docker3`:

```
auto newbridge
iface newbridge inet static
    address 10.11.12.2
    netmask 255.255.255.0
    bridge_ports ovs_bridge
```

By putting the `newbridge` configuration information into the network start script, we accomplish two tasks. First, we create the bridge that Docker is expecting to use before the actual Docker service starts. Without this, the Docker service would fail to start because it couldn't find the bridge. Second, this configuration allows us to bind the OVS to `newbridge` at the same time that the bridge is created by specifying the bridge's `bridge_ports`. Because this configuration was done manually before through the `ip link` command, the binding would not persist through a system reboot.

5

Container Linking and Docker DNS

In this chapter, we will cover the following recipes:

- Verifying a host-based DNS configuration inside a container
- Overriding the default name resolution settings
- Configuring links for name and service resolution
- Leveraging Docker DNS
- Creating Docker DNS aliases

Introduction

I've made a point in earlier chapters to point out that Docker does a lot of things for you in the network space. As we've already seen, having Docker manage IP allocations through IPAM is a huge benefit that's not inherently obvious when you start using Docker. Another thing that Docker provides for you is DNS resolution. As we'll see in this chapter, there are multiple levels of name and service resolution that Docker can provide. As Docker has matured, so have the options to provide these types of services. In this chapter, we'll start to review basic name resolution and how a container knows which DNS server to use. We'll then cover container linking and see how Docker can tell containers about other containers and the services they host. Finally, we'll walk through some of the DNS enhancements that came along with the addition of user-defined networks.

Verifying a host-based DNS configuration inside a container

You might not realize it but Docker, by default, is providing your containers a means to do basic name resolution. Docker passes name resolution options from the Docker host, directly into the container. The result is that a spawned container can natively resolve anything that the Docker host itself can. The mechanics used by Docker to achieve name resolution in a container are elegantly simple. In this recipe, we'll walk through how this is done and how you can verify that it's working as expected.

Getting ready

In this recipe, we'll be demonstrating the configuration on a single Docker host. It is assumed that this host has Docker installed and that Docker is in its default configuration. We'll be altering name resolution settings on the host, so you'll need root-level access.

How to do it...

Let's start a new container on our host `docker1` and examine how the container handles name resolution:

```
user@docker1:~$ docker run -d -P --name=web8 \
jonlangemak/web_server_8_dns
d65baf205669c871d1216dc091edd1452a318b6522388e045c211344815c280a
user@docker1:~$
user@docker1:~$ docker exec web8 host www.google.com
www.google.com has address 216.58.216.196
www.google.com has IPv6 address 2607:f8b0:4009:80e::2004
user@docker1:~ $
```

It would appear that the container has the ability to resolve DNS names. If we look at our local Docker host and run the same test, we should get similar results:

```
user@docker1:~$ host www.google.com
www.google.com has address 216.58.216.196
www.google.com has IPv6 address 2607:f8b0:4009:80e::2004
user@docker1:~$
```

In addition, just like our Docker host, the container can also resolve local DNS records associated with the local domain `lab.lab`:

```
user@docker1:~$ docker exec web8 host docker4
```

docker4.lab.lab has address **192.168.50.102**

user@docker1:~$

You'll notice that I didn't need to specify a fully qualified domain name in order to resolve the host name `docker4` in the domain `lab.lab`. At this point, it's safe to assume that the container is receiving some sort of intelligent update from the Docker host that provides it relevant information about the local DNS configuration.

> Note that the `resolv.conf` file is generally where you define a Linux system's name resolution parameters. In many cases, it is altered automatically by configuration information from other places. However, regardless of how it's altered, it should always be the source of truth for how the system handles name resolution.

To see what the container is receiving, let's examine the container's `resolv.conf` file:

```
user@docker1:~$ docker exec -t web8 more /etc/resolv.conf
::::::::::::::
/etc/resolv.conf
::::::::::::::
# Dynamic resolv.conf(5) file for glibc resolver(3) generated by
resolvconf(8)
#     DO NOT EDIT THIS FILE BY HAND -- YOUR CHANGES WILL BE OVERWRITTEN
nameserver 10.20.30.13
search lab.lab
user@docker1:~$
```

As you can see, the container has learned that the local DNS server is `10.20.30.13` and that the local DNS search domain is `lab.lab`. Where did it get this information? The solution is rather simple. When a container starts, Docker generates instances of the following three files for each container spawned and saves it with the container configuration:

- `/etc/hostname`
- `/etc/hosts`
- `/etc/resolv.conf`

These files are stored as part of the container configuration and then mounted into the container. We can use the `findmnt` tool from within the container to examine the source of the mounts:

```
root@docker1:~# docker exec web8 findmnt -o SOURCE
...<Additional output removed for brevity>...
```

```
/dev/mapper/docker1--vg-root [/var/lib/docker/containers/
c803f130b7a2450609672c23762bce3499dec9abcfdc540a43a7eb560adaf62a/resolv.
conf
```

```
/dev/mapper/docker1--vg-root [/var/lib/docker/containers/
c803f130b7a2450609672c23762bce3499dec9abcfdc540a43a7eb560adaf62a/
hostname]
```

```
/dev/mapper/docker1--vg-root [/var/lib/docker/containers/
c803f130b7a2450609672c23762bce3499dec9abcfdc540a43a7eb560adaf62a/hosts]
```

```
root@docker1:~#
```

So while the container thinks that it has local copies of the `hostname`, `hosts`, and `resolv.conf` file in its `/etc/` directory, the real files are actually located in the container's configuration directory (`/var/lib/docker/containers/`) on the Docker host.

When you tell Docker to run a container, it does the following three things:

- It examines the Docker host's `/etc/resolv.conf` file and places a copy of it in the containers directory

- It creates a `hostname` file in the container's directory and assigns the container a unique `hostname`

- It creates a `hosts` file in the container's directory and adds relevant records including localhost and a record referencing the host itself

Each time the container is restarted, the container's `resolv.conf` file is updated based on the values found in the Docker host's `resolv.conf` file. This means that any changes made to the `resolv.conf` file are lost each time the container is restarted. The `hostname` and `hosts` configuration files are also rewritten each time the container is restarted losing any changes made during the previous run.

To validate the configuration files a given container is using, we can inspect the container's configuration for these variables:

```
user@docker1:~$ docker inspect web8 | grep HostsPath
```

```
"HostsPath": "/var/lib/docker/containers/
c803f130b7a2450609672c23762bce3499dec9abcfdc540a43a7eb560adaf62a/hosts",
```

```
user@docker1:~$ docker inspect web8 | grep HostnamePath
```

```
"HostnamePath": "/var/lib/docker/containers/
c803f130b7a2450609672c23762bce3499dec9abcfdc540a43a7eb560adaf62a/
hostname",
```

```
user@docker1:~$ docker inspect web8 | grep ResolvConfPath
```

```
"ResolvConfPath": "/var/lib/docker/containers/
c803f130b7a2450609672c23762bce3499dec9abcfdc540a43a7eb560adaf62a/resolv.
conf",
```

```
user@docker1:~$
```

As expected, these are the same mount paths we saw when we ran the `findmnt` command from within the container itself. These represent the exact mount path for each file into the containers `/etc/` directory for each respective file.

Overriding the default name resolution settings

The method Docker uses to provide name resolution to containers works very well in most cases. However, there could be some instances where you want Docker to provide the containers with a DNS server other than the one the Docker host is configured to use. In these cases, Docker offers you a couple of options. You can tell the Docker service to provide a different DNS server for all the containers the service spawns. You can also manually override this setting at container runtime by providing a DNS server as an option to the `docker run` subcommand. In this recipe, we'll show you your options for changing the default name resolution behavior as well as how to verify the settings worked.

Getting ready

In this recipe, we'll be demonstrating the configuration on a single Docker host. It is assumed that this host has Docker installed and that Docker is in its default configuration. We'll be altering name resolution settings on the host, so you'll need root-level access.

How to do it...

As we saw in the first recipe in this chapter, by default, Docker provides containers with the DNS server that the Docker host itself uses. This comes in the form of copying the host's `resolv.conf` file and providing it to each spawned container. Along with the name server setting, this file also includes definitions for DNS search domains. Both of these options can be configured at the service level to cover any spawned containers as well as at the individual level.

For the purpose of comparison, let's start by examining the Docker host's DNS configuration:

```
root@docker1:~# more /etc/resolv.conf
# Dynamic resolv.conf(5) file for glibc resolver(3) generated by
resolvconf(8)
#     DO NOT EDIT THIS FILE BY HAND -- YOUR CHANGES WILL BE OVERWRITTEN
nameserver 10.20.30.13
search lab.lab
root@docker1:~#
```

With this configuration, we would expect that any container spawned on this host would receive the same name server and DNS search domain. Let's spawn a container named web8 to verify that this is working as expected:

```
root@docker1:~# docker run -d -P --name=web8 \
jonlangemak/web_server_8_dns
156bc29d28a98e2fbccffc1352ec390bdc8b9b40b84e4c5f58cbebed6fb63474
root@docker1:~#
root@docker1:~# docker exec -t web8 more /etc/resolv.conf
::::::::::::::
/etc/resolv.conf
::::::::::::::
# Dynamic resolv.conf(5) file for glibc resolver(3) generated by
resolvconf(8)
#     DO NOT EDIT THIS FILE BY HAND -- YOUR CHANGES WILL BE OVERWRITTEN
nameserver 10.20.30.13
search lab.lab
```

As expected, the container receives the same configuration. Let's now inspect the container and see if we see any DNS-related options defined:

```
user@docker1:~$ docker inspect web8 | grep Dns
            "Dns": [],
            "DnsOptions": [],
            "DnsSearch": [],
user@docker1:~$
```

Because we're using the default configuration, there is no reason to configure anything specific within the container in regard to DNS server or search domain. Each time the container starts, Docker will apply the settings for the host's resolv.conf file to the container's DNS configuration files.

If we'd prefer to have Docker give containers a different DNS server or DNS search domain, we can do so through Docker options. In this case, the two we're interested in are:

- --dns=<DNS Server>: Specify a DNS server address that Docker should provide to the containers

- --dns-search=<DNS Search Domain>: Specify a DNS search domain that Docker should provide to the containers

Let's configure Docker to provide containers with a public DNS server (4.2.2.2) and a search domain of lab.external. We can do so by passing the following options to the Docker systemd drop-in file:

```
ExecStart=/usr/bin/dockerd --dns=4.2.2.2 --dns-search=lab.external
```

Once the options are configured, reload the systemd configuration, restart the service to load the new options, and restart our container `web8`:

```
user@docker1:~$ sudo systemctl daemon-reload
user@docker1:~$ sudo systemctl restart docker
user@docker1:~$ docker start web8
web8
user@docker1:~$ docker exec -t web8 more /etc/resolv.conf
search lab.external
nameserver 4.2.2.2
user@docker1:~$
```

You'll note that, despite this container initially having the host's DNS server (`10.20.30.13`) and search domain (`lab.lab`), it now has the service-level DNS options we just specified. If you recall earlier, we saw that, when we inspected this container, it didn't define a specific DNS server or search domain. Since none was specified, Docker now uses the settings from the Docker options that take priority. Although this provides some level of flexibility, it's not yet truly flexible. At this point, any and all containers spawned on this server will be provided with the same DNS server and search domain. To be truly flexible, we should be able to have Docker alter the name resolution configuration on a per container level. As luck would have it, these options can also be provided directly at container runtime.

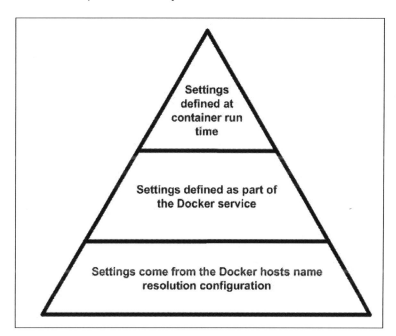

The preceding figure defines the priority Docker uses when deciding what name resolution settings to apply to a container when it's started. As we've seen in earlier chapters, settings defined at container runtime always take priority. If the settings aren't defined there, Docker then looks to see if they are configured at the service level. If the settings aren't there, it falls back to the default method of relying on the Docker host's DNS settings.

For instance, we can launch a container named `web2` and provide different options:

```
root@docker1:~# docker run -d --dns=8.8.8.8 --dns-search=lab.dmz \
-P --name=web8-2 jonlangemak/web_server_8_dns
1e46d66a47b89d541fa6b022a84d702974414925f5e2dd56eeb840c2aed4880f
root@docker1:~#
```

If we inspect the container, we'll see that we now have the `dns` and `dns-search` fields defined as part of the container configuration:

```
root@docker1:~# docker inspect web8-2
...<Additional output removed for brevity>...
            "Dns": [
                "8.8.8.8"
            ],
            "DnsOptions": [],
            "DnsSearch": [
                "lab.dmz"
            ],
...<Additional output removed for brevity>...
root@docker1:~#
```

This ensures that, if the container is restarted, it will still have the same DNS settings that were initially provided the first time the container was run. Let's make some slight changes to the Docker service to verify the priority is working as expected. Let's change our Docker options to look like this:

```
ExecStart=/usr/bin/dockerd --dns-search=lab.external
```

Now restart the service and run the following container:

```
user@docker1:~$ sudo systemctl daemon-reload
user@docker1:~$ sudo systemctl restart docker
root@docker1:~#
root@docker1:~# docker run -d -P --name=web8-3 \
jonlangemak/web_server_8_dns
5e380f8da17a410eaf41b772fde4e955d113d10e2794512cd20aa5e551d9b24c
root@docker1:~#
```

Because we didn't provide any DNS-related options at container runtime, the next place we'd check would be the service-level options. Our Docker service-level options include a DNS search domain of `lab.external`. We'd expect the container to receive that search domain. However, since we don't have a DNS server defined, we'll need to fall back to the one configured on the Docker host itself.

And now examine its `resolv.conf` file to make sure things worked as expected:

```
user@docker1:~$ docker exec -t web8-3 more /etc/resolv.conf
search lab.external
nameserver 10.20.30.13
user@docker1:~$
```

Configuring links for name and service resolution

Container linking provides a means for one container to easily communicate with another container on the same host. As we've seen in previous examples, most container-to-container communication has occurred through IP addresses. Container linking improves on this by allowing linked containers to communicate with each other by name. In addition to providing basic name resolution, it also provides a means to see what services a linked container is providing. In this recipe, we'll review how to create container links as well as discuss some of their limitations.

Getting ready

In this recipe, we'll be demonstrating the configuration on a single Docker host. It is assumed that this host has Docker installed and that Docker is in its default configuration. We'll be altering name resolution settings on the host, so you'll need root-level access.

How to do it...

The phrase *container linking* might imply to some that it involves some kind of network configuration or modification. In reality, container linking has very little to do with container networking. In the default mode, container linking provides a means for one container to resolve the name of another. For instance, let's start two containers on our lab host `docker1`:

```
root@docker1:~# docker run -d -P --name=web1 jonlangemak/web_server_1
88f9c862966874247c8e2ba90c18ac673828b5faac93ff08090adc070f6d2922 root@
docker1:~# docker run -d -P --name=web2 --link=web1 \
jonlangemak/web_server_2
00066ea46367c07fc73f73bdcdff043bd4c2ac1d898f4354020cbcfefd408449
root@docker1:~#
```

Notice how, when I started the second container, I used a new flag named `--link` and referenced the container `web1`. We would now say that `web2` was linked to `web1`. However, they're not really linked in any sort of way. A better description might be to say that `web2` is now aware of `web1`. Let's connect to the container `web2` to show you what I mean:

```
root@docker1:~# docker exec -it web2 /bin/bash
root@00066ea46367:/# ping web1 -c 2
PING web1 (172.17.0.2): 48 data bytes
56 bytes from 172.17.0.2: icmp_seq=0 ttl=64 time=0.163 ms
56 bytes from 172.17.0.2: icmp_seq=1 ttl=64 time=0.092 ms
--- web1 ping statistics ---
2 packets transmitted, 2 packets received, 0% packet loss
round-trip min/avg/max/stddev = 0.092/0.128/0.163/0.036 ms
root@00066ea46367:/#
```

It appears that the `web2` container is now able to resolve the container `web1` by name. This is because the linking process inserted records into the `web2` container's `hosts` file:

```
root@00066ea46367:/# more /etc/hosts
127.0.0.1       localhost
::1     localhost ip6-localhost ip6-loopback
fe00::0 ip6-localnet
ff00::0 ip6-mcastprefix
ff02::1 ip6-allnodes
ff02::2 ip6-allrouters
172.17.0.2      web1 88f9c8629668
172.17.0.3      00066ea46367
root@00066ea46367:/#
```

With this configuration, the `web2` container can reach the `web1` container either by the name we gave the container at runtime (`web1`) or the unique `hostname` Docker generated for the container (`88f9c8629668`).

In addition to the `hosts` file being updated, `web2` also generates some new environmental variables:

```
root@00066ea46367:/# printenv
WEB1_ENV_APACHE_LOG_DIR=/var/log/apache2
HOSTNAME=00066ea46367
APACHE_RUN_USER=www-data
WEB1_PORT_80_TCP=tcp://172.17.0.2:80
```

```
WEB1_PORT_80_TCP_PORT=80
LS_COLORS=
WEB1_PORT=tcp://172.17.0.2:80
WEB1_ENV_APACHE_RUN_GROUP=www-data
APACHE_LOG_DIR=/var/log/apache2
PATH=/usr/local/sbin:/usr/local/bin:/usr/sbin:/usr/bin:/sbin:/bin
PWD=/
WEB1_PORT_80_TCP_PROTO=tcp
APACHE_RUN_GROUP=www-data
SHLVL=1
HOME=/root
WEB1_PORT_80_TCP_ADDR=172.17.0.2
WEB1_ENV_APACHE_RUN_USER=www-data
WEB1_NAME=/web2/web1
_=/usr/bin/printenv
root@00066ea46367:/#
```

You'll notice many new environmental variables. Docker will copy any environmental variables from the linked container that were defined as part of the container. This includes:

- Environmental variables described in the Docker image. More specifically, any ENV variables from the images Dockerfile
- Environmental variables passed to the container at runtime through the `--env` or `-e` flag

In this case, these three variables were defined as ENV variables in the image's Dockerfile:

```
APACHE_RUN_USER=www-data
APACHE_RUN_GROUP=www-data
APACHE_LOG_DIR=/var/log/apache2
```

Because both container images have the same ENV variables defined, we'll see the local variables as well as the same environmental variables from the container web1 prefixed with WEB1_ENV_:

```
WEB1_ENV_APACHE_RUN_USER=www-data
WEB1_ENV_APACHE_RUN_GROUP=www-data
WEB1_ENV_APACHE_LOG_DIR=/var/log/apache2
```

In addition, Docker also created six other environmental variables that describe the `web1` container as well as any of its exposed ports:

```
WEB1_PORT=tcp://172.17.0.2:80
WEB1_PORT_80_TCP=tcp://172.17.0.2:80
WEB1_PORT_80_TCP_ADDR=172.17.0.2
WEB1_PORT_80_TCP_PORT=80
WEB1_PORT_80_TCP_PROTO=tcp
WEB1_NAME=/web2/web1
```

Linking also allows you to specify aliases. For instance, let's stop, remove, and respawn container `web2` using a slightly different syntax for linking:

```
user@docker1:~$ docker stop web2
web2
user@docker1:~$ docker rm web2
web2
user@docker1:~$ docker run -d -P --name=web2 --link=web1:webserver \
jonlangemak/web_server_2
e102fe52f8a08a02b01329605dcada3005208d9d63acea257b8d99b3ef78e71b
user@docker1:~$
```

Notice that, after the link definition, we inserted a `:webserver`. The name after the colon represents the alias for the link. In this case, I've specified an alias for the container `web1` as `webserver`.

If we examine the `web2` container, we'll see that the alias is now also listed in the `hosts` file:

```
root@c258c7a0884d:/# more /etc/hosts
...<Additional output removed for brevity>...
172.17.0.2      webserver 88f9c8629668 web1
172.17.0.3      c258c7a0884d
root@c258c7a0884d:/#
```

Aliases also impact the environmental variables created during linking. Rather than using the container name, they'll instead use the alias:

```
user@docker1:~$ docker exec web2 printenv
...<Additional output removed for brevity>...
WEBSERVER_PORT_80_TCP_ADDR=172.17.0.2
WEBSERVER_PORT_80_TCP_PORT=80
WEBSERVER_PORT_80_TCP_PROTO=tcp
```

…<Additional output removed for brevity>…

user@docker1:~$

At this point, you might be wondering how dynamic this is. After all, Docker is providing this functionality by updating static files in each container. What happens if a container's IP address changes? For instance, let's stop the container web1 and start a new container named web3 using the same image:

```
user@docker1:~$ docker stop web1
web1
user@docker1:~$ docker run -d -P --name=web3 jonlangemak/web_server_1
69fa80be8b113a079e19ca05c8be9e18eec97b7bbb871b700da4482770482715
user@docker1:~$
```

If you'll recall from earlier, the container web1 had an IP address of 172.17.0.2 allocated to it. Since I stopped the container, Docker will release that IP address reservation making it available to be reassigned to the next container we start. Let's check the IP address assigned to the container web3:

```
user@docker1:~$ docker exec web3 ip addr show dev eth0
79: eth0@if80: <BROADCAST,MULTICAST,UP,LOWER_UP> mtu 1500 qdisc noqueue
state UP
    link/ether 02:42:ac:11:00:02 brd ff:ff:ff:ff:ff:ff
    inet 172.17.0.2/16 scope global eth0
       valid_lft forever preferred_lft forever
    inet6 fe80::42:acff:fe11:2/64 scope link
       valid_lft forever preferred_lft forever
user@docker1:~$
```

As expected, web3 took the now open IP address of 172.17.0.2 that previously belonged to the web1 container. We can also verify that the container web2 still believes that this IP address belongs to the web1 container:

```
user@docker1:~$ docker exec -t web2 more /etc/hosts | grep 172.17.0.2
172.17.0.2      webserver 88f9c8629668 web1
user@docker1:~$
```

If we start the container web1 once again, we should see that it will get a new IP address allocated to it:

```
user@docker1:~$ docker start web1
web1
user@docker1:~$ docker exec web1 ip addr show dev eth0
```

```
81: eth0@if82: <BROADCAST,MULTICAST,UP,LOWER_UP> mtu 1500 qdisc noqueue
state UP
    link/ether 02:42:ac:11:00:04 brd ff:ff:ff:ff:ff:ff
    inet 172.17.0.4/16 scope global eth0
       valid_lft forever preferred_lft forever
    inet6 fe80::42:acff:fe11:4/64 scope link
       valid_lft forever preferred_lft forever
user@docker1:~$
```

If we check the container web2 again, we should see that Docker has updated it to reference the web1 container's new IP address:

```
user@docker1:~$ docker exec web2 more /etc/hosts | grep web1
172.17.0.4      webserver 88f9c8629668 web1
user@docker1:~$
```

However, while Docker takes care of updating the hosts file with the new IP address, it will not take care of updating any of the environmental variables to reflect the new IP address:

```
user@docker1:~$ docker exec web2 printenv
…<Additional output removed for brevity>…
WEBSERVER_PORT=tcp://172.17.0.2:80
WEBSERVER_PORT_80_TCP=tcp://172.17.0.2:80
WEBSERVER_PORT_80_TCP_ADDR=172.17.0.2
…<Additional output removed for brevity>…
user@docker1:~$
```

In addition, it should be pointed out that the link is only one way. That is, this link does not cause the container web1 to become aware of the web2 container. Web1 will not receive the host records or the environmental variables referencing the web2 container:

```
user@docker1:~$ docker exec -it web1 ping web2
ping: unknown host
user@docker1:~$
```

Another reason to provision links is when you use Docker **Inter-Container Connectivity** (ICC) mode set to false. As we've discussed previously, ICC prevents any containers on the same bridge from talking directly to each other. This forces them to talk to each other only though published ports. Linking provides a mechanism to override the default ICC rules. To demonstrate, let's stop and remove all the containers on our host docker1 and then add the following Docker option to the systemd drop-in file:

```
ExecStart=/usr/bin/dockerd --icc=false
```

Now reload the systemd configuration, restart the service, and start the following containers:

```
docker run -d -P --name=web1 jonlangemak/web_server_1
docker run -d -P --name=web2 jonlangemak/web_server_2
```

With ICC mode on, you'll notice that containers can't talk directly to each other:

```
user@docker1:~$ docker exec web1 ip addr show dev eth0
87: eth0@if88: <BROADCAST,MULTICAST,UP,LOWER_UP> mtu 1500 qdisc noqueue
state UP
    link/ether 02:42:ac:11:00:02 brd ff:ff:ff:ff:ff:ff
    inet 172.17.0.2/16 scope global eth0
       valid_lft forever preferred_lft forever
    inet6 fe80::42:acff:fe11:2/64 scope link
       valid_lft forever preferred_lft forever
user@docker1:~$ docker exec -it web2 curl http://172.17.0.2
user@docker1:~$
```

In the preceding example, web2 is not able to access the web servers on web1. Now, let's delete and recreate the web2 container, this time linking it to web1:

```
user@docker1:~$ docker stop web2
web2
user@docker1:~$ docker rm web2
web2
user@docker1:~$ docker run -d -P --name=web2 --link=web1 \
jonlangemak/web_server_2
4c77916bb08dfc586105cee7ae328c30828e25fcec1df55f8adba8545cbb2d30
user@docker1:~$ docker exec -it web2 curl http://172.17.0.2
<body>
  <html>
     <h1><span style="color:#FF0000;font-size:72px;">Web Server #1 -
Running on port 80</span>
     </h1>
</body>
  </html>
user@docker1:~$
```

We can see that, with the link in place, the communication is allowed as expected. Once again, just like the link, this access is allowed in one direction.

It should be noted that linking works differently when using user-defined networks. In this recipe, we covered what are now being named **legacy links**. Linking with user-defined networks will be covered in the next two recipes.

Leveraging Docker DNS

The introduction of user-defined networks signaled a big change in Docker networking. While the ability to provision custom networks was the big news, there were also major enhancements in name resolution. User-defined networks can benefit from what's being named **embedded DNS**. The Docker engine itself now has the ability to provide name resolution to all of the containers. This is a marked improvement from the legacy solution where the only means for name resolution was external DNS or linking, which relied on the `hosts` file. In this recipe, we'll walk through how to use and configure embedded DNS.

Getting ready

In this recipe, we'll be demonstrating the configuration on a single Docker host. It is assumed that this host has Docker installed and that Docker is in its default configuration. We'll be altering name resolution settings on the host, so you'll need root-level access.

How to do it...

As mentioned, the embedded DNS system only works on user-defined Docker networks. That being said, let's provision a user-defined network and then start a simple container on it:

```
user@docker1:~$ docker network create -d bridge mybridge1
0d75f46594eb2df57304cf3a2b55890fbf4b47058c8e43a0a99f64e4ede98f5f
user@docker1:~$ docker run -d -P --name=web1 --net=mybridge1 \
jonlangemak/web_server_1
3a65d84a16331a5a84dbed4ec29d9b6042dde5649c37bc160bfe0b5662ad7d65
user@docker1:~$
```

As we saw in an earlier recipe, by default, Docker pulls the name resolution configuration from the Docker host and provides it to the container. This behavior can be changed by providing different DNS servers or search domains either at the service level or at container runtime. In the case of containers connected to a user-defined network, the DNS settings provided to the container are slightly different. For instance, let's look at the `resolv.conf` file for the container we just connected to the user-defined bridge `mybridge1`:

```
user@docker1:~$ docker exec -t web1 more /etc/resolv.conf
search lab.lab
```

```
nameserver 127.0.0.11
```

options ndots:0

user@docker1:~$

Notice how the name server for this container is now `127.0.0.11`. This IP address represents Docker's embedded DNS server and will be used for any container, which is connected to a user-defined network. It is a requirement that any container connected to a user-defined network should use the embedded DNS server.

Containers not initially started on a user-defined network will get updated the moment they connect to a user-defined network. For instance, let's start another container named `web2` but have it use the default `docker0` bridge:

```
user@docker1:~$ docker run -dP --name=web2 jonlangemak/web_server_2
d0c414477881f03efac26392ffbdfb6f32914597a0a7ba578474606d5825df3f
user@docker1:~$ docker exec -t web2 more /etc/resolv.conf
:::::::::::::::
/etc/resolv.conf
:::::::::::::::
# Dynamic resolv.conf(5) file for glibc resolver(3) generated by
resolvconf(8)
#       DO NOT EDIT THIS FILE BY HAND -- YOUR CHANGES WILL BE OVERWRITTEN
nameserver 10.20.30.13
search lab.lab
```

user@docker1:~$

If we now connect the `web2` container to our user-defined network, Docker will update the name server to reflect the embedded DNS server:

```
user@docker1:~$ docker network connect mybridge1 web2
user@docker1:~$ docker exec -t web2 more /etc/resolv.conf
search lab.lab
nameserver 127.0.0.11
```

options ndots:0

user@docker1:~$

Since both our containers are now connected to the same user-defined network, they can now reach each other by name:

```
user@docker1:~$ docker exec -t web1 ping web2 -c 2
PING web2 (172.18.0.3): 48 data bytes
```

```
56 bytes from 172.18.0.3: icmp_seq=0 ttl=64 time=0.107 ms
56 bytes from 172.18.0.3: icmp_seq=1 ttl=64 time=0.087 ms
--- web2 ping statistics ---
2 packets transmitted, 2 packets received, 0% packet loss
round-trip min/avg/max/stddev = 0.087/0.097/0.107/0.000 ms

user@docker1:~$ docker exec -t web2 ping web1 -c 2
PING web1 (172.18.0.2): 48 data bytes
56 bytes from 172.18.0.2: icmp_seq=0 ttl=64 time=0.060 ms
56 bytes from 172.18.0.2: icmp_seq=1 ttl=64 time=0.119 ms
--- web1 ping statistics ---
2 packets transmitted, 2 packets received, 0% packet loss
round-trip min/avg/max/stddev = 0.060/0.089/0.119/0.030 ms
user@docker1:~$
```

You'll note that the name resolution is bidirectional, and it works inherently without the use of any links. That being said, with user-defined networks, we can still define links for the purpose of creating local aliases. For instance, let's stop and remove both containers web1 and web2 and reprovision them as follows:

```
user@docker1:~$ docker run  d  P   name=web1   net=mybridge1 \
--link=web2:thesecondserver jonlangemak/web_server_1
fd21c53def0c2255fc20991fef25766db9e072c2bd503c7adf21a1bd9e0c8a0a
user@docker1:~$ docker run -d -P --name=web2 --net=mybridge1 \
--link=web1:thefirstserver jonlangemak/web_server_2
6e8f6ab4dec7110774029abbd69df40c84f67bcb6a38a633e0a9faffb5bf625e
user@docker1:~$
```

The first interesting item to point out is that Docker lets us link to a container that did not yet exist. When we ran the container web1, we asked Docker to link it to the container web2. At that point, web2 didn't exist. This is a notable difference in how links work with the embedded DNS server. In legacy linking, Docker needed to know the target container information prior to making the link. This was because it had to manually update the source container's host file and environmental variables. The second interesting item is that aliases are no longer listed in the container's hosts file. If we look at the hosts file on each container, we'll see that the linking no longer generates entries:

```
user@docker1:~$ docker exec -t web1 more /etc/resolv.conf
search lab.lab
nameserver 127.0.0.11
options ndots:0
```

```
user@docker1:~$ docker exec -t web1 more /etc/hosts
...<Additional output removed for brevity>...
172.18.0.2          9cee9ce88cc3
user@docker1:~$
user@docker1:~$ docker exec -t web2 more /etc/hosts
...<Additional output removed for brevity>...
172.18.0.3          2d4b63452c8a
user@docker1:~$
```

All of the resolution is now occurring in the embedded DNS server. This includes keeping track of defined aliases and their scope. So even without host records, each container is able to resolve the other containers alias through the embedded DNS server:

```
user@docker1:~$ docker exec -t web1 ping thesecondserver -c2
PING thesecondserver (172.18.0.3): 48 data bytes
56 bytes from 172.18.0.3: icmp_seq=0 ttl=64 time=0.067 ms
56 bytes from 172.18.0.3: icmp_seq=1 ttl=64 time=0.067 ms
--- thesecondserver ping statistics ---
2 packets transmitted, 2 packets received, 0% packet loss
round-trip min/avg/max/stddev = 0.067/0.067/0.067/0.000 ms


user@docker1:~$ docker exec -t web2 ping thefirstserver -c 2
PING thefirstserver (172.18.0.2): 48 data bytes
56 bytes from 172.18.0.2: icmp_seq=0 ttl=64 time=0.062 ms
56 bytes from 172.18.0.2: icmp_seq=1 ttl=64 time=0.042 ms
--- thefirstserver ping statistics ---
2 packets transmitted, 2 packets received, 0% packet loss
round-trip min/avg/max/stddev = 0.042/0.052/0.062/0.000 ms
user@docker1:~$
```

The aliases created have a scope that is local to the container itself. For instance, a third container on the same user-defined network is not able to resolve the aliases created as part of the links:

```
user@docker1:~$ docker run -d -P --name=web3 --net=mybridge1 \
jonlangemak/web_server_1
d039722a155b5d0a702818ce4292270f30061b928e05740d80bb0c9cb50dd64f
user@docker1:~$ docker exec -it web3 ping thefirstserver -c 2
ping: unknown host
user@docker1:~$ docker exec -it web3 ping thesecondserver -c 2
ping: unknown host
user@docker1:~$
```

You'll recall that legacy linking also automatically created a set of environmental variables on the source container. These environmental variables referenced the target container and any ports it might be exposing. Linking in user-defined networks does not create these environmental variables:

```
user@docker1:~$ docker exec web1 printenv
PATH=/usr/local/sbin:/usr/local/bin:/usr/sbin:/usr/bin:/sbin:/bin
HOSTNAME=4eba77b66d60
APACHE_RUN_USER=www-data
APACHE_RUN_GROUP=www-data
APACHE_LOG_DIR=/var/log/apache2
HOME=/root
user@docker1:~$
```

As we saw in the previous recipe, keeping these variables up to date wasn't achievable even with legacy links. That being said, it's not a total surprise that the functionality doesn't exist when dealing with user-defined networks.

In addition to providing local container resolution, the embedded DNS server also handles any external requests. As we saw in the preceding example, the search domain from the Docker host (`lab.lab` in my case) was still being passed down to the containers and configured in their `resolv.conf` file. The name server learned from the host becomes a forwarder for the embedded DNS server. This allows the embedded DNS server to process any container name resolution requests and hand off external requests to the name server used by the Docker host. This behavior can be overridden either at the service level or by passing the `--dns` or `--dns-search` flag to a container at runtime. For instance, we can start two more instances of the `web1` container and specify a specific DNS server in either case:

```
user@docker1:~$ docker run -dP --net=mybridge1 --name=web4 \
--dns=10.20.30.13 jonlangemak/web_server_1
19e157b46373d24ca5bbd3684107a41f22dea53c91e91e2b0d8404e4f2ccfd68
user@docker1:~$ docker run -dP --net=mybridge1 --name=web5 \
--dns=8.8.8.8 jonlangemak/web_server_1
700f8ac4e7a20204100c8f0f48710e0aab8ac0f05b86f057b04b1bbfe8141c26
user@docker1:~$
```

 Note that web4 would receive `10.20.30.13` as a DNS forwarder even if we didn't specify it explicitly. This is because that's also the DNS server used by the Docker host and when not specified the container inherits from the host. It is specified here for the sake of the example.

Now if we try to resolve a local DNS record on either container, we can see that in the case of web1 it works since it has the local DNS server defined, whereas the lookup on web2 fails because 8.8.8.8 doesn't know about the lab.lab domain:

```
user@docker1:~$ docker exec -it web4 ping docker1.lab.lab -c 2
PING docker1.lab.lab (10.10.10.101): 48 data bytes
56 bytes from 10.10.10.101: icmp_seq=0 ttl=64 time=0.080 ms
56 bytes from 10.10.10.101: icmp_seq=1 ttl=64 time=0.078 ms
--- docker1.lab.lab ping statistics ---
2 packets transmitted, 2 packets received, 0% packet loss
round-trip min/avg/max/stddev = 0.078/0.079/0.080/0.000 ms

user@docker1:~$ docker exec -it web5 ping docker1.lab.lab -c 2
ping: unknown host
user@docker1:~$
```

Creating Docker DNS aliases

Before embedded DNS, the only way to alias a container to a different name was to use links. As we've seen in previous recipes, this is still the method used to create localized or container-specific aliases. However, what if you wanted to have an alias with a larger scope, one that any container connected to a given network could resolve? The embedded DNS server offers what are referred to as network-scoped aliases, which are resolvable within a given user-defined network. In this recipe, we'll show you how to create network-scoped aliases within user-defined networks.

Getting ready

In this recipe, we'll be demonstrating the configuration on a single Docker host. It is assumed that this host has Docker installed and that Docker is in its default configuration. We'll be altering name resolution settings on the host, so you'll need root-level access.

How to do it...

Network aliases can be defined in a couple of different ways. They can be defined at container runtime or when you connect a container to a network. Once again, network aliases are a feature only provided when a container implements a user-defined network. You cannot create a network alias without specifying a user-defined network at the same time. Docker will prevent you from specifying them at container runtime:

```
user@docker1:~$ docker run -dP --name=web1 --net-alias=webserver1 \
```

```
jonlangemak/web_server_1
460f587d0fb3e70842b37736639c150b6d333fd0b647345aa7ed9e0505ebfd2d
```

docker: Error response from daemon: Network-scoped alias is supported only for containers in user defined networks.

```
user@docker1:~$
```

If we create a user-defined network and specify it as part of the container configuration, the command will execute successfully:

```
user@docker1:~$ docker network create -d bridge mybridge1
663f9fe0b4a0dbf7a0be3c4eaf8da262f7e2b3235de252ed5a5b481b68416ca2
user@docker1:~$ docker run -dP --name=web1 --net=mybridge1 \
--net-alias=webserver1 jonlangemak/web_server_1
05025adf381c7933f427e647a512f60198b29a3cd07a1d6126bc9a6d4de0a279
user@docker1:~$
```

Once the alias is created, we can see it as part of the specific container's configuration. For instance, if we now inspect the container web1, we'll see a defined alias under its network configuration:

```
user@docker1:~$ docker inspect web1
...<Additional output removed for brevity>...
                "mybridge1": {
                    "IPAMConfig": null,
                    "Links": null,
                    "Aliases": [
                        "webserver1",
                        "6916ac68c459"
                    ],
                    "NetworkID":
"a75b46cc785b88ddfbc83ad7b6ab7ced88bbafef3f64e3e4314904fb95aa9e5c",
                    "EndpointID":
"620bc4bf9962b7c6a1e59a3dad8d3ebf25831ea00fea4874a9a5fcc750db5534",
                    "Gateway": "172.18.0.1",
                    "IPAddress": "172.18.0.2",
...<Additional output removed for brevity>...
user@docker1:~$
```

Now, let's start another container named web2 and see if we can resolve the alias:

```
user@docker1:~$ docker run -dP --name=web2 --net=mybridge1 \
```

```
jonlangemak/web_server_2
9b6d23ce868bf62999030a8c1eb29c3ca7b3836e8e3cbb7247d4d8e12955f117
user@docker1:~$ docker exec -it web2 ping webserver1 -c 2
PING webserver1 (172.18.0.2): 48 data bytes
56 bytes from 172.18.0.2: icmp_seq=0 ttl=64 time=0.104 ms
56 bytes from 172.18.0.2: icmp_seq=1 ttl=64 time=0.091 ms
--- webserver1 ping statistics ---
2 packets transmitted, 2 packets received, 0% packet loss
round-trip min/avg/max/stddev = 0.091/0.098/0.104/0.000 ms
user@docker1:~$
```

There are a couple of interesting things to point out here. First, this method for defining aliases is vastly different than the linking method in more than just scope. With links, a source container specified what it wanted a target container to be aliases to. In the case of network aliases, a source container sets its own alias.

Second, this only worked because the container web2 is on the same user-defined network as web1. Because the alias' scope is the entire user-defined network, this means that the same container could go by different aliases on a different user-defined networks. For instance, let's create another user-defined network:

```
user@docker1:~$ docker network create -d bridge mybridge2
d867d7ad3a1f639cde8926405acd3a36e99352f0e2a45871db5263caf3b59c44
user@docker1:~$
```

Now, let's attach the container web1 to it:

```
user@docker1:~$ docker network connect --alias=fooserver mybridge2 web1
```

Recall that we said you can define network-scoped aliases as part of the network connect subcommand as well:

```
user@docker1:~$ docker inspect web1
...<Additional output removed for brevity>...
                "mybridge1": {
                    "IPAMConfig": null,
                    "Links": null,
                    "Aliases": [
                        "webserver1",
                        "6916ac68c459"
                    ],
```

```
                       "NetworkID":
"a75b46cc785b88ddfbc83ad7b6ab7ced88bbafef3f64e3e4314904fb95aa9e5c",

                       "EndpointID":
"620bc4bf9962b7c6a1e59a3dad8d3ebf25831ea00fea4874a9a5fcc750db5534",

                   "Gateway": "172.18.0.1",

                   "IPAddress": "172.18.0.2",

                   "IPPrefixLen": 16,

                   "IPv6Gateway": "",

                   "GlobalIPv6Address": "",

                   "GlobalIPv6PrefixLen": 0,

                   "MacAddress": "02:42:ac:12:00:02"
               },
           "mybridge2": {
                   "IPAMConfig": {},

                   "Links": null,

                   "Aliases": [

                       "fooserver",

                       "6916ac68c459"

                   ],
                   "NetworkID":
"daf24590cc8f9c9bf859eb31dab42554c6c14c1c1e4396b3511524fe89789a58",

                   "EndpointID":
"a36572ec71077377cebfe750f4e533e0316669352894b93df101dcdabebf9fa7",

                   "Gateway": "172.19.0.1",

                   "IPAddress": "172.19.0.2",

user@docker1:~$
```

Note that the container web1 now has two aliases, one on each network. Because the container web2 is only connected to one network, it is still only able to resolve the alias associated with the mybridge1 network:

```
user@docker1:~$ docker exec -it web2 ping webserver1 -c 2
PING webserver1 (172.18.0.2): 48 data bytes
56 bytes from 172.18.0.2: icmp_seq=0 ttl=64 time=0.079 ms
56 bytes from 172.18.0.2: icmp_seq=1 ttl=64 time=0.123 ms
--- webserver1 ping statistics ---
2 packets transmitted, 2 packets received, 0% packet loss
round-trip min/avg/max/stddev = 0.079/0.101/0.123/0.000 ms
```

```
user@docker1:~$ docker exec -it web2 ping fooserver -c 2
ping: unknown host
user@docker1:~$
```

However, once we connect web2 to the mybridge2 network, it is now able to resolve both aliases:

```
user@docker1:~$ docker network connect mybridge2 web2
user@docker1:~$ docker exec -it web2 ping webserver1 -c 2
PING webserver1 (172.18.0.2): 48 data bytes
56 bytes from 172.18.0.2: icmp_seq=0 ttl=64 time=0.064 ms
56 bytes from 172.18.0.2: icmp_seq=1 ttl=64 time=0.097 ms
--- webserver1 ping statistics ---
2 packets transmitted, 2 packets received, 0% packet loss
round-trip min/avg/max/stddev = 0.064/0.081/0.097/0.000 ms
user@docker1:~$ docker exec -it web2 ping fooserver -c 2
PING fooserver (172.19.0.2): 48 data bytes
56 bytes from 172.19.0.2: icmp_seq=0 ttl=64 time=0.080 ms
56 bytes from 172.19.0.2: icmp_seq=1 ttl=64 time=0.087 ms
--- fooserver ping statistics ---
2 packets transmitted, 2 packets received, 0% packet loss
round-trip min/avg/max/stddev = 0.080/0.083/0.087/0.000 ms
user@docker1:~$
```

Interestingly, Docker also lets you define the same alias to multiple containers. For instance, let's now start a third container named web3 and connect it to mybridge1 using the same alias as web1 (webserver1):

```
user@docker1:~$ docker run -dP --name=web3 --net=mybridge1 \
--net-alias=webserver1 jonlangemak/web_server_1
cdf22ba64231553dd7e876b5718e155b1312cca68a621049e04265f5326e063c
user@docker1:~$
```

The alias is now defined for the container web1 as well as web2. However, attempts to resolve the alias from web2 still point to web1:

```
user@docker1:~$ docker exec -it web2 ping webserver1 -c 2
PING webserver1 (172.18.0.2): 48 data bytes
56 bytes from 172.18.0.2: icmp_seq=0 ttl=64 time=0.066 ms
56 bytes from 172.18.0.2: icmp_seq=1 ttl=64 time=0.088 ms
--- webserver1 ping statistics ---
```

```
2 packets transmitted, 2 packets received, 0% packet loss
round-trip min/avg/max/stddev = 0.066/0.077/0.088/0.000 ms
user@docker1:~$
```

If we disconnect or stop the container web1, we should see that the resolution now changes to web3 since it's still active on the network and has the same alias:

```
user@docker1:~$ docker stop web1
web1
user@docker1:~$ docker exec -it web2 ping webserver1 -c 2
PING webserver1 (172.18.0.4): 48 data bytes
56 bytes from 172.18.0.4: icmp_seq=0 ttl=64 time=0.085 ms
56 bytes from 172.18.0.4: icmp_seq=1 ttl=64 time=0.091 ms
--- webserver1 ping statistics ---
2 packets transmitted, 2 packets received, 0% packet loss
round-trip min/avg/max/stddev = 0.085/0.088/0.091/0.000 ms
user@docker1:~$
```

This functionality can provide you with some interesting options in terms of high availability or failover, especially when coupled with the overlay network type.

It should be noted that this functionality works for all user-defined network types including the overlay network type. We've used bridges in these examples to keep the examples simple.

6

Securing Container Networks

In this chapter, we will cover the following recipes:

- ▶ Enabling and disabling ICC
- ▶ Disabling outbound masquerading
- ▶ Managing netfilter to Docker integration
- ▶ Creating custom iptables rules
- ▶ Exposing services through a load balancer

Introduction

As you move toward container-based applications, one of the items you'll want to put some serious consideration toward is network security. Containers, in particular, can lead to a proliferation in the number of network endpoints that need to be secured. Granted, not all endpoints are fully exposed to the network. However, those that aren't, by default, talk directly to each other, which can cause other concerns. There are many ways to tackle network security when it comes to container-based applications, and this chapter doesn't aim to address all possible solutions. Rather, this chapter aims to review configuration options and relevant network topologies that can be combined in a number of different ways based on your own network security requirements. We'll discuss in detail some features that we were exposed to in earlier chapters such as ICC mode and outbound masquerading. In addition, we'll cover a couple of different techniques to limit the network exposure of your containers.

Enabling and disabling ICC

In earlier chapters, we were exposed to the concept of ICC mode, but didn't have much information on the mechanics of how it worked. ICC is a Docker-native way of isolating all containers connected to the same network. The isolation provided prevents containers from talking directly to each other while still allowing their exposed ports to be published as well as allowing outbound connectivity. In this recipe, we'll review our options for ICC-based configuration in both the default `docker0` bridge context as well as with user-defined networks.

Getting ready

We'll be using two Docker hosts in this recipe to demonstrate how ICC works in different network configurations. It is assumed that both Docker hosts used in this lab are in their default configuration. In some cases, the changes we make may require you to have root-level access to the system.

How to do it...

ICC mode can be configured on both the native `docker0` bridge as well as any user-defined networks that utilize the bridge driver. In this recipe, we'll review how to configure ICC mode on the `docker0` bridge. As we've seen in earlier chapters, settings related to the `docker0` bridge need to be made at the service level. This is because the `docker0` bridge is created as part of service initialization. This also means that, to make changes to it, we'll need to edit the Docker service configuration and then restart the service for them to take effect. Before we make any changes, let's take the opportunity to review the default ICC configuration. To do this, let's first view the `docker0` bridge configuration:

```
user@docker1:~$ docker network inspect bridge
[
    {
        "Name": "bridge",
        "Id":
"d88fa0a96585792f98023881978abaa8c5d05e4e2bbd7b4b44a6e7b0ed7d346b",
        "Scope": "local",
        "Driver": "bridge",
        "EnableIPv6": false,
        "IPAM": {
            "Driver": "default",
            "Options": null,
            "Config": [
                {
```

```
                "Subnet": "172.17.0.0/16",
                "Gateway": "172.17.0.1"
            }
        ]
    },
    "Internal": false,
    "Containers": {},
    "Options": {
        "com.docker.network.bridge.default_bridge": "true",
        "com.docker.network.bridge.enable_icc": "true",
        "com.docker.network.bridge.enable_ip_masquerade": "true",
        "com.docker.network.bridge.host_binding_ipv4": "0.0.0.0",
        "com.docker.network.bridge.name": "docker0",
        "com.docker.network.driver.mtu": "1500"
    },
    "Labels": {}
    }
]
user@docker1:~$
```

> It's important to remember that the `docker network` subcommand is used to manage all Docker networks. A common misconception is that it can only be used to manage user-defined networks.

As we can see, the `docker0` bridge is configured for ICC mode on (`true`). This means that Docker will not interfere or prevent containers connected to this bridge to talk directly to one another. To prove this out, let's start two containers:

```
user@docker1:~$ docker run -d --name=web1 jonlangemak/web_server_1
417dd2587dfe3e664b67a46a87f90714546bec9c4e35861476d5e4fa77e77e61
user@docker1:~$ docker run -d --name=web2 jonlangemak/web_server_2
a54db26074c00e6771d0676bb8093b1a22eb95a435049916becd425ea9587014
user@docker1:~$
```

Notice that we didn't specify the `-P` flag, which tells Docker to not publish any of the containers exposed ports. Now, let's get each container's IP address, so we can validate connectivity:

```
user@docker1:~$ docker exec web1 ip addr show dev eth0 | grep inet
    inet 172.17.0.2/16 scope global eth0
    inet6 fe80::42:acff:fe11:2/64 scope link
```

```
user@docker1:~$ docker exec web2 ip addr show dev eth0 | grep inet
    inet 172.17.0.3/16 scope global eth0
    inet6 fe80::42:acff:fe11:3/64 scope link
user@docker1:~$
```

Now that we know the IP addresses, we can verify that each container can access the other on any service in which the container is listening:

```
user@docker1:~$ docker exec -it web1 ping 172.17.0.3 -c 2
PING 172.17.0.3 (172.17.0.3): 48 data bytes
56 bytes from 172.17.0.3: icmp_seq=0 ttl=64 time=0.198 ms
56 bytes from 172.17.0.3: icmp_seq=1 ttl=64 time=0.082 ms
--- 172.17.0.3 ping statistics ---
2 packets transmitted, 2 packets received, 0% packet loss
round-trip min/avg/max/stddev = 0.082/0.140/0.198/0.058 ms
user@docker1:~$
user@docker1:~$ docker exec web2 curl -s http://172.17.0.2
<body>
  <html>
      <h1><span style="color:#FF0000;font-size:72px;">Web Server #1 -
Running on port 80</span>
      </h1>
</body>
  </html>
user@docker1:~$
```

Based on these tests, we can assume that the containers are allowed to talk to each other on any protocol that is listening. This is the expected behavior when ICC mode is enabled. Now, let's change the service level setting and recheck our configuration. To do this, set the following configuration in your systemd drop in file for the Docker service:

```
ExecStart=/usr/bin/dockerd --icc=false
```

Now reload the systemd configuration, restart the Docker service, and check the ICC setting:

```
user@docker1:~$ sudo systemctl daemon-reload
user@docker1:~$ sudo systemctl restart docker
user@docker1:~$ docker network inspect bridge
...<Additional output removed for brevity>...
        "Options": {
```

```
       "com.docker.network.bridge.default_bridge": "true",
       "com.docker.network.bridge.enable_icc": "false",
       "com.docker.network.bridge.enable_ip_masquerade": "true",
       "com.docker.network.bridge.host_binding_ipv4": "0.0.0.0",
       "com.docker.network.bridge.name": "docker0",
       "com.docker.network.driver.mtu": "1500"
...<Additional output removed for brevity>...
user@docker1:~$
```

Now that we've confirmed that ICC is disabled, let's start up our two containers once again and run the same connectivity tests:

```
user@docker1:~$ docker start web1
web1
user@docker1:~$ docker start web2
web2
user@docker1:~$
user@docker1:~$ docker exec -it web1 ping 172.17.0.3 -c 2
PING 172.17.0.3 (172.17.0.3): 48 data bytes
user@docker1:~$ docker exec -it web2 curl -m 1 http://172.17.0.2
curl: (28) connect() timed out!
user@docker1:~$
```

As you can see, we have no connectivity between the two containers. However, the Docker host itself is still able to access the services:

```
user@docker1:~$ curl http://172.17.0.2
<body>
  <html>
      <h1><span style="color:#FF0000;font-size:72px;">Web Server #1 -
Running on port 80</span>
      </h1>
</body>
  </html>
user@docker1:~$ curl http://172.17.0.3
<body>
  <html>
      <h1><span style="color:#FF0000;font-size:72px;">Web Server #2 -
Running on port 80</span>
```

```
  </h1>
</body>
  </html>
user@docker1:~$
```

We can inspect the netfilter rules that are used to implement ICC by looking at the `iptables` rules `FORWARD` chain of the filter table:

```
user@docker1:~$ sudo iptables -S FORWARD

-P FORWARD ACCEPT

-A FORWARD -j DOCKER-ISOLATION

-A FORWARD -o docker0 -j DOCKER

-A FORWARD -o docker0 -m conntrack --ctstate RELATED,ESTABLISHED -j
ACCEPT

-A FORWARD -i docker0 ! -o docker0 -j ACCEPT

-A FORWARD -i docker0 -o docker0 -j DROP

user@docker1:~$
```

The preceding bolded rule is what prevents container–to-container communication on the `docker0` bridge. If we had inspected this `iptables` chain before disabling ICC, we would have seen this rule set to `ACCEPT` as shown following:

```
user@docker1:~$ sudo iptables -S FORWARD

-P FORWARD ACCEPT

-A FORWARD -j DOCKER-ISOLATION

-A FORWARD -i docker0 -o docker0 -j ACCEPT

-A FORWARD -o docker0 -j DOCKER

-A FORWARD -o docker0 -m conntrack --ctstate RELATED,ESTABLISHED -j
ACCEPT

-A FORWARD -i docker0 ! -o docker0 -j ACCEPT

user@docker1:~$
```

As we saw earlier, linking containers allowed you to bypass this rule and allow a source container to access a target container. If we remove the two containers we can restart them with a link as follows:

```
user@docker1:~$ docker run -d --name=web1 jonlangemak/web_server_1

9846614b3bac6a2255e135d19f20162022a40d95bd62a0264ef4aaa89e24592f

user@docker1:~$ docker run -d --name=web2 --link=web1 jonlangemak/web_
server_2

b343b570189a0445215ad5406e9a2746975da39a1f1d47beba4d20f14d687d83

user@docker1:~$
```

Now if we examine the rules with `iptables`, we can see two new rules added to the filter table:

```
user@docker1:~$ sudo iptables -S
-P INPUT ACCEPT
-P FORWARD ACCEPT
-P OUTPUT ACCEPT
-N DOCKER
-N DOCKER-ISOLATION
-A FORWARD -j DOCKER-ISOLATION
-A FORWARD -o docker0 -j DOCKER
-A FORWARD -o docker0 -m conntrack --ctstate RELATED,ESTABLISHED -j
ACCEPT
-A FORWARD -i docker0 ! -o docker0 -j ACCEPT
-A FORWARD -i docker0 -o docker0 -j DROP
-A DOCKER -s 172.17.0.3/32 -d 172.17.0.2/32 -i docker0 -o docker0 -p tcp
-m tcp --dport 80 -j ACCEPT
-A DOCKER -s 172.17.0.2/32 -d 172.17.0.3/32 -i docker0 -o docker0 -p tcp
-m tcp --sport 80 -j ACCEPT
-A DOCKER-ISOLATION -j RETURN
user@docker1:~$
```

These two new rules allow web2 to access web1 on any exposed port. Notice how the first rule defines the access from web2 (172.17.0.3) to web1 (172.17.0.2) with a destination port of 80. The second rule flips the IPs and specifies port 80 as the source port, allowing the traffic to return to web2.

> Earlier, when we discussed user-defined networks, you saw that we could pass the ICC flag to a user-defined bridge. However, disabling ICC mode is not currently supported with the overlay driver.

Disabling outbound masquerading

By default, containers are allowed to access the outside network by masquerading or hiding their real IP address behind that of the Docker host. This is accomplished through netfilter `masquerade` rules that hide container traffic behind the Docker host interface referenced in the next hop. We saw a detailed example of this in *Chapter 2, Configuring and Monitoring Docker Networks*, when we discussed container-to-container connectivity across hosts. While this type of configuration is ideal in many respects, there are some cases when you might prefer to disable the outbound masquerading capability. For instance, if you prefer to not allow your containers to have outbound connectivity at all, disabling masquerading would prevent containers from talking to the outside network. This, however, only prevents outbound traffic due to lack of return routing. A better option might be to treat containers like any other individual network endpoint and use existing security appliances to define network policy. In this recipe, we'll discuss how to disable IP masquerading as well as how to provide containers with unique IP addressing as they traverse the outside network.

Getting ready

We'll be using a single Docker host in this example. It is assumed that the Docker host used in this lab is in its default configuration. You'll also need access to change Docker service-level settings. In some cases, the changes we make may require you to have root-level access to the system. We'll also be making changes to the network equipment to which the Docker host connects.

How to do it...

You'll recall that IP masquerading in Docker is handled through a netfilter `masquerade` rule. On a Docker host in its default configuration, we can see this rule by examining the ruleset with `iptables`:

```
user@docker1:~$ sudo iptables -t nat -S
-P PREROUTING ACCEPT
-P INPUT ACCEPT
-P OUTPUT ACCEPT
-P POSTROUTING ACCEPT
-N DOCKER
-A PREROUTING -m addrtype --dst-type LOCAL -j DOCKER
-A OUTPUT ! -d 127.0.0.0/8 -m addrtype --dst-type LOCAL -j DOCKER
-A POSTROUTING -s 172.17.0.0/16 ! -o docker0 -j MASQUERADE
-A DOCKER -i docker0 -j RETURN
user@docker1:~$
```

This rule specifies the source of the traffic as the docker0 bridge subnet and only NAT traffic can be headed off the host. The MASQUERADE target tells the host to source NAT the traffic to the Docker host's next hop interface. That is, if the host has multiple IP interfaces, the container's traffic will source NAT to whichever interface is used as the next hop. This means that container traffic could potentially be hidden behind different IP addresses based on the Docker host interface and routing table configuration. For instance, consider a Docker host with two interfaces, as shown in the following figure:

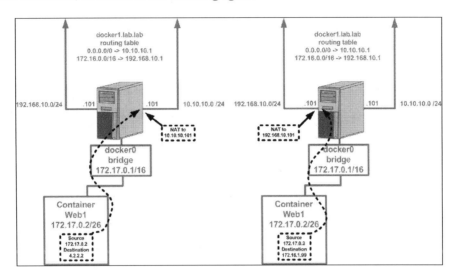

In the left-hand side example, traffic is taking the default route since the destination of 4.2.2.2 doesn't match a more specific prefix in the host's routing table. In this case, the host performs a source NAT and changes the source of the traffic from 172.17.0.2 to 10.10.10.101 as it traverses the Docker host to the outside network. However, if the destination falls into 172.17.0.0/16, the container traffic will instead be hidden behind the 192.168.10.101 interface, as shown in the example on the right.

The default behavior of Docker can be changed by manipulating the --ip-masq Docker option. By default, the option is considered to be true and can be overridden by specifying the option and setting it to false. We can do this by specifying the option in our Docker systemd drop in file, as follows:

```
ExecStart=/usr/bin/dockerd --ip-masq=false
```

Now reload the systemd configuration, restart the Docker service, and check the ICC setting:

```
user@docker1:~$ sudo systemctl daemon-reload
user@docker1:~$ sudo systemctl restart docker
user@docker1:~$
user@docker1:~$ sudo iptables -t nat -S
```

```
-P PREROUTING ACCEPT

-P INPUT ACCEPT

-P OUTPUT ACCEPT

-P POSTROUTING ACCEPT

-N DOCKER

-A PREROUTING -m addrtype --dst-type LOCAL -j DOCKER

-A OUTPUT ! -d 127.0.0.0/8 -m addrtype --dst-type LOCAL -j DOCKERuser@
docker1:~$
```

Notice that the `masquerade` rule is now gone. Traffic generated from a container on this host would attempt to route out through the Docker host with its actual source IP address. A `tcpdump` on the Docker host would capture this traffic exiting the host's `eth0` interface with the original container IP address:

```
user@docker1:~$ sudo tcpdump -n -i eth0 dst 4.2.2.2

tcpdump: verbose output suppressed, use -v or -vv for full protocol
decode

listening on eth0, link-type EN10MB (Ethernet), capture size 65535 bytes

09:06:10.243523 IP 172.17.0.2 > 4.2.2.2: ICMP echo request, id 3072, seq
0, length 56

09:06:11.244572 IP 172.17.0.2 > 4.2.2.2: ICMP echo request, id 3072, seq
256, length 56
```

Since the outside network doesn't know where `172.17.0.0/16` is, this request will never receive a response effectively preventing the container from communicating to the outside world.

While this may be a useful means to prevent communication to the outside world, it's not entirely ideal. For starters, you're still allowing the traffic out; the response just won't know where to go as it attempts to return to the source. Also, you've impacted all of the containers, from all networks, on the Docker host. If the `docker0` bridge had a routable subnet allocated to it, and the outside network knew where that subnet lived, you could use existing security tooling to make security policy decisions.

For instance, let's assume that the `docker0` bridge were to be allocated a subnet of `172.10.10.0/24` and we left IP masquerading disabled. We could do this by changing the Docker options to also specify a new bridge IP address:

```
ExecStart=/usr/bin/dockerd --ip-masq=false --bip=172.10.10.1/24
```

As before, traffic leaving a container and destined for the outside network would be unchanged as it traversed the Docker host. Let's assume a small network topology, as the one shown in the following figure:

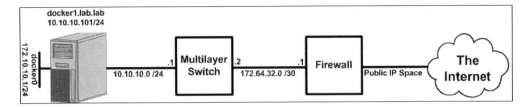

Let's assume a flow from the container to `4.2.2.2`. In this case, egress traffic should work inherently:

- Container generates traffic toward `4.2.2.2` and uses its default gateway that is the `docker0` bridge IP address

- The Docker host does a route lookup, fails to find a specific prefix match, and forwards the traffic to its default gateway that is the switch.

- The switch does a route lookup, fails to find a specific prefix match, and forwards the traffic to its default route that is the firewall.

- The firewall does a route lookup, fails to find a specific prefix match, ensures that the traffic is allowed in the policy, performs a hide NAT to a public IP address, and forwards the traffic to its default route that is the Internet.

So without any additional configuration, egress traffic should reach its destination. The problem is with the return traffic. When the response from the Internet destination gets back to the firewall, it will attempt to determine how to route back to the source. This route lookup will likely fail causing the firewall to drop the traffic.

 In some cases, edge network equipment (the firewall in this case) routes all private IP addressing back to the inside (the switch in this case). In those scenarios, the firewall might forward the return traffic to the switch, but the switch won't have a specific return route causing the same problem.

In order for this to work, the firewall and the switch need to know how to return the traffic to the specific container. To do this, we need to add specific routes on each device pointing the `docker0` bridge subnet back to the `docker1` host:

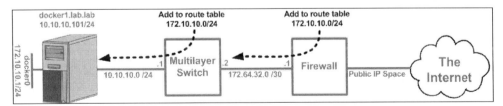

Once these routes are in place, containers spun up on the Docker host should have connectivity to outside networks:

```
user@docker1:~$ docker run -it --name=web1 jonlangemak/web_server_1 /bin/
bash
root@132530812e1f:/# ping 4.2.2.2
PING 4.2.2.2 (4.2.2.2): 48 data bytes
56 bytes from 4.2.2.2: icmp_seq=0 ttl=50 time=33.805 ms
56 bytes from 4.2.2.2: icmp_seq=1 ttl=50 time=40.431 ms
```

A `tcpdump` on the Docker host will show that the traffic is leaving with the original container IP address:

```
user@docker1:~$ sudo tcpdump -n -i eth0 dst 4.2.2.2
tcpdump: verbose output suppressed, use -v or -vv for full protocol
decode
listening on eth0, link-type EN10MB (Ethernet), capture size 65535 bytes
10:54:42.197828 IP 172.10.10.2 > 4.2.2.2: ICMP echo request, id 3328, seq
0, length 56
10:54:43.198882 IP 172.10.10.2 > 4.2.2.2: ICMP echo request, id 3328, seq
256, length 56
```

This type of configuration offers the ability to use existing security appliances to decide whether containers can reach certain resources on the outside networks. However, this is also a function of how close the security appliance is to your Docker host. For instance, in this configuration the containers on the Docker host would be able to reach any other network endpoints connected to the switch. The enforcement point (the firewall, in this example) only allows you to limit the container's connectivity to the Internet. In addition, assigning routable IP space each Docker host might introduce IP assignment constraints if you have large scale.

Managing netfilter to Docker integration

By default, Docker performs most of the netfilter configuration for you. It takes care of things such as publishing ports and outbound masquerading, as well as allows you to block or allow ICC. However, this is all optional and you can tell Docker not to modify or add to any of your existing `iptables` rules. If you do this, you'll need to generate your own rules to provide similar functionality. This may be appealing to you if you're already using `iptables` rules extensively and don't want Docker to automatically make changes to your configuration. In this recipe we'll discuss how to disable automatic `iptables` rule generation for Docker and show you how to manually create similar rules.

Getting ready

We'll be using a single Docker host in this example. It is assumed that the Docker host used in this lab is in its default configuration. You'll also need access to change Docker service-level settings. In some cases, the changes we make may require you to have root-level access to the system.

How to do it...

As we've already seen, Docker takes care of a lot of the heavy lifting for you when it comes to network configuration. It also allows you the ability to configure these things on your own if need be. Before we look at doing it ourselves, let's confirm what Docker is actually configuring on our behalf with regard to `iptables` rules. Let's run the following containers:

```
user@docker1:~$ docker run -dP --name=web1 jonlangemak/web_server_1
f5b7b389890398588c55754a09aa401087604a8aa98dbf55d84915c6125d5e62
user@docker1:~$ docker run -dP --name=web2 jonlangemak/web_server_2
e1c866892e7f3f25dee8e6ba89ec526fa3caf6200cdfc705ce47917f12095470
user@docker1:~$
```

Running these containers would yield the following topology:

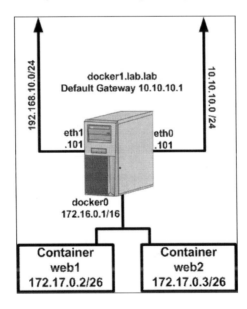

The examples given later will not use the host's `eth1` interface directly. It is displayed to illustrate how the rules generated by Docker are written in a manner that encompasses all physical interfaces on the Docker host.

As we've mentioned before, Docker uses `iptables` to handle the following items:

- Outbound container connectivity (masquerading)
- Inbound port publishing
- Container–to–container connectivity

Since we're using the default configuration and we have published ports on both containers, we should be able to see all three of these items configured in `iptables`. Let's take a look at the NAT table to start with:

 In most cases, I prefer to print the rules and interpret them rather than have them listed in formatted columns. There are trade-offs to each approach, but if you prefer the list mode, you can replace the `-S` with `-vL`.

```
user@docker1:~$ sudo iptables -t nat -S
-P PREROUTING ACCEPT
-P INPUT ACCEPT
-P OUTPUT ACCEPT
-P POSTROUTING ACCEPT
-N DOCKER
-A PREROUTING -m addrtype --dst-type LOCAL -j DOCKER
-A OUTPUT ! -d 127.0.0.0/8 -m addrtype --dst-type LOCAL -j DOCKER
-A POSTROUTING -s 172.17.0.0/16 ! -o docker0 -j MASQUERADE
-A POSTROUTING -s 172.17.0.2/32 -d 172.17.0.2/32 -p tcp -m tcp --dport 80
-j MASQUERADE
-A POSTROUTING -s 172.17.0.3/32 -d 172.17.0.3/32 -p tcp -m tcp --dport 80
-j MASQUERADE
-A DOCKER -i docker0 -j RETURN
-A DOCKER ! -i docker0 -p tcp -m tcp --dport 32768 -j DNAT --to-
destination 172.17.0.2:80
-A DOCKER ! -i docker0 -p tcp -m tcp --dport 32769 -j DNAT --to-
destination 172.17.0.3:80
user@docker1:~$
```

Let's review the importance of each of the bolded lines in the preceding output. The first bolded line takes care of the outbound hide NAT or `MASQUERADE`:

```
-A POSTROUTING -s 172.17.0.0/16 ! -o docker0 -j MASQUERADE
```

The rule is looking for traffic that matches two characteristics:

▸ The source IP address must match the IP address space of the docker0 bridge

▸ The traffic is not exiting through the docker0 bridge. That is, it's leaving through another interface such as eth0 or eth1

The jump statement at the end specifies a target of MASQUERADE, which will source NAT the container traffic to one of the host's IP interfaces based on the routing table.

The next two bolded lines provide similar functionality and provide the NAT required for publishing ports on each respective container. Let's examine one of them:

```
-A DOCKER ! -i docker0 -p tcp -m tcp --dport 32768 -j DNAT --to-destination 172.17.0.2:80
```

The rule is looking for traffic that matches three characteristics:

▸ The traffic is not entering through the docker0 bridge

▸ The traffic is TCP

▸ The traffic has a destination port of 32768

The jump statement at the end specifies a target of DNAT and a destination of the container with its real service port (80). Notice that both of these rules are generic in terms of the Docker host's physical interfaces. As we saw earlier, both port publishing and outbound masquerading can occur on any interface on the host unless we 'specifically limit the scope.

The next table we want to review is the filter table:

```
user@docker1:~$ sudo iptables -t filter -S

-P INPUT ACCEPT

-P FORWARD ACCEPT

-P OUTPUT ACCEPT

-N DOCKER

-N DOCKER-ISOLATION

-A FORWARD -j DOCKER-ISOLATION

-A FORWARD -o docker0 -j DOCKER

-A FORWARD -o docker0 -m conntrack --ctstate RELATED,ESTABLISHED -j
ACCEPT

-A FORWARD -i docker0 ! -o docker0 -j ACCEPT

-A FORWARD -i docker0 -o docker0 -j ACCEPT

-A DOCKER -d 172.17.0.2/32 ! -i docker0 -o docker0 -p tcp -m tcp --dport
80 -j ACCEPT

-A DOCKER -d 172.17.0.3/32 ! -i docker0 -o docker0 -p tcp -m tcp --dport
80 -j ACCEPT
```

```
-A DOCKER-ISOLATION -j RETURN
user@docker1:~$
```

Again, you'll note that the chain policy is set to ACCEPT for the default chains. In the case of the filter table, it has a more drastic impact on functionality. This means that everything is being allowed unless specifically denied in a rule. In other words, if there were no rules defined everything would still work. Docker inserts these rules in case your default policy is not set to ACCEPT. Later on, when we manually create the rules, we'll set the default policy to DROP so that you can see the impact the rules have. The preceding rules require a little more explaining, especially if you aren't familiar with how iptables rules work. Let's review the bolded lines one at a time.

The first bolded line takes care of allowing traffic from the outside network back into the containers. In this case, the rule is specific to instances where the container itself is generating traffic toward, and expecting a response, from the outside network:

```
-A FORWARD -o docker0 -m conntrack --ctstate RELATED,ESTABLISHED -j
ACCEPT
```

The rule is looking for traffic that matches two characteristics:

- ▶ The traffic is exiting through the docker0 bridge
- ▶ The traffic has a connection state of RELATED or ESTABLISHED. This would include sessions that are part of an existing flow or related to it

The jump statement at the end references a target of ACCEPT, which will allow the flow through.

The second bolded line allows the container's connectivity to the outside network:

```
-A FORWARD -i docker0 ! -o docker0 -j ACCEPT
```

The rule is looking for traffic that matches two characteristics:

- ▶ The traffic is entering through the docker0 bridge
- ▶ The traffic is not exiting through the docker0 bridge

This is a very generic way of identifying traffic that came from the containers and is leaving through any other interface than the docker0 bridge. The jump statement at the end references a target of ACCEPT, which will allow the flow through. This rule, in conjunction with the first rule, will allow a flow generated from a container toward the outside network to work.

The third bolded line allows inter-container connectivity:

```
-A FORWARD -i docker0 -o docker0 -j ACCEPT
```

The rule is looking for traffic that matches two characteristics:

- The traffic is entering through the docker0 bridge
- The traffic is exiting through the docker0 bridge

This is another generic means to identify traffic that is originated from a container on the docker0 bridge as well as destined for a target on the docker0 bridge. The jump statement at the end references a target of ACCEPT, which will allow the flow through. This is the same rule that's turned into a DROP target when you disable ICC mode as we saw in earlier chapters.

The last two bolded lines allow the published ports to reach the containers. Let's examine one of them:

```
-A DOCKER -d 172.17.0.2/32 ! -i docker0 -o docker0 -p tcp -m tcp --dport
80 -j ACCEPT
```

The rule is looking for traffic that matches five characteristics:

- The traffic is destined to the container whose port was published
- The traffic is not entering through the docker0 bridge
- The traffic is exiting through the docker0 bridge
- The protocol is TCP
- The port number is 80

This rule specifically allows the published port to work by allowing access to the container's service port (80). The jump statement at the end references a target of ACCEPT, which will allow the flow through.

Manually creating the required iptables rules

Now that we've seen how Docker automatically handles rule generation, let's walk through an example of how to build this connectivity on our own. To do this, we first need to instruct Docker to not create any iptables rules. To do this, we set the --iptables Docker option to false in the Docker systemd drop in file:

```
ExecStart=/usr/bin/dockerd --iptables=false
```

We'll need to reload the systemd drop in file and restart the Docker service for Docker to reread the service parameters. To ensure that you start with a blank slate, if possible, restart the server or flush all the iptables rules out manually (if you're not comfortable with managing the iptables rules, the best approach is just to reboot the server to clear them out). We'll assume for the rest of the example that we're working with an empty ruleset. Once Docker is restarted, you can restart your two containers and ensure that there are no iptables rules present on the system:

```
user@docker1:~$ docker start web1
```

```
web1
user@docker1:~$ docker start web2
web2
user@docker1:~$ sudo iptables -S
-P INPUT ACCEPT
-P FORWARD ACCEPT
-P OUTPUT ACCEPT
user@docker1:~$
```

As you can see, there are no `iptables` rules currently defined. We can also see that our default chain policy in the filter table is set to ACCEPT. Let's now change the default policy in the filter table to DROP for each chain. Along with that, let's also include a rule to allow SSH to and from the host so as not to break our connectivity:

```
user@docker1:~$ sudo iptables -A INPUT -i eth0 -p tcp --dport 22 \
-m state --state NEW,ESTABLISHED -j ACCEPT
user@docker1:~$ sudo iptables -A OUTPUT -o eth0 -p tcp --sport 22 \
-m state --state ESTABLISHED -j ACCEPT
user@docker1:~$ sudo iptables -P INPUT DROP
user@docker1:~$ sudo iptables -P FORWARD DROP
user@docker1:~$ sudo iptables -P OUTPUT DROP
```

Let's now check the filter table once again to make sure that the rules were accepted:

```
user@docker1:~$ sudo iptables -S
-P INPUT DROP
-P FORWARD DROP
-P OUTPUT DROP
-A INPUT -i eth0 -p tcp -m tcp --dport 22 -m state --state
NEW,ESTABLISHED -j ACCEPT
-A OUTPUT -o eth0 -p tcp -m tcp --sport 22 -m state --state ESTABLISHED
-j ACCEPT
user@docker1:~$
```

At this point, the containers web1 and web2 will no longer be able to reach each other:

```
user@docker1:~$ docker exec -it web1 ping 172.17.0.3 -c 2
PING 172.17.0.3 (172.17.0.3): 48 data bytes
user@docker1:~$
```

Depending on your operating system, you might notice that web1 actually is able to ping web2 at this point. The most likely reason for this is that the br_netfilter kernel module has not been loaded. Without this module bridged packets will not be inspected by netfilter. To resolve this, you can manually load the module by using the `sudo modprobe br_netfilter` command. To make the module load at each boot, you could add it to the /etc/modules file as well. When Docker is managing the iptables ruleset, it takes care of loading the module for you.

Now, let's start building the ruleset to recreate the connectivity that Docker previously built for us automatically. The first thing we want to do is allow containers inbound and outbound access. We'll do that with these two rules:

```
user@docker1:~$ sudo iptables -A FORWARD -i docker0 ! \
-o docker0 -j ACCEPT
user@docker1:~$ sudo iptables -A FORWARD -o docker0 \
-m conntrack --ctstate RELATED,ESTABLISHED -j ACCEPT
```

Although these two rules will allow containers to generate and receive traffic from the outside network, the connectivity still won't work at this point. In order for this to work, we need to apply the masquerade rule so that the container traffic will be hidden behind an interface on the docker0 host. If we don't do this, the traffic will never get returned as the outside network knows nothing about the 172.17.0.0/16 network in which the containers live:

```
user@docker1:~$ sudo iptables -t nat -A POSTROUTING \
-s 172.17.0.0/16 ! -o docker0 -j MASQUERADE
```

With this in place, the containers will now be able to reach network endpoints on the outside network:

```
user@docker1:~$ docker exec -it web1 ping 4.2.2.2 -c 2
PING 4.2.2.2 (4.2.2.2): 48 data bytes
56 bytes from 4.2.2.2: icmp_seq=0 ttl=50 time=36.261 ms
56 bytes from 4.2.2.2: icmp_seq=1 ttl=50 time=55.271 ms
--- 4.2.2.2 ping statistics ---
2 packets transmitted, 2 packets received, 0% packet loss
round-trip min/avg/max/stddev = 36.261/45.766/55.271/9.505 ms
user@docker1:~$
```

However, the containers still cannot communicate directly with each other:

```
user@docker1:~$ docker exec -it web1 ping 172.17.0.3 -c 2
PING 172.17.0.3 (172.17.0.3): 48 data bytes
user@docker1:~$ docker exec -it web1 curl -S http://172.17.0.3
```

```
user@docker1:~$
```

We need to add one final rule:

```
sudo iptables -A FORWARD -i docker0 -o docker0 -j ACCEPT
```

Since traffic between containers both enters and leaves the `docker0` bridge, this will allow the inter-container connectivity:

```
user@docker1:~$ docker exec -it web1 ping 172.17.0.3 -c 2
PING 172.17.0.3 (172.17.0.3): 48 data bytes
56 bytes from 172.17.0.3: icmp_seq=0 ttl=64 time=0.092 ms
56 bytes from 172.17.0.3: icmp_seq=1 ttl=64 time=0.086 ms
--- 172.17.0.3 ping statistics ---
2 packets transmitted, 2 packets received, 0% packet loss
round-trip min/avg/max/stddev = 0.086/0.089/0.092/0.000 ms
user@docker1:~$
user@docker1:~$ docker exec -it web1 curl http://172.17.0.3
<body>
  <html>
    <h1><span style="color:#FF0000;font-size:72px;">Web Server #2 -
Running on port 80</span>
    </h1>
</body>
  </html>
user@docker1:~$
```

The only configuration remaining is to provide a mechanism to publish ports. We can do that by first provisioning a destination NAT on the Docker host itself. Even though Docker is not provisioning the NAT rules, it's still keeping track of the port allocations on your behalf. At container runtime if you choose to publish a port, Docker will allocate a port mapping for you even though it is not handling the publishing. It is wise to use the port Docker allocates to prevent overlaps:

```
user@docker1:~$ docker port web1
80/tcp -> 0.0.0.0:32768
user@docker1:~$ docker port web2
80/tcp -> 0.0.0.0:32769
user@docker1:~$
user@docker1:~$ sudo iptables -t nat -A PREROUTING ! -i docker0 \
-p tcp -m tcp --dport 32768 -j DNAT --to-destination 172.17.0.2:80
```

```
user@docker1:~$ sudo iptables -t nat -A PREROUTING ! -i docker0 \
-p tcp -m tcp --dport 32769 -j DNAT --to-destination 172.17.0.3:80
user@docker1:~$
```

Using the ports Docker allocated, we can define an inbound NAT rule for each container that translates inbound connectivity to an external port on the Docker host to the real container IP and service port. Finally, we just need to allow inbound traffic:

```
user@docker1:~$ sudo iptables -A FORWARD -d 172.17.0.2/32 ! -i docker0 -o
docker0 -p tcp -m tcp --dport 80 -j ACCEPT
user@docker1:~$ sudo iptables -A FORWARD -d 172.17.0.3/32 ! -i docker0 -o
docker0 -p tcp -m tcp --dport 80 -j ACCEPT
```

Once these rules are configured, we can now test the connectivity from outside the Docker host on the published ports:

Creating custom iptables rules

In the previous recipe, we covered how Docker handles `iptables` rules for the most common container networking needs. However, there may be cases where you wish to extend the default `iptables` configuration to either allow more access or limit the scope of connectivity. In this recipe, we'll walk through a couple of examples of how to implement custom `iptables` rules. We'll focus on limiting the scope of sources connecting to services running on your containers as well as allowing the Docker host itself to connect to those services.

 The examples provided later are designed to demonstrate the options you have to configure `iptables` rulesets. The way they are implemented in these examples may or may not make sense in your environment and can be deployed in different ways and places based on your security needs.

Getting ready

We'll be using the same Docker host with the same configuration from the previous recipe. The Docker service should be configured with the `--iptables=false` service option, and there should be two containers defined—web1 and web2. If you are unsure how to get to this state, please see the previous recipe. In order to define a new `iptables` policy, we'll also need to flush all the existing `iptables` rules out of the NAT and the FILTER table. The easiest way to do this is to reboot the host.

 Flushing the `iptables` rules when your default policy is deny will disconnect any remote administration sessions. Be careful not to accidentally disconnect yourself if you are managing the system without console access!

If you prefer not to reboot, you can change the default filter policy back to `allow`. Then, flush the filter and NAT table as follows:

```
sudo iptables -P INPUT ACCEPT
sudo iptables -P FORWARD ACCEPT
sudo iptables -P OUTPUT ACCEPT
sudo iptables -t filter -F
sudo iptables -t nat -F
```

How to do it...

At this point, you should once again have a Docker host with two containers running and an empty default `iptables` policy. To begin, let's once again change the default filter policy to `deny` while ensuring that we still allow our management connection over SSH:

```
user@docker1:~$ sudo iptables -A INPUT -i eth0 -p tcp --dport 22 \
-m state --state NEW,ESTABLISHED -j ACCEPT
user@docker1:~$ sudo iptables -A OUTPUT -o eth0 -p tcp --sport 22 \
-m state --state ESTABLISHED -j ACCEPT
user@docker1:~$ sudo iptables -P INPUT DROP
user@docker1:~$ sudo iptables -P FORWARD DROP
user@docker1:~$ sudo iptables -P OUTPUT DROP
```

Because we'll be focusing on policy around the filter table, let's put in the NAT policy unchanged from the previous recipe. These NATs cover both outbound masquerading and inbound masquerading for the destination NATs for the service in each container:

```
user@docker1:~$ sudo iptables -t nat -A POSTROUTING -s \
```

```
172.17.0.0/16 ! -o docker0 -j MASQUERADE
user@docker1:~$ sudo iptables -t nat -A PREROUTING ! -i docker0 \
-p tcp -m tcp --dport 32768 -j DNAT --to-destination 172.17.0.2:80
user@docker1:~$ sudo iptables -t nat -A PREROUTING ! -i docker0 \
-p tcp -m tcp --dport 32769 -j DNAT --to-destination 172.17.0.3:80
```

One of the items you might be interested in configuring is limiting the scope of what the containers can access on the outside network. You'll notice that, in previous examples, the containers were allowed to talk to anything externally. This was allowed since the filter rule was rather generic:

```
sudo iptables -A FORWARD -i docker0 ! -o docker0 -j ACCEPT
```

This rule allows the containers to talk to anything out of any interface besides docker0. Rather than allowing this, we can specify only the ports we want to allow outbound. So for instance, if we publish port 80, we can then define a reverse or outbound rule, which only allows that specific return traffic. Let's first recreate the inbound rules we used in the previous example:

```
user@docker1:~$ sudo iptables -A FORWARD -d 172.17.0.2/32 \
! -i docker0 -o docker0 -p tcp -m tcp --dport 80 -j ACCEPT
user@docker1:~$ sudo iptables -A FORWARD -d 172.17.0.3/32 \
! -i docker0 -o docker0 -p tcp -m tcp --dport 80 -j ACCEPT
```

Now we can easily replace the more generic outbound rule with specific rules that only allow the return traffic on port 80. For example, let's put in a rule that allows the container web1 to return traffic only on port 80:

```
user@docker1:~$ sudo iptables -A FORWARD -s 172.17.0.2/32 -i \
docker0 ! -o docker0 -p tcp -m tcp --sport 80 -j ACCEPT
```

If we check, we should see that from the outside network we can get to the service on web1:

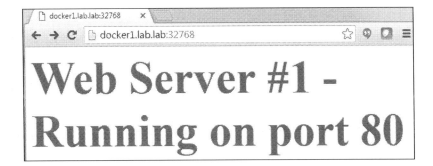

However, the container `web1` is not able to talk to anything on the outside network except on port `80` at this point because we didn't use the generic outbound rule:

```
user@docker1:~$ docker exec -it web1 ping 4.2.2.2 -c 2
PING 4.2.2.2 (4.2.2.2): 48 data bytes
user@docker1:~$
```

To fix this, we can add specific rules to allow things like ICMP sourced from the `web1` container:

```
user@docker1:~$ sudo iptables -A FORWARD -s 172.17.0.2/32 -i \
docker0 ! -o docker0 -p icmp -j ACCEPT
```

The above rule coupled with the state-aware return rule from the previous recipe will allow the web1 container to initiate and receive return ICMP traffic.

```
user@docker1:~$ sudo iptables -A FORWARD -o docker0 -m conntrack \
--ctstate RELATED,ESTABLISHED -j ACCEPT
user@docker1:~$ docker exec -it web1 ping 4.2.2.2 -c 2
PING 4.2.2.2 (4.2.2.2): 48 data bytes
56 bytes from 4.2.2.2: icmp_seq=0 ttl=50 time=33.892 ms
56 bytes from 4.2.2.2: icmp_seq=1 ttl=50 time=34.326 ms
--- 4.2.2.2 ping statistics ---
2 packets transmitted, 2 packets received, 0% packet loss
round-trip min/avg/max/stddev = 33.892/34.109/34.326/0.217 ms
user@docker1:~$
```

In the case of the `web2` container, its web server can still not be accessed from the outside network. If we wish to limit the source of traffic which can talk to the web server we could do that by altering the inbound port `80` rule, or by specifying a destination in the outbound port `80` rule. We could for instance limit the source of the traffic to a single device on the outside network by specifying a destination in the egress rule:

```
user@docker1:~$ sudo iptables -A FORWARD -s 172.17.0.3/32 -d \
10.20.30.13 -i docker0 ! -o docker0 -p tcp -m tcp --sport 80 \
-j ACCEPT
```

Now if we try from a lab device on the outside network with the IP address of `10.20.30.13`, we should be able to access the web server:

```
[user@lab1 ~]# ip addr show dev eth0 | grep inet
```

```
    inet 10.20.30.13/24 brd 10.20.30.255 scope global eth0
 [user@lab2 ~]# curl http://docker1.lab.lab:32769
<body>
  <html>
    <h1><span style="color:#FF0000;font-size:72px;">Web Server #2 -
Running on port 80</span>
    </h1>
</body>
  </html>
[user@lab1 ~]#
```

But if we try from a different lab server with a different IP address, the connection will fail:

```
[user@lab2 ~]# ip addr show dev eth0 | grep inet
    inet 10.20.30.14/24 brd 10.20.30.255 scope global eth0
[user@lab2 ~]# curl http://docker1.lab.lab:32769
[user@lab2 ~]#
```

Again, this rule could be implemented either as an inbound or outbound rule.

When managing the `iptables` rules in this manner, you might have noticed that the Docker host itself no longer has connectivity to the containers and the services they are hosting:

```
user@docker1:~$ ping 172.17.0.2 -c 2
PING 172.17.0.2 (172.17.0.2) 56(84) bytes of data.
ping: sendmsg: Operation not permitted
ping: sendmsg: Operation not permitted
--- 172.17.0.2 ping statistics ---
2 packets transmitted, 0 received, 100% packet loss, time 999ms
user@docker1:~$
```

This is because all of the rules we've been writing in the filter table have been in the forward chain. The forward chain only applies to traffic the host is forwarding, not traffic that is originated or destined to the host itself. To fix this, we can put rules in the `INPUT` and `OUTPUT` chains of the filter table. To allow ICMP to and from the containers, we can specify rules like this:

```
user@docker1:~$ sudo iptables -A OUTPUT -o docker0 -p icmp -m \
state --state NEW,ESTABLISHED -j ACCEPT
```

```
user@docker1:~$ sudo iptables -A INPUT -i docker0 -p icmp -m \
state --state ESTABLISHED -j ACCEPT
```

The rule being added to the output chain looks for traffic headed out of the `docker0` bridge (toward the containers), that is of protocol ICMP, and is a new or established flow. The rule being added to the input chain looks for traffic headed into the `docker0` bridge (toward the host), that is of protocol ICMP, and is an established flow. Since the traffic is being originated from the Docker host, these rules will match and allow the ICMP traffic to the container to work:

```
user@docker1:~$ ping 172.17.0.2 -c 2
PING 172.17.0.2 (172.17.0.2) 56(84) bytes of data.
64 bytes from 172.17.0.2: icmp_seq=1 ttl=64 time=0.081 ms
64 bytes from 172.17.0.2: icmp_seq=2 ttl=64 time=0.021 ms
--- 172.17.0.2 ping statistics ---
2 packets transmitted, 2 received, 0% packet loss, time 999ms
rtt min/avg/max/mdev = 0.021/0.051/0.081/0.030 ms
user@docker1:~$
```

However, this still will not allow the containers themselves to ping the default gateway. This is because the rule we added to the input chain matching traffic coming into the `docker0` bridge is only looking for established sessions. To have this work bidirectionally, you'd need to add the NEW flag to the second rule so that it would also match new flows generated by the containers toward the host:

```
user@docker1:~$ sudo iptables -A INPUT -i docker0 -p icmp -m \
state --state NEW,ESTABLISHED -j ACCEPT
```

Since the rule we added to the output chain already specifies new or established flows, ICMP connectivity from the containers to the host will now also work:

```
user@docker1:~$ docker exec -it web1 ping
PING 172.17.0.1 (172.17.0.1): 48 data bytes
56 bytes from 172.17.0.1: icmp_seq=0 ttl=64 time=0.073 ms
56 bytes from 172.17.0.1: icmp_seq=1 ttl=64 time=0.079 ms
^C--- 172.17.0.1 ping statistics ---
2 packets transmitted, 2 packets received, 0% packet loss
round-trip min/avg/max/stddev = 0.073/0.076/0.079/0.000 ms
user@docker1:~$
```

Exposing services through a load balancer

Another way to isolate your containers is to frontend them with a load balancer. This mode of operation offers several advantages. First, the load balancer can provide intelligent load balancing to multiple backend nodes. If a container dies, the load balancer can remove it from the load balancing pool. Second, you're effectively hiding your containers behind a load balancing **Virtual IP (VIP)** address. Clients believe that they are interacting directly with the application running in the container while they are actually interacting with the load balancer. In many cases, a load balancer can provide or offload security features, such as SSL and web application firewall that make scaling a container-based application easier to accomplish in a secure fashion. In this recipe, we'll learn how this can be done and some of the features available in Docker that make this easier to do.

Getting ready

We'll be using multiple Docker hosts in the following examples. We'll also be using a user-defined overlay network. It will be assumed that you know how to configure the Docker hosts for overlay networking. If you do not, please see the *Creating a user-defined overlay network* recipe in *Chapter 3, User-Defined Networks*.

How to do it...

Load balancing is not a new concept and is one that is well-understood in the physical and virtual machine space. However, load balancing with containers adds in an extra layer of complexity, which can make things drastically more complicated. To start with, let's look how load balancing typically works without containers:

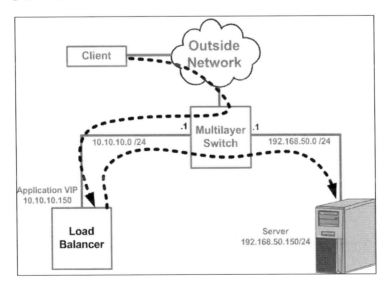

In this case, we have a simple load balancer configuration where the load balancer is providing VIP for a single backend pool member (192.168.50.150). The flow works like this:

- ▶ The client generates a request toward the VIP (10.10.10.150) hosted on the load balancer
- ▶ The load balancer receives the request, ensures that it has VIP for that IP, and then generates a request to the backend pool member(s) for that VIP on behalf of the client
- ▶ The server receives the request sourced from the load balancer and responds directly back to the load balancer
- ▶ The load balancer then responds back to the client

In most cases, the conversation involves two distinct sessions, one between the client and the load balancer and another between the load balancer and the server. Each of these is a distinct TCP session.

Now, let's show an example of how this might work in the container space. Examine the topology shown in the following figure:

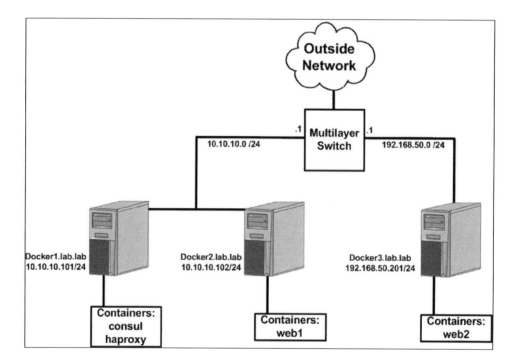

In this example, we'll be using both container-based application servers as backend pool members as well as a container-based load balancer. Let's make the following assumptions:

▸ The hosts `docker2` and `docker3` will provide hosting for many different web presentation containers that support many different VIPs

▸ We will use one load balancer container (`haproxy` instance) for each VIP we wish to define

▸ Each presentation server exposes port `80`

Given this, we can assume that host network mode is out of the question for both the load balancer host (`docker1`) as well as the hosting hosts (`docker2` and `docker3`) since it would require containers exposing services on a large number of ports. Before the introduction of user-defined networks, this would leave us with having to deal with port mapping on the `docker0` bridge.

That would quickly become a problem both to manage as well as troubleshoot. For instance, the topology might really look like this:

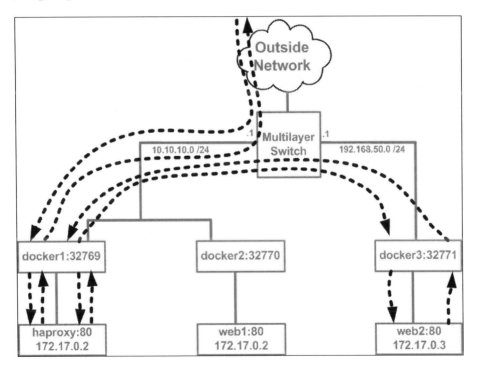

In this case, the load balancer VIP would be a published port on the host `docker1`, that is, `32769`. The web servers themselves are also publishing ports to expose their web servers. Let's walk through what a load balancing request might look like:

- A client from the outside network generates a request to `http://docker1.lab.lab:32769`.

- The `docker1` host receives the request and translates the packet through the published port on the `haproxy` container. This changes the destination IP and port to `172.17.0.2:80`.

- The `haproxy` container receives the request and determines that the VIP being accessed has a backend pool containing `docker2:23770` and `docker3:32771`. It selects the `docker3` host for this session and sends a request towards `docker3:32771`.

- As the request traverses the host `docker1`, it performs an outbound MASQUERADE and hides the container behind the host's IP interface.

- The request is sent to the host's default gateway (the MLS), which, in turn, forwards the request down to the host `docker3`.

- The `docker3` host receives the request and translates the packet through the published port on the `web2` container. This changes the destination IP and port to `172.17.0.3:80`.

- The `web2` container receives the request and responds back toward `docker1`

- The `docker3` host receives the reply and translates the packet back through the inbound published port.

- The request is received at `docker1` translated back through the outbound MASQUERADE, and is delivered at the `haproxy` container.

- The `haproxy` container then responds back to the client. The `docker1` host translates the `haproxy` container's response back to its own IP address on port `32769` and the response makes its way back to the client.

While doable, it's a lot to keep track of. In addition, the load balancer node needs to be aware of the published port and IP address of each backend container. If a container gets restarted, the published port can change effectively making it unreachable. Troubleshooting this with a large backend pool would be a headache as well.

So while this is certainly doable, the introduction of user-defined networks can make this much more manageable. For instance, we could leverage an overlay type network for the backend pool members and completely remove the need for much of the port publishing and outbound masquerading. That topology would look more like this:

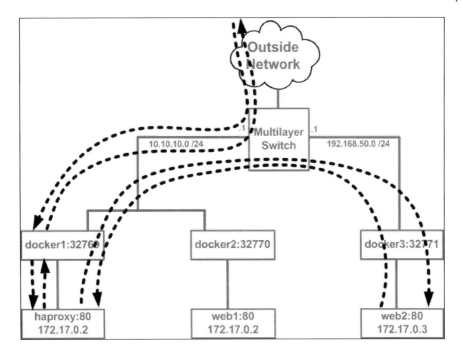

Let's see what it would take to build this kind of configuration. The first thing we need to do is to define a user-defined overlay type network on one of the nodes. We'll define it on `docker1` and call it `presentation_backend`:

```
user@docker1:~$ docker network create -d overlay \
--internal presentation_backend
bd9e9b5b5e064aee2ddaa58507fa6c15f49e4b0a28ea58ffb3da4cc63e6f8908
user@docker1:~$
```

> Note that how I passed the `--internal` flag when I created this network. You'll recall from *Chapter 3, User-Defined Networks*, that this means that only containers connected to this network will be able to access it.

The next thing we want to do is to create the two web containers which will serve as the backend pool members for the load balancer. We'll do that on hosts `docker2` and `docker3`:

```
user@docker2:~$ docker run -dP --name=web1 --net \
presentation_backend jonlangemak/web_server_1
6cc8862f5288b14e84a0dd9ff5424a3988de52da5ef6a07ae593c9621baf2202
user@docker2:~$
```

```
user@docker3:~$ docker run -dP --name=web2 --net \
presentation_backend jonlangemak/web_server_2
e2504f08f234220dd6b14424d51bfc0cd4d065f75fcbaf46c7b6dece96676d46
user@docker3:~$
```

The remaining component left to deploy is the load balancer. As mentioned, `haproxy` has a container image of their load balancer, so we'll use that for this example. Before we run the container we need to come up with a configuration that we can pass into the container for `haproxy` to use. This is done through mounting a volume into the container as we'll see shortly. The configuration file is named `haproxy.cfg` and my example configuration looks like this:

```
global
    log 127.0.0.1    local0
defaults
    log       global
    mode      http
    option    httplog
    timeout connect 5000
    timeout client 50000
    timeout server 50000
    stats enable
    stats auth user:docker
    stats uri /lbstats
frontend all
    bind *:80
    use_backend pres_containers


backend pres_containers
    balance roundrobin
    server web1 web1:80 check
    server web2 web2:80 check
    option httpchk HEAD /index.html HTTP/1.0
```

A couple of items are worth pointing out in the preceding configuration:

- ▸ We bind the `haproxy` service to all interfaces on port `80`
- ▸ Any request hitting the container on port `80` will get load balanced to a pool named `pres_containers`

- The `pres_containers` pool load balances in a round-robin method between two servers:

    ❏ web1 on port `80`

    ❏ web2 on port `80`

One of the interesting items here is that we can define the pool members by name. This is a huge advantage that comes along with user-defined networks and means that we don't need to worry about tracking container IP addressing.

I put this config file in a folder in my home directory named `haproxy`:

```
user@docker1:~/haproxy$ pwd
/home/user/haproxy
user@docker1:~/haproxy$ ls
haproxy.cfg
user@docker1:~/haproxy$
```

Once the configuration file is in pace, we can run the container as follows:

```
user@docker1:~$ docker run -d --name haproxy --net \
presentation_backend -p 80:80 -v \
~/haproxy:/usr/local/etc/haproxy/ haproxy
d34667aa1118c70cd333810d9c8adf0986d58dab9d71630d68e6e15816741d2b
user@docker1:~$
```

You might be wondering why I'm specifying a port mapping when connecting the container to an `internal` type network. Recall from earlier chapters that port mappings are global across all network types. In other words, even though I'm not using it currently, it's still a characteristic of the container. So if I ever connect a network type to the container that can use the port mapping, it will. In this case, I first need to connect the container to the overlay network to ensure that it has reachability to the backend web servers. If the `haproxy` container is unable to resolve the pool member names when it starts, it will fail to load.

At this point, the `haproxy` container has reachability to its pool members, but we have no way to access the `haproxy` container externally. To do that, we'll connect another interface to the container that can use the port mapping. In this case, that will be the `docker0` bridge:

```
user@docker1:~$ docker network connect bridge haproxy
user@docker1:~
```

At this point, the `haproxy` container should be available externally at the following URLs:

- Load balanced VIP: `http://docker1.lab.lab`
- HAProxy stats: `http://docker1.lab.lab/lbstats`

If we check the stats page, we should see that the `haproxy` container can reach each backend web server across the overlay. We can see that the health check for each is coming back with a `200 OK` status:

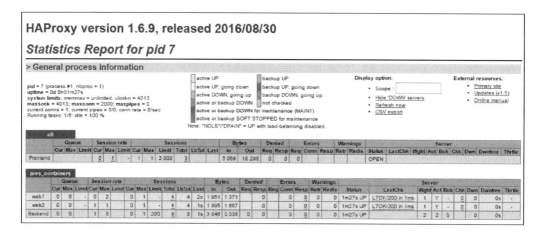

Now if we check VIP itself and hit refresh a couple of times, we should see the web page presented from each container:

This type of topology provides us several notable advantages over the first concept we had around container load balancing. The use of the overlay-based network not only provided name-based resolution of containers but also significantly reduced the complexity of the traffic path. Granted, the traffic took the same physical path in either case, but we didn't need to rely on so many different NATs for the traffic to work. It also made the entire solution far more dynamic. This type of design can be easily replicated to provide load balancing for many different backend overlay networks.

7
Working with Weave Net

In this chapter, we will cover the following recipes:

- Installing and configuring Weave
- Running Weave-connected containers
- Understanding Weave IPAM
- Working with WeaveDNS
- Weave security
- Using the Weave network plugin

Introduction

Weave Net (Weave for short) is a third-party network solution for Docker. Early on, it provided users additional network functionality outside of what Docker natively offered. For instance, Weave provided overlay networks and **WeaveDNS** before Docker began supporting user-defined overlay networks and embedded DNS. However, with the more recent releases, Docker has started to gain feature parity from a network perspective with Weave. That being said, Weave still has a lot to offer and is an interesting example of how a third-party tool can interact with Docker to provide container networking. In this chapter, we'll walk through the basics of installing and configuring Weave to work with Docker as well as describe some of Weaves functionality from a network perspective. While we'll spend some time demonstrating some of the features of Weave this is not intended to be a how-to guide for the entire Weave solution. There are many features of Weave that will not be covered in this chapter. I recommend you check out their website for the most up-to-date information on features and functionality (`https://www.weave.works/`).

Installing and configuring Weave

In this recipe, we'll walk through the installation of Weave as well as how to provision Weave services on your Docker hosts. We'll also show how Weave handles connecting hosts that wish to participate in the Weave network.

Getting ready

In this example, we'll be using the same lab topology we used in *Chapter 3, User-Defined Networks*, where we discussed user-defined overlay networks:

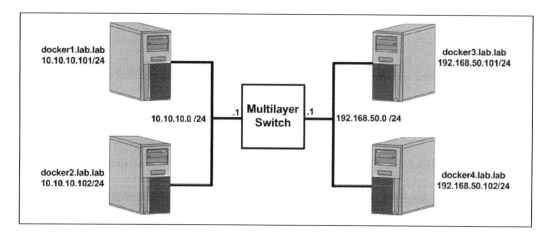

You'll need a couple of hosts, preferably with some of them being on different subnets. It is assumed that the Docker hosts used in this lab are in their default configuration. In some cases, the changes we make may require you to have root-level access to the system.

How to do it...

Weave is installed and managed through the Weave CLI tool. Once downloaded, it manages not only Weave-related configuration but also the provisioning of Weave services. On each host you wish to configure, you simply run the following three commands:

- Download the Weave binary to your local system:

```
user@docker1:~$ sudo curl -L git.io/weave -o \
/usr/local/bin/weave
```

- Make the file executable:

```
user@docker1:~$ sudo chmod +x /usr/local/bin/weave
```

- Run Weave:

```
user@docker1:~$ weave launch
```

If all of these commands complete successfully, your Docker host is now ready to use Weave for Docker networking. To verify, you can check the Weave status using the `weave status` command:

```
user@docker1:~$ weave status
        Version: 1.7.1 (up to date; next check at 2016/10/11 01:26:42)

        Service: router
       Protocol: weave 1..2
           Name: 12:d2:fe:7a:c1:f2(docker1)
     Encryption: disabled
  PeerDiscovery: enabled
        Targets: 0
    Connections: 0
          Peers: 1
 TrustedSubnets: none

        Service: ipam
         Status: idle
          Range: 10.32.0.0/12
  DefaultSubnet: 10.32.0.0/12

        Service: dns
         Domain: weave.local.
       Upstream: 10.20.30.13
            TTL: 1
        Entries: 0

        Service: proxy
        Address: unix:///var/run/weave/weave.sock

        Service: plugin
     DriverName: weave
user@docker1:~$
```

This output provides you with information regarding all five of Weave's network-related services. Those are `router`, `ipam`, `dns`, `proxy`, and `plugin`. At this point, you might be wondering where all these services are running. Keeping with the Docker theme, they're all running inside containers on the host:

```
user@docker1:~$ docker ps
CONTAINER ID   IMAGE                        COMMAND                CREATED        STATUS       PORTS   NAMES
f1e01dffdf19   weaveworks/plugin:1.7.1      "/home/weave/plugin"   2 minutes ago  Up 2 minutes         weaveplugin
299b487060e3   weaveworks/weaveexec:1.7.1   "/home/weave/weavepro" 2 minutes ago  Up 2 minutes         weaveproxy
a51314370dd8   weaveworks/weave:1.7.1       "/home/weave/weaver ." 2 minutes ago  Up 2 minutes         weave
user@docker1:~$
```

As you can see, there are three Weave-related containers running on the host. Running the `weave launch` command spawned all three containers. Each container provides unique services that Weave uses to network containers. The `weaveproxy` container serves as a shim layer allowing Weave to be leveraged directly from the Docker CLI. The `weaveplugin` container implements a custom network driver for Docker. The "`weave`" container is commonly called the Weave router and provides all the other services that are related to Weave networking.

Each of these containers can be configured and run independently. Running Weave with the `weave launch` command assumes that you'd like to use all three containers and deploys them with a sane set of defaults. However, if you ever wish to change the settings related to a specific container, you'd need to launch the containers independently. This can be done in this manner:

```
weave launch-router
```

```
weave launch-proxy
```

```
weave launch-plugin
```

If at any time you wish to clean up the Weave configuration on a particular host, you can issue the `weave reset` command, which will clean up all the Weave-related service containers. To start our example, we'll only be using the Weave router container. Let's clear out the Weave configuration and then start just that container on our host `docker1`:

```
user@docker1:~$ weave reset
```

```
user@docker1:~$ weave launch-router
```

```
e5af31a8416cef117832af1ec22424293824ad8733bb7a61d0c210fb38c4ba1e
```

```
user@docker1:~$
```

The Weave router (weave container) is the only container we need to provide the majority of the network functionality. Let's take a look at the configuration options that are passed to the Weave router by default by inspecting the weave container configuration:

```
user@docker1:~$ docker inspect weave
...<Additional output removed for brevity>...
        "Args": [
            "--port",
```

```
        "6783",
        "--name",
        "12:d2:fe:7a:c1:f2",
        "--nickname",
        "docker1",
        "--datapath",
        "datapath",
        "--ipalloc-range",
        "10.32.0.0/12",
        "--dns-effective-listen-address",
        "172.17.0.1",
        "--dns-listen-address",
        "172.17.0.1:53",
        "--http-addr",
        "127.0.0.1:6784",
        "--resolv-conf",
        "/var/run/weave/etc/resolv.conf"
...<Additional output removed for brevity>...
user@docker1:~$
```

There are some items worth pointing out in the preceding output. The IP allocation range is given as `10.32.0.0/12`. This is significantly different than the `172.17.0.0/16` we're used to dealing with by default on the `docker0` bridge. Also, there's an IP address defined to be used as the DNS listen address. Recall that Weave also provides WeaveDNS, which can be used to resolve the names of other containers on the Weave network by name. Notice that this IP address is that of the `docker0` bridge interface on the host.

Let's now configure another one of our hosts as part of the Weave network:

```
user@docker2:~$ sudo curl -L git.io/weave -o /usr/local/bin/weave
user@docker2:~$ sudo chmod +x /usr/local/bin/weave
user@docker2:~$ weave launch-router 10.10.10.101
48e5035629b5124c8d3bedf09fca946b333bb54aff56704ceecef009b53dd449
user@docker2:~$
```

Note that we installed Weave in the same manner as before, but when we launched the router container, we did so by specifying the IP address of the first Docker host. In Weave, this is how we peer multiple hosts together. Any host you wish to connect to the Weave network just needs to specify the IP address of any existing node on the Weave network. If we check the status of Weave on this newly attached node, we should see that it shows as connected:

```
user@docker2:~$ weave status
        Version: 1.7.1 (up to date; next check at 2016/10/11 03:36:22)
```

```
       Service: router
      Protocol: weave 1..2
          Name: e6:b1:90:cd:76:da(docker2)
    Encryption: disabled
 PeerDiscovery: enabled
       Targets: 1
   Connections: 1 (1 established)
         Peers: 2 (with 2 established connections)
TrustedSubnets: none
...<Additional output removed for brevity>...
user@docker2:~$
```

We can proceed to connect the other two remaining nodes in the same way after Weave is installed:

```
user@docker3:~$ weave launch-router 10.10.10.102
user@docker4:~$ weave launch-router 192.168.50.101
```

In each case, we specify the previously joined Weave node as the peer of the node we are attempting to join. In our case, our join pattern looks like what's shown in the following image:

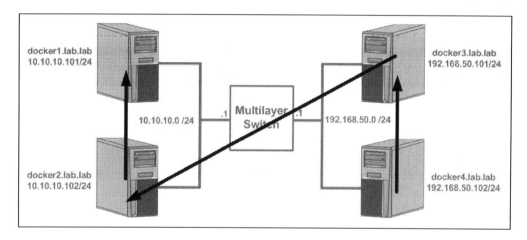

However, we could have had each node join any other existing node and achieved the same result. That is, joining nodes docker2, docker3, and docker4 to docker1 would have yielded the same end state. This is because Weave only needs to talk to an existing node to get information about the current state of the Weave network. Since all of the existing members have that information, it doesn't matter which one they talk to in order to join a new node to the Weave network. If we check the status of any of the Weave nodes now, we should see that we have a total of four peers:

```
user@docker4:~$ weave status
```

```
      Version: 1.7.1 (up to date; next check at 2016/10/11 03:25:22)


      Service: router
     Protocol: weave 1..2
         Name: 42:ec:92:86:1a:31(docker4)
   Encryption: disabled
PeerDiscovery: enabled
      Targets: 1
  Connections: 3 (3 established)
        Peers: 4 (with 12 established connections)
TrustedSubnets: none
...<Additional output removed for brevity>...
user@docker4:~$
```

We can see that this node has three connections, one to each of the other joined nodes. This gives us a total of four peers with twelve connections, three per Weave node. So despite only configuring peering between three nodes, we end up with a full mesh for container connectivity between all the hosts:

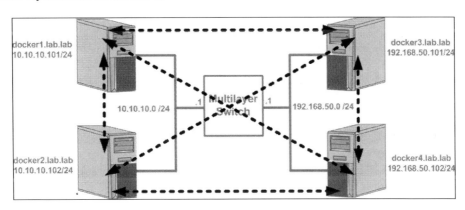

Now the configuration of Weave is complete, and we have a full mesh network between all of our Weave-enabled Docker hosts. You can verify the connections that each host has with the other peers using the `weave status connections` command:

```
user@docker1:~$ weave status connections
-> 192.168.50.102:6783    established fastdp 42:ec:92:86:1a:31(docker4)
<- 10.10.10.102:45632     established fastdp e6:b1:90:cd:76:da(docker2)
<- 192.168.50.101:38411   established fastdp ae:af:a6:36:18:37(docker3)
user@docker1:~$
```

You'll note that this configuration did not require the configuration of a standalone key-value store.

It should also be noted that Weave peers can be managed manually using the Weave CLI `connect` and `forget` commands. If you fail to specify an existing member of the Weave network when you instantiate Weave, you can use Weave connect to manually connect to an existing member. Also, if you remove a member from the Weave network and don't expect it to return, you can tell the network to entirely forget the peer with the `forget` command.

Running Weave-connected containers

Weave is an interesting example showcasing the different ways in which a third-party solution can interact with Docker. It offers several different approaches to interacting with Docker. The first is the Weave CLI from which you can not only configure Weave, but also spawn containers much like you would through the Docker CLI. The second is the network plugin, which ties directly into Docker and allows you to provision containers from Docker onto the Weave network. In this recipe, we'll walk through how to connect containers to the Weave network using the Weave CLI. The Weave network plugin will be covered in its own recipe later in this chapter.

> Weave also offers an API proxy service that allows Weave to insert itself as a shim in between Docker and the Docker CLI transparently. That configuration will not be covered in this chapter, but they have extensive documentation about that functionality at this link:
>
> `https://www.weave.works/docs/net/latest/weave-docker-api/`

Getting ready

It is assumed that you're building off of the lab we created in the first recipe of this chapter. It is also assumed that the hosts have Docker and Weave installed. The Weave peering we defined in the previous chapter is also assumed to be in place.

How to do it...

When using the Weave CLI to manage container connectivity, there are two approaches you can take to connect a container to the Weave network.

The first is to use the `weave` command to run a container. Weave accomplishes this by passing anything you specify after `weave run` to `docker run`. The advantage to this approach is that Weave is made aware of the connection since it's the one actually telling Docker to run the container.

This puts Weave in a perfect position to ensure that the container is started with the proper configuration for it to work on the Weave network. For instance, we can start a container named web1 on the host docker1 using this syntax:

```
user@docker1:~$ weave run -dP --name=web1 jonlangemak/web_server_1
```

Note that the syntax for the run command is identical to that of Docker.

 Despite the similarities, there are a couple of differences worth noting. Weave can only start containers in the background or -d mode. Also, you can not specify the --rm flag to remove the container after it finishes execution.

Once the container is started in this manner, let's look at the container's interface configuration:

```
user@docker1:~$ docker exec web1 ip addr
...<Loopback interface removed for brevity>...
20: eth0@if21: <BROADCAST,MULTICAST,UP,LOWER_UP> mtu 1500 qdisc noqueue
state UP
    link/ether 02:42:ac:11:00:02 brd ff:ff:ff:ff:ff:ff
    inet 172.17.0.2/16 scope global eth0
        valid_lft forever preferred_lft forever
    inet6 fe80::42:acff:fe11:2/64 scope link
        valid_lft forever preferred_lft forever
22: ethwe@if23: <BROADCAST,MULTICAST,UP,LOWER_UP> mtu 1410 qdisc noqueue
state UP
    link/ether a6:f2:d0:36:6f:bd brd ff:ff:ff:ff:ff:ff
    inet 10.32.0.1/12 scope global ethwe
        valid_lft forever preferred_lft forever
    inet6 fe80::a4f2:d0ff:fe36:6fbd/64 scope link
        valid_lft forever preferred_lft forever
user@docker1:~$
```

Note that the container now has an additional interface named ethwe, which has an IP address of 10.32.0.1/12. This is the Weave network interface and is added in addition to the Docker network interface (eth0). If we check, we'll note that since we passed the -P flag, Docker has published the containers-exposed port to several the eth0 interface:

```
user@docker1:~$ docker port web1
80/tcp -> 0.0.0.0:32785
user@docker1:~$ sudo iptables -t nat -S
```

```
...<Additional output removed for brevity>...
-A DOCKER ! -i docker0 -p tcp -m tcp --dport 32768 -j DNAT --to-
destination 172.17.0.2:80
user@docker1:~$
```

This proves that all of the port publishing functionality we saw earlier is still done through Docker networking constructs. The Weave interface is just added in addition to the existing Docker native network interfaces.

The second approach to connecting a container to the Weave network can be accomplished in two different ways but yields essentially the same result. Existing Docker containers can be added to the Weave network by either starting a currently stopped container using the Weave CLI, or by attaching a running container to Weave. Let's look at each approach. First, let's start a container on the host `docker2` in the same way we normally do using the Docker CLI and then restart it using Weave:

```
user@docker2:~$ docker run -dP --name=web2 jonlangemak/web_server_2
5795d42b58802516fba16eed9445950123224326d5ba19202f23378a6d84eb1f
user@docker2:~$ docker stop web2
web2
user@docker2:~$ weave start web2
web2
user@docker2:~$ docker exec web2 ip addr
...<Loopback interface removed for brevity>...
15: eth0@if16: <BROADCAST,MULTICAST,UP,LOWER_UP> mtu 1500 qdisc noqueue
state UP
    link/ether 02:42:ac:11:00:02 brd ff:ff:ff:ff:ff:ff
    inet 172.17.0.2/16 scope global eth0
       valid_lft forever preferred_lft forever
    inet6 fe80::42:acff:fe11:2/64 scope link
       valid_lft forever preferred_lft forever
17: ethwe@if18: <BROADCAST,MULTICAST,UP,LOWER_UP> mtu 1410 qdisc noqueue
state UP
    link/ether e2:22:e0:f8:0b:96 brd ff:ff:ff:ff:ff:ff
    inet 10.44.0.0/12 scope global ethwe
       valid_lft forever preferred_lft forever
    inet6 fe80::e022:e0ff:fef8:b96/64 scope link
       valid_lft forever preferred_lft forever
user@docker2:~$
```

So as you can see, Weave has taken care of adding the Weave interface to the container when it was restarted using the Weave CLI. Similarly, we can start a second instance of our web1 container on the host docker3 and then dynamically connect it to the Weave network with the weave attach command:

```
user@docker3:~$ docker run -dP --name=web1 jonlangemak/web_server_1
dabdf098964edc3407c5084e56527f214c69ff0b6d4f451013c09452e450311d
user@docker3:~$ docker exec web1 ip addr
...<Loopback interface removed for brevity>...
5: eth0@if6: <BROADCAST,MULTICAST,UP,LOWER_UP> mtu 1500 qdisc noqueue
state UP
    link/ether 02:42:ac:11:00:02 brd ff:ff:ff:ff:ff:ff
    inet 172.17.0.2/16 scope global eth0
       valid_lft forever preferred_lft forever
    inet6 fe80::42:acff:fe11:2/64 scope link
       valid_lft forever preferred_lft forever
user@docker3:~$
user@docker3:~$ weave attach web1
10.36.0.0
user@docker3:~$ docker exec web1 ip addr
...<Loopback interface removed for brevity>...
5: eth0@if6: <BROADCAST,MULTICAST,UP,LOWER_UP> mtu 1500 qdisc noqueue
state UP
    link/ether 02:42:ac:11:00:02 brd ff:ff:ff:ff:ff:ff
    inet 172.17.0.2/16 scope global eth0
       valid_lft forever preferred_lft forever
    inet6 fe80::42:acff:fe11:2/64 scope link
       valid_lft forever preferred_lft forever
15: ethwe@if16: <BROADCAST,MULTICAST,UP,LOWER_UP> mtu 1410 qdisc noqueue
state UP
    link/ether de:d6:1c:03:63:ba brd ff:ff:ff:ff:ff:ff
    inet 10.36.0.0/12 scope global ethwe
       valid_lft forever preferred_lft forever
    inet6 fe80::dcd6:1cff:fe03:63ba/64 scope link
       valid_lft forever preferred_lft forever
user@docker3:~$
```

As we can see in the preceding output, the container did not have an ethwe interface until we manually attached it to the Weave network. The attachment was done dynamically without the need to restart the container. In addition to adding containers to the Weave network, you may also dynamically remove them from Weave using the weave detach command.

At this point, you should have connectivity between all of the containers that are now connected to the Weave network. In my case, they were allocated the following IP addresses:

- web1 on host docker1: 10.32.0.1
- web2 on host docker2: 10.44.0.0
- web1 on host docker3: 10.36.0.0

```
user@docker1:~$ docker exec -it web1 ping 10.44.0.0 -c 2
PING 10.40.0.0 (10.40.0.0): 48 data bytes
56 bytes from 10.40.0.0: icmp_seq=0 ttl=64 time=0.447 ms
56 bytes from 10.40.0.0: icmp_seq=1 ttl=64 time=0.681 ms
--- 10.40.0.0 ping statistics ---
2 packets transmitted, 2 packets received, 0% packet loss
round-trip min/avg/max/stddev = 0.447/0.564/0.681/0.117 ms
user@docker1:~$ docker exec -it web1 ping 10.36.0.0 -c 2
PING 10.44.0.0 (10.44.0.0): 48 data bytes
56 bytes from 10.44.0.0: icmp_seq=0 ttl=64 time=1.676 ms
56 bytes from 10.44.0.0: icmp_seq=1 ttl=64 time=0.839 ms
--- 10.44.0.0 ping statistics ---
2 packets transmitted, 2 packets received, 0% packet loss
round-trip min/avg/max/stddev = 0.839/1.257/1.676/0.419 ms
user@docker1:~$
```

This proves that the Weave network is working as expected and the containers are on the correct network segment.

Understanding Weave IPAM

As we saw multiple times in earlier chapters, IPAM is a critical component of any container networking solution. The criticality of IPAM becomes even clearer when you start using common networks across multiple Docker hosts. As the number of IP allocations begins to scale being able to resolve these containers by names also becomes vital. Much like Docker, Weave has its own integrated IPAM for their container network solution. In this chapter, we'll show how to configure and leverage Weave IPAM to manage IP allocations across the Weave network.

Getting ready

It is assumed that you're building off of the lab we created in the first recipe of this chapter. It is also assumed that the hosts have Docker and Weave installed. Docker should be in its default configuration, and Weave should be installed but not yet peered. If you need to remove the peering defined in previous examples, issue the `weave reset` command on each host.

How to do it...

Weave's solution to IPAM relies on the Weave network as a whole using one large subnet, which is then carved into smaller pieces and allocated directly to each host. The host then allocates container IP addresses out of the IP address pool it was allocated. In order for this to work, the Weave cluster has to agree on what IP allocations to assign to each host. It does this by first reaching a consensus within the cluster. If you have a general idea of how large your cluster will be, you can provide specifics to Weave during initialization that help it make a better decision.

The goal of this recipe is not to get into specifics on optimizing the consensus algorithm that Weave uses with IPAM. For specifics on that, see the following link:
https://www.weave.works/docs/net/latest/ipam/

For the sake of this recipe, we'll assume that you don't know how big your cluster will be and we'll work off the premise that it will start with two hosts and expand from there.

It's important to understand that the IPAM in Weave sits idle until you provision your first container. For instance, let's start by configuring Weave on the host `docker1`:

```
user@docker1:~$ weave launch-router --ipalloc-range 172.16.16.0/24
469c81f786ac38618003e4bd08eb7303c1f8fa84d38cc134fdb352c589cbc42d
user@docker1:~$
```

The first thing you should notice is the addition of the parameter `--ipalloc-range`. As we mentioned earlier, Weave works off the concept of one large subnet. By default, this subnet is `10.32.0.0/12`. This default setting can be overridden during Weave initialization by passing the `--ipalloc-range` flag to Weave. To make these examples a little easier to understand, I decided to change the default subnet to something more manageable; in this case, `172.16.16.0/24`.

Let's also run the same command on the host `docker2` but pass it the IP address of the host `docker1`, so it can immediately peer:

```
user@docker2:~$ weave launch-router --ipalloc-range \
172.16.16.0/24 10.10.10.101
```

```
9bfb1cb0295ba87fe88b7373a8ff502b1f90149741b2f43487d66898ffad775d
user@docker2:~$
```

Note that I once again passed the same subnet to Weave. It is critical that the IP allocation range on each host running Weave is identical. Only hosts that agree on the same IP allocation range will be able to function properly. Let's now check the status of the Weave services:

```
user@docker2:~$ weave status
…<Additional output removed for brevity>…
Connections: 1 (1 established)
        Peers: 2 (with 2 established connections)
  TrustedSubnets: none


        Service: ipam
         Status: idle
          Range: 172.16.16.0/24
  DefaultSubnet: 172.16.16.0/24
…<Additional output removed for brevity>…
user@docker2:~$
```

The output shows two peers indicating that our peering to `docker1` was successful. Note that the IPAM service shows a status of `idle`. The `idle` status means that Weave is waiting for more peers to join before it makes any decisions about what hosts will get what IP allocations. Let's see what happens when we run a container:

```
user@docker2:~$ weave run -dP --name=web2 jonlangemak/web_server_2
379402b05db83315285df7ef516e0417635b24923bba3038b53f4e58a46b4b0d
user@docker2:~$
```

If we check the Weave status again, we should see that IPAM has now changed from **idle** to **ready**:

```
user@docker2:~$ weave status
…<Additional output removed for brevity>…
    Connections: 1 (1 established)
          Peers: 2 (with 2 established connections)
  TrustedSubnets: none


        Service: ipam
         Status: ready
```

```
       Range: 172.16.16.0/24
  DefaultSubnet: 172.16.16.0/24
…<Additional output removed for brevity>…
user@docker2:~$
```

Running the first container connected to the Weave network has forced Weave to come to a consensus. At this point, Weave has decided that the cluster size is two and has made its best effort to allocate the available IP addressing between the hosts. Let's run a container on the host `docker1` as well and then check the IP addresses that were allocated to each container:

```
user@docker1:~$ weave run -dP --name=web1 jonlangemak/web_server_1
fbb3eac421159308f41d795638c3a4689c92a9401718fd1988083bfc12047844
user@docker1:~$ weave ps
weave:expose 12:d2:fe:7a:c1:f2
fbb3eac42115 02:a7:38:ab:73:23 172.16.16.1/24
user@docker1:~$
```

Using the **weave ps** command, we can see that the container we just spawned on the host `docker1` received an IP address of `172.16.16.1/24`. If we check the IP address of the container web2 on the host `docker2`, we'll see that it got an IP address of `172.16.16.128/24`:

```
user@docker2:~$ weave ps
weave:expose e6:b1:90:cd:76:da
dde411fe4c7b c6:42:74:89:71:da 172.16.16.128/24
user@docker2:~$
```

This makes perfect sense. Weave knew that it had two members in the network so it splits the allocation directly in half, essentially giving each host its own `/25` network allocation. `docker1` started allocating out of the first half of the `/24` and `docker2` started right at the beginning of the second half.

Despite fully allocating the entire space, it does not mean that we are now out of IP space. These initial allocations are more like reservations and can be changed based on the size of the Weave network. For instance, we can now add the host `docker3` to the Weave network and start another instance of the web1 container on it:

```
user@docker3:~$ weave launch-router --ipalloc-range \
172.16.16.0/24 10.10.10.101
8e8739f48854d87ba14b9dcf220a3c33df1149ce1d868819df31b0fe5fec2163
user@docker3:~$ weave run -dP --name=web1 jonlangemak/web_server_1
0c2193f2d7569943171764155e0e93272f5715c257adba75ed544283a2794d3e
user@docker3:~$ weave ps
```

```
weave:expose ae:af:a6:36:18:37
0c2193f2d756 76:8d:4c:ee:08:db 172.16.16.224/24
user@docker3:~$
```

Because the network now has more members, Weave just further splits the initial allocation into smaller chunks. Based on the IP addresses being allocated to the containers on each host, we can see that Weave tries to keep the allocations within valid subnets. The following image shows what would happen to the IP allocations as the third and fourth hosts joined the Weave network:

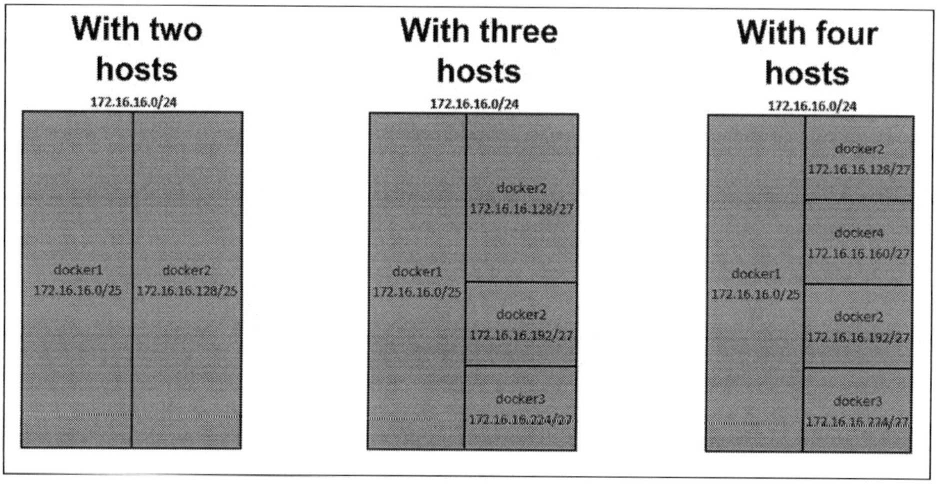

It's important to keep in mind that while the allocations given to each server are flexible, they all use the same mask as the initial allocation when they assign the IP address to the container. This ensures that the containers all assume that they are on the same network and have direct connectivity to each other removing the need to have routes pointing to other hosts.

To prove that the initial IP allocation must be the same across all hosts, we can try joining the last host, docker4, using a different subnet:

```
user@docker4:~$ weave launch-router --ipalloc-range 172.64.65.0/24
10.10.10.101
9716c02c66459872e60447a6a3b6da7fd622bd516873146a874214057fe11035
user@docker4:~$ weave status
...<Additional output removed for brevity>...
        Service: router
       Protocol: weave 1..2
           Name: 42:ec:92:86:1a:31(docker4)
     Encryption: disabled
```

```
      PeerDiscovery: enabled
           Targets: 1
      Connections: 1 (1 failed)
...<Additional output removed for brevity>...
user@docker4:~$
```

If we check the Weave router's container for logs, we'll see that it's unable to join the existing Weave network because of having the wrong IP allocation defined:

```
user@docker4:~$ docker logs weave

...<Additional output removed for brevity>...

INFO: 2016/10/11 02:16:09.821503 ->[192.168.50.101:6783|ae:af:a6:36:18
:37(docker3)]: connection shutting down due to error: Incompatible IP
allocation ranges (received: 172.16.16.0/24, ours: 172.64.65.0/24)

...<Additional output removed for brevity>...
```

The only way to join the existing Weave network would be to use the same initial IP allocation as all of the existing nodes.

Finally, it's important to call out that it's not a requirement to use Weave IPAM in this fashion. You can allocate IP addressing manually by specifying an IP address during a weave run like this:

```
user@docker1:~$ weave run 1.1.1.1/24 -dP --name=wrongip \
jonlangemak/web_server_1
259004af91e3b0367bede723c9eb9d3fbdc0c4ad726efe7aea812b79eb408777
user@docker1:~$
```

When specifying individual IP addresses, you can choose any IP address you like. As you'll see in a later recipe, you can also specify a subnet for allocation and have Weave keep track of that subnet allocation in IPAM. When assigning an IP address from a subnet the subnet must be part of the initial Weave allocation.

If you wish to manually allocate IP addresses to some containers, it may be wise to configure an additional Weave parameter during the initial Weave configuration to limit the scope of the dynamic allocations. You may pass the --ipalloc-default-subnet parameter to Weave during launch to limit the scope of which IP addresses are dynamically assigned to hosts. For instance, you might pass this:

```
weave launch-router --ipalloc-range 172.16.16.0/24 \
--ipalloc-default-subnet 172.16.16.0/25
```

This would configure the Weave subnet to be `172.16.16.0/25` leaving the rest of the larger network available for manual allocation. We'll see in a later recipe that this type of configuration plays a big role in how Weave handles network isolation across the Weave network.

Working with WeaveDNS

Naturally, the next thing to consider after IPAM is name resolution. Regardless of scale, having some way to locate and identify containers by something other than an IP address becomes a necessity. Much like newer versions of Docker, Weave offers its own DNS service for resolving container names that live on Weave networks. In this recipe, we'll review the default configuration for WeaveDNS as well as show how it's implemented and some relevant configuration settings to get you up and running.

Getting ready

It is assumed that you're building off the lab we created in the first recipe of this chapter. It is also assumed that the hosts have Docker and Weave installed. Docker should be in its default configuration and Weave should be installed with all four hosts successfully peered together, as we did in the first recipe of this chapter.

How to do it...

If you've been following along up until this point in the chapter, you've already provisioned WeaveDNS. WeaveDNS comes along with the Weave router container and is enabled by default. We can see this by looking at the Weave status:

```
user@docker1:~$ weave status
...<Additional output removed for brevity>...
        Service: dns
         Domain: weave.local.
       Upstream: 10.20.30.13
            TTL: 1
        Entries: 0
...<Additional output removed for brevity>...
```

When Weave provisions the DNS service, it starts with some sane defaults. In this case, it's detected that my hosts DNS server is `10.20.30.13`, and so it has configured that as an upstream resolver. It's also selected `weave.local` as the domain name. If we start a container using the weave run syntax, Weave will make sure that the container is provisioned in a manner that allows it to consume this DNS service. For instance, let's start a container on the host `docker1`:

```
user@docker1:~$ weave run -dP --name=web1 jonlangemak/web_server_1
```

```
c0cf29fb07610b6ffc4e55fdd4305f2b79a89566acd0ae0a6de09df06979ef36
user@docker1:~$ docker exec -t web1 more /etc/resolv.conf
nameserver 172.17.0.1
user@docker1:~$
```

After starting the container, we can see that Weave has configured the container's `resolv.conf` file differently than Docker would have. Recall that Docker, by default, in nonuser-defined networks, will give a container the same DNS configuration as the Docker hosts itself. In this case, Weave has given the container a name server of `172.17.0.1`, which is, by default, the IP address assigned to the `docker0` bridge. You might be wondering how Weave expects the container to resolve its own DNS system by talking to the `docker0` bridge. The solution is quite simple. The Weave router container is run in host mode and has a service bound to port `53`:

```
user@docker1:~$ docker network inspect host
…<Additional output removed for brevity>…
"Containers": {
"03e3e82a5e0ced0b973e2b31ed9c2d3b8fe648919e263965d61ee7c425d9627c": {
          "Name": "weave",
…<Additional output removed for brevity>…
```

If we check the ports bound on the host, we can see that the weave router is exposing port `53`:

```
user@docker1:~$ sudo netstat -plnt
Active Internet connections (only servers)
…<some columns removed to increase readability>…
Proto Local Address State        PID/Program name
tcp    172.17.0.1:53 LISTEN       2227/weaver
```

This means that the WeaveDNS service in the Weave container will be listening on the `docker0` bridge interface for DNS requests. Let's start another container on the host docker2:

```
user@docker2:~$ weave run -dP --name=web2 jonlangemak/web_server_2
b81472e86d8ac62511689185fe4e4f36ac4a3c41e49d8777745a60cce6a4ac05
user@docker2:~$ docker exec -it web2 ping web1 -c 2
PING web1.weave.local (10.32.0.1): 48 data bytes
56 bytes from 10.32.0.1: icmp_seq=0 ttl=64 time=0.486 ms
56 bytes from 10.32.0.1: icmp_seq=1 ttl=64 time=0.582 ms
--- web1.weave.local ping statistics ---
2 packets transmitted, 2 packets received, 0% packet loss
```

```
round-trip min/avg/max/stddev = 0.486/0.534/0.582/0.048 ms
user@docker2:~$
```

As long as both containers are on the Weave network and have the appropriate settings, Weave will automatically generate a DNS record with the containers name. We can view all the name records Weave is aware of using the `weave status dns` command from any Weave-enabled host:

```
user@docker2:~$ weave status dns
web1          10.32.0.1        86029a1305f1 12:d2:fe:7a:c1:f2
web2          10.44.0.0        56927d3bf002 e6:b1:90:cd:76:da
user@docker2:~$
```

Here, we can see the container name, the IP address, the container ID, and the MAC address of the destination host's Weave network interface.

This works well but relies on the container being configured with the appropriate settings. This is another scenario where using the Weave CLI is rather helpful since it ensures that these settings are in place at container runtime. For instance, if we start another container on the host `docker3` with the Docker CLI and then attach it to Docker, it won't get a DNS record:

```
user@docker3:~$ docker run -dP --name=web1 jonlangemak/web_server_1
cd3b043bd70c0f60a03ec24c7835314ca2003145e1ca6d58bd06b5d0c6803a5c
user@docker3:~$ weave attach web1
10.36.0.0
user@docker3:~$ docker exec -it web1 ping web2
ping: unknown host
user@docker3:~$
```

This doesn't work for two reasons. First, the container doesn't know where to look for Weave DNS, and it is trying to resolve it through the DNS server Docker provided. In this case, that's the one configured on the Docker host:

```
user@docker3:~$ docker exec -it web1 more /etc/resolv.conf
# Dynamic resolv.conf(5) file for glibc resolver(3) generated by
resolvconf(8)
#     DO NOT EDIT THIS FILE BY HAND -- YOUR CHANGES WILL BE OVERWRITTEN
nameserver 10.20.30.13
search lab.lab
user@docker3:~$
```

Second, Weave did not register a record in WeaveDNS when the container was attached. In order for Weave to generate a record for the container in WeaveDNS, the container must be in the same domain. To do this, when Weave runs a container through its CLI, it passes the hostname of the container along with a domain name. We can mimic this behavior by provisioning a hostname when we run the container in Docker. For instance:

```
user@docker3:~$ docker stop web1
user@docker3:~$ docker rm web1
user@docker3:~$ docker run -dP --hostname=web1.weave.local \
--name=web1 jonlangemak/web_server_1
04bb1ba21b692b4117a9b0503e050d7f73149b154476ed5a0bce0d049c3c9357
user@docker3:~$
```

Now when we attach the container to the Weave network, we should see a DNS record generated for it:

```
user@docker3:~$ weave attach web1
10.36.0.0
user@docker3:~$ weave status dns
web1          10.32.0.1        86029a1305f1 12:d2:fe:7a:c1:f2
web1          10.36.0.0        5bab5eae10b0 ae:af:a6:36:18:37
web2          10.44.0.0        56927d3bf002 e6:b1:90:cd:76:da
user@docker3:~$
```

 If you wanted to have this container also be able to resolve records in WeaveDNS, you'd also need to pass the `--dns=172.17.0.1` flag to the container to ensure that its DNS server is set to the IP address of the `docker0` bridge.

You might have noticed that we now have two entries in WeaveDNS for the same container name. This is how Weave provides for basic load balancing within the Weave network. For instance, if we head back to the `docker2` host, let's try and ping the name `web1` a couple of different times:

```
user@docker2:~$ docker exec -it web2 ping web1 -c 1
PING web1.weave.local (10.32.0.1): 48 data bytes
56 bytes from 10.32.0.1: icmp_seq=0 ttl=64 time=0.494 ms
--- web1.weave.local ping statistics ---
1 packets transmitted, 1 packets received, 0% packet loss
round-trip min/avg/max/stddev = 0.494/0.494/0.494/0.000 ms
user@docker2:~$ docker exec -it web2 ping web1 -c 1
```

```
PING web1.weave.local (10.36.0.0): 48 data bytes
56 bytes from 10.36.0.0: icmp_seq=0 ttl=64 time=0.796 ms
--- web1.weave.local ping statistics ---
1 packets transmitted, 1 packets received, 0% packet loss
round-trip min/avg/max/stddev = 0.796/0.796/0.796/0.000 ms
user@docker2:~$ docker exec -it web2 ping web1 -c 1
PING web1.weave.local (10.32.0.1): 48 data bytes
56 bytes from 10.32.0.1: icmp_seq=0 ttl=64 time=0.507 ms
--- web1.weave.local ping statistics ---
1 packets transmitted, 1 packets received, 0% packet loss
round-trip min/avg/max/stddev = 0.507/0.507/0.507/0.000 ms
user@docker2:~$
```

Note how the container is resolving to a different IP address during the second ping attempt. Since there are multiple records in WeaveDNS for the same name, we can provide basic load balancing functionality just using DNS. Weave will also track the state of the containers and pull dead containers out of WeaveDNS. For instance, if we kill the container on the host docker3, we should see one of the web1 records fall out of DNS leaving only a single record for web1:

```
user@docker3:~$ docker stop web1
web1
user@docker3:~$ weave status dns
web1         10.32.0.1       86029a1305f1 12:d2:fe:7a:c1:f2
web2         10.44.0.0       56927d3bf002 e6:b1:90:cd:76:da
user@docker3:~$
```

 There are many different configuration options available to you for customizing how WeaveDNS works. To see the entire guide, check out the documentation at https://www.weave.works/docs/net/latest/weavedns/.

Weave security

Weave offers a couple of features that fall under the umbrella of security. Since Weave is an overlay-based network solution, it offers the ability to encrypt the overlay traffic as it traverses the physical or underlay network. This can be particularly useful when your containers may need to traverse a public network. In addition, Weave allows you to isolate containers within certain network segments. Weave relies on using different subnets for each isolated segment to achieve this. In this recipe, we'll walk through how to configure both overlay encryption as well as how to provide isolation for different containers across the Weave network.

Getting ready

It is assumed that you're building off the lab we created in the first recipe of this chapter. It is also assumed that the hosts have Docker and Weave installed. Docker should be in its default configuration, and Weave should be installed but not yet peered. If you need to remove the peering defined in previous examples, issue the `weave reset` command on each host.

How to do it...

Configuring Weave to encrypt the overlay network is fairly straightforward to accomplish; however, it must be done during the initial configuration of Weave. Using the same lab topology from the previous recipes, let's run the following commands to build the Weave network:

- On the host `docker1`:

```
weave launch-router --password notverysecurepwd \
--trusted-subnets 192.168.50.0/24 --ipalloc-range \
172.16.16.0/24 --ipalloc-default-subnet 172.16.16.128/25
```

- On the hosts `docker2`, `docker3`,and `docker4`:

```
weave launch-router --password notverysecurepwd \
--trusted-subnets 192.168.50.0/24 --ipalloc-range \
172.16.16.0/24 --ipalloc-default-subnet \
172.16.16.128/25 10.10.10.101
```

You'll note that the command we run on the hosts is largely the same with the exception of the last three hosts specifying `docker1` as a peer in order to build the Weave network. In either case, there are a few additional parameters we've passed to the router during Weave initialization:

- `--password`: This is what enables the encryption for the communication between Weave nodes. You should, unlike in my example, pick a very secure password to use. This needs to be the same on every node running weave.

- `--trusted-subnets`: This allows you to define subnets of hosts as trusted, which means they don't require their communication to be encrypted. When Weave does encryption it falls back to a slower data path than what is normally used. Since using the `--password` parameter turns on encryption end to end, it might make sense to define some subnets as not needing encryption

- `--ipalloc-range`: Here, we define the larger Weave network to be `172.16.16.0/24`. We saw this command used in earlier recipes:

- `--ipalloc-default-subnet`: This instructs Weave to, by default, allocate container IP addresses out of a smaller subnet of the larger Weave allocation. In this case, that's `172.16.16.128/25`.

Now, let's run the following containers on each host:

- `docker1`:

```
weave run -dP --name=web1tenant1 jonlangemak/web_server_1
```

- `docker2`:

```
weave run -dP --name=web2tenant1 jonlangemak/web_server_2
```

- `docker3`:

```
weave run net:172.16.16.0/25 -dP --name=web1tenant2 \
jonlangemak/web_server_1
```

- `docker4`:

```
weave run net:172.16.16.0/25 -dP --name=web2tenant2 \
jonlangemak/web_server_2
```

You'll note that on the host `docker3` and `docker4`, I added the `net:172.16.16.0/25` parameter. Recall when we started the Weave network, we told Weave to by default allocate IP addresses out of `172.16.16.128/25`. We can override this at container runtime and provide a new subnet for Weave to use so long as it's within the larger Weave network. In this case, the containers on `docker1` and `docker2` will get an IP address within `172.16.16.128/25` because that is the default. The containers on `docker3` and `docker4` will get an IP address within `172.16.16.0/25` since we overrode the default. We can confirm this once you've started all the containers:

```
user@docker4:~$ weave status dns
web1tenant1   172.16.16.129    26c58ef399c3 12:d2:fe:7a:c1:f2
web1tenant2   172.16.16.64     4c569073d663 ae:af:a6:36:18:37
web2tenant1   172.16.16.224    211c2e0b388e e6:b1:90:cd:76:da
web2tenant2   172.16.16.32     191207a9fb61 42:ec:92:86:1a:31
user@docker4:~$
```

As I mentioned earlier, using distinct subnets is how Weave provides for container segmentation. In this case, the topology would look like this:

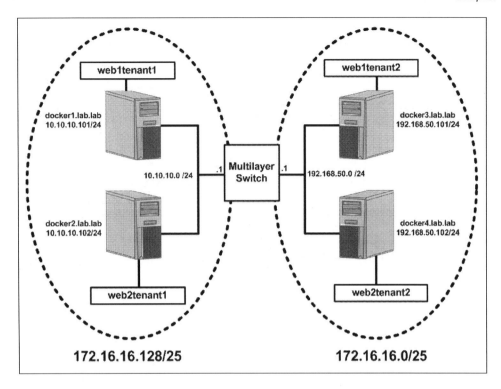

The dotted lines symbolize the isolation that Weave is providing for us in the overlay network. Since the `tenant1` containers live is a separate subnet from the `tenant2` containers, they will not have connectivity. In this manner, Weave is using basic networking to allow for container isolation. We can prove this works with a few tests:

```
user@docker4:~$ docker exec -it web2tenant2 curl http://web1tenant2
<body>
  <html>
    <h1><span style="color:#FF0000;font-size:72px;">Web Server #1 -
Running on port 80</span>
    </h1>
</body>
  </html>
user@docker4:~$ docker exec -it web2tenant2 curl http://web1tenant1
user@docker4:~$ docker exec -it web2tenant2 curl http://web2tenant1
user@docker4:~$
user@docker4:~$ docker exec -it web2tenant2 ping web1tenant1 -c 1
PING web1tenant1.weave.local (172.16.16.129): 48 data bytes
```

```
--- web1tenant1.weave.local ping statistics ---
1 packets transmitted, 0 packets received, 100% packet loss
user@docker4:~$
```

You'll notice that when the `web2tenant2` container attempts to access a service within its own tenant (subnet), it works as expected. Attempts to access a service in `tenant1` receive no response. However, since DNS is shared across the Weave network, the container can still resolve the IP address of the containers in `tenant1`.

This also illustrates an example of encryption and how we can specify certain hosts as being trusted. Regardless of which subnetwork the containers live in, Weave still builds connectivity between all of the hosts. Since we enabled encryption during Weave initialization, all of those connections should now be encrypted. However, we also specified a trusted network. The trusted network defines nodes that do not require encryption between themselves. In our case, we specified `192.168.50.0/24` as being trusted. Since there are two nodes that have those IP addresses, `docker3` and `docker4`, we should see that the connectivity between them is unencrypted. We can validate that using the weave status connections command on the hosts. We should get the following response:

- docker1 (truncated output):

```
<- 10.10.10.102:45888      established encrypted   sleeve
<- 192.168.50.101:57880    established encrypted   sleeve
<- 192.168.50.102:45357    established encrypted   sleeve
```

- docker2 (truncated output):

```
<- 192.168.50.101:35207    established encrypted   sleeve
<- 192.168.50.102:34640    established encrypted   sleeve
-> 10.10.10.101:6783       established encrypted   sleeve
```

- docker3 (truncated output):

```
-> 10.10.10.101:6783       established encrypted   sleeve
-> 192.168.50.102:6783     established unencrypted fastdp
-> 10.10.10.102:6783       established encrypted   sleeve
```

- docker4 (truncated output):

```
-> 10.10.10.102:6783       established encrypted   sleeve
<- 192.168.50.101:36315    established unencrypted fastdp
-> 10.10.10.101:6783       established encrypted   sleeve
```

You can see that all the connections show as encrypted with the exception of the connections between the host `docker3` (`192.168.50.101`) and the host `docker4` (`192.168.50.102`). Since both hosts need to agree on what a trusted network is, the hosts `docker1` and `docker2` will never agree for their connections to be unencrypted.

Using the Weave network plugin

One of the things that sets Weave apart is that it can be operated in several different manners. As we've seen in the previous recipes of this chapter, Weave has its own CLI which we can use to provision containers directly onto the Weave network. While this is certainly a tight integration that works well, it requires that you leverage the Weave CLI or Weave API proxy to integrate with Docker. In addition to these options, Weave has also written a native Docker network plugin. This plugin allows you to work with Weave directly from Docker. That is, once the plugin is registered, you no longer need to use the Weave CLI to provision containers into Weave. In this recipe, we'll review how to install and work with the Weave network plugin.

Getting ready

It is assumed that you're building off the lab we created in the first recipe of this chapter. It is also assumed that the hosts have Docker and Weave installed. Docker should be in its default configuration, Weave should be installed, with all four hosts successfully peered together, as we did in the first recipe of this chapter.

How to do it...

Like the other components of Weave, leveraging the Docker plugin couldn't be easier. All you need to do is to tell Weave to launch it. For instance, if I decided to use the Docker plugin on the host `docker1`, I could launch the plugin like this:

```
user@docker1:~$ weave launch-plugin
3ef9ee01cc26173f2208b667fddc216e655795fd0438ef4af63dfa11d27e2546
user@docker1:~$
```

Much like the other services, the plugin comes in the form of a container. After running the preceding command, you should see the plugin running as a container named `weaveplugin`:

```
user@docker1:~$ docker ps
CONTAINER ID    IMAGE                      COMMAND                CREATED          STATUS          PORTS    NAMES
24a2b91bc651    weaveworks/plugin:1.7.1    "/home/weave/plugin"   22 seconds ago   Up 21 seconds            weaveplugin
5f8fbc859596    weaveworks/weave:1.7.1     "/home/weave/weaver -" 59 seconds ago   Up 58 seconds            weave
user@docker1:~$
```

Once running, you should also see it registered as a network plugin:

```
user@docker1:~$ docker info
...<Additional output removed for brevity>...
Plugins:
 Volume: local
 Network: host weavemesh overlay bridge null
```

…<Additional output removed for brevity>…

user@docker1:~$

We can also see it as a defined network type using the `docker network` subcommand:

```
user@docker1:~$ docker network ls
NETWORK ID          NAME                DRIVER              SCOPE
79105142fbf0        bridge              bridge              local
bb090c21339c        host                host                local
9ae306e2af0a        none                null                local
20864e3185f5        weave               weavemesh           local
user@docker1:~$
```

At this point, connecting containers to the Weave network can be done directly through Docker. All you need to do is specify the network name of `weave` when you start a container. For instance, we can run:

```
user@docker1:~$ docker run -dP --name=web1 --net=weave \
jonlangemak/web_server_1
4d84cb472379757ae4dac5bf6659ec66c9ae6df200811d56f65ffc957b10f748
user@docker1:~$
```

If we look at the container interfaces we should see the two interfaces we're accustomed to seeing with Weave connected containers:

```
user@docker1:~$ docker exec web1 ip addr
…<loopback interface removed for brevity>…
83: ethwe0@if84: <BROADCAST,MULTICAST,UP,LOWER_UP> mtu 1410 qdisc noqueue
state UP
    link/ether 9e:b2:99:c4:ac:c4 brd ff:ff:ff:ff:ff:ff
    inet 10.32.0.1/12 scope global ethwe0
        valid_lft forever preferred_lft forever
    inet6 fe80::9cb2:99ff:fec4:acc4/64 scope link
        valid_lft forever preferred_lft forever
86: eth1@if87: <BROADCAST,MULTICAST,UP,LOWER_UP> mtu 1500 qdisc noqueue
state UP
    link/ether 02:42:ac:12:00:02 brd ff:ff:ff:ff:ff:ff
    inet 172.18.0.2/16 scope global eth1
        valid_lft forever preferred_lft forever
    inet6 fe80::42:acff:fe12:2/64 scope link
        valid_lft forever preferred_lft forever
user@docker1:~$
```

However, you might note that the IP address for `eth1` is not on the `docker0` bridge, but rather on `docker_gwbridge` we saw used in earlier chapters when we showed the Docker overlay driver. The benefit of using the gateway bridge rather than the `docker0` bridge is that the gateway bridge has ICC disabled by default. This prevents Weave connected containers that are supposed to be isolated from accidentally cross talking across the `docker0` bridge if you had ICC mode enabled.

A downside to the plugin approach is that Weave isn't in the middle to tell Docker about the DNS-related configurations, which means that the containers aren't registering their names. Even if they were, they also aren't receiving the proper name resolution settings required to resolve WeaveDNS. There are two ways we can specify the proper settings to the container. In either case, we need to manually specify the parameters at container runtime. The first method involves manually specifying all the required parameters yourself. Manually, it's done as follows:

```
user@docker1:~$ docker run -dP --name=web1 \
--hostname=web1.weave.local --net=weave --dns=172.17.0.1 \
--dns-search=weave.local jonlangemak/web_server_1
6a907ee64c129d36e112d0199eb2184663f5cf90522ff151aa10c2a1e6320e16
user@docker1:~$
```

In order to register with DNS, you need the four bolded settings shown in the preceding code:

- `--hostname=web1.weave.local`: If you don't set the hostname of the container to a name within `weave.local`, the DNS server won't register the name.

- `--net=weave`: It has to be on the Weave network for any of this to work.

- `--dns=172.17.0.1`: We need to tell it to use the Weave DNS server listening on the `docker0` bridge IP address. However, you might have noticed that this container doesn't actually have an IP address on the `docker0` bridge. Rather, since we're connected to the `docker-gwbridge`, we have an IP address in the `172.18.0.0/16` network. In either case, since both bridges have IP interfaces the container can route through the `docker_gwbridge` to get to the IP interface on the `docker0` bridge.

- `--dns-search=weave.local`: This allows the container to resolve names without specifying the **Fully Qualified Domain Name (FQDN)**.

Once a container is started with these settings, you should see records registering in WeaveDNS:

```
user@docker1:~$ weave status dns
web1          10.32.0.1        7b02c0262786 12:d2:fe:7a:c1:f2
user@docker1:~$
```

The second solution is still manual but involves pulling the DNS information from Weave itself. Rather than specifying the DNS server and the search domain, you can inject it right from Weave. Weave has a command named `dns-args` that will return the relevant information for you. So rather than specifying it, we can simply inject that command as part of the container parameters like this:

```
user@docker2:~$ docker run --hostname=web2.weave.local \
--net=weave $(weave dns-args) --name=web2 -dP \
jonlangemak/web_server_2
597ffde17581b7203204594dca84c9461c83cb7a9076ed3d1ed3fcb598c2b77d
user@docker2:~$
```

Granted, this doesn't prevent the need to specify the network or the FQDN of the container, but it does trim down some of the typing. At this point, you should see all of the records defined in WeaveDNS and be able to access services across the Weave network by name:

```
user@docker1:~$ weave status dns
web1            10.32.0.1          7b02c0262786 12:d2:fe:7a:c1:f2
web2            10.32.0.2          b154e3671feb 12:d2:fe:7a:c1:f2
user@docker1:~$
user@docker2:~$ docker exec -it web2 ping web1 -c 2
PING web1 (10.32.0.1): 48 data bytes
56 bytes from 10.32.0.1: icmp_seq=0 ttl=64 time=0.139 ms
56 bytes from 10.32.0.1: icmp_seq=1 ttl=64 time=0.130 ms
--- web1 ping statistics ---
2 packets transmitted, 2 packets received, 0% packet loss
round-trip min/avg/max/stddev = 0.130/0.135/0.139/0.000 ms
user@docker1:~$
```

You might note that these container's DNS configuration isn't exactly as you expected. For instance, the `resolv.conf` file does not show the DNS server we specified at container runtime:

```
user@docker1:~$ docker exec web1 more /etc/resolv.conf
::::::::::::::
/etc/resolv.conf
::::::::::::::
search weave.local
nameserver 127.0.0.11
options ndots:0
user@docker1:~$
```

However, if you inspect the container's configuration, you'll see that the correct DNS server is properly defined:

```
user@docker1:~$ docker inspect web1
...<Additional output removed for brevity>...
            "Dns": [
                "172.17.0.1"
            ],
...<Additional output removed for brevity>...
user@docker1:~$
```

Recall that user-defined networks require the use of Docker's embedded DNS system. The IP address we saw in the containers `resolv.conf` file references Docker's embedded DNS server. In turn, when we specify a DNS server for a container, the embedded DNS server adds that server as a forwarder in embedded DNS. This means that, although the request is still hitting the embedded DNS server first, the request is being forwarded on to WeaveDNS for resolution.

 The Weave plugin also allows you to create additional user-defined networks using the Weave driver. However, since Docker sees those as global in scope, they require the use of an external key store. If you're interested in using Weave in that fashion, please refer to the Weave documentation at `https://www.weave.works/docs/net/latest/plugin/`.

8

Working with Flannel

In this chapter, we will cover the following recipes:

- Installing and configuring Flannel
- Integrating Flannel with Docker
- Using the VXLAN backend
- Using the host gateway backend
- Specifying Flannel options

Introduction

Flannel is a third-party network solution for Docker that was developed by the team at **CoreOS**. Flannel was one of the earlier projects that aimed to give each container a uniquely routable IP address. This removes the requirement for inter-host container-to-container communication to use published ports. Much like some of the other solutions we've reviewed, Flannel uses a key-value store to keep track of allocations and various other configuration settings. However, unlike Weave, Flannel offers no direct integration with the Docker service offering no plugin. Rather, Flannel relies on you telling Docker to use the Flannel network to provision containers. In this chapter, we'll walk through how to install Flannel as well as walk through its various configuration options.

Installing and configuring Flannel

In this recipe, we'll walk through the installation of Flannel. Flannel requires the installation of a key store and Flannel service. Due to the dependencies of each of these, they need to be configured as actual services on the Docker hosts. To do this, we'll leverage `systemd` unit files to define each respective service.

Getting ready

In this example, we'll be using the same lab topology we used in *Chapter 3, User-Defined Networks*, where we discussed user-defined overlay networks:

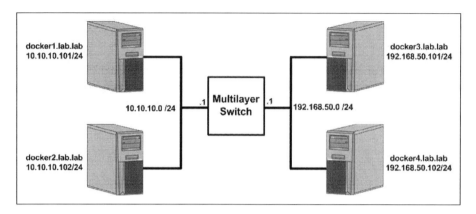

You'll need a couple of hosts, preferably with some of them being on different subnets. It is assumed that the Docker hosts used in this lab are in their default configuration. In some cases, the changes we make may require you to have root-level access to the system.

How to do it...

As mentioned, Flannel relies on a key-value store to provide information to all the nodes participating in the Flannel network. In other examples, we've run a container-based key-value store such as Consul to provide this functionality. Since Flannel was built by CoreOS, we'll be leveraging their key-value store named etcd. And while etcd is offered in a container format, we can't easily use the container-based version due to some of the prerequisites required for Flannel to work. That being said, we'll be downloading the binaries for both etcd and Flannel and running them as services on our hosts.

Let's start with etcd since it's a perquisite for Flannel. The first thing you need to do is download the code. In this example, we'll be leveraging etcd version 3.0.12 and running the key-value store on the host docker1. To download the binary, we'll run this command:

```
user@docker1:~$ curl -LO \
https://github.com/coreos/etcd/releases/download/v3.0.12/\
etcd-v3.0.12-linux-amd64.tar.gz
```

Once downloaded, we can extract the binaries from the archive using this command:

```
user@docker1:~$ tar xzvf etcd-v3.0.12-linux-amd64.tar.gz
```

And then we can move the binaries we need into the correct location to make them executable. In this case, the location is /usr/bin and the binaries we want are the etcd service itself as well as its command-line tool named etcdctl:

```
user@docker1:~$ cd etcd-v3.0.12-linux-amd64
user@docker1:~/etcd-v2.3.7-linux-amd64$ sudo mv etcd /usr/bin/
user@docker1:~/etcd-v2.3.7-linux-amd64$ sudo mv etcdctl /usr/bin/
```

Now that we have all the pieces in place, the last thing we need to do is to create a service on the system that will take care of running etcd. Since our version of Ubuntu is using systemd, we'll need to create a unit file for the etcd service. To create the service definition, you can create a service unit file in the /lib/systemd/system/ directory:

```
user@docker1:~$  sudo vi /lib/systemd/system/etcd.service
```

Then, you can create a service definition to run etcd. An example unit file for the etcd service is shown as follows:

```
[Unit]
Description=etcd key-value store
Documentation=https://github.com/coreos/etcd
After=network.target


[Service]
Environment=DAEMON_ARGS=
Environment=ETCD_NAME=%H
Environment=ETCD_ADVERTISE_CLIENT_URLS=http://0.0.0.0:2379
Environment=ETCD_LISTEN_CLIENT_URLS=http://0.0.0.0:2379
Environment=ETCD_LISTEN_PEER_URLS=http://0.0.0.0:2378
Environment=ETCD_DATA_DIR=/var/lib/etcd/default
Type=notify
ExecStart=/usr/bin/etcd $DAEMON_ARGS
Restart=always
RestartSec=10s
LimitNOFILE=65536


[Install]
WantedBy=multi-user.target
```

Keep in mind that `systemd` can be configured in many different ways based on your requirements. The unit file given earlier demonstrates one way to configure `etcd` as a service.

Once the unit file is in place, we can reload `systemd` and then enable and start the service:

```
user@docker1:~$ sudo systemctl daemon-reload
user@docker1:~$ sudo systemctl enable etcd
user@docker1:~$ sudo systemctl start etcd
```

If for some reason the service doesn't start or stay started, you can check the status of the service by using the `systemctl status etcd` command:

```
user@docker1:~$ systemctl status etcd
  etcd.service - etcd key-value store
   Loaded: loaded (/lib/systemd/system/etcd.service; enabled; vendor
preset: enabled)
   Active: active (running) since Tue 2016-10-11 13:41:01 CDT; 1h 30min
ago
     Docs: https://github.com/coreos/etcd
 Main PID: 17486 (etcd)
    Tasks: 8
   Memory: 8.5M
      CPU: 22.095s
   CGroup: /system.slice/etcd.service
           └─17486 /usr/bin/etcd


Oct 11 13:41:01 docker1 etcd[17486]: setting up the initial cluster
version to 3.0
Oct 11 13:41:01 docker1 etcd[17486]: published {Name:docker1 ClientURLs:[
http://0.0.0.0:2379]} to cluster cdf818194e3a8c32
Oct 11 13:41:01 docker1 etcd[17486]: ready to serve client requests
Oct 11 13:41:01 docker1 etcd[17486]: serving insecure client requests on
0.0.0.0:2379, this is strongly  iscouraged!
Oct 11 13:41:01 docker1 systemd[1]: Started etcd key-value store.
Oct 11 13:41:01 docker1 etcd[17486]: set the initial cluster version to
3.0
Oct 11 13:41:01 docker1 etcd[17486]: enabled capabilities for version 3.0
Oct 11 15:04:20 docker1 etcd[17486]: start to snapshot (applied: 10001,
lastsnap: 0)
```

```
Oct 11 15:04:20 docker1 etcd[17486]: saved snapshot at index 10001
Oct 11 15:04:20 docker1 etcd[17486]: compacted raft log at 5001
user@docker1:~$
```

Later on, if you're having issues with Flannel-enabled nodes being able to talk to `etcd`, check and make sure that `etcd` is allowing access on all interfaces (`0.0.0.0`) as shown in the preceding bolded output. This is defined in the sample unit file provided, but if not defined, `etcd` will default to only listen on the local loopback interface (`127.0.0.1`). This will prevent remote servers from accessing the service.

 Since the key-value store configuration is being done explicitly to demonstrate Flannel, we won't be covering the basics of key-value stores. These configuration options are enough to get you up and running on a single node and are not intended to be used in a production environment. Please make sure that you understand how `etcd` works before using it in a production setting.

Once the `etcd` service is started, we can then use the `etcdctl` command-line tool to configure some of the base settings in Flannel:

```
user@docker1:~$ etcdctl mk /coreos.com/network/config \
'{"Network":"10.100.0.0/16"}'
```

We'll discuss these configuration options in a later recipe, but for now, just know that the subnet we defined as the `Network` parameter defines the Flannel global scope.

Now that we have `etcd` configured, we can focus on configuring Flannel itself. The configuration of Flannel as a service on the system is very similar to what we just did for `etcd`. The major difference is that we'll be doing this same configuration on all four lab hosts, whereas the key-value store was only configured on a single host. We'll show the installation of Flannel on a single host, `docker4`, but you'll need to repeat these steps on each host in your lab environment that you wish to be a member of the Flannel network:

First, we'll download the Flannel binary. In this example, we'll be using version 0.5.5:

```
user@docker4:~$ cd /tmp/
user@docker4:/tmp$ curl -LO \
https://github.com/coreos/flannel/releases/download/v0.6.2/\
flannel-v0.6.2-linux-amd64.tar.gz
```

Then, we need to extract the files from the archive and move the `flanneld` binary to the correct location. Note that there is no command-line tool to interact with Flannel as there was with `etcd`:

```
user@docker4:/tmp$ tar xzvf flannel-v0.6.2-linux-amd64.tar.gz
user@docker4:/tmp$ sudo mv flanneld /usr/bin/
```

As with `etcd`, we want to define a `systemd` unit file so that we can run `flanneld` as a service on each host. To create the service definition, you can create another service unit file in the `/lib/systemd/system/` directory:

```
user@docker4:/tmp$ sudo vi /lib/systemd/system/flanneld.service
```

Then, you can create a service definition to run `etcd`. An example unit file for the `etcd` service is shown as follows:

```
[Unit]
Description=Flannel Network Fabric
Documentation=https://github.com/coreos/flannel
Before=docker.service
After=etcd.service


[Service]
Environment='DAEMON_ARGS=---etcd-endpoints=http://10.10.10.101:2379'
Type=notify
ExecStart=/usr/bin/flanneld $DAEMON_ARGS
Restart=always
RestartSec=10s
LimitNOFILE=65536


[Install]
WantedBy=multi-user.target
```

Once the unit file is in pace, we can reload `systemd` and then enable and start the service:

```
user@docker4:/tmp$ sudo systemctl daemon-reload
user@docker4:/tmp$ sudo systemctl enable flanneld
user@docker4:/tmp$ sudo systemctl start flanneld
```

If, for some reason, the service doesn't start or stay started, you can check the status of the service using the `systemctl status flanneld` command:

```
user@docker4:/tmp$ systemctl status flanneld
  flanneld.service - Flannel Network Fabric
   Loaded: loaded (/lib/systemd/system/flanneld.service; enabled; vendor
preset: enabled)
   Active: active (running) since Wed 2016-10-12 08:50:54 CDT; 6s ago
     Docs: https://github.com/coreos/flannel
 Main PID: 25161 (flanneld)
```

```
  Tasks: 6
 Memory: 3.3M
    CPU: 12ms
 CGroup: /system.slice/flanneld.service
        └─25161 /usr/bin/flanneld --etcd-endpoints=ht
tp://10.10.10.101:2379
```

Oct 12 08:50:54 docker4 systemd[1]: Starting Flannel Network Fabric...

Oct 12 08:50:54 docker4 flanneld[25161]: I1012 08:50:54.409928 25161 main.go:126] Installing signal handlers

Oct 12 08:50:54 docker4 flanneld[25161]: I1012 08:50:54.410384 25161 manager.go:133] Determining IP address of default interface

Oct 12 08:50:54 docker4 flanneld[25161]: I1012 08:50:54.410793 25161 manager.go:163] Using 192.168.50.102 as external interface

Oct 12 08:50:54 docker4 flanneld[25161]: I1012 08:50:54.411688 25161 manager.go:164] Using 192.168.50.102 as external endpoint

Oct 12 08:50:54 docker4 flanneld[25161]: I1012 08:50:54.423706 25161 local_manager.go:179] **Picking subnet in range 10.100.1.0 ... 10.100.255.0**

Oct 12 08:50:54 docker4 flanneld[25161]: I1012 08:50:54.429636 25161 manager.go:246] **Lease acquired: 10.100.15.0/24**

Oct 12 08:50:54 docker4 flanneld[25161]: I1012 08:50:54.430507 25161 network.go:98] Watching for new subnet leases

Oct 12 08:50:54 docker4 systemd[1]: **Started Flannel Network Fabric.**

user@docker4:/tmp$

You should see similar output in your log indicating that Flannel found a lease within the global scope allocation you configured in `etcd`. These leases are local to each host and I often refer to them as local scopes or networks. The next step is to complete this configuration on the remaining hosts. By checking the Flannel log on each host, I can tell what subnets were allocated to each host. In my case, this is what I ended up with:

- docker1: `10.100.93.0/24`
- docker2: `10.100.58.0/24`
- docker3: `10.100.90.0/24`
- docker4: `10.100.15.0/24`

At this point, Flannel is fully configured. In the next recipe, we'll discuss how to configure Docker to consume the Flannel network.

Integrating Flannel with Docker

As we mentioned earlier, there is currently no direct integration between Flannel and Docker. That being said, we'll need to find a way to get the containers onto the Flannel network without Docker directly knowing that's what's happening. In this recipe, we'll show how this is done, discuss some of the perquisites that led to our current configuration, and see how Flannel handles host-to-host communication.

Getting ready

It is assumed that you're building off the lab described in the previous recipe. In some cases the changes we make may require you to have root-level access to the system.

How to do it...

In the previous recipe, we configured Flannel, but we didn't examine what the Flannel configuration actually did from a network perspective. Let's take a quick look at the configuration of one of our Flannel-enabled hosts to see what's changed:

```
user@docker4:~$ ip addr
...<loopback interface removed for brevity>...
2: eth0: <BROADCAST,MULTICAST,UP,LOWER_UP> mtu 1500 qdisc pfifo_fast
state UP group default qlen 1000
    link/ether d2:fe:5e:b2:f6:43 brd ff:ff:ff:ff:ff:ff
    inet 192.168.50.102/24 brd 192.168.50.255 scope global eth0
        valid_lft forever preferred_lft forever
    inet6 fe80::d0fe:5eff:feb2:f643/64 scope link
        valid_lft forever preferred_lft forever
3: flannel0: <POINTOPOINT,MULTICAST,NOARP,UP,LOWER_UP> mtu 1472 qdisc
pfifo_fast state UNKNOWN group default qlen 500
    link/none
    inet 10.100.15.0/16 scope global flannel0
        valid_lft forever preferred_lft forever
4: docker0: <NO-CARRIER,BROADCAST,MULTICAST,UP> mtu 1500 qdisc noqueue
state DOWN group default
    link/ether 02:42:16:78:74:cf brd ff:ff:ff:ff:ff:ff
    inet 172.17.0.1/16 scope global docker0
        valid_lft forever preferred_lft forever
user@docker4:~$
```

You'll note the addition of a new interface named `flannel0`. You'll also note that it has an IP address within the `/24` local scope that was assigned to this host. If we dig a little deeper, we can use `ethtool` to determine that this interface is a virtual `tun` interface:

```
user@docker4:~$ ethtool -i flannel0
driver: tun
version: 1.6
firmware-version:
bus-info: tun
supports-statistics: no
supports-test: no
supports-eeprom-access: no
supports-register-dump: no
supports-priv-flags: no
user@docker4:~$
```

Flannel creates this interface on each host where the Flannel service is running. Note that the subnet mask of the `flannel0` interface is a `/16`, which covers the entire global scope allocation we defined in `etcd`. Despite allocating the host a `/24` scope, the host believes that the entire `/16` is reachable through the `flannel0` interface:

```
user@docker4:~$ ip route
default via 192.168.50.1 dev eth0
10.100.0.0/16 dev flannel0  proto kernel  scope link  src 10.100.93.0
172.17.0.0/16 dev docker0  proto kernel  scope link  src 172.17.0.1
192.168.50.0/24 dev eth0  proto kernel  scope link  src 192.168.50.102
user@docker4:~$
```

Having the interface present creates this route, which ensures that traffic headed to any of the assigned local scopes on other hosts goes through the `flannel0` interface. We can prove that this works by pinging the other `flannel0` interfaces on the other hosts:

```
user@docker4:~$ ping 10.100.93.0 -c 2
PING 10.100.93.0 (10.100.93.0) 56(84) bytes of data.
64 bytes from 10.100.93.0: icmp_seq=1 ttl=62 time=0.901 ms
64 bytes from 10.100.93.0: icmp_seq=2 ttl=62 time=0.930 ms
--- 10.100.93.0 ping statistics ---
2 packets transmitted, 2 received, 0% packet loss, time 1001ms
rtt min/avg/max/mdev = 0.901/0.915/0.930/0.033 ms
user@docker4:~$
```

Since the physical network has no knowledge of the 10.100.0.0/16 network space, Flannel must encapsulate the traffic as it traverses the physical network. In order to do this, it needs to know what physical Docker host has a given scope assigned to it. Recall from the Flannel logs we examined in the previous recipe that Flannel chose an external interface for each host based on the host's default route:

```
I0707 09:07:01.733912 02195 main.go:130] Determining IP address of
default interface
```

```
I0707 09:07:01.734374 02195 main.go:188] Using 192.168.50.102 as external
interface
```

This information, along with the scope assigned to each host, is registered in the key-value store. Using this information, Flannel can determine which host has which scope assigned and can use the external interface of that host as a destination to send the encapsulated traffic towards.

 Flannel supports multiple backends or transport mechanisms. By default, it encapsulates traffic in UDP on port 8285. In the upcoming recipes, we'll discuss other backend options.

Now that we know how Flannel works, we need to sort out how to get the actual Docker containers onto the Flannel network. The easiest way to do this is to have Docker use the assigned scope as the subnet for the docker0 bridge. Flannel writes the scope information out to a file saved in /run/flannel/subnet.env:

```
user@docker4:~$ more /run/flannel/subnet.env
```

```
FLANNEL_NETWORK=10.100.0.0/16
```

FLANNEL_SUBNET=10.100.15.1/24

FLANNEL_MTU=1472

```
FLANNEL_IPMASQ=false
```

```
user@docker4:~$
```

Using this information, we can configure Docker to use the correct subnet for its bridge interface. Flannel offers two ways to do this. The first involves generating a new Docker configuration file using a script that was included along with the Flannel binary. The script allows you to output a new Docker configuration file that uses the information from the subnet.env file. For example, we can use the script to generate a new configuration as follows:

```
user@docker4:~$ cd /tmp
```

```
user@docker4:/tmp$ ls
```

```
flannel-v0.6.2-linux-amd64.tar.gz  mk-docker-opts.sh  README.md
```

```
user@docker4:~/flannel-0.5.5$ ./mk-docker-opts.sh -c -d \
```

example_docker_config

```
user@docker4:/tmp$ more example_docker_config
DOCKER_OPTS=" --bip=10.100.15.1/24 --ip-masq=true --mtu=1472"
user@docker4:/tmp$
```

In systems that don't leverage `systemd` Docker will, in most cases, automatically check the file `/etc/default/docker` for service-level options. This means that we could simply have Flannel write the earlier-mentioned configuration file out to `/etc/default/docker`, which will allow Docker to consume the new settings when the service reloads. However, since our system uses `systemd`, this method would require updating our Docker drop-in file (`/etc/systemd/system/docker.service.d/docker.conf`) to look like this:

```
[Service]
EnvironmentFile=/etc/default/docker
ExecStart=
ExecStart=/usr/bin/dockerd $DOCKER_OPTS
```

The bolded lines indicate that the service should check the file `etc/default/docker` and then load the variable `$DOCKER_OPTS` to be passed to the service at runtime. If you use this method, it might be wise to define all your service-level options in `etc/default/docker` for the sake of simplicity.

 It should be noted that this first approach relies on running the script to generate the configuration file. If you are running the script manually to generate the file, there's a chance that the configuration file will get out of date if the Flannel configuration changes. The second approach shown later is more dynamic since the `/run/flannel/subnet.env` file is updated by the Flannel service.

Although the first approach certainly works, I prefer to use a slightly different method where I just load the variables from the `/run/flannel/subnet.env` file and consume them within the drop-in file. To do this, we change our Docker drop-in file to look like this:

```
[Service]
EnvironmentFile=/run/flannel/subnet.env
ExecStart=
ExecStart=/usr/bin/dockerd --bip=${FLANNEL_SUBNET} --mtu=${FLANNEL_MTU}
```

By specifying `/run/flannel/subnet.env` as an `EnvironmentFile`, we make the variables defined in the file available for consumption within the service definition. Then, we just use them as options to pass to the service when it starts. If we make these changes on our Docker host, reload the `systemd` configuration, and restart the Docker service, we should see that our `docker0` interface now reflects the Flannel subnet:

```
user@docker4:~$ ip addr show dev docker0
```

```
8: docker0: <NO-CARRIER,BROADCAST,MULTICAST,UP> mtu 1500 qdisc noqueue
state DOWN group default
    link/ether 02:42:24:0a:e3:c8 brd ff:ff:ff:ff:ff:ff
    inet 10.100.15.1/24 scope global docker0
       valid_lft forever preferred_lft forever
user@docker4:~$
```

You can also manually update the Docker service-level parameters yourself based on the Flannel configuration. Just make sure that you use the information from the `/run/flannel/subnet.env` file. Regardless of which method you choose, make sure that the `docker0` bridge is using the configuration specified by Flannel on all four of the Docker hosts. Our topology should now look like this:

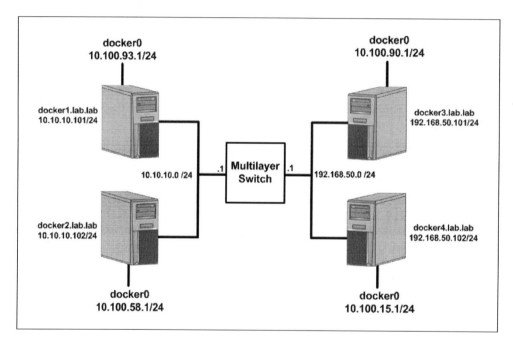

Since each Docker host only uses the Flannel-assigned scope for its subnet, each host believes the remaining subnets included in the global Flannel network are still reachable through the `flannel0` interface. Only the specific `/24` for the assigned local scope is reachable through the `docker0` bridge locally:

```
user@docker4:~$ ip route
default via 192.168.50.1 dev eth0 onlink
10.100.0.0/16 dev flannel0  proto kernel   scope link src 10.100.15.0
10.100.15.0/24 dev docker0  proto kernel   scope link src 10.100.15.1
192.168.50.0/24 dev eth0  proto kernel   scope link src 192.168.50.102
user@docker4:~$
```

We can verify the operation of Flannel at this point by running two different containers on two different hosts:

```
user@docker1:~$ docker run -dP --name=web1 jonlangemak/web_server_1

7e44a55c7ea7704d97a8804bfa211344c66f9fb83b3ac17f697c504b3b193e2d

user@docker1:~$

user@docker4:~$ docker run -dP --name=web2 jonlangemak/web_server_2

39a47920588b5e0d77ca9d2838988e2d8de893dee6198759f9ddbd3b38cea80d

user@docker4:~$
```

We can now reach the services running on each container directly by IP address. First, find the IP address of one of the containers:

```
user@docker1:~$ docker exec -it web1 ip addr show dev eth0

12: eth0@if13: <BROADCAST,MULTICAST,UP,LOWER_UP> mtu 1472 qdisc noqueue
state UP

    link/ether 02:42:0a:64:5d:02 brd ff:ff:ff:ff:ff:ff

    inet 10.100.93.2/24 scope global eth0

       valid_lft forever preferred_lft forever

    inet6 fe80::42:aff:fe64:5d02/64 scope link

       valid_lft forever preferred_lft forever

user@docker1:~$
```

Then, access the service from the second container:

```
user@docker4:~$ docker exec -it web2 curl http://10.100.93.2

<body>

  <html>

    <h1><span style="color:#FF0000;font-size:72px;">Web Server #1 -
Running on port 80</span>

    </h1>

</body>

  </html>

user@docker4:~$
```

Connectivity is working as expected. Now that we have the entire Flannel configuration working with Docker, it's important to call out the order in which we did things. Other solutions we've looked at were able to containerize certain pieces of their solution. For instance, Weave was able to offer their services in a container format rather than requiring local services as we did with Flannel. With Flannel, each component has a perquisite in order to work.

For instance, we need the `etcd` service running before Flannel will register. That by itself is not a huge concern and, if both `etcd` and Flannel ran in containers, you could solve that piece pretty easily. However, since the changes Docker needs to make to its bridge IP address are done at the service level, Docker needs to know about the Flannel scope before starting. This means that we can't run the `etcd` and Flannel services inside Docker containers because we can't start Docker without the information that Flannel generates based on reading keys from `etcd`. In this case, the prerequisites for each component are important to understand.

When running Flannel in CoreOS, they are able to run these components in containers. The solution for this is detailed in their documentation at this line under the *under the hood* section:

`https://coreos.com/flannel/docs/latest/flannel-config.html`

Using the VXLAN backend

As mentioned earlier, Flannel supports multiple different backend configurations. A backend is considered to be the means by which Flannel passes traffic between Flannel-enabled hosts. By default, this is done through UDP as we saw in the previous recipe. However, Flannel also supports VXLAN. The advantage to using VXLAN over UDP is that newer hosts support VXLAN in the kernel. In this recipe, we'll demonstrate how to change the Flannel backend type to VXLAN.

Getting ready

It is assumed that you're building off the lab described in the previous recipes in this chapter. You'll need Flannel-enabled hosts that are integrated with Docker as described in the first two recipes of this chapter. In some cases, the changes we make may require you to have root-level access to the system.

How to do it...

The type of backend you wish to use is defined when you first instantiate your network within `etcd`. Since we didn't specify a type when we defined the network `10.100.0.0/16`, Flannel defaulted to using the UDP backend. This can be changed by updating the configuration we initially set in `etcd`. Recall that our Flannel network was first defined with this command:

```
etcdctl mk /coreos.com/network/config '{"Network":"10.10.0.0/16"}'
```

Note how we used the `mk` command of `etcdctl` to make the key. If we wanted to change the backend type to VXLAN, we could run this command:

```
etcdctl set /coreos.com/network/config '{"Network":"10.100.0.0/16",
"Backend": {"Type": "vxlan"}}'
```

Note that, since we're updating the object, we now use the `set` command in place of `mk`. While sometimes hard to see when in plain text form, the properly formatted JSON that we're passing to `etcd` looks like this:

```
{
    "Network": "10.100.0.0/16",
    "Backend": {
        "Type": "vxlan",
    }
}
```

This defines the type of this backend to be VXLAN. While the preceding configuration by itself would be sufficient to change the backend type, there are sometimes additional parameters that we can specify as part of the backend. For instance, when defining the type as VXLAN, we can also specify a **VXLAN Identifier** (**VNI**) and a UDP port. If not specified, the VNI defaults to 1 and the port defaults to the 8472. For the sake of demonstration, we'll apply the defaults as part of our configuration:

```
user@docker1:~$ etcdctl set /coreos.com/network/config \
'{"Network":"10.100.0.0/16", "Backend": {"Type": "vxlan","VNI": 1,
"Port": 8472}}'
```

This in properly formatted JSON looks like this:

```
{
    "Network": "10.100.0.0/16",
    "Backend": {
        "Type": "vxlan",
        "VNI": 1,
        "Port": 8472
    }
}
```

If we run the command the local `etcd` instances configuration will be updated. We can verify that `etcd` has the proper configuration by querying `etcd` through the `etcdctl` command-line tool. To read the configuration, we can use the `etcdctl get` subcommand:

```
user@docker1:~$ etcdctl get /coreos.com/network/config
{"Network":"10.100.0.0/16", "Backend": {"Type": "vxlan", "VNI": 1,
"Port": 8472}}
user@docker1:~$
```

Although we've successfully updated `etcd`, the Flannel services on each node will not act on this new configuration. This is because the Flannel service on each host only reads these variables when the service starts. In order for this change to take effect, we need to restart the Flannel service on each node:

```
user@docker4:~$ sudo systemctl restart flanneld
```

Make sure that you restart the Flannel service on each host. Hosts will not be able to communicate if some are using the VXLAN backend and others are using the UDP backend. Once restarted, we can check our Docker host's interfaces once again:

```
user@docker4:~$ ip addr show
…<Additional output removed for brevity>…
11: flannel.1: <BROADCAST,MULTICAST,UP,LOWER_UP> mtu 1450 qdisc noqueue
state UNKNOWN group default
    link/ether 2e:28:e7:34:1a:ff brd ff:ff:ff:ff:ff:ff
    inet 10.100.15.0/16 scope global flannel.1
       valid_lft forever preferred_lft forever
    inet6 fe80::2c28:e7ff:fe34:1aff/64 scope link
       valid_lft forever preferred_lft forever
```

Here, we can see that the host now has a new interface named `flannel.1`. If we check the interface with `ethtool`, we can see that it is using the VXLAN driver:

```
user@docker4:~$ ethtool -i flannel.1
driver: vxlan
version: 0.1
firmware-version:
bus-info:
supports-statistics: no
supports-test: no
supports-eeprom-access: no
supports-register-dump: no
supports-priv-flags: no
user@docker4:~$
```

And we should still be able to access the services using the Flannel IP addresses:

```
user@docker4:~$ docker exec -it web2 curl http://10.100.93.2
<body>
  <html>
    <h1><span style="color:#FF0000;font-size:72px;">Web Server #1 -
Running on port 80</span>
    </h1>
</body>
  </html>
user@docker4:~$
```

 If you were to specify a different VNI, the Flannel interface would be defined as `flannel.<VNI number>`.

It is important to know that Flannel does not take care of cleaning up artifacts from older configurations. For instance, if you change the VXLAN ID in `etcd` and restart the Flannel service, you will end up with two interfaces on the same network. You'll want to manually delete the old interface that was named using the old VNI. In addition, if you change the subnet allocated to Flannel, you'll want to restart the Docker service after you restart the Flannel service. Recall that Docker reads configuration variables from Flannel when the Docker service loads. If those change you'll need to reload the configuration for them to take effect.

Using the host gateway backend

As we've seen already, Flannel supports two types of overlay network. Using either UDP or VXLAN encapsulation, Flannel can build an overlay network between Docker hosts. The obvious advantage to this is that you can provision networks across disparate Docker nodes without having to touch the physical underlay network. However, some types of overlay networks also introduce a significant performance penalty, especially for processes that perform encapsulation in user space. Host gateway mode aims to solve that problem by not using an overlay network. This, however, comes with its own limitations. In this recipe, we'll review what host gateway mode can provide as well as show how to configure it.

In this recipe, we'll be slightly modifying the lab we've been using up until this point. The lab topology will look like this:

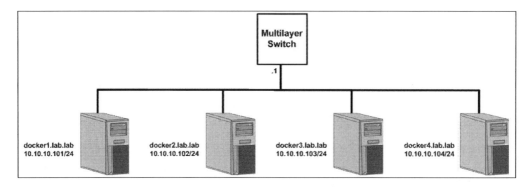

In this case, the hosts `docker3` and `docker4` now have IP addresses on the same subnet as `docker1` and `docker2`. That is, all of the hosts are now layer 2 adjacent to each other and can talk directly without the need to route through a gateway. Once you have your hosts reconfigured in this topology, we'll want to wipe the Flannel configuration. To do that, perform these steps:

- On the host running the `etcd` service:

```
sudo systemctl stop etcd
sudo rm -rf /var/lib/etcd/default
sudo systemctl start etcd
```

- On all of the hosts running the Flannel service:

```
sudo systemctl stop flanneld
sudo ip link delete flannel.1
sudo systemctl --no-block start flanneld
```

You'll note that we passed the `systemctl` command with the `--no-block` parameter when we started `flanneld`. Since we deleted the Flannel configuration from `etcd`, the Flannel service is searching for configuration to use for initialization. Due to the way the service is defined (as type notify), passing this parameter is required to prevent the command from hanging on the CLI.

How to do it...

At this point, your Flannel nodes will be searching for their configuration. Since we deleted the `etcd` data store, the key that tells the Flannel nodes how to configure the service is currently missing, and the Flannel service will continue to poll the `etcd` host until we make the appropriate configuration. We can verify this by checking the logs on one of the hosts:

```
user@docker4:~$ journalctl -f -u flanneld
-- Logs begin at Wed 2016-10-12 12:39:35 CDT. -
Oct 12 12:39:36 docker4 flanneld[873]: I1012 12:39:36.843784 00873
manager.go:163] Using 10.10.10.104 as external interface
Oct 12 12:39:36 docker4 flanneld[873]: I1012 12:39:36.844160 00873
manager.go:164] Using 10.10.10.104 as external endpoint
Oct 12 12:41:22 docker4 flanneld[873]: E1012 12:41:22.102872 00873
network.go:106] failed to retrieve network config: 100: Key not found (/
coreos.com) [4]
Oct 12 12:41:23 docker4 flanneld[873]: E1012 12:41:23.104904 00873
network.go:106] failed to retrieve network config: 100: Key not found (/
coreos.com) [4]
```

It's important to note that at this point Flannel has already decided what its external endpoint IP address will be by seeing which interface supports the default route for the host:

```
user@docker4:~$ ip route
default via 10.10.10.1 dev eth0
10.10.10.0/24 dev eth0  proto kernel  scope link  src 10.10.10.104
user@docker4:~$
```

Since that happens to be `eth0`, Flannel picks that interface's IP address as its external address. To configure host gateway mode, we can put the following configuration into `etcd`:

```
{
    "Network":"10.100.0.0/16",
    "Backend":{
        "Type":"host-gw"
    }
}
```

As we've seen before, we still specify a network. The only difference is that we supply a `type` of `host-gw`. The command to insert this into `etcd` looks like this:

```
user@docker1:~$ etcdctl set /coreos.com/network/config \
'{"Network":"10.100.0.0/16", "Backend": {"Type": "host-gw"}}'
```

After we insert this configuration, the Flannel nodes should all pick up the new configuration. Let's examine the service logs for Flannel on the host `docker4` to verify this:

```
user@docker4:~$ journalctl -r -u flanneld
-- Logs begin at Wed 2016-10-12 12:39:35 CDT, end at Wed 2016-10-12
12:55:38 CDT. --
Oct 12 12:55:06 docker4 flanneld[873]: I1012 12:55:06.797289 00873
network.go:83] Subnet added: 10.100.23.0/24 via 10.10.10.103
Oct 12 12:55:06 docker4 flanneld[873]: I1012 12:55:06.796982 00873
network.go:83] Subnet added: 10.100.20.0/24 via 10.10.10.101
Oct 12 12:55:06 docker4 flanneld[873]: I1012 12:55:06.796468 00873
network.go:83] Subnet added: 10.100.43.0/24 via 10.10.10.102
Oct 12 12:55:06 docker4 flanneld[873]: I1012 12:55:06.785464 00873
network.go:51] Watching for new subnet leases
Oct 12 12:55:06 docker4 flanneld[873]: I1012 12:55:06.784436 00873
manager.go:246] Lease acquired: 10.100.3.0/24
Oct 12 12:55:06 docker4 flanneld[873]: I1012 12:55:06.779349 00873 local_
manager.go:179] Picking subnet in range 10.100.1.0 ... 10.100.255.0
```

> The `journalctl` command is useful for seeing all the logs related to a service being managed by `systemd`. In the preceding example, we passed the `-r` parameter to show the logs in reverse order (the most current on top). We also passed the `-u` parameter to specify which service we want to see the logs for.

The oldest log entry we see is this host's Flannel service picking and registering a scope within the `10.100.0.0/16` subnet. This works in the same manner as it did with both the UDP and the VXLAN backend. The next three log entries show Flannel detecting the registrations of the other three Flannel nodes scopes. Since `etcd` is tracking each Flannel node's external IP address, as well as their registered scope, all of the Flannel hosts now know what external IP address can be used to reach each registered Flannel scope. In overlay mode (UDP or VXLAN), this external IP address was used as the destination for encapsulated traffic. In host gateway mode, this external IP address is used as route destination. If we inspect the routing table, we can see a route entry for each host:

```
user@docker4:~$ ip route
default via 10.10.10.1 dev eth0 onlink
10.10.10.0/24 dev eth0  proto kernel  scope link  src 10.10.10.104
10.100.20.0/24 via 10.10.10.101 dev eth0
10.100.23.0/24 via 10.10.10.103 dev eth0
10.100.43.0/24 via 10.10.10.102 dev eth0
user@docker4:~$
```

In this configuration, Flannel simply relies on basic routing to provide reachability to all the Flannel registered scopes. In this case, the host `docker4` has routes to all the other Docker hosts in order to reach their Flannel network scope:

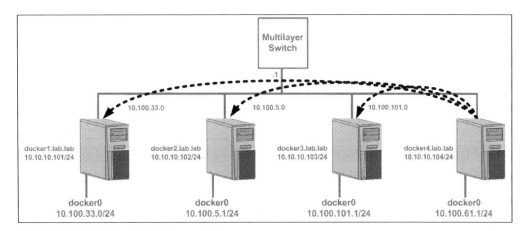

Not only is this far less complex than dealing with overlay networks, but it can also be much more performant than requiring each host to do encapsulation for the overlay network. The downside of this approach is that each host needs to have an interface on the same network in order for this to work. If the hosts are not on the same network, Flannel cannot add these routes because it would require the upstream network device (the host's default gateway) to also have routing information about how to reach the remote host. And while the Flannel node can point a static route at its default gateway, the physical network has no knowledge of the `10.100.0.0/16` network and will fail to deliver the traffic. The net effect is that host gateway mode limits the location of where you can place Flannel-enabled Docker hosts.

Finally, it's important to point out that Flannel may have changed state after the Docker service was already running. If that's the case, you'll want to restart Docker to make sure that it picks up the new variables from Flannel. If you rebooted your hosts when you reconfigured their network interfaces, you probably just need to start the Docker service. The service likely failed to load when the system booted because of the lack of Flannel configuration information which should now be present.

 Flannel also has backends for various cloud providers such as GCE and AWS. You can view their documentation to find more specific information about those backend types.

Specifying Flannel options

In addition to configuring different backend types you can also specify other options both through etcd as well as through the Flannel client itself. These options allow you to limit the IP allocation scopes as well as specify a specific interface to use as a Flannel node's external IP endpoint. In this recipe, we'll review the additional configuration options available to you both locally and globally.

Getting ready

We will keep building off the lab in the previous chapter where we configured the host gateway backend. However, the lab topology is going to revert to the previous configuration with Docker hosts docker3 and docker4 being in the 192.168.50.0/24 subnet:

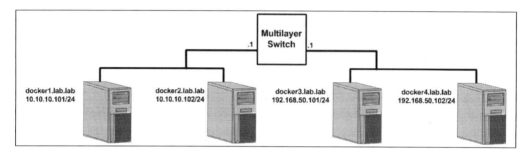

Once you have your hosts configured in this topology, we'll want to wipe out the Flannel configuration. To do that, perform these steps:

- On the host running the etcd service:

```
sudo systemctl stop etcd
sudo rm -rf /var/lib/etcd/default
sudo systemctl start etcd
```

- On all the hosts running the Flannel service:

```
sudo systemctl stop flanneld
sudo ip link delete flannel.1
sudo systemctl --no-block start flanneld
```

In some cases, the changes we make may require you to have root-level access to the system.

How to do it...

The previous recipes showed several examples of how to specify an overall Flannel network or global scope as well change the backend network type. We also saw some backend network types allowed for additional configuration options. In addition to the options we've seen, we can also configure other parameters globally that dictate how Flannel works overall. There are three other main parameters that can influence the scopes assigned to the Flannel nodes:

- `SubnetLen`: This parameter is specified in the form of an integer and dictates the size of the scope assigned to each node. As we've seen, this defaults to a `/24`

- `SubnetMin`: This parameter is specified in the form of a string and dictates the beginning IP range in which the scope allocations should begin

- `SubnetMax`: This parameter is specified in the form of a string and dictates the end of the IP range at which the subnet allocation should end

Using these options in combination with the `Network` flag gives us quite a bit of flexibility when we assign networks. For instance, let's use this configuration:

```
{
    "Network":"10.100.0.0/16",
    "SubnetLen":25,
    "SubnetMin":"10.100.0.0",
    "SubnetMax":"10.100.1.0",
    "Backend":{
        "Type":"host-gw"
    }
}
```

This defines that each Flannel node should get a scope allocation of a `/25`, the first subnet should start at `10.100.0.0`, and the last subnet should end at `10.100.1.0`. You might have noticed that, in this case, we only have space for three subnets within that allocation:

- `10.100.0.0/25`
- `10.100.0.128./25`
- `10.100.1.0/25`

This was done intentionally to show what happens when Flannel runs out of space in the global scope. Let's now put this configuration in `etcd` using this command:

```
user@docker1:~$ etcdctl set /coreos.com/network/config \
 '{"Network":"10.100.0.0/16","SubnetLen": 25, "SubnetMin": "10.100.0.0",
"SubnetMax": "10.100.1.0", "Backend": {"Type": "host-gw"}}'
```

Once in place, you should see that the majority of the hosts receive local scope allocations. However, if we check our hosts, we'll see that one has failed to receive an allocation. In my case, that's the host `docker4`. We can see this within the Flannel services logs:

```
user@docker4:~$ journalctl -r -u flanneld
-- Logs begin at Wed 2016-10-12 12:39:35 CDT, end at Wed 2016-10-12
13:17:42 CDT. --
Oct 12 13:17:42 docker4 flanneld[1422]: E1012 13:17:42.650086 01422
network.go:106] failed to register network: failed to acquire lease: out
of subnets
Oct 12 13:17:42 docker4 flanneld[1422]: I1012 13:17:42.649604 01422
local_manager.go:179] Picking subnet in range 10.100.0.0 ... 10.100.1.0
```

Since we only allowed space for three allocations in the global scope, the fourth host is unable to receive a local scope and will continue to request one until one becomes available. This could be remedied by updating the `SubnetMax` parameter to `10.100.1.128` and restarting the Flannel service on the host that failed to receive a local scope allocation.

As I mentioned, there are also configuration parameters that we can pass to the Flannel service on each host.

 The Flannel client supports a variety of parameters, all of which can be viewed by running `flanneld --help`. These cover new and upcoming features as well as configurations related to SSL-based communication, which will be important to review when running these types of services on infrastructure you don't control.

From a network perspective, perhaps the most valuable configuration option would be the `--iface` parameter, which allows you to specify which host interface you wish to use as Flannel's external endpoint. To view the importance of this, let's look at a quick example of our multihost lab topology:

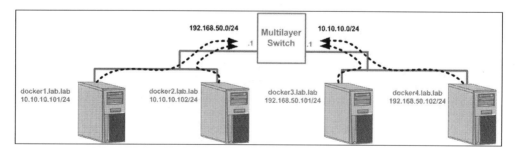

If you recall, in host gateway mode Flannel requires that all the Flannel nodes be layer 2 adjacent or on the same network. In this case, there are two hosts on the `10.10.10.0/24` network on the left and two hosts on the `192.168.50.0/24` network on the right. In order to talk to each other, they need to route through the multilayer switch. A scenario like this typically calls for an overlay backend mode that would tunnel the container traffic across the multilayer switch. However, if host gateway mode is a requirement for performance or other reasons, you might still be able to use it if you can provide additional interfaces to your hosts. For instance, imagine that these hosts were really virtual machines, and it was relatively easy for us to provision another interface on each host, call it `eth1`:

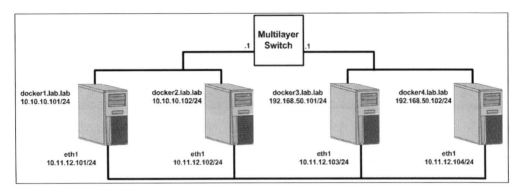

This interface could be dedicated to Flannel traffic allowing each host to still be layer 2 adjacent for the sake of Flannel traffic while still maintaining their existing default route through `eth0`. However, just provisioning the interface is not enough. Recall that Flannel by default picks its external endpoint interface by referencing the default route of the host. Since the default route is unchanged in this model, Flannel will be unable to add the appropriate routes:

```
user@docker4:~$ journalctl -ru flanneld
-- Logs begin at Wed 2016-10-12 14:24:51 CDT, end at Wed 2016-10-12
14:31:14 CDT. --
Oct 12 14:31:14 docker4 flanneld[1491]: E1012 14:31:14.463106 01491
network.go:116] Error adding route to 10.100.1.128/25 via 10.10.10.102:
network is unreachable
Oct 12 14:31:14 docker4 flanneld[1491]: I1012 14:31:14.462801 01491
network.go:83] Subnet added: 10.100.1.128/25 via 10.10.10.102
Oct 12 14:31:14 docker4 flanneld[1491]: E1012 14:31:14.462589 01491
network.go:116] Error adding route to 10.100.0.128/25 via 10.10.10.101:
network is unreachable
Oct 12 14:31:14 docker4 flanneld[1491]: I1012 14:31:14.462008 01491
network.go:83] Subnet added: 10.100.0.128/25 via 10.10.10.101
```

Since Flannel is still using the `eth0` interface as its external endpoint IP address, it knows that the hosts on the other subnet aren't directly reachable. We can fix this by telling Flannel to use the `eth1` interface by passing the `--iface` option to the Flannel service.

For instance, we can change the Flannel configuration by updating the Flannel service definition (`/lib/systemd/system/flanneld.service`) to look like this:

```
[Unit]
Description=Flannel Network Fabric
Documentation=https://github.com/coreos/flannel
Before=docker.service
After=etcd.service

[Service]
Environment= 'DAEMON_ARGS=--etcd-endpoints=http://10.10.10.101:2379
--iface=eth1'
Type=notify
ExecStart=/usr/bin/flanneld $DAEMON_ARGS
Restart=always
RestartSec=10s
LimitNOFILE=65536

[Install]
WantedBy=multi-user.target
```

With this configuration, Flannel will use the `eth1` interface for its external endpoint, allowing all the hosts to communicate directly across the `10.11.12.0/24` network. You can then load the new configuration by reloading the `systemd` configuration and restarting the service on all hosts:

```
sudo systemctl daemon-reload
sudo systemctl restart flanneld
```

Keep in mind that Flannel uses the external endpoint IP address to keep track of Flannel nodes. Changing this means that Flannel will allocate a new scope to each Flannel node. It's best to configure these options before joining a Flannel node. In our case, since `etcd` is already configured, we'll want to once again delete the existing `etcd` configuration and reconfigure it in order for the scope to become available:

```
user@docker1:~$ sudo systemctl stop etcd
user@docker1:~$ sudo rm -rf /var/lib/etcd/default
user@docker1:~$ sudo systemctl start etcd
```

```
user@docker1:~$ etcdctl set /coreos.com/network/config \
 '{"Network":"10.100.0.0/16","SubnetLen": 25, "SubnetMin": "10.100.0.0",
"SubnetMax": "10.100.1.128", "Backend": {"Type": "host-gw"}}'
```

If you check a host, you should now see that it has three Flannel routes—one for each assigned scope of the other three hosts:

```
user@docker1:~$ ip route
default via 10.10.10.1 dev eth0 onlink
10.10.10.0/24 dev eth0   proto kernel   scope link src 10.10.10.101
10.11.12.0/24 dev eth1   proto kernel   scope link src 10.11.12.101
10.100.0.0/25 via 10.11.12.102 dev eth1
10.100.1.0/25 via 10.11.12.104 dev eth1
10.100.1.128/25 via 10.11.12.103 dev eth1
10.100.0.128/25 dev docker0   proto kernel   scope link src 10.100.75.1
user@docker1:~$
```

In addition, if you'll be using Flannel through NAT, you might also want to look at the `--public-ip` option, which allows you to define a node's public IP address. This is particularly relevant in cloud environments where the server's real IP address may be hidden behind NAT.

9
Exploring Network Features

In this chapter, we will cover the following recipes:

- Working with prerelease versions of Docker
- Understanding MacVLAN interfaces
- Working with the Docker MacVLAN network driver
- Understanding IPVLAN interfaces
- Working with the Docker IPVLAN network driver
- Tagging VLAN IDs with MacVLAN and IPVLAN networks

Introduction

Although many of the features we've discussed in earlier chapters have been here since day one, many have been very recently introduced. Docker is a rapidly evolving piece of open source software with many contributors. To manage the introduction, testing, and potential release of features, Docker releases code in a couple of different ways. In this chapter, we'll show how you can explore features that are not yet in the production or release version of the software. As part of this, we'll review two of the newer networking features that have been introduced to Docker. One of which, MacVLAN, was recently merged into the release version of the software as of version 1.12. The second, IPVLAN, is still in the prerelease software channel. After we review how to consume the Docker prerelease software channels, we'll discuss the basic operation of both MacVLAN and IPVLAN network interfaces and then discuss how they are implemented as drivers in Docker.

Working with prerelease versions of Docker

Docker offers two different channels in which you can preview unreleased code. This gives users a chance to review features that are both slated for release as well as features that are entirely experimental and may never make it into an actual release version. Reviewing these features and providing feedback on them is an important piece of open source software development. Docker takes the feedback it receives seriously and lots of great ideas that have been tested in these channels make it into the production code release. In this recipe, we'll review how to install both the test and the experimental Docker releases.

Getting ready

In this recipe, we'll be using a freshly installed Ubuntu 16.04 host. Although not a requirement, it is recommended that you install prerelease versions of Docker on a host that does not currently have Docker installed. If the installer script detects Docker is already installed, it will warn you not to install the experimental or test code. That being said, I recommend that testing of software from these channels occurs on dedicated development servers. In many cases, virtual machines are used for this purpose. If you use a virtual machine, I recommend you to install your base operating system and then snapshot the VM to give yourself a restore point. If something goes wrong with the installation, you can always revert to this snapshot to start from a known good system.

As Docker calls out in their documentation:

> *Experimental features are not ready for production. They are provided for test and evaluation in your sandbox environments.*

Please keep this in mind when using either of the nonproduction trains of code. It is strongly encouraged that you provide feedback on GitHub on any and all features present in either channel.

How to do it...

As mentioned, there are two different prerelease software channels available to end users.

- `https://experimental.docker.com/`: This is the URL for the script to download and install the experimental version of Docker. This version includes features that are entirely experimental. Many of these futures may at some later point be integrated into a production release. However, many will not and are in this channel solely for experimentation.

- `https://test.docker.com/`: This is the URL for the script to download and install the test version of Docker. Docker also refers to this as the **Release Candidate (RC)** version of code. This is code has features that are slated to be released but have not yet been integrated into the production or release version of Docker.

To install either version, you simply download the script from the URL and pass it to the shell. For instance:

- To install the experimental release, run this command:

```
curl -sSL https://experimental.docker.com/ | sh
```

- To install the test or release candidate, release run this command:

```
curl -sSL https://test.docker.com/ | sh
```

 As a point of interest, you can also use a similar configuration to download the production version of Docker. In addition to `https://test.docker.com/` and `https://experimental.docker.com/`, there is also `https://get.docker.com/` that will install the production release of the software.

As mentioned, the use of these scripts should be done on machines that do not currently have Docker installed. After installation, you can verify the appropriate release was installed by examining the output of `docker info`. For example, when installing the experimental release, you can see the experimental flag set in the output:

```
user@docker-test:~$ sudo docker info
Containers: 0
 Running: 0
 Paused: 0
 Stopped: 0
Images: 0
Server Version: 1.12.2
...<Additional output removed for brevity>...
Experimental: true
Insecure Registries:
 127.0.0.0/8
user@docker-test:~$
```

In the test or RC version, you'll see similar output; however, there will not be an experimental variable listed in the output of Docker info:

```
user@docker-test:~$ sudo docker info
Containers: 0
 Running: 0
 Paused: 0
 Stopped: 0
Images: 0
Server Version: 1.12.2-rc3
...<Additional output removed for brevity>...
Insecure Registries:
 127.0.0.0/8
user@docker-test:~$
```

After installation via the script, you should find that Docker is installed and running just as if you had installed Docker through your operating systems default package manager. While the script should prompt you toward the end of the installation, it is advisable to add your user account to the Docker group. This prevents you from having to escalate your privileges with sudo to use the Docker CLI commands. To add your user account to the Docker group, use this command:

```
user@docker-test:~$ sudo usermod -aG docker <your username>
```

Make sure that you log off and back in for the setting to take effect.

Keep in mind that these scripts can also be used to update to latest version of either channel. In those scenarios, the script will still prompt you about the possibility of installing over an existing Docker installation, but it will provide verbiage to indicate that you can ignore the message:

```
user@docker-test:~$ curl -sSL https://test.docker.com/ | sh
Warning: the "docker" command appears to already exist on this system.

If you already have Docker installed, this script can cause trouble,
which is why we're displaying this warning and provide the opportunity to
cancel the installation.

If you installed the current Docker package using this script and are
using it again to update Docker, you can safely ignore this message.

You may press Ctrl+C now to abort this script.
+ sleep 20
```

Although this is not the only way to get the test and experimental code, it is certainly the easiest. You may also download the prebuilt binaries or build the binary yourself. Information on how to do both is available on Docker's GitHub page at `https://github.com/docker/docker/tree/master/experimental`.

Understanding MacVLAN interfaces

The first feature we'll be looking at is MacVLAN. In this recipe, we'll be implementing MacVLAN outside of Docker to gain a better understanding of how it works. Understanding how MacVLAN works outside of Docker will be critical in understanding how Docker consumes MacVLAN. In the next recipe, we'll walk through the Docker network driver implementation of MacVLAN.

Getting ready

In this recipe, we'll be using two Linux hosts (`net1` and `net2`) to demonstrate MacVLAN functionality. Our lab topology will look as follows:

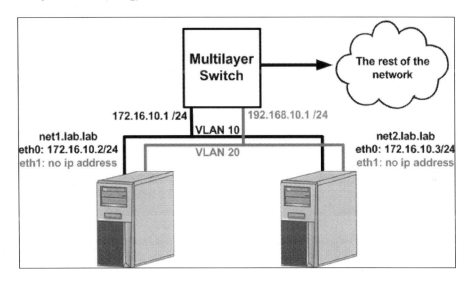

It is assumed that the hosts are in a base configuration and each host has two network interfaces. The `eth0` interface will have a static IP address defined and serve as each hosts default gateway. The `eth1` interface will be configured with no IP address. For reference, you can find the network configuration file (`/etc/network/interfaces`) for each host following:

- `net1.lab.lab`

```
auto eth0
```

```
iface eth0 inet static
        address 172.16.10.2
        netmask 255.255.255.0
        gateway 172.16.10.1
        dns-nameservers 10.20.30.13
        dns-search lab.lab


auto eth1
iface eth1 inet manual
```

- net2.lab.lab

```
auto eth0
iface eth0 inet static
        address 172.16.10.3
        netmask 255.255.255.0
        gateway 172.16.10.1
        dns-nameservers 10.20.30.13
        dns-search lab.lab


auto eth1
iface eth1 inet manual
```

 While we'll cover all of the steps needed to create the topology in this recipe, you may wish to refer to *Chapter 1, Linux Networking Constructs*, if some of the steps aren't clear. *Chapter 1, Linux Networking Constructs*, covers the base Linux networking constructs and the CLI tools in much greater depth.

How to do it...

MacVLAN represents an entirely different way to configure interfaces from what we've seen up until this point. Earlier Linux networking configurations we examined relied on constructs that loosely mimicked physical network constructs. MacVLAN interfaces are logical in nature and are bound to an existing network interface. The interface supporting the MacVLAN interfaces is referred to as the **parent** interface and can support one or more MacVLAN logical interfaces. Let's look at a quick example of configuring a MacVLAN interface on one of our lab hosts.

Configuring MacVLAN type interfaces is done in a very similar manner to all other types on Linux network interfaces. Using the `ip` command-line tool, we can use the `link` subcommand to define the interface:

```
user@net1:~$ sudo ip link add macvlan1 link eth0 type macvlan
```

This syntax should be familiar to you from the first chapter of the book where we defined multiple different interface types. Once created, the next step is to configure it with an IP address. This is also done through the `ip` command:

```
user@net1:~$ sudo ip address add 172.16.10.5/24 dev macvlan1
```

And finally, we need to make sure that bring the interface up.

```
user@net1:~$ sudo ip link set dev macvlan1 up
```

The interface is now up and we can examine the configuration with the `ip addr show` command:

```
user@net1:~$ ip addr show
1: …<loopback interface configuration removed for brevity>…
2: eth0: <BROADCAST,MULTICAST,UP,LOWER_UP> mtu 1500 qdisc pfifo_fast
state UP group default qlen 1000
    link/ether 00:0c:29:2d:dd:79 brd ff:ff:ff:ff:ff:ff
    inet 172.16.10.2/24 brd 172.16.10.255 scope global eth0
      valid_lft forever preferred_lft forever
    inet6 fe80::20c:29ff:fe2d:dd79/64 scope link
      valid_lft forever preferred_lft forever
3: eth1: <BROADCAST,MULTICAST,UP,LOWER_UP> mtu 1500 qdisc pfifo_fast
state UP group default qlen 1000
    link/ether 00:0c:29:2d:dd:83 brd ff:ff:ff:ff:ff:ff
    inet6 fe80::20c:29ff:fe2d:dd83/64 scope link
      valid_lft forever preferred_lft forever
4: macvlan1@eth0: <BROADCAST,MULTICAST,UP,LOWER_UP> mtu 1500 qdisc
noqueue state UNKNOWN group default
    link/ether da:aa:c0:18:55:4a brd ff:ff:ff:ff:ff:ff
    inet 172.16.10.5/24 scope global macvlan1
      valid_lft forever preferred_lft forever
    inet6 fe80::d8aa:c0ff:fe18:554a/64 scope link
      valid_lft forever preferred_lft forever
user@net1:~$
```

There are a couple of interesting items to point out now that we have the interface configured. First, the name of the MacVLAN interface makes it easy to identify the interfaces parent interface. Recall that we mentioned that each MacVLAN interface had to be associated with a parent interface. In this case, we can tell that the parent of this MacVLAN interface is `eth0` by looking at the name listed after the `macvlan1@` in the MacVLAN interface name. Second, the IP address assigned to the MacVLAN interfaces is in the same subnet as the parent interface (`eth0`). This is intentional to allow external connectivity. Let's define a second MacVLAN interface on the same parent interface to demonstrate what sort of connectivity is allowed:

```
user@net1:~$ sudo ip link add macvlan2 link eth0 type macvlan
user@net1:~$ sudo ip address add 172.16.10.6/24 dev macvlan2
user@net1:~$ sudo ip link set dev macvlan2 up
```

Our network topology is as follows:

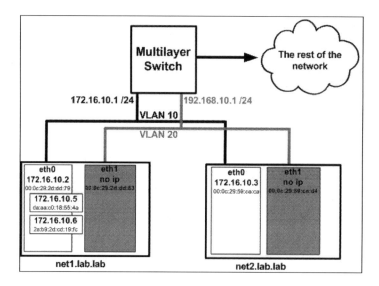

We have two MacVLAN interfaces bound to net1's `eth0` interface. If we try to reach either interface from an external subnet, the connectivity should work as expected:

```
user@test_server:~$ ip addr show dev eth0 |grep inet
     inet 10.20.30.13/24 brd 10.20.30.255 scope global eth0
user@test_server:~$ ping 172.16.10.5 -c 2
PING 172.16.10.5 (172.16.10.5) 56(84) bytes of data.
64 bytes from 172.16.10.5: icmp_seq=1 ttl=63 time=0.423 ms
```

```
64 bytes from 172.16.10.5: icmp_seq=2 ttl=63 time=0.458 ms
--- 172.16.10.5 ping statistics ---
2 packets transmitted, 2 received, 0% packet loss, time 1000ms
rtt min/avg/max/mdev = 0.423/0.440/0.458/0.027 ms
user@test_server:~$ ping 172.16.10.6 -c 2
PING 172.16.10.6 (172.16.10.6) 56(84) bytes of data.
64 bytes from 172.16.10.6: icmp_seq=1 ttl=63 time=0.510 ms
64 bytes from 172.16.10.6: icmp_seq=2 ttl=63 time=0.532 ms
--- 172.16.10.6 ping statistics ---
2 packets transmitted, 2 received, 0% packet loss, time 1000ms
rtt min/avg/max/mdev = 0.510/0.521/0.532/0.011 ms
```

In the preceding output, I attempted to reach both `172.16.10.5` and `172.16.10.6` from a test server that lives off subnet from the `net1` host. In both cases, we were able to reach the IP address of the MacVLAN interfaces implying that routing is working as expected. This is why, we gave the MacVLAN interfaces IP addresses within the existing subnet of the servers `eth0` interface. Since the multilayer switch knew that `172.16.10.0/24` lives out of VLAN 10, it simply has to issue an ARP request for the new IP addresses on VLAN 10 to get their MAC addresses. The Linux host already has a default route pointing back to the switch that allows the return traffic to reach the test server. However, this is by no means a requirement of MacVLAN interfaces. I could have easily chosen another IP subnet to use for the interfaces, but that would have prevented external routing from inherently working.

Another item to point out is that the parent interface does not need to have an IP address associated with it. For instance, let's extend the topology by building two more MacVLAN interfaces. One on the host `net1` and another on the host `net2`:

```
user@net1:~$ sudo ip link add macvlan3 link eth1 type macvlan
user@net1:~$ sudo ip address add 192.168.10.5/24 dev macvlan3
user@net1:~$ sudo ip link set dev macvlan3 up


user@net2:~$ sudo ip link add macvlan4 link eth1 type macvlan
user@net2:~$ sudo ip address add 192.168.10.6/24 dev macvlan4
user@net2:~$ sudo ip link set dev macvlan4 up
```

Our topology is as follows:

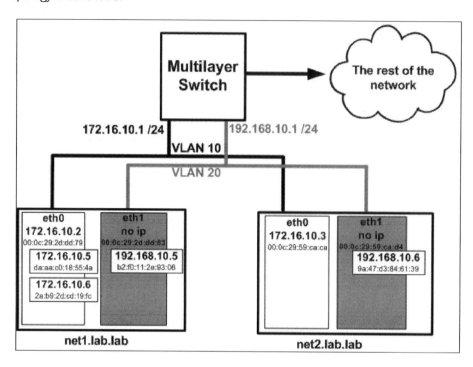

Despite not having an IP address defined on the physical interface, the hosts now see the `192.168.10.0/24` network as being defined and believe the network to be locally connected:

```
user@net1:~$ ip route
default via 172.16.10.1 dev eth0
172.16.10.0/24 dev eth0   proto kernel  scope link  src 172.16.10.2
172.16.10.0/24 dev macvlan1  proto kernel  scope link  src 172.16.10.5
172.16.10.0/24 dev macvlan2  proto kernel  scope link  src 172.16.10.6
192.168.10.0/24 dev macvlan3  proto kernel  scope link  src 192.168.10.5
user@net1:~$
```

This means that the two hosts can reach each other directly through their associated IP addresses on that subnet:

```
user@net1:~$ ping 192.168.10.6 -c 2
PING 192.168.10.6 (192.168.10.6) 56(84) bytes of data.
64 bytes from 192.168.10.6: icmp_seq=1 ttl=64 time=0.405 ms
64 bytes from 192.168.10.6: icmp_seq=2 ttl=64 time=0.432 ms
```

```
--- 192.168.10.6 ping statistics ---
2 packets transmitted, 2 received, 0% packet loss, time 1000ms
rtt min/avg/max/mdev = 0.405/0.418/0.432/0.024 ms
user@net1:~$
```

At this point, you might be wondering why you would use a MacVLAN interface type. From the looks of it, it's doesn't appear that much different than just creating logical subinterfaces. The real difference is in how the interface is built. Typically, subinterfaces all use the same MAC address of the parent interfaces. You might have noted in the earlier output and diagrams that the MacVLAN interfaces have different MAC addresses than their associated parent interface. We can validate this on the upstream multilayer switch (gateway) as well:

```
switch# show ip arp vlan 10
Protocol   Address          Age (min)   Hardware Addr   Type   Interface
Internet   172.16.10.6              8   a2b1.0cd4.4e73  ARPA   Vlan10
Internet   172.16.10.5              8   4e19.f07f.33e0  ARPA   Vlan10
Internet   172.16.10.2              0   000c.292d.dd79  ARPA   Vlan10
Internet   172.16.10.3             62   000c.2959.caca  ARPA   Vlan10
Internet   172.16.10.1              -   0021.d7c5.f245  ARPA   Vlan10
```

In testing, you might find that the Linux host is presenting the same MAC address for each IP address in your configuration. Depending on what operating system you are running, you may need to change the following kernel parameters in order to prevent the host from presenting the same MAC address:

```
echo 1 | sudo tee /proc/sys/net/ipv4/conf/all/arp_ignore
echo 2 | sudo tee /proc/sys/net/ipv4/conf/all/arp_
announce
echo 2 | sudo tee /proc/sys/net/ipv4/conf/all/rp_filter
```

Keep in mind that the applying these settings in this manner won't persist through a reboot.

Looking at the MAC addresses, we can see that the parent interface (`172.16.10.2`) and both MacVLAN interfaces (`172.16.10.5 and .6`) have different MAC addresses. MacVLAN allows you to present multiple interfaces using different MAC addresses. The net result is that you can have multiple IP interfaces, each with their own unique MAC address, that all use the same physical interface.

Since the parent interface is responsible for multiple MAC addresses it needs to be in promiscuous mode. The host should automatically put an interface into promiscuous mode when it's chosen as a parent interface. You can verify it by checking the ip link details:

```
user@net2:~$ ip -d link
```

```
...<output removed for brevity>...
2: eth1: <BROADCAST,MULTICAST,UP,LOWER_UP> mtu 1500 qdisc pfifo_fast
state UP mode DEFAULT group default qlen 1000
    link/ether 00:0c:29:59:ca:d4 brd ff:ff:ff:ff:ff:ff promiscuity 1
...<output removed for brevity>...
```

 If having the parent interface in promiscuous mode is a concern, you might be interested in the later recipes of this chapter where we discuss IPVLAN configurations.

As with other Linux interface types we've seen, MacVLAN interfaces are also namespace aware. This can lead to some interesting configuration options. Let's now look at deploying MacVLAN interfaces within unique network namespaces.

Let's start by deleting all of our existing MacVLAN interfaces:

```
user@net1:~$ sudo ip link del macvlan1
user@net1:~$ sudo ip link del macvlan2
user@net1:~$ sudo ip link del macvlan3
user@net2:~$ sudo ip link del macvlan4
```

Much like we did in *Chapter 1, Linux Networking Constructs*, we can create an interface and then move it into a namespace. We start by creating the namespace:

```
user@net1:~$ sudo ip netns add namespace1
```

Then, we create the MacVLAN interface:

```
user@net1:~$ sudo ip link add macvlan1 link eth0 type macvlan
```

Next, we move the interface into the newly created network namespace:

```
user@net1:~$ sudo ip link set macvlan1 netns namespace1
```

And finally, from within the namespace, we assign it an IP address and bring it up:

```
user@net1:~$ sudo ip netns exec namespace1 ip address \
add 172.16.10.5/24 dev macvlan1
user@net1:~$ sudo ip netns exec namespace1 ip link set \
dev macvlan1 up
```

Let's also create a second interface within a second namespace for testing purposes:

```
user@net1:~$ sudo ip netns add namespace2
user@net1:~$ sudo ip link add macvlan2 link eth0 type macvlan
user@net1:~$ sudo ip link set macvlan2 netns namespace2
```

```
user@net1:~$ sudo ip netns exec namespace2 ip address \
add 172.16.10.6/24 dev macvlan2
user@net1:~$ sudo ip netns exec namespace2 ip link set \
dev macvlan2 up
```

> As you play around with different configurations, it's common to create and delete the same interface a number of times. In doing so, you'll likely generate interfaces with the same IP address, but different MAC addresses. Since we're presenting these MAC address to the upstream physical network, always make sure that the upstream device or gateway has the most recent ARP entry for the IP you are trying to reach. It's common for many switches and routers to have long ARP timeout values during which they won't ARP for the newer MAC entry.

At this point, we have a topology that looks something like this:

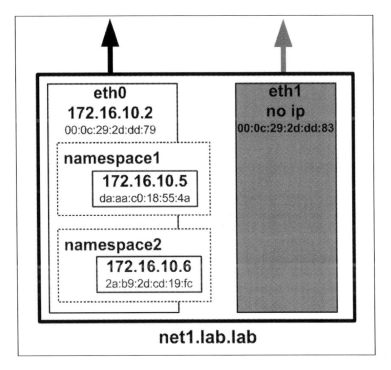

The parent interface (eth0) has an IP address as before, but this time, the MacVLAN interfaces live within their own unique namespaces. Despite being in separate namespaces, they still share the same parent since this was done before moving them into the namespace.

At this point, you should note that external hosts can no longer ping all of the IP addresses. Rather, you can only reach the etho IP address of 172.16.10.2. The reason for this is simple. As you'll recall, namespaces are comparable to a **Virtual Routing and Forwarding (VRF)** and have their own routing table. If you examine, the routing table of both of the namespaces, you'll see that neither of them have a default route:

```
user@net1:~$ sudo ip netns exec namespace1 ip route
172.16.10.0/24 dev macvlan1  proto kernel  scope link  src 172.16.10.5
user@net1:~$ sudo ip netns exec namespace2 ip route
172.16.10.0/24 dev macvlan2  proto kernel  scope link  src 172.16.10.6
user@net1:~$
```

In order for these interfaces to be reachable off network, we'll need to give each namespace a default route pointing to the gateway on that subnet (172.16.10.1). Again, this is the benefit of addressing the MacVLAN interfaces in the same subnet as the parent interface. The routing is already there on the physical network. Add the routes and test again:

```
user@net1:~$ sudo ip netns exec namespace1 ip route \
add 0.0.0.0/0 via 172.16.10.1
user@net1:~$ sudo ip netns exec namespace2 ip route \
add 0.0.0.0/0 via 172.16.10.1
```

From the external test host (some output removed for brevity):

```
user@test_server:~$ ping 172.16.10.2 -c 2
PING 172.16.10.2 (172.16.10.2) 56(84) bytes of data.
64 bytes from 172.16.10.2: icmp_seq=1 ttl=63 time=0.459 ms
64 bytes from 172.16.10.2: icmp_seq=2 ttl=63 time=0.441 ms
user@test_server:~$ ping 172.16.10.5 -c 2
PING 172.16.10.5 (172.16.10.5) 56(84) bytes of data.
64 bytes from 172.16.10.5: icmp_seq=1 ttl=63 time=0.521 ms
64 bytes from 172.16.10.5: icmp_seq=2 ttl=63 time=0.528 ms
user@test_server:~$ ping 172.16.10.6 -c 2
PING 172.16.10.6 (172.16.10.6) 56(84) bytes of data.
64 bytes from 172.16.10.6: icmp_seq=1 ttl=63 time=0.524 ms
64 bytes from 172.16.10.6: icmp_seq=2 ttl=63 time=0.551 ms
```

So while external connectivity appears to be working as expected, you'll note that none of the interfaces can talk to each other:

```
user@net1:~$ sudo ip netns exec namespace2 ping 172.16.10.5
PING 172.16.10.5 (172.16.10.5) 56(84) bytes of data.
```

```
--- 172.16.10.5 ping statistics ---
5 packets transmitted, 0 received, 100% packet loss, time 0ms
user@net1:~$ sudo ip netns exec namespace2 ping 172.16.10.2
PING 172.16.10.2 (172.16.10.2) 56(84) bytes of data.
--- 172.16.10.2 ping statistics ---
5 packets transmitted, 0 received, 100% packet loss, time 0ms
user@net1:~$
```

This seems odd because they all share the same parent interface. The problem is in how the MacVLAN interfaces were configured. The MacVLAN interface type supports four different modes:

- **VEPA**: The **Virtual Ethernet Port Aggregator (VEPA)** mode forces all traffic sourced from the MacVLAN interfaces out of the parent interface regardless of destination. Even traffic destined to another MacVLAN interface sharing the same parent interface is subject to this policy. In a layer 2 scenario, the communication between two MacVLAN interfaces would likely be blocked because of standard spanning tree rules. You could potentially route between the two on an upstream router.

- **Bridge**: The MacVLAN bridge mode mimics a standard Linux bridge. Communication between two MacVLAN interfaces on the same parent interface is allowed to occur directly without transiting the parent interface off the host. This is useful for scenarios where you expect a high level of interface to interface communication across the same parent interface.

- **Private**: This mode resembles VEPA mode with the added capability of entirely blocking communication between interfaces on the same parent interface. Even if you allow the traffic to transit the parent and then hairpin back into the host, the communication will be dropped.

- **Passthru**: Intended as a means to directly tie the parent interface to the MacVLAN interface. In this mode, only a single MacVLAN interface per parent is allowed and the MacVLAN interface inherits the MAC address from the parent.

While not easy to discern without knowing where to look, our MacVLAN interfaces happen to be of type VEPA, which happens to be the default. We can see this by passing the details (-d) flag to the `ip` command:

```
user@net1:~$ sudo ip netns exec namespace1 ip -d link show
1: lo: <LOOPBACK> mtu 65536 qdisc noop state DOWN mode DEFAULT group
default
    link/loopback 00:00:00:00:00:00 brd 00:00:00:00:00:00 promiscuity 0
20: macvlan1@if2: <BROADCAST,MULTICAST,UP,LOWER_UP> mtu 1500 qdisc
noqueue state UNKNOWN mode DEFAULT group default
    link/ether 36:90:37:f6:08:cc brd ff:ff:ff:ff:ff:ff promiscuity 0
```

```
        macvlan   mode vepa
user@net1:~$
```

In our case, the VEPA mode is what's preventing the two namespace interfaces from talking directly to each other. More commonly, MacVLAN interfaces are defined as type `bridge` to allowed communication between interfaces on the same parent. However, even in this mode, the child interfaces are not allowed to communicate directly with the IP address assigned directly to the parent interface (in this case `172.16.10.2`). This should be a separate paragraph.

```
user@net1:~$ sudo ip netns del namespace1
user@net1:~$ sudo ip netns del namespace2
```

Now we can recreate both interfaces specifying the `bridge` mode for each MacVLAN interface:

```
user@net1:~$ sudo ip netns add namespace1
user@net1:~$ sudo ip link add macvlan1 link eth0 type \
macvlan mode bridge
user@net1:~$ sudo ip link set macvlan1 netns namespace1
user@net1:~$ sudo ip netns exec namespace1 ip address \
add 172.16.10.5/24 dev macvlan1
user@net1:~$ sudo ip netns exec namespace1 ip link set \
dev macvlan1 up


user@net1:~$ sudo ip netns add namespace2
user@net1:~$ sudo ip link add macvlan2 link eth0 type \
macvlan mode bridge
user@net1:~$ sudo ip link set macvlan2 netns namespace2
user@net1:~$ sudo ip netns exec namespace2 sudo ip address \
add 172.16.10.6/24 dev macvlan2
user@net1:~$ sudo ip netns exec namespace2 ip link set \
dev macvlan2 up
```

After specifying the `bridge` mode, we can verify that the two interfaces can directly to one another:

```
user@net1:~$ sudo ip netns exec namespace1 ping 172.16.10.6 -c 2
PING 172.16.10.6 (172.16.10.6) 56(84) bytes of data.
64 bytes from 172.16.10.6: icmp_seq=1 ttl=64 time=0.041 ms
```

```
64 bytes from 172.16.10.6: icmp_seq=2 ttl=64 time=0.030 ms
--- 172.16.10.6 ping statistics ---
2 packets transmitted, 2 received, 0% packet loss, time 999ms
rtt min/avg/max/mdev = 0.030/0.035/0.041/0.008 ms
user@net1:~$
```

However, we also note that we still cannot reach the hosts IP address defined on the parent interface (eth0):

```
user@net1:~$ sudo ip netns exec namespace1 ping 172.16.10.2 -c 2
PING 172.16.10.2 (172.16.10.2) 56(84) bytes of data.
--- 172.16.10.2 ping statistics ---
2 packets transmitted, 0 received, 100% packet loss, time 1008ms
user@net1:~$
```

Working with the Docker MacVLAN network driver

When I began writing this book, the current version of Docker was 1.10 and at that time MacVLAN functionality was included in the release candidate version of Docker. Since then, version 1.12 has been released, which pushed MacVLAN into the release version of the software. That being said, the only requirement to use the MacVLAN driver is to ensure that you have a 1.12 or newer version of Docker installed. In this chapter, we'll review how to consume the MacVLAN network driver for containers provisioned from Docker.

Getting ready

In this recipe, we'll be using two Linux hosts running Docker. Our lab topology will consist of two Docker hosts that live on the same network. It will look like this:

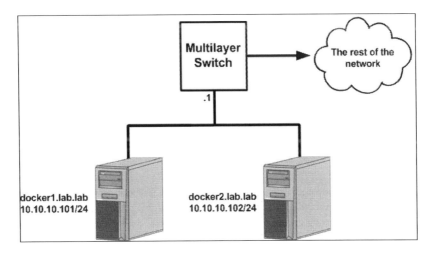

It is assumed that each host is running a version of Docker that is 1.12 or greater in order to have access to the MacVLAN driver. The hosts should have a single IP interface and Docker should be in its default configuration. In some cases, the changes we make may require you to have root-level access to the system.

How to do it...

Much like all of the other user-defined network types, the MacVLAN driver is handled through the `docker network` subcommand. Creating a MacVLAN type network is just as easy as creating any other network type, but there are a few things to keep in mind that are specific to this driver.

- You need to specify the upstream gateway when defining the network. Remember that MacVLAN interfaces are presented on the same interface of the parent. They'll need the host or interfaces upstream gateway to access external subnets.

- In other user-defined network types, Docker would generate a subnet for you to use if you decided not to specify one. While that is still the case with the MacVLAN driver, it will not function properly unless you specify the network in which your parent interface has access to. Like we saw in the last recipe, MacVLAN relies on the upstream network device knowing how to route the MacVLAN interfaces. This is accomplished by defining the MacVLAN interfaces for your containers on the same subnet as the parent interface. You may also chose to use a parent interface that does not have a defined IP address. In these cases, just make sure that the gateway you specify when defining the network in Docker is reachable out of the parent interface.

- As an option to the driver, you need to specify the interface that you wish to use as the parent interface for all containers attached with MacVLAN interfaces. If you do not specify a parent interface as an option, Docker will create a dummy network interface and use this as the parent interface. This will prevent any communication to outside networks from this network.

- The `--internal flag` is available when creating networks with the MacVLAN driver. When specified the parent interface is defined as a dummy interface, which prevents traffic from leaving the host.

- There is a one-to-one relationship with MacVLAN user-defined networks and parent interfaces. That is, you can only define one MacVLAN type network on a given parent interface.

- Some switch vendors limit the number of MAC addresses that can be learned per port. While this number is typically extremely high, make sure that you take this into consideration when using this network type.

- As with other user-defined network types, you can specify an IP range or a set of auxiliary addresses that you wish Docker's IPAM not to allocate to containers. In MacVLAN mode, these settings are much more significant because you are presenting containers directly onto the physical network.

Taking these points into consideration with our current lab topology, we can define the network as follows on each host:

```
user@docker1:~$ docker network create -d macvlan \
--subnet 10.10.10.0/24 --ip-range 10.10.10.0/25 \
--gateway=10.10.10.1 --aux-address docker1=10.10.10.101 \
--aux-address docker2=10.10.10.102 -o parent=eth0 macvlan_net


user@docker2:~$ docker network create -d macvlan \
--subnet 10.10.10.0/24 --ip-range 10.10.10.128/25 \
--gateway=10.10.10.1 --aux-address docker1=10.10.10.101 \
--aux-address docker2=10.10.10.102 -o parent=eth0 macvlan_net
```

With this configuration, each host on the network will use one half of the available defined subnet, which in this case is a /25. Since Dockers IPAM automatically reserves the gateway IP address for us, there's no need to prevent it from being allocated by defining it as an auxiliary address. However, since the Docker hosts interfaces themselves do live within this range, we do need to reserve those with auxiliary addresses.

We can now define containers on each host and verify that they can communicate with each other:

```
user@docker1:~$ docker run -d --name=web1 \
--net=macvlan_net jonlangemak/web_server_1
user@docker1:~$ docker exec web1 ip addr
1: lo: <LOOPBACK,UP,LOWER_UP> mtu 65536 qdisc noqueue state UNKNOWN qlen 1
    link/loopback 00:00:00:00:00:00 brd 00:00:00:00:00:00
    inet 127.0.0.1/8 scope host lo
       valid_lft forever preferred_lft forever
    inet6 ::1/128 scope host
       valid_lft forever preferred_lft forever
7: eth0@if2: <BROADCAST,MULTICAST,UP,LOWER_UP> mtu 1500 qdisc noqueue state UNKNOWN
    link/ether 02:42:0a:0a:0a:02 brd ff:ff:ff:ff:ff:ff
    inet 10.10.10.2/24 scope global eth0
       valid_lft forever preferred_lft forever
    inet6 fe80::42:aff:fe0a:a02/64 scope link
       valid_lft forever preferred_lft forever
user@docker1:~$
```

```
user@docker2:~$ docker run -d --name=web2 \
--net=macvlan_net jonlangemak/web_server_2
user@docker2:~$ docker exec web2 ip addr
1: lo: <LOOPBACK,UP,LOWER_UP> mtu 65536 qdisc noqueue state UNKNOWN qlen
1
    link/loopback 00:00:00:00:00:00 brd 00:00:00:00:00:00
    inet 127.0.0.1/8 scope host lo
       valid_lft forever preferred_lft forever
    inet6 ::1/128 scope host
       valid_lft forever preferred_lft forever
4: eth0@if2: <BROADCAST,MULTICAST,UP,LOWER_UP> mtu 1500 qdisc noqueue
state UNKNOWN
    link/ether 02:42:0a:0a:0a:80 brd ff:ff:ff:ff:ff:ff
    inet 10.10.10.128/24 scope global eth0
       valid_lft forever preferred_lft forever
    inet6 fe80::42:aff:fe0a:a80/64 scope link
       valid_lft forever preferred_lft forever
user@docker2:~$
```

You'll note that there isn't a need to publish ports when the containers are run. Since the container has a uniquely routable IP address at this point, port publishing is not required. Any container can offer any service on its own unique IP address.

Much like other network types, Docker creates a network namespace for each container, which it then maps the containers MacVLAN interface into. Our topology at this point looks like this:

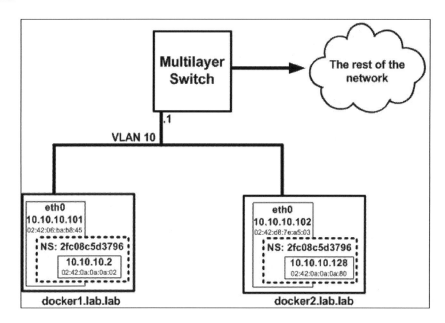

The namespace name can be found by inspecting the container itself or by linking the Docker `netns` directory, as we saw in earlier chapters, so the `ip netns` subcommand can query Docker-defined network namespaces.

From an external testing host that lives off subnet, we can verify that each containers services are reachable via the containers IP address:

```
user@test_server:~$ curl http://10.10.10.2
<body>
  <html>
    <h1><span style="color:#FF0000;font-size:72px;">Web Server #1 -
Running on port 80</span>
    </h1>
</body>
  </html>
user@test_server:~$ curl http://10.10.10.128
<body>
  <html>
    <h1><span style="color:#FF0000;font-size:72px;">Web Server #2 -
Running on port 80</span>
    </h1>
</body>
  </html>
[root@tools ~]#
```

However, you will note that containers attached to MacVLAN networks are not accessible from the local host despite being on the same interface:

```
user@docker1:~$ ping 10.10.10.2
PING 10.10.10.2 (10.10.10.2) 56(84) bytes of data.
From 10.10.10.101 icmp_seq=1 Destination Host Unreachable
--- 10.10.10.2 ping statistics ---
5 packets transmitted, 0 received, +1 errors, 100% packet loss, time 0ms
user@docker1:~$
```

The current implementation of Docker support MacVLAN only in the MacVLAN bridge mode. We can verify that this is the operating mode of the MacVLAN interfaces by checking the details of the interface within the container:

```
user@docker1:~$ docker exec web1 ip -d link show
```

```
1: lo: <LOOPBACK,UP,LOWER_UP> mtu 65536 qdisc noqueue state UNKNOWN
    link/loopback 00:00:00:00:00:00 brd 00:00:00:00:00:00
5: eth0@if2: <BROADCAST,MULTICAST,UP,LOWER_UP> mtu 1500 qdisc noqueue
state UNKNOWN
    link/ether 02:42:0a:0a:0a:02 brd ff:ff:ff:ff:ff:ff
    macvlan  mode bridge
user@docker1:~$
```

Understanding IPVLAN interfaces

An alternative to MacVLAN is IPVLAN. IPVLAN comes in two flavors. The first is L2 mode, which operates very similarly to MacVLAN with the exception of how MAC addresses are assigned. With IPVLAN mode, all logical IP interfaces use the same MAC address. This allows you to keep the parent NIC out of promiscuous mode and also prevents you from running into any possible NIC or switch port MAC limitations. The second mode is IPVLAN layer 3. In layer 3 mode, IPVLAN acts like a router and forwards unicast packets in and out of IPVLAN connected networks. In this recipe, we'll cover the basic IPVLAN networking construct to get an idea of how it works and how it can be implemented.

Getting ready

In this recipe, we'll be using the same Linux hosts (net1 and net2) from the *Understanding MacVLAN interfaces* recipe in this chapter. Please refer to *Understanding MacVLAN* recipe's *Getting ready* section for more information about the topology.

 Older versions of the iproute2 toolset did not include full support for IPVLAN. If the commands are not working for the IPVLAN configuration there's a good chance you're on an older version without support. You likely need to update in order to get a newer version that has full support. The older versions have some support for IPVLAN but lack the ability to define a mode (L2 or L3).

How to do it...

As mentioned, IPVLAN in L2 mode is almost identical to MacVLAN in terms of functionality. The major difference is in the fact that IPVLAN leverages the same MAC address for all IPVLAN interfaces attached to the same master. You'll recall that MacVLAN interfaces leveraged a different MAC address for each MacVLAN interface attached to the same parent.

We can create the same interfaces we did in MacVLAN recipe to show that the interface addresses are created with an identical MAC address:

```
user@net1:~$ sudo ip link add ipvlan1 link eth0  type ipvlan mode l2
```

```
user@net1:~$ sudo ip address add 172.16.10.5/24 dev ipvlan1
user@net1:~$ sudo ip link set dev ipvlan1 up


user@net1:~$ sudo ip link add ipvlan2 link eth0 type ipvlan mode l2
user@net1:~$ sudo ip address add 172.16.10.6/24 dev ipvlan2
user@net1:~$ sudo ip link set dev ipvlan2 up
```

Note that the only difference in the configuration is that we're specifying the type as IPVLAN and the mode as L2. In the case of IPVLAN, the default mode is L3, so we need to specify L2 in order to get the interfaces to operate in that fashion. Since IPVLAN interfaces inherit the MAC address of the parent, our topology should look like this:

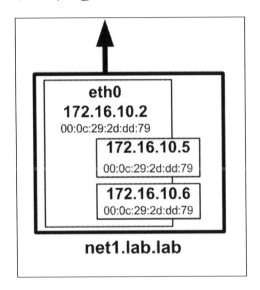

We can prove this just by checking the interface themselves:

```
user@net1:~$ ip -d link
...<loopback interface removed for brevity>...
2: eth0: <BROADCAST,MULTICAST,UP,LOWER_UP> mtu 1500 qdisc pfifo_fast
state UP mode DEFAULT group default qlen 1000
    link/ether 00:0c:29:2d:dd:79 brd ff:ff:ff:ff:ff:ff promiscuity 1
addrgenmode eui64
3: eth1: <BROADCAST,MULTICAST,UP,LOWER_UP> mtu 1500 qdisc pfifo_fast
state UP mode DEFAULT group default qlen 1000
    link/ether 00:0c:29:2d:dd:83 brd ff:ff:ff:ff:ff:ff promiscuity 0
addrgenmode eui64
28: ipvlan1@eth0: <BROADCAST,MULTICAST,UP,LOWER_UP> mtu 1500 qdisc
noqueue state UNKNOWN mode DEFAULT group default
```

```
    link/ether 00:0c:29:2d:dd:79 brd ff:ff:ff:ff:ff:ff promiscuity 0

    ipvlan  mode 12 addrgenmode eui64
29: ipvlan2@eth0: <BROADCAST,MULTICAST,UP,LOWER_UP> mtu 1500 qdisc
noqueue state UNKNOWN mode DEFAULT group default
    link/ether 00:0c:29:2d:dd:79 brd ff:ff:ff:ff:ff:ff promiscuity 0

    ipvlan  mode 12 addrgenmode eui64
user@net1:~$
```

If we were to initiate traffic toward these IPs from off of the local subnet we could validate that each IP is reporting the same MAC address by checking the ARP table on the upstream gateway:

```
switch#show ip arp vlan 10
Protocol  Address          Age (min)  Hardware Addr    Type   Interface
Internet  172.16.10.6          0      000c.292d.dd79   ARPA   Vlan30
Internet  172.16.10.5          0      000c.292d.dd79   ARPA   Vlan30
Internet  172.16.10.2        111      000c.292d.dd79   ARPA   Vlan30
Internet  172.16.10.3        110      000c.2959.caca   ARPA   Vlan30
Internet  172.16.10.1          -      0021.d7c5.f245   ARPA   Vlan30
```

And while we won't show an example here, IPVLAN interfaces in L2 mode are also namespace aware just like we saw in the last couple of recipes with the MacVLAN interface type. The only difference would be in the interface MAC addresses as we saw in the preceding code. The same restrictions apply in regard to the parent interface being unable to talk to the child interfaces and vice versa.

Now that we know how IPVLAN in L2 mode works, let's discuss IPVLAN L3 mode. L3 mode is significantly different than what we've seen up to this point. As the name L3 mode suggests, this interface type routes traffic between all attached subinterfaces. This is easiest to comprehend in a namespace configuration. For instance, let's look at this quick lab topology:

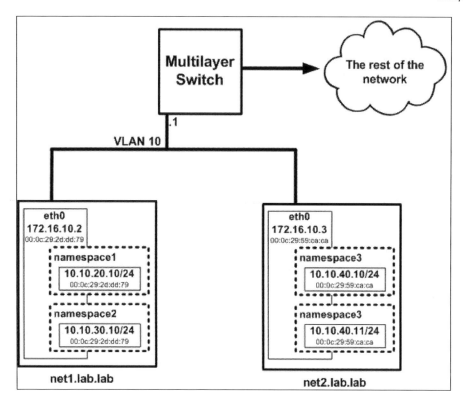

In the preceding image, you can see that I've created four unique namespaces across our two lab hosts. I also created four unique IPVLAN interfaces, mapped them into the different namespaces, and gave them each a unique IP address. Since these are IPVLAN interfaces, you'll note that all of the IPVLAN interfaces share the MAC address of the parent interface. To build this topology, I used the following configuration on each respective host:

```
user@net1:~$ sudo ip link del dev ipvlan1
user@net1:~$ sudo ip link del dev ipvlan2
user@net1:~$ sudo ip netns add namespace1
user@net1:~$ sudo ip netns add namespace2
user@net1:~$ sudo ip link add ipvlan1 link eth0 type ipvlan mode l3
user@net1:~$ sudo ip link add ipvlan2 link eth0 type ipvlan mode l3
user@net1:~$ sudo ip link set ipvlan1 netns namespace1
user@net1:~$ sudo ip link set ipvlan2 netns namespace2
user@net1:~$ sudo ip netns exec namespace1 ip address \
add 10.10.20.10/24 dev ipvlan1
user@net1:~$ sudo ip netns exec namespace1 ip link set dev ipvlan1 up
```

```
user@net1:~$ sudo ip netns exec namespace2 sudo ip address \
add 10.10.30.10/24 dev ipvlan2
user@net1:~$ sudo ip netns exec namespace2 ip link set dev ipvlan2 up

user@net2:~$ sudo ip netns add namespace3
user@net2:~$ sudo ip netns add namespace4
user@net2:~$ sudo ip link add ipvlan3 link eth0 type ipvlan mode l3
user@net2:~$ sudo ip link add ipvlan4 link eth0 type ipvlan mode l3
user@net2:~$ sudo ip link set ipvlan3 netns namespace3
user@net2:~$ sudo ip link set ipvlan4 netns namespace4
user@net2:~$ sudo ip netns exec namespace3 ip address \
add 10.10.40.10/24 dev ipvlan3
user@net2:~$ sudo ip netns exec namespace3 ip link set dev ipvlan3 up
user@net2:~$ sudo ip netns exec namespace4 sudo ip address \
add 10.10.40.11/24 dev ipvlan4
user@net2:~$ sudo ip netns exec namespace4 ip link set dev ipvlan4 up
```

Once this is configured, you'll note that the only interfaces that can communicate with one another are those on the host net2 (10.10.40.10 and 10.10.40.11). Let's look at this topology logically to understand why:

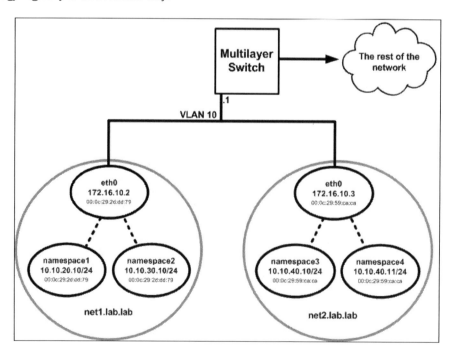

Looking at this logically, it starts to look like a routed network. You'll notice that all the IP addresses assigned are unique without any overlap. As I mentioned earlier, IPVLAN L3 mode acts like a router. From a conceptual perspective, you can think of the parent interface as that router. If we look at this from a layer 3 perspective, it makes sense that only the interfaces in namespaces 3 and 4 can talk because they are in the same broadcast domain. The other namespaces would need to route through a gateway to talk to each other. Let's check the routing table on all of the namespaces to see where things stand:

```
user@net1:~$ sudo ip netns exec namespace1 ip route
10.10.20.0/24 dev ipvlan1  proto kernel  scope link  src 10.10.20.10
user@net1:~$ sudo ip netns exec namespace2 ip route
10.10.30.0/24 dev ipvlan2  proto kernel  scope link  src 10.10.30.10
user@net2:~$ sudo ip netns exec namespace3 ip route
10.10.40.0/24 dev ipvlan3  proto kernel  scope link  src 10.10.40.10
user@net2:~$ sudo ip netns exec namespace4 ip route
10.10.40.0/24 dev ipvlan4  proto kernel  scope link  src 10.10.40.11
```

As expected, each namespace only knows about the local network. So in order for these interfaces to communicate, they need to have at the very least a default route. This is where things get a little interesting. IPVLAN interfaces do not allow broadcast or multicast traffic. This means that if we defined the gateway of the interface to be the upstream switch, it would never be able to reach it because it wouldn't be able to ARP for it. However, since the parent is acting like a sort of router, we can have the namespaces use the IPVLAN interface itself as a gateway. We can do that by adding default routes in this fashion:

```
user@net1:~$ sudo ip netns exec namespace1 ip route add \
default dev ipvlan1
user@net1:~$ sudo ip netns exec namespace2 ip route add \
default dev ipvlan2
user@net2:~$ sudo ip netns exec namespace3 ip route add \
default dev ipvlan3
user@net2:~$ sudo ip netns exec namespace4 ip route add \
default dev ipvlan4
```

After adding these routes, you'll also need to add routes on each Linux host to tell them where to go to reach these remote subnets. Since the two hosts in this example are layer 2 adjacent, the best place to do this on the host itself. While you could also rely on the default route and configure these routes on the upstream network device that would not be ideal. You would effectively be routing in and out of the same L3 interface on the gateway, which isn't great network design practice. If the hosts had not been layer 2 adjacent adding the routes on the multilayer switch would have been required:

```
user@net1:~$ sudo ip route add 10.10.40.0/24 via 172.16.10.3
```

```
user@net2:~$ sudo ip route add 10.10.20.0/24 via 172.16.10.2
user@net2:~$ sudo ip route add 10.10.30.0/24 via 172.16.10.2
```

After you have all of the routes installed, you should be able to reach all of the namespaces from any of the other namespaces:

```
user@net1:~$ sudo ip netns exec namespace1 ping 10.10.30.10 -c 2
PING 10.10.30.10 (10.10.30.10) 56(84) bytes of data.
64 bytes from 10.10.30.10: icmp_seq=1 ttl=64 time=0.047 ms
64 bytes from 10.10.30.10: icmp_seq=2 ttl=64 time=0.033 ms
--- 10.10.30.10 ping statistics ---
2 packets transmitted, 2 received, 0% packet loss, time 999ms
rtt min/avg/max/mdev = 0.033/0.040/0.047/0.007 ms
user@net1:~$ sudo ip netns exec namespace1 ping 10.10.40.10 -c 2
PING 10.10.40.10 (10.10.40.10) 56(84) bytes of data.
64 bytes from 10.10.40.10: icmp_seq=1 ttl=64 time=0.258 ms
64 bytes from 10.10.40.10: icmp_seq=2 ttl=64 time=0.366 ms
--- 10.10.40.10 ping statistics ---
2 packets transmitted, 2 received, +3 duplicates, 0% packet loss, time
1001ms
rtt min/avg/max/mdev = 0.258/0.307/0.366/0.042 ms
user@net1:~$ sudo ip netns exec namespace1 ping 10.10.40.11 -c 2
PING 10.10.40.11 (10.10.40.11) 56(84) bytes of data.
64 bytes from 10.10.40.11: icmp_seq=1 ttl=64 time=0.246 ms
64 bytes from 10.10.40.11: icmp_seq=2 ttl=64 time=0.366 ms
--- 10.10.40.11 ping statistics ---
2 packets transmitted, 2 received, +3 duplicates, 0% packet loss, time
1001ms
rtt min/avg/max/mdev = 0.246/0.293/0.366/0.046 ms
user@net1:~$ s
```

As you can see, IPVLAN L3 mode is a different animal than what we've seen up until this point. Unlike MacVLAN or IPVLAN L2, you'll need to tell the network how to reach these new interfaces.

Working with the Docker IPVLAN network driver

As we've seen in the previous recipe, IPVLAN offers some interesting modes of operations that can be relevant to large-scale container deployments. As of now, Docker support IPVLAN in its experimental software channel. In this recipe, we'll review how you can consume IPVLAN attached containers with the Docker IPVLAN driver.

Getting ready

In this recipe, we'll be using two Linux hosts running Docker. Our lab topology will look like this:

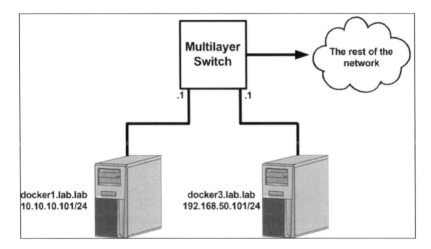

It is assumed that each host is running the experimental channel of Docker in order to get access to the experimental IPVLAN network driver. Please see recipe 1 in regard to the use and consumption of the experimental software channel. The hosts should have a single IP interface and Docker should be in its default configuration. In some cases, the changes we make may require you to have root-level access to the system.

How to do it...

Once you have your hosts running the experimental code, verify that you are on the correct version by viewing the output of `docker info`:

```
user@docker1:~$ docker info
...<Additional output removed for brevity>...
Server Version: 1.12.2
```

…<Additional output removed for brevity>…

Experimental: true

user@docker1:~$

At the time of this writing, you need to be on an experimental version of Docker for the IPVLAN driver to be present.

The Docker IPVLAN network driver offers both the layer 2 and layer 3 mode of operation. Since the IPVLAN L2 mode closely mimics the MacVLAN configuration we reviewed earlier, we'll focus on implementing the L3 mode in this recipe. The first thing we need to do is to define the networks. Before doing so, there are a few things to keep in mind when using the IPVLAN network driver:

- While it will allow you to specify a gateway when defining the network, the setting is ignored. Recall from the previous recipe that you need to use the IPVLAN interface itself as the gateway rather than the upstream network device. Docker will take care of configuring this for you.

- As an option to the driver, you need to specify the interface that you wish to use as the parent interface for all containers attached with IPVLAN interfaces. If you do not specify a parent interface as an option, Docker will create a dummy network interface and use this as the parent interface. This will prevent any communication to outside networks from this network.

- The `--internal` flag is available when creating networks with the IPVLAN driver. When specified the parent interface is defined as a dummy interface, which prevents traffic from leaving the host.

- If you do not specify a subnet, Docker IPAM will select one for you. This is not advised as these are routable subnets. IPAM on different Docker hosts will likely pick the same subnet. Always specify the subnet you wish to define.

- There is a one-to-one relationship with IPVLAN user-defined networks and parent interfaces. That is, you can only define one IPVLAN type network on a given parent interface.

You'll note that many of the preceding points are similar to the ones that apply to the Docker MacVLAN driver. A significant difference lies in the fact that we do not want to use the same network as the parent interface. In our examples, we'll use the subnet 10.10.20.0/24 on the host docker1 and the subnet 10.10.30.0/24 on the host docker3. Let's define the networks on each host now:

```
user@docker1:~$ docker network  create -d ipvlan -o parent=eth0 \
--subnet=10.10.20.0/24 -o ipvlan_mode=l3 ipvlan_net
16a6ed2b8d2bdffad04be17e53e498cc48b71ca0bdaed03a565542ba1214bc37


user@docker3:~$ docker network  create -d ipvlan -o parent=eth0 \
```

```
--subnet=10.10.30.0/24 -o ipvlan_mode=l3 ipvlan_net
6ad00282883a83d1f715b0f725ae9115cbd11034ec59347524bebb4b673ac8a2
```

Once created, we can start a container on each host that uses the IPVLAN network:

```
user@docker1:~$ docker run -d --name=web1 --net=ipvlan_net \
jonlangemak/web_server_1
93b6be9e83ee2b1eaef26abd2fb4c653a87a75cea4b9cd6bf26376057d77f00f


user@docker3:~$ docker run -d --name=web2 --net=ipvlan_net \
jonlangemak/web_server_2
89b8b453849d12346b9694bb50e8376f30c2befe4db8836a0fd6e3950f57595c
```

You'll notice that we once again do not need to deal with publishing ports. The container is assigned a fully routable IP address and can present any service it wishes on that IP. The IP addresses assigned to the container will come out of the specified subnet. In this case, our topology looks like this:

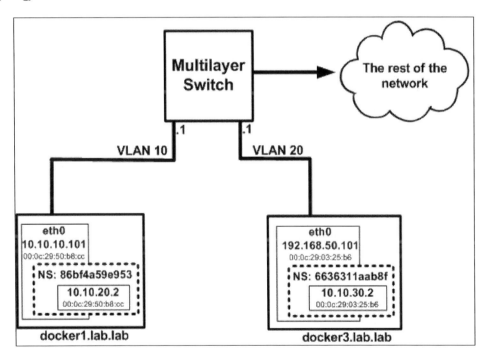

Once running, you'll notice that the containers don't have any connectivity. This is because the network doesn't know how to reach each of the IPVLAN networks. For this to work, we need to tell the upstream network device how to reach each subnet. To do this, we'll add the following routes on the multilayer switch:

```
ip route 10.10.20.0 255.255.255.0 10.10.10.101
```

```
ip route 10.10.30.0 255.255.255.0 192.168.50.101
```

Once this routing is in place, we'll be able to route to the remote containers and access any service they are offering:

```
user@docker1:~$ docker exec web1 curl -s http://10.10.30.2
<body>
   <html>
      <h1><span style="color:#FF0000;font-size:72px;">Web Server #2 -
Running on port 80</span>
      </h1>
</body>
   </html>
user@docker1:~$
```

You'll notice that in this mode, the container can also reach the hosts interface:

```
user@docker1:~$ docker exec -it web1 ping 10.10.10.101 -c 2
PING 10.10.10.101 (10.10.10.101): 48 data bytes
56 bytes from 10.10.10.101: icmp_seq=0 ttl=63 time=0.232 ms
56 bytes from 10.10.10.101: icmp_seq=1 ttl=63 time=0.321 ms
--- 10.10.10.101 ping statistics ---
2 packets transmitted, 2 packets received, 0% packet loss
round-trip min/avg/max/stddev = 0.232/0.277/0.321/0.045 ms
user@docker1:~$
```

While this works, it's important to know that this is happening by traversing the parent interface out to the multilayer switch and then coming back in. We can see that the upstream switch (gateway) is generating ICMP redirects if we try the ping in the reverse direction:

```
user@docker1:~$ ping 10.10.20.2 -c 2
PING 10.10.20.2 (10.10.20.2) 56(84) bytes of data.
From 10.10.10.1: icmp_seq=1 Redirect Host(New nexthop: 10.10.10.101)
64 bytes from 10.10.20.2: icmp_seq=1 ttl=64 time=0.270 ms
From 10.10.10.1: icmp_seq=2 Redirect Host(New nexthop: 10.10.10.101)
64 bytes from 10.10.20.2: icmp_seq=2 ttl=64 time=0.368 ms
--- 10.10.20.2 ping statistics ---
2 packets transmitted, 2 received, 0% packet loss, time 1000ms
rtt min/avg/max/mdev = 0.270/0.319/0.368/0.049 ms
user@docker1:~$
```

So while host-to-container connectivity works, it's not the best model if you require the host to communicate with the containers locally.

Tagging VLAN IDs with MacVLAN and IPVLAN networks

One feature that's available with both MacVLAN and IPVLAN Docker network types is the ability to tag containers on a particular VLAN. This is possible since both network types leverage a parent interface. In this recipe, we'll show you how you can create Docker network types that are VLAN tagged or VLAN aware. Since this functionality works the same in the case of either network type, we'll focus on configuring this with MacVLAN type networks.

Getting ready

In this recipe, we'll be a single Docker host to demonstrate how the Linux host can send VLAN tagged frames to upstream network devices. Our lab topology will be as follows:

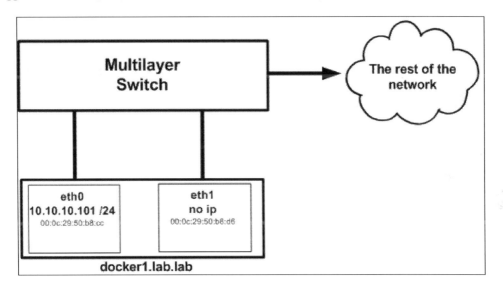

It is assumed that this host is running version 1.12. The host has two network interfaces, eth0 with an IP address of 10.10.10.101 and eth1 that is up, but has no IP address configured on it.

How to do it...

One of the interesting features comes along with MacVLAN and IPVLAN network drivers is the ability to provision subinterfaces. A subinterface is a logical partition of what's typically a physical interface. The standard way of partitioning a physical interface is to leverage VLANs. You'll commonly hear this referred to as dot1q trunking or VLAN tagging. To do this, the upstream network interface has to be prepared to receive tagged frames and be able to interpret the tag. In all of our previous examples, the upstream network port was hard-coded to a particular VLAN. This is the case with the `eth0` interface of this server. It is plugged into a port on the switch that is statically configured for VLAN 10. In addition to this, the switch also has an IP interface on VLAN 10, which in our case is `10.10.10.1/24`. It acts as the server's default gateway. Frames sent from the servers `eth0` interface are received by the switch and end up in VLAN 10. That piece is pretty straightforward.

The other option is to have the server tell the switch what VLAN it wishes to be in. To do this, we create a subinterface on the server that is specific to a given VLAN. Traffic leaving that interface is tagged with the VLAN number and sent on its way to the switch. In order for this to work, the switch port needs to be configured as a **trunk**. Trunks are interfaces that can carry multiple VLANs and are VLAN tag (dot1q) aware. When the switch receives the frame, it references the VLAN tag in the frame and puts the traffic into the right VLAN based on the tag. Logically, you might depict a trunk configuration as follows:

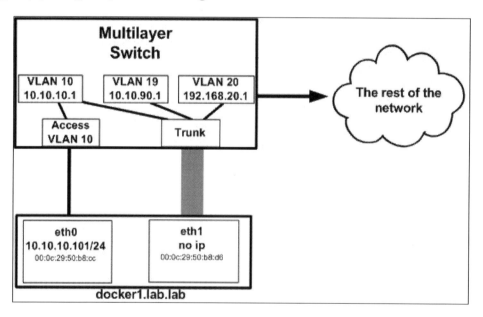

We depict the `eth1` interface as a wide channel that can support connectivity to a large number of VLANs. We can see that the trunk port can connect to all of the possible VLAN interfaces based on the tag it receives. The `eth0` interface is statically bound to the VLAN 10 interface.

It is wise in production environments to limit the VLANs allowed on a trunk port. Not doing so would mean someone could potentially gain access to any VLAN on the switch just by specifying the right dot1q tag.

This functionality has been around for a long time, and Linux system administrators are likely familiar with the manual process used to create VLAN tagged subinterfaces. The interesting piece is that Docker can now manage this for you. For instance, we can create two different MacVLAN networks:

```
user@docker1:~$ docker network create -d macvlan -o parent=eth1.19 \
  --subnet=10.10.90.0/24 --gateway=10.10.90.1 vlan19
8f545359f4ca19ee7349f301e5af2c84d959e936a5b54526b8692d0842a94378
```

```
user@docker1:~$ docker network create -d macvlan -o parent=eth1.20 \
--subnet=192.168.20.0/24 --gateway=192.168.20.1 vlan20
df45e517a6f499d589cfedabe7d4a4ef5a80ed9c88693f255f8ceb91fe0bbb0f
user@docker1:~$
```

The interfaces are defined much like any other MacVLAN interface. What's different is that we specified the `.19` and `.20` on the parent interface names. Specifying a dot with numbers after an interface name is the common syntax for defining subinterfaces. If we look at the hosts network interface, we should see the addition of two new interfaces:

```
user@docker1:~$ ip -d link show
...<Additional output removed for brevity>...
5: eth1.19@eth1: <BROADCAST,MULTICAST,UP,LOWER_UP> mtu 1500 qdisc noqueue
state UP mode DEFAULT group default
    link/ether 00:0c:29:50:b8:d6 brd ff:ff:ff:ff:ff:ff promiscuity 0
    vlan protocol 802.1Q id 19 <REORDER_HDR> addrgenmode eui64
6: eth1.20@eth1: <BROADCAST,MULTICAST,UP,LOWER_UP> mtu 1500 qdisc noqueue
state UP mode DEFAULT group default
    link/ether 00:0c:29:50:b8:d6 brd ff:ff:ff:ff:ff:ff promiscuity 0
    vlan protocol 802.1Q id 20 <REORDER_HDR> addrgenmode eui64
user@docker1:~$
```

We can tell from this output that these are either MacVLAN or IPVLAN interfaces whose parent happens to be the physical interface `eth1`.

If we launch containers on both of these networks, we'll see that they end up within either VLAN 19 or VLAN 20 based on which network we specify:

```
user@docker1:~$ docker run --net=vlan19 --name=web1 -d \
jonlangemak/web_server_1
7f54eec28098eb6e589c8d9601784671b9988b767ebec5791540e1a476ea5345
user@docker1:~$
user@docker1:~$ docker run --net=vlan20 --name=web2 -d \
jonlangemak/web_server_2
a895165c46343873fa11bebc355a7826ef02d2f24809727fb4038a14dd5e7d4a
user@docker1:~$
user@docker1:~$ docker exec web1 ip addr show dev eth0
7: eth0@if5: <BROADCAST,MULTICAST,UP,LOWER_UP> mtu 1500 qdisc noqueue
state UNKNOWN
    link/ether 02:42:0a:0a:5a:02 brd ff:ff:ff:ff:ff:ff
    inet 10.10.90.2/24 scope global eth0
      valid_lft forever preferred_lft forever
    inet6 fe80::42:aff:fe0a:5a02/64 scope link
      valid_lft forever preferred_lft forever
user@docker1:~$
user@docker1:~$ docker exec web2 ip addr show dev eth0
8: eth0@if6: <BROADCAST,MULTICAST,UP,LOWER_UP> mtu 1500 qdisc noqueue
state UNKNOWN
    link/ether 02:42:c0:a8:14:02 brd ff:ff:ff:ff:ff:ff
    inet 192.168.20.2/24 scope global eth0
      valid_lft forever preferred_lft forever
    inet6 fe80::42:c0ff:fea8:1402/64 scope link
      valid_lft forever preferred_lft forever
user@docker1:~$
```

And if we attempt to send traffic to either of their gateways, we'll find that both are reachable:

```
user@docker1:~$ docker exec -it web1 ping 10.10.90.1 -c 2
PING 10.10.90.1 (10.10.90.1): 48 data bytes
56 bytes from 10.10.90.1: icmp_seq=0 ttl=255 time=0.654 ms
56 bytes from 10.10.90.1: icmp_seq=1 ttl=255 time=0.847 ms
```

```
--- 10.10.90.1 ping statistics ---
2 packets transmitted, 2 packets received, 0% packet loss
round-trip min/avg/max/stddev = 0.654/0.750/0.847/0.097 ms
user@docker1:~$ docker exec -it web2 ping 192.168.20.1 -c 2
PING 192.168.20.1 (192.168.20.1): 48 data bytes
56 bytes from 192.168.20.1: icmp_seq=0 ttl=255 time=0.703 ms
56 bytes from 192.168.20.1: icmp_seq=1 ttl=255 time=0.814 ms
--- 192.168.20.1 ping statistics ---
2 packets transmitted, 2 packets received, 0% packet loss
round-trip min/avg/max/stddev = 0.703/0.758/0.814/0.056 ms
user@docker1:~$
```

If we capture the frames as they leave the server, we'll even be able to see the dot1q (VLAN) tag in the layer 2 header:

As with other network constructs Docker creates, Docker will also take care of the cleanup in the case that you delete these user-defined networks. In addition, if you prefer to build the subinterface yourself, Docker can consume interfaces that you have already created so long as the name is the same as the parent you specify.

Being able to specify VLAN tags as part of a user-defined network is a big deal and makes presenting containers to the physical network a much easier task.

10
Leveraging IPv6

In this chapter, we will cover the following recipes:

- IPv6 command-line basics
- Enabling IPv6 capabilities in Docker
- Working with IPv6-enabled containers
- Configuring NDP proxying
- User-defined networks and IPv6

Introduction

Up until this point in the book, we've focused solely on IPv4 networking. However, IPv4 is not the only IP protocol available to us. Although IPv4 is still the most widely understood protocol, IPv6 has started to gain significant attraction. Public IPv4 space is exhausted and many are starting to foresee issues with running out of private IPv4 allocations as well. IPv6 looks to overcome this problem by defining a much larger set of usable IP space. However, IPv6 does some things differently from IPv4 making some believe that implementing IPv6 would be cumbersome. I would argue that as you look to deploy container technology, you should also be looking at how to effectively leverage IPv6. Although IPv6 is a different animal, it will soon become a requirement in many networks. With containers representing the possibility of introducing many more IP endpoints on your network making the transition sooner rather than later is a good idea. In this chapter, we'll look at what IPv6 features Docker currently supports.

IPv6 command-line basics

Even if you understand the basics of the IPv6 protocol, working with IPv6 on a Linux host for the first time can be a bit daunting. Much like IPv4, IPv6 has its own unique set of command-line tools that can be leveraged to configure and troubleshoot IPv6 connectivity. Some of these tools are the same that we used with IPv4 and just use a slightly different syntax. Other tools are completely unique to IPv6. In this recipe, we'll walk through configuring and verifying basic IPv6 connectivity.

Getting ready

In this recipe, we'll be using a small lab consisting of two Linux hosts:

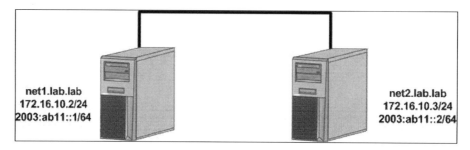

net1.lab.lab
172.16.10.2/24
2003:ab11::1/64

net2.lab.lab
172.16.10.3/24
2003:ab11::2/64

Each host has both an IPv4 address as well as an IPv6 address assigned to its physical interface. You'll need root-level access to each host to make network configuration changes.

 The intent of this recipe is not to teach the basics of IPv6 or IPv6 network design. The examples in this recipe are for example purposes only. Although we may cover some of the basics during the examples, it is assumed that the reader has a base understanding of how the IPv6 protocol works.

How to do it...

As shown in the preceding figure, each Linux host has been assigned both an IPv4 and an IPv6 IP address. These were both configured as part of the host's network configuration script. The following are sample configurations from each of the two lab hosts:

- `net1.lab.lab`

```
auto eth0
iface eth0 inet static
        address 172.16.10.2
        netmask 255.255.255.0
```

```
                gateway 172.16.10.1

                dns-nameservers 10.20.30.13

                dns-search lab.lab
```

iface eth0 inet6 static

        address 2003:ab11::1

        netmask 64

- net2.lab.lab

```
auto eth0

iface eth0 inet static

                address 172.16.10.3

                netmask 255.255.255.0

                gateway 172.16.10.1

                dns-nameservers 10.20.30.13

                dns-search lab.lab
```

iface eth0 inet6 static

        address 2003:ab11::2

        netmask 64

Note that in each case, we're adding the IPv6 address to the existing physical network interface. In this type of configuration, both the IPv4 and IPv6 addresses coexist on the same NIC. This is commonly referred to as running **dual stack** since both protocols share the same physical adapter. Once configured, you'll need to reload the interfaces for the configuration to take effect. You should then be able to confirm that each host has the correct configuration by either using the `ifconfig` tool or the `ip` (`iproute2`) toolset:

```
user@net1:~$ ifconfig eth0

eth0      Link encap:Ethernet   HWaddr 00:0c:29:2d:dd:79

inet addr:172.16.10.2  Bcast:172.16.10.255  Mask:255.255.255.0
```
        inet6 addr: fe80::20c:29ff:fe2d:dd79/64 Scope:Link

        inet6 addr: 2003:ab11::1/64 Scope:Global
```
          UP BROADCAST RUNNING MULTICAST  MTU:1500  Metric:1

          RX packets:308 errors:0 dropped:0 overruns:0 frame:0

          TX packets:348 errors:0 dropped:0 overruns:0 carrier:0

          collisions:0 txqueuelen:1000

          RX bytes:32151 (32.1 KB)  TX bytes:36732 (36.7 KB)

user@net1:~$
```

```
user@net2:~$ ip -6 addr show dev eth0
2: eth0: <BROADCAST,MULTICAST,UP,LOWER_UP> mtu 1500 qlen 1000
    inet6 2003:ab11::2/64 scope global
        valid_lft forever preferred_lft forever
    inet6 fe80::20c:29ff:fe59:caca/64 scope link
        valid_lft forever preferred_lft forever
user@net2:~$
```

The advantage of using the older `ifconfig` tool is that you can see the IPv4 and IPv6 interface information at the same time. When using the `ip` tool, you need to specify that you wish to see IPv6 information by passing the `-6` flag. We'll see this is the same case later on when we use the `ip` tool for configuration of IPv6 interfaces.

In either case, both hosts now appear to be configured for IPv6 on their `eth0` interfaces. However, note that we actually have two IPv6 addresses defined. You'll notice that one address has a scope of local and the other has a scope of global. In IPv6, each IP interface gets assigned both a global and a local IPv6 address. The locally scoped interface is only valid for communication on the link it is assigned on and is commonly used to reach neighboring devices on the same segment. In most cases, the link local address is dynamically determined by the host itself. This means that an IPv6-enabled interface almost always has a link local IPv6 address defined even if you haven't specifically configured a global IPv6 address on the interface. Packets using link local IP addresses are never forwarded by a router which restricts them to the segment they are defined on. For the majority of our discussion, we'll be focusing on the global address.

 Any further reference to an IPv6 address is referring to a globally scoped IPv6 address unless otherwise noted.

Since both of our hosts are on the same subnet, we should be able to reach one server from the other using IPv6:

```
user@net1:~$ ping6 2003:ab11::2 -c 2
PING 2003:ab11::2(2003:ab11::2) 56 data bytes
64 bytes from 2003:ab11::2: icmp_seq=1 ttl=64 time=0.422 ms
64 bytes from 2003:ab11::2: icmp_seq=2 ttl=64 time=0.401 ms
--- 2003:ab11::2 ping statistics ---
2 packets transmitted, 2 received, 0% packet loss, time 999ms
rtt min/avg/max/mdev = 0.401/0.411/0.422/0.022 ms
user@net1:~$
```

Note that instead of using the standard ping tool, we're using the `ping6` tool to verify IPv6 reachability.

The last thing we want to check is the neighbor discovery table. Another major change with IPv6 is that it doesn't use ARP to find the hardware or MAC address of an IP endpoint. The major reason for this is that IPv6 does not support broadcast traffic. ARP relies on broadcasts to work, so it couldn't be used in IPv6. Instead, IPv6 uses neighbor discovery, which leverages multicast.

That being said, you need to look at the neighbor discovery table rather than the ARP table when troubleshooting local network. To do this, we can use the familiar `iproute2` toolset:

```
user@net1:~$ ip -6 neighbor show
fe80::20c:29ff:fe59:caca dev eth0 lladdr 00:0c:29:59:ca:ca DELAY
2003:ab11::2 dev eth0 lladdr 00:0c:29:59:ca:ca REACHABLE
user@net1:~$
```

Much like the ARP table, the neighbor table shows us the hardware or MAC address of the IPv6 address we wish to reach. Note that as before we passed the `-6` flag to the `ip` command to tell it we wanted IPv6 information.

Now that we have basic connectivity, let's add a new IPv6 interface to each host. To do that, we follow almost the same steps we did when we added an IPv4 interface. For instance, adding a dummy interface is almost identical:

```
user@net1:~$ sudo ip link add ipv6_dummy type dummy
user@net1:~$ sudo ip -6 address add 2003:cd11::1/64 dev ipv6_dummy
user@net1:~$ sudo ip link set ipv6_dummy up
```

Note that the only difference is that we need to tell `iproute2` that we're specifying a IPv6 address by once again passing the `-6` flag. In all other regards, the configuration is identical to how we did this in IPv4. Let's configure another dummy interface on the second host as well:

```
user@net2:~$ sudo ip link add ipv6_dummy type dummy
user@net2:~$ sudo ip -6 address add 2003:ef11::1/64 dev ipv6_dummy
user@net2:~$ sudo ip link set ipv6_dummy up
```

At this point, our topology now looks as follows:

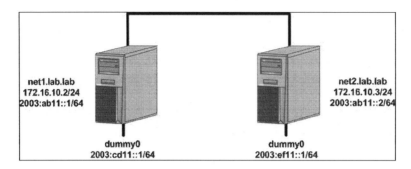

Let's now check the IPv6 routing table on each host. As before we can also use the `iproute2` tool to check the IPv6 routing table:

```
user@net1:~$ ip -6 route
2003:ab11::/64 dev eth0   proto kernel   metric 256   pref medium
2003:cd11::/64 dev ipv6_dummy   proto kernel   metric 256   pref medium
fe80::/64 dev eth0   proto kernel   metric 256   pref medium
fe80::/64 dev ipv6_dummy   proto kernel   metric 256   pref medium
user@net1:~$


user@net2:~$ ip -6 route
2003:ab11::/64 dev eth0   proto kernel   metric 256   pref medium
2003:ef11::/64 dev ipv6_dummy   proto kernel   metric 256   pref medium
fe80::/64 dev eth0   proto kernel   metric 256   pref medium
fe80::/64 dev ipv6_dummy   proto kernel   metric 256   pref medium
user@net2:~$
```

As we can see, each host knows about its directly connected interfaces but does not know about the other hosts dummy interface. In order for either host to reach the other hosts dummy interface, we're going to need to route to get to it. Since these hosts are directly connected, this could be solved by adding a default IPv6 route. Each default route would reference the other host as the next hop. Although that's doable, let's instead add specific routes to each host that reference the network that the dummy interface is in:

```
user@net1:~$ sudo ip -6 route add 2003:ef11::/64 via 2003:ab11::2
user@net2:~$ sudo ip -6 route add 2003:cd11::/64 via 2003:ab11::1
```

After adding these routes, either host should be able to reach the other hosts `ipv6_dummy` interface:

```
user@net1:~$ ping6 2003:ef11::1 -c 2
```

```
PING 2003:ef11::1(2003:ef11::1) 56 data bytes
64 bytes from 2003:ef11::1: icmp_seq=1 ttl=64 time=0.811 ms
64 bytes from 2003:ef11::1: icmp_seq=2 ttl=64 time=0.408 ms
--- 2003:ef11::1 ping statistics ---
2 packets transmitted, 2 received, 0% packet loss, time 999ms
rtt min/avg/max/mdev = 0.408/0.609/0.811/0.203 ms
user@net1:~$
```

 You'll likely notice that just adding one route on a single host will allow that host to reach the dummy interface on the other host. This is because we only need the route to get the traffic off the initiating host. The traffic will be sourced by the hosts `eth0` interface (`2003:ab11::/64`), which the other host knows how to get to inherently. If the ping was sourced from the dummy interface, you'd need both routes for this to work.

Now that we've configured and verified basic connectivity, let's take one final step and rebuild these interfaces using network namespaces. To do that, let's first clean up the dummy interfaces since we'll be reusing those IPv6 subnets inside the namespaces:

```
user@net1:~$ sudo ip link del dev ipv6_dummy
user@net2:~$ sudo ip link del dev ipv6_dummy
```

The configuration we're after will look as follows:

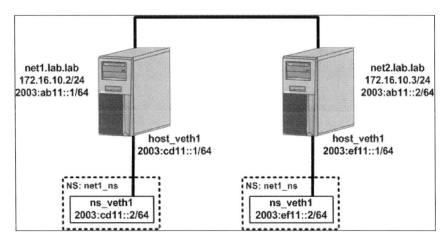

Although very similar to the last configuration, there are two major differences. You'll notice that we are now using network namespaces to encapsulate the new interfaces. In doing so, we've configured the IPv6 address for the new interface on one side of a VETH pair. The other end of the VETH pair lives on the host in the default network namespace.

If you aren't comfortable with some of these Linux networking constructs, please review *Chapter 1*, *Linux Networking Constructs*, where we discuss namespaces and VETH interfaces in much greater detail.

To configure this, we'll apply the following configuration:

Add a new network namespace named `net1_ns`:

```
user@net1:~$ sudo ip netns add net1_ns
```

Create a VETH pair naming one end `host_veth1` and the other end `ns_veth1`:

```
user@net1:~$ sudo ip link add host_veth1 type veth peer name ns_veth1
```

Move the namespace side of the VETH pair into the namespace:

```
user@net1:~$ sudo ip link set dev ns_veth1 netns net1_ns
```

Within the namespace, give the VETH interface an IP address:

```
user@net1:~$ sudo ip netns exec net1_ns ip -6 address \
add 2003:cd11::2/64 dev ns_veth1
```

Within the namespace, bring the interface up:

```
user@net1:~$ sudo ip netns exec net1_ns ip link set ns_veth1 up
```

Within the namespace, add a route to reach the namespace on the other host:

```
user@net1:~$ sudo ip netns exec net1_ns ip -6 route \
add 2003:ef11::/64 via 2003:cd11::1
```

Give the host side of the VETH pair an IP address:

```
user@net1:~$ sudo ip -6 address add 2003:cd11::1/64 dev host_veth1
```

Bring the host side of VETH interface up:

```
user@net1:~$ sudo ip link set host_veth1 up
```

Note that we only added a route within the namespace to reach the other namespace. We did not add the same route on the Linux host. This is because we already did this earlier in the recipe in order to reach the dummy interface. If you removed that route, you'll need to add it back for this to work.

We must now perform a similar configuration on the second host:

```
user@net2:~$ sudo ip netns add net2_ns
user@net2:~$ sudo ip link add host_veth1 type veth peer name ns_veth1
user@net2:~$ sudo ip link set dev ns_veth1 netns net2_ns
user@net2:~$ sudo ip netns exec net2_ns ip -6 address add \
2003:ef11::2/64 dev ns_veth1
user@net2:~$ sudo ip netns exec net2_ns ip link set ns_veth1 up
user@net2:~$ sudo ip netns exec net2_ns ip -6 route add \
2003:cd11::/64 via 2003:ef11::1
user@net2:~$ sudo ip -6 address add 2003:ef11::1/64 dev host_veth1
user@net2:~$ sudo ip link set host_veth1 up
```

Once this is added, you should be able to verify that each namespace has the routing information required to reach the other hosts namespace:

```
user@net1:~$ sudo ip netns exec net1_ns ip -6 route
2003:cd11::/64 dev ns_veth1  proto kernel  metric 256  pref medium
2003:ef11::/64 via 2003:cd11::1 dev ns_veth1  metric 1024  pref medium
fe80::/64 dev ns_veth1  proto kernel  metric 256  pref medium
user@net1:~$
user@net2:~$ sudo ip netns exec net2_ns ip -6 route
2003:cd11::/64 via 2003:ef11::1 dev ns_veth1  metric 1024  pref medium
2003:ef11::/64 dev ns_veth1  proto kernel  metric 256  pref medium
fe80::/64 dev ns_veth1  proto kernel  metric 256  pref medium
user@net2:~$
```

But when we try to reach from namespace to namespace, the connection fails:

```
user@net1:~$ sudo ip netns exec net1_ns ping6 2003:ef11::2 -c 2
PING 2003:ef11::2(2003:ef11::2) 56 data bytes
--- 2003:ef11::2 ping statistics ---
2 packets transmitted, 0 received, 100% packet loss, time 1007ms
user@net1:~$
```

This is because we're now trying to use the Linux host as a router. If you recall from earlier chapters when we want the Linux kernel to forward or route packets we have to enable that functionality. This is done by changing these two kernel parameters on each host:

```
user@net1:~$ sudo sysctl net.ipv6.conf.default.forwarding=1
net.ipv6.conf.default.forwarding = 1
user@net1:~$ sudo sysctl net.ipv6.conf.all.forwarding=1
```

```
net.ipv6.conf.all.forwarding = 1
```

 Keep in mind that these settings won't persist through a reboot when defined in this manner.

Once these settings are made on both hosts, your ping should now begin to work:

```
user@net1:~$ sudo ip netns exec net1_ns ping6 2003:ef11::2 -c 2
PING 2003:ef11::2(2003:ef11::2) 56 data bytes
64 bytes from 2003:ef11::2: icmp_seq=1 ttl=62 time=0.540 ms
64 bytes from 2003:ef11::2: icmp_seq=2 ttl=62 time=0.480 ms
--- 2003:ef11::2 ping statistics ---
2 packets transmitted, 2 received, 0% packet loss, time 999ms
rtt min/avg/max/mdev = 0.480/0.510/0.540/0.030 ms
user@net1:~$
```

As an interesting side note, check your neighbor table on the host once you've enabled IPv6 forwarding in the kernel:

```
user@net1:~$ ip -6 neighbor
2003:ab11::2 dev eth0 lladdr 00:0c:29:59:ca:ca router STALE
2003:cd11::2 dev host_veth1 lladdr a6:14:b5:39:da:96 STALE
fe80::20c:29ff:fe59:caca dev eth0 lladdr 00:0c:29:59:ca:ca router STALE
fe80::a414:b5ff:fe39:da96 dev host_veth1 lladdr a6:14:b5:39:da:96 STALE
user@net1:~$
```

Can you notice anything different about the neighbor entry for the other Linux host? It now has the `router` flag as part of the neighbor definition. The Linux host advertises itself as a router on the segment when IPv6 forwarding is enabled in the kernel.

Enabling IPv6 capabilities in Docker

IPv6 functionality is disabled by default in Docker. Much like other features we reviewed earlier, enabling it requires doing so at the service level. Once enabled, Docker will provision the host interfaces associated with Docker, as well as the containers themselves, with IPv6 addressing.

Getting ready

In this recipe, we'll be using a small lab consisting of two Docker hosts:

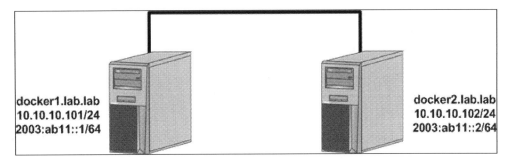

Each host has both an IPv4 address as well as an IPv6 address assigned to its physical interface. You'll need root-level access to each host to make network configuration changes. It is assumed that Docker is installed, and it's a default configuration.

How to do it...

As mentioned, Docker will not provision containers with an IPv6 address unless told to do so. To enable IPv6 in Docker, we need to pass a service-level flag to the Docker service.

 If you need a refresher on defining Docker service-level parameters, see the last recipe in *Chapter 2, Configuring and Monitoring Docker Networks*, where we discuss configuring these on a system running `systemd`.

In addition to enabling IPv6 functionality, you also need to define a subnet for the `docker0` bridge. To do this, we'll modify our `systemd` drop-in file for Docker and make sure that it has the following options:

- On the host `docker1`:

```
ExecStart=/usr/bin/dockerd --ipv6 --fixed-cidr-v6=2003:cd11::/64
```

- On the host `docker2`:

```
ExecStart=/usr/bin/dockerd --ipv6 --fixed-cidr-v6=2003:ef11::/64
```

If we apply this configuration, reload the `systemd` configuration and restart the Docker service on each host, we should see that the `docker0` bridge has taken the first available IP address from the defined IPv6 CIDR range:

```
user@docker1:~$ ip -6 addr show dev docker0
3: docker0: <NO-CARRIER,BROADCAST,MULTICAST,UP> mtu 1500
    inet6 2003:cd11::1/64 scope global tentative
       valid_lft forever preferred_lft forever
    inet6 fe80::1/64 scope link tentative
```

```
              valid_lft forever preferred_lft forever
user@docker1:~$


user@docker2:~$ ip -6 addr show dev docker0
5: docker0: <NO-CARRIER,BROADCAST,MULTICAST,UP> mtu 1500
    inet6 2003:ef11::1/64 scope global tentative
          valid_lft forever preferred_lft forever
    inet6 fe80::1/64 scope link tentative
          valid_lft forever preferred_lft forever
user@docker2:~$
```

At this point, our topology looks a lot like it did in the first recipe:

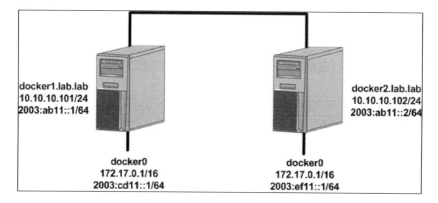

Docker will issue an IPv6 address along with an IPv4 address to each container it creates. Let's spin up a container on the first host to see what I mean:

```
user@docker1:~$ docker run -d --name=web1 jonlangemak/web_server_1
50d522d176ebca2eac0f7e826ffb2e36e754ce27b3d3b4145aa8a11c6a13cf15
user@docker1:~$
```

Note that we did not pass the -P flag to the containers to publish the containers exposed ports. If we test locally, we can validate that the host can reach the service within the container from both the containers IPv4 and IPv6 address:

```
user@docker1:~$ docker exec web1 ifconfig eth0
eth0      Link encap:Ethernet  HWaddr 02:42:ac:11:00:02
          inet addr:172.17.0.2  Bcast:0.0.0.0  Mask:255.255.0.0
          inet6 addr: fe80::42:acff:fe11:2/64 Scope:Link
          inet6 addr: 2003:cd11::242:ac11:2/64 Scope:Global
          UP BROADCAST RUNNING MULTICAST  MTU:1500  Metric:1
```

```
         RX packets:16 errors:0 dropped:0 overruns:0 frame:0
         TX packets:8 errors:0 dropped:0 overruns:0 carrier:0
         collisions:0 txqueuelen:0
         RX bytes:1792 (1.7 KB)  TX bytes:648 (648.0 B)
```

```
user@docker1:~$ curl http://172.17.0.2
<body>
   <html>
      <h1><span style="color:#FF0000;font-size:72px;">Web Server #1 -
Running on port 80</span>
      </h1>
</body>
   </html>
user@docker1:~$ curl -g http://[2003:cd11::242:ac11:2]
<body>
   <html>
      <h1><span style="color:#FF0000;font-size:72px;">Web Server #1 -
Running on port 80</span>
      </h1>
</body>
   </html>
user@docker1:~$
```

 When using `curl` with IPv6 addresses, you need to put the IPv6 address inside of brackets and then tell `curl` not to glob by passing the `-g` flag.

As we can see, the behavior with the IPv6 address is the same as it is with the IPv4 address. Following suit, containers on the same host can talk directly to each other across the docker0 bridge using their assigned IPv6 address. Let's start a second container on the same host:

```
user@docker1:~$ docker run -d --name=web2 jonlangemak/web_server_2
```

A quick validation will prove to us that these two containers are allowed to talk directly to one another with their IPv6 addresses just as expected:

```
user@docker1:~$ docker exec web2 ip -6 addr show dev eth0
10: eth0@if11: <BROADCAST,MULTICAST,UP,LOWER_UP> mtu 1500
    inet6 2003:cd11::242:ac11:3/64 scope global nodad
```

```
        valid_lft forever preferred_lft forever
    inet6 fe80::42:acff:fe11:3/64 scope link
        valid_lft forever preferred_lft forever
user@docker1:~$
user@docker1:~$ docker exec -it web1 curl -g \
http://[2003:cd11::242:ac11:3]
<body>
  <html>
    <h1><span style="color:#FF0000;font-size:72px;">Web Server #2 -
Running on port 80</span>
    </h1>
</body>
  </html>
user@docker1:~$
```

Working with IPv6-enabled containers

In the previous recipe, we saw how Docker handles the basic allocation of IPv6-enabled containers. The behavior we've seen up to this point has closely mimicked what we saw in earlier chapters when only dealing with IPv4 addressed containers. However, this is not the case for all of the network functionality. Docker does not currently have complete feature parity between IPv4 and IPv6. Namely, as we'll see in this recipe, Docker does not have `iptables` (ip6tables) integration for IPv6 enabled containers. In this chapter, we'll review some of the network features that we previously visited with IPv4 only enabled containers and see how they act when using IPv6 addressing.

Getting ready

In this recipe, we'll be building off of the lab we built in the previous recipe. You'll need root-level access to each host to make network configuration changes. It is assumed that Docker is installed, and it's a default configuration.

How to do it...

As mentioned, Docker does not currently have host firewall, specifically netfilter or `iptables`, integration for IPv6. This means that several of the features we relied on previously with IPv4 behave differently when dealing with a containers IPv6 address. Let's start with some of the basic functionality. In the previous recipe, we saw that two containers on the same host, connected to the `docker0` bridge, could talk directly with one another.

This behavior was expected and works in much the same manner when using IPv4 addresses. If we wanted to prevent this communication, we might look to disable **Inter-Container Communication (ICC)** in the Docker service. Let's update our Docker options on the host docker1 to set ICC to `false`:

```
ExecStart=/usr/bin/dockerd --icc=false --ipv6 --fixed-cidr-
v6=2003:cd11::/64
```

Then, we can reload the `systemd` configuration, restart the Docker service, and restart the containers:

```
user@docker1:~$ docker start web1
web1
user@docker1:~$ docker start web2
web2
user@docker1:~$ docker exec web2 ifconfig eth0
eth0      Link encap:Ethernet  HWaddr 02:42:ac:11:00:03
          inet addr:172.17.0.3  Bcast:0.0.0.0  Mask:255.255.0.0
          inet6 addr: fe80::42:acff:fe11:3/64 Scope:Link
          inet6 addr: 2003:cd11::242:ac11:3/64 Scope:Global
          UP BROADCAST RUNNING MULTICAST  MTU:1500  Metric:1
          RX packets:12 errors:0 dropped:0 overruns:0 frame:0
          TX packets:8 errors:0 dropped:0 overruns:0 carrier:0
          collisions:0 txqueuelen:0
          RX bytes:1128 (1.1 KB)  TX bytes:648 (648.0 B)


user@docker1:~$
user@docker1:~$ docker exec -it web1 curl http://172.17.0.3
curl: (7) couldn't connect to host
user@docker1:~$ docker exec -it web1 curl -g \
http://[2003:cd11::242:ac11:3]
<body>
  <html>
    <h1><span style="color:#FF0000;font-size:72px;">Web Server #2 -
Running on port 80</span>
    </h1>
</body>
  </html>
user@docker1:~$
```

As we can see, the attempt on IPv4 fails and the subsequent IPv6 attempt works. Since Docker is not managing any firewall rules related to the containers IPv6 address, there is nothing to prevent direct connectivity between IPv6 addresses.

Since Docker isn't managing IPv6-related firewall rules, you might also assume that features like outbound masquerade and port publishing no longer work as well. And while this is true in the sense that Docker is not creating IPv6 associated NAT rules and firewall policy, it does not mean that a containers IPv6 address is not reachable from the outside network. Let's walk through an example to show you what I mean. Let's start a container on the second Docker host:

```
user@docker2:~$ docker run -dP --name=web2 jonlangemak/web_server_2
5e2910c002db3f21aa75439db18e5823081788e69d1e507c766a0c0233f6fa63
user@docker2:~$
user@docker2:~$ docker port web2
80/tcp -> 0.0.0.0:32769
user@docker2:~$
```

Note that when we ran the container on the host `docker2` that we passed the `-P` flag to tell Docker to publish the exposed ports of the container. If we check the port mapping, we can see that the host has chosen port `32768`. Note that the port mapping indicates an IP address of `0.0.0.0`, which typically indicates any IPv4 address. Let's perform some quick tests from the other Docker host to validate what is and isn't working:

```
user@docker1:~$ curl http://10.10.10.102:32769
<body>
   <html>
      <h1><span style="color:#FF0000;font-size:72px;">Web Server #2 -
Running on port 80</span>
      </h1>
</body>
   </html>
user@docker1:~$
```

As expected, the IPv4 port mapping works. We're able to access the containers service through the Docker hosts IPv4 address by leveraging the `iptables` NAT rule to map port `32769` to the actual service port of `80`. Let's now try the same example but using the hosts IPv6 address:

```
user@docker1:~$ curl -g http://[2003:ab11::2]:32769
<body>
   <html>
```

```
    <h1><span style="color:#FF0000;font-size:72px;">Web Server #2 -
Running on port 80</span>
    </h1>
</body>
  </html>
user@docker1:~$
```

Surprisingly, this also works. You might be wondering how this is working considering that Docker doesn't manage or integrate with any of the hosts IPv6 firewall policy. The answer is actually quite simple. If we look at the second Docker hosts open ports, we'll see that there is a `docker-proxy` service bound to port `32769`:

```
user@docker2:~$ sudo netstat -plnt
...<output removed for brevity>...
Active Internet connections (only servers)
Local Address      Foreign Address      State      PID/Program name
0.0.0.0:22         0.0.0.0:*            LISTEN     1387/sshd
127.0.0.1:6010     0.0.0.0:*            LISTEN     3658/0
:::22              :::*                 LISTEN     1387/sshd
::1:6010           :::*                 LISTEN     3658/0
:::32769           :::*                 LISTEN     2390/docker-proxy
user@docker2:~$
```

As we saw in earlier chapters, the `docker-proxy` service facilitates inter container and published port connectivity. In order for this to work, the `docker-proxy` service has to bind to the port in which the container publishes. Recall that services listening on all IPv4 interfaces use the syntax of `0.0.0.0` to represent all IPv4 interfaces. In a similar fashion, IPv6 interfaces use the syntax of `:::` to indicate the same thing. You'll note that the `docker-proxy` port references all IPv6 interfaces. Although this may differ based on your operating system, binding to all IPv6 interfaces also implies binding to all IPv4 interfaces. That is, the preceding `docker-proxy` service is actually listening on all of the hosts IPv4 and IPv6 interfaces.

 Keep in mind that `docker-proxy` is not typically used for inbound services. Those rely on the `iptables` NAT rules to map the published port to the container. However, in the case that those rules don't exist, the host is still listening on all of its interfaces for traffic to port `32769`.

The net result of this is that despite not having an IPv6 NAT rule, I'm still able to access the containers service through the Docker hosts interfaces. In this manner, published ports with IPv6 still work. However, this only works when using the `docker-proxy`. That mode of operation, while still the default, is intended to be removed in favor of hairpin NAT. We can enable hairpin NAT on the Docker host by passing the `--userland-proxy=false` parameter to Docker as a service-level option. Doing so would prevent this means of IPv6 port publishing from working.

Finally, the lack of firewall integration also means that we no longer have support for the outbound masquerade feature. In IPv4, this feature allowed containers to talk to the outside network without having to worry about routing or IP address overlapping. Container traffic leaving the host was always hidden behind one of the hosts IP interfaces. However, this was not a mandated configuration. As we saw in earlier chapters, you could very easily disable the outbound masquerade feature and provision the `docker0` bridge with a routable IP address and subnet. So long as the outside, or external, network knew how to reach that subnet, a container could very easily have a unique routable IP address.

One of the reasons IPv6 came to be was because of the rapid depletion of IPv4 addresses. NAT in IPv4 served as a largely successful, although equally troublesome, temporary stop gap to the address depletion problem. This means that many believe that we shouldn't be implementing any sort of NAT in regard to IPv6 whatsoever. Rather, all IPv6 prefixes should be natively routable and reachable without the obfuscation of an IP translation. Lacking IPv6 firewall integration, natively routing IPv6 traffic to each host is the current means in which Docker can facilitate reachability across multiple Docker hosts and the outside network. This requires that each Docker host uses a unique IPv6 CIDR range and that the Docker hosts know how to reach all of the other Docker hosts defined CIDR range. While this typically requires the physical network to have network reachability information, in our simple lab example each host just requires a static route to the other hosts CIDR. Much like we did in the first recipe, we'll add an IPv6 route on each host so both know how to reach the IPv6 subnet of the other `docker0` bridge:

```
user@docker1:~$ sudo ip -6 route add 2003:ef11::/64 via 2003:ab11::2
user@docker2:~$ sudo ip -6 route add 2003:cd11::/64 via 2003:ab11::1
```

After adding the routes, each Docker host knows how to get to the other host's IPv6 `docker0` bridge subnet:

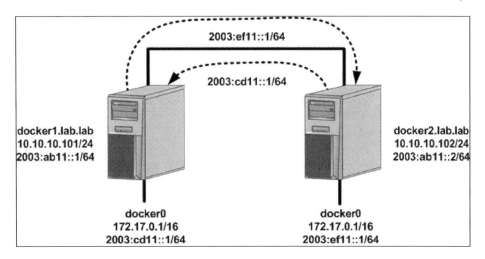

If we now check, we should have reachability between containers on each host:

```
user@docker2:~$ docker exec web2 ifconfig eth0
eth0      Link encap:Ethernet  HWaddr 02:42:ac:11:00:02
          inet addr:172.17.0.2  Bcast:0.0.0.0  Mask:255.255.0.0
          inet6 addr: fe80::42:acff:fe11:2/64 Scope:Link
          inet6 addr: 2003:ef11::242:ac11:2/64 Scope:Global
          UP BROADCAST RUNNING MULTICAST  MTU:1500  Metric:1
          RX packets:43 errors:0 dropped:0 overruns:0 frame:0
          TX packets:34 errors:0 dropped:0 overruns:0 carrier:0
          collisions:0 txqueuelen:0
          RX bytes:3514 (3.5 KB)  TX bytes:4155 (4.1 KB)


user@docker2:~$
user@docker1:~$ docker exec -it web1 curl -g http://
[2003:ef11::242:ac11:2]
<body>
  <html>
    <h1><span style="color:#FF0000;font-size:72px;">Web Server #2 -
Running on port 80</span>
    </h1>
</body>
  </html>
user@docker1:~$
```

As we can see, the container on the host `docker1` was able to successfully route directly to the container running on the host `docker2`. So as long as each Docker host has the appropriate routing information, containers will be able to route directly to one another.

The downside of this approach is that the container is now a fully exposed network endpoint. We no longer get the advantage of exposing only certain ports to the outside network through Docker published ports. If you want to ensure that only certain ports are exposed on your IPv6 interfaces the userland proxy may be your best option at this point. Keep these options in mind when designing services around IPv6 connectivity.

Configuring NDP proxying

As we saw in the last recipe, one of the major differences with IPv6 support in Docker is the lack of the firewall integration. Without that integration, we lose things like outbound masquerade and full port publishing capabilities. And while this may not be necessary in all cases, there is a certain convenience factor that is lost when not using this. For instance, when running in IPv4 only mode, an administrator could install Docker and immediately connect your containers to the outside network. This is because the container was only ever seen through the Docker host's IP addresses for both inbound (published port) and outbound (masquerade) connectivity. This meant that there was no need to inform the outside network about additional subnets because the outside network only ever saw the Docker host's IP addresses. In the IPv6 model, the outside network has to know about the container subnets in order to route to them. In this chapter, we'll review how to configure NDP proxying as a workaround to this problem.

Getting ready

In this recipe, we'll be using this lab topology:

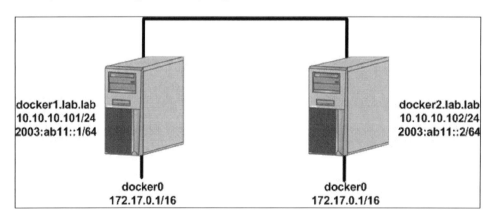

You'll need root-level access to each host to make network configuration changes. It is assumed that Docker is installed, and it's a default configuration.

How to do it...

The preceding topology shows that our hosts are dual stack connected to the network, but Docker has not yet been configured to use IPv6. Like we saw in the previous recipe, configuring Docker for IPv6 would also typically mean configuring routing on the outside network, so it knows how to reach the IPv6 CIDR you define for the docker0 bridge to use. However, assume for a moment that this isn't possible. Assume that you have no control over the outside network, which means you can't advertise or notify other network endpoints about any newly defined IPv6 subnet on your Docker host.

Let's also assume that while you can't advertise any newly defined IPv6 networks, you are however able to reserve additional IPv6 space within the existing networks. For instance, the hosts currently have interfaces defined within the 2003:ab11::/64 network. If we carve up this space, we can split it into four /66 networks:

- 2003:ab11::/66
- 2003:ab11:0:0:4000::/66
- 2003:ab11:0:0:8000::/66
- 2003:ab11:0:0:c000::/66

Let's assume for a second that we are allowed to reserve the last two subnets for our use. We can now enable IPv6 within Docker and allocate these two networks as the IPv6 CIDR ranges. Here are the configuration options for each Docker host:

- docker1

ExecStart=/usr/bin/dockerd --ipv6 --fixed-cidr-
v6=2003:ab11:0:0:8000::/66

- docker2

ExecStart=/usr/bin/dockerd --ipv6 --fixed-cidr-
v6=2003:ab11:0:0:c000::/66

After loading the new configuration into `systemd` and restarting the Docker service, our lab topology would now look like this:

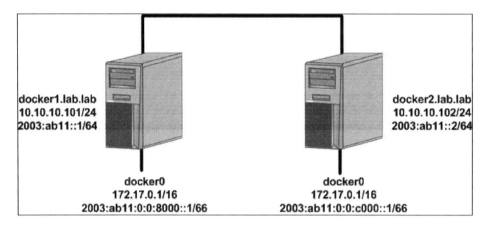

Let's launch a container on both hosts:

```
user@docker1:~$ docker run -d --name=web1 jonlangemak/web_server_1
user@docker2:~$ docker run -d --name=web2 jonlangemak/web_server_2
```

Now determine the allocated IPv6 address of the `web1` container:

```
user@docker1:~$ docker exec web1 ip -6 addr show dev eth0
4: eth0@if5: <BROADCAST,MULTICAST,UP,LOWER_UP> mtu 1500
    inet6 2003:ab11::8000:242:ac11:2/66 scope global nodad
       valid_lft forever preferred_lft forever
    inet6 fe80::42:acff:fe11:2/64 scope link
       valid_lft forever preferred_lft forever
user@docker1:~$
```

Now, let's try and reach that container from the `web2` container:

```
user@docker2:~$ docker exec -it web2 ping6 \
2003:ab11::8000:242:ac11:2  -c 2
PING 2003:ab11::8000:242:ac11:2 (2003:ab11::8000:242:ac11:2): 48 data
bytes
56 bytes from 2003:ab11::c000:0:0:1: Destination unreachable: Address
unreachable
56 bytes from 2003:ab11::c000:0:0:1: Destination unreachable: Address
unreachable
--- 2003:ab11::8000:242:ac11:2 ping statistics ---
2 packets transmitted, 0 packets received, 100% packet loss
user@docker2:~$
```

This fails because the Docker hosts believe that the destination address is directly connected to their eth0 interface. When the web2 container attempts the connection, the following actions occur:

- The container does a route lookup and determines that the address 2003:ab11::8000:242:ac11:2 does not fall within its local subnet of 2003:ab11:0:0:c000::1/66, so it forwards the traffic to its default gateway (the docker0 bridge interface)

- The host receives the traffic and does a route lookup and determines that the destination address of 2003:ab11::8000:242:ac11:2 falls within its local subnet of 2003:ab11::/64 (eth0) and uses NDP to try and find the host with that destination IP address

- The host receives no response to this query and the flow fails

We can verify that this is what's happening by checking the docker2 host's IPv6 neighbor table:

```
user@docker2:~$ ip -6 neighbor show
fe80::20c:29ff:fe50:b8cc dev eth0 lladdr 00:0c:29:50:b8:cc STALE
2003:ab11::c000:242:ac11:2 dev docker0 lladdr 02:42:ac:11:00:02 REACHABLE
2003:ab11::8000:242:ac11:2 dev eth0   FAILED
fe80::42:acff:fe11:2 dev docker0 lladdr 02:42:ac:11:00:02 REACHABLE
user@docker2:~$
```

Following the normal routing logic, everything is working the way it should. However IPv6 has a feature called NDP proxy, which can help solve this problem. Those of you familiar with proxy ARP in IPv4 will find NDP proxy to provide similar functionality. Essentially, NDP proxy allows a host to answer neighbor requests on behalf of another endpoint. In our case, we can tell both Docker hosts to answer on behalf of the containers. To do this, we need to first enable NDP proxy on the host itself. This is done by enabling the kernel parameter net.ipv6.conf. eth0.proxy_ndp, as shown in the following code:

```
user@docker1:~$ sudo sysctl net.ipv6.conf.eth0.proxy_ndp=1
net.ipv6.conf.eth0.proxy_ndp = 1
user@docker1:~$
user@docker2:~$ sudo sysctl net.ipv6.conf.eth0.proxy_ndp=1
net.ipv6.conf.eth0.proxy_ndp = 1
user@docker2:~$
```

 Keep in mind that these settings won't persist through a reboot when defined in this manner.

Once that is enabled, we need to manually tell each host what IPv6 address to answer for. We do that by adding proxy entries to each host's neighbor table. In the preceding example, we need to do that for both the source and the destination container in order to allow for bidirectional traffic flow. First, add the entry on the host `docker1` for the destination:

```
user@docker1:~$ sudo ip -6 neigh add proxy \
2003:ab11::8000:242:ac11:2 dev eth0
```

Then, determine the IPv6 address of the `web2` container, which will act as the source of the traffic and add a proxy entry for that on the host `docker2`:

```
user@docker2:~$ docker exec web2 ip -6 addr show dev eth0
6: eth0@if7: <BROADCAST,MULTICAST,UP,LOWER_UP> mtu 1500
    inet6 2003:ab11::c000:242:ac11:2/66 scope global nodad
       valid_lft forever preferred_lft forever
    inet6 fe80::42:acff:fe11:2/64 scope link
       valid_lft forever preferred_lft forever
user@docker2:~$
user@docker2:~$ sudo ip -6 neigh add proxy \
2003:ab11::c000:242:ac11:2 dev eth0
```

This will tell each Docker host to reply to the neighbor solicitation requests on behalf of the containers. Ping tests should now work as expected:

```
user@docker2:~$ docker exec -it web2 ping6 \
2003:ab11::8000:242:ac11:2 -c 2
PING 2003:ab11::8000:242:ac11:2 (2003:ab11::8000:242:ac11:2): 48 data
bytes
56 bytes from 2003:ab11::8000:242:ac11:2: icmp_seq=0 ttl=62 time=0.462 ms
56 bytes from 2003:ab11::8000:242:ac11:2: icmp_seq=1 ttl=62 time=0.660 ms
--- 2003:ab11::8000:242:ac11:2 ping statistics ---
2 packets transmitted, 2 packets received, 0% packet loss
round-trip min/avg/max/stddev = 0.462/0.561/0.660/0.099 ms
user@docker2:~$
```

And we should see the relevant neighbor entry on each host:

```
user@docker1:~$ ip -6 neighbor show
fe80::20c:29ff:fe7f:3d64 dev eth0 lladdr 00:0c:29:7f:3d:64 router
REACHABLE
2003:ab11::8000:242:ac11:2 dev docker0 lladdr 02:42:ac:11:00:02 REACHABLE
fe80::42:acff:fe11:2 dev docker0 lladdr 02:42:ac:11:00:02 DELAY
```

```
2003:ab11::c000:242:ac11:2 dev eth0 lladdr 00:0c:29:7f:3d:64 REACHABLE
user@docker1:~$
user@docker2:~$ ip -6 neighbor show
fe80::42:acff:fe11:2 dev docker0 lladdr 02:42:ac:11:00:02 REACHABLE
2003:ab11::c000:242:ac11:2 dev docker0 lladdr 02:42:ac:11:00:02 REACHABLE
fe80::20c:29ff:fe50:b8cc dev eth0 lladdr 00:0c:29:50:b8:cc router
REACHABLE
2003:ab11::8000:242:ac11:2 dev eth0 lladdr 00:0c:29:50:b8:cc REACHABLE
user@docker2:~$
```

Much like proxy ARP, NDP proxy works by the host providing its own MAC address in response to the neighbor discovery request. We can see that in both cases, the MAC address in the neighbor table is actually each host's eth0 MAC address:

```
user@docker1:~$ ip link show dev eth0
2: eth0: <BROADCAST,MULTICAST,UP,LOWER_UP> mtu 1500 qdisc pfifo_fast
state UP mode DEFAULT group default qlen 1000
    link/ether 00:0c:29:50:b8:cc brd ff:ff:ff:ff:ff:ff
user@docker1:~$
user@docker2:~$ ip link show dev eth0
2: eth0: <BROADCAST,MULTICAST,UP,LOWER_UP> mtu 1500 qdisc pfifo_fast
state UP mode DEFAULT group default qlen 1000
    link/ether 00:0c:29:7f:3d:64 brd ff:ff:ff:ff:ff:ff
user@docker2:~$
```

This approach works fairly well in cases where you can't advertise your Docker IPv6 subnet to the outside network. However, it relies on individual proxy entries for each IPv6 address you wish to proxy. For each container spawned you would need to generate an additional IPv6 proxy address.

User-defined networks and IPv6

Much like we saw with IPv4, user-defined networks can leverage IPv6 addressing. That is, all of the network-related parameters relate to both IPv4 and IPv6. In this chapter, we'll walk through defining a user-defined IPv6 network and demonstrate some of the related configuration options.

Getting ready

In this recipe, we'll be using a single Docker host. It is assumed that Docker is installed and is its default configuration. It is not required that the Docker service be enabled with the `--ipv6` service-level parameter in order to use IPv6 addressing on user-defined networks.

How to do it...

When working with user-defined networks, we can define configuration for both IPv4 and IPv6. In addition, when we run containers we can specify both their IPv4 and IPv6 addresses. To demonstrate this, let's first define a user-defined network that has both IPv4 and IPv6 addressing:

```
user@docker1:~$ docker network create -d bridge \
--subnet 2003:ab11:0:0:c000::/66 --subnet 192.168.127.0/24 \
--ipv6 ipv6_bridge
```

The syntax of this command should be familiar to you from *Chapter 3*, *User-Defined Networks*, where we discussed user-defined networks. However, there are a couple of things to point out.

First, you'll notice that we've defined the `--subnet` parameter twice. In doing so, we defined both an IPv4 subnet as well as an IPv6 subnet. The `--gateway` and `--aux-address` fields can be used in a similar fashion when defining IPv4 and IPv6 addresses. Second, we defined an option to enable IPv6 on this network. If you do not define this option to enable IPv6 the gateway interface of the host will not be defined.

Once defined, let's start a container on the network to see what our configuration looks like:

```
user@docker1:~$ docker run -d --name=web1 --net=ipv6_bridge \
--ip 192.168.127.10 --ip6 2003:ab11::c000:0:0:10 \
jonlangemak/web_server_1
```

This syntax should also look familiar to you. Note that we specified that this container should be a member of the user-defined network `ipv6_bridge`. In doing so, we can also define both an IPv4 and IPv6 address for the container using the `--ip` and `--ip6` parameters.

If we inspect the network, we should see the container attached as well as all of the relevant information related to both the network definition as well as the containers network interfaces:

```
user@docker1:~$ docker network inspect ipv6_bridge
[
    {
        "Name": "ipv6_bridge",
        "Id":
```

```
"0c6e760998ea6c5b99ba39f3c7ce63b113dab2276645e5fb7a2207f06273401a",
        "Scope": "local",
        "Driver": "bridge",
        "IPAM": {
            "Driver": "default",
            "Options": {},
            "Config": [
                {
                    "Subnet": "192.168.127.0/24"
                },
                {
                    "Subnet": "2003:ab11:0:0:c000::/66"
                }
            ]
        },
        "Containers": {
"38e7ac1a0d0ce849a782c5045caf770c3310aca42e069e02a55d0c4a601e6b5a": {
                "Name": "web1",
                "EndpointID":
"a80ac4b00d34d462ed98084a238980b3a75093591630b5832f105d400fabb4bb",
                "MacAddress": "02:42:c0:a8:7f:0a",
                "IPv4Address": "192.168.127.10/24",
                "IPv6Address": "2003:ab11::c000:0:0:10/66"
            }
        },
        "Options": {
            "com.docker.network.enable_ipv6": "true"
        }
    }
]
user@docker1:~$
```

By checking the host's network configuration, we should see that a new bridge has been created that matches up with these networks:

```
user@docker1:~$ ip addr show
...<Additional output removed for brevity>...
```

```
9: br-0b2efacf6f85: <BROADCAST,MULTICAST,UP,LOWER_UP> mtu 1500 qdisc
noqueue state UP group default
    link/ether 02:42:09:bc:9f:77 brd ff:ff:ff:ff:ff:ff
    inet 192.168.127.1/24 scope global br-0b2efacf6f85
       valid_lft forever preferred_lft forever
    inet6 2003:ab11::c000:0:0:1/66 scope global
       valid_lft forever preferred_lft forever
    inet6 fe80::42:9ff:febc:9f77/64 scope link
       valid_lft forever preferred_lft forever
    inet6 fe80::1/64 scope link
       valid_lft forever preferred_lft forever
...<Additional output removed for brevity>...
user@docker1:~$
```

If we check the container itself, we'll note that these interfaces are what the containers on this network will use for both their IPv4 and IPv6 default gateway:

```
user@docker1:~$ docker exec web1 ip route
default via 192.168.127.1 dev eth0
192.168.127.0/24 dev eth0  proto kernel  scope link  src 192.168.127.10
user@docker1:~$ docker exec web1 ip -6 route
2003:ab11:0:0:c000::/66 dev eth0  proto kernel  metric 256
fe80::/64 dev eth0  proto kernel  metric 256
default via 2003:ab11::c000:0:0:1 dev eth0  metric 1024
user@docker1:~$
```

Just like the default network modes, user-defined networks do not support host firewall integration to support outbound masquerade or inbound port publishing. IPv6 connectivity on and off of the host is the same as the docker0 bridge in regard to having to route the IPv6 traffic natively.

You'll also note that if you start a second container on the host that embedded DNS works for both IPv4 and IPv6 addressing:

```
user@docker1:~$ docker run -d --name=web2 --net=ipv6_bridge \
jonlangemak/web_server_1
user@docker1:~$
user@docker1:~$ docker exec -it web2 ping web1 -c 2
PING web1 (192.168.127.10): 48 data bytes
56 bytes from 192.168.127.10: icmp_seq=0 ttl=64 time=0.113 ms
```

```
56 bytes from 192.168.127.10: icmp_seq=1 ttl=64 time=0.111 ms
--- web1 ping statistics ---
2 packets transmitted, 2 packets received, 0% packet loss
round-trip min/avg/max/stddev = 0.111/0.112/0.113/0.000 ms
user@docker1:~$
user@docker1:~$ docker exec -it web2 ping6 web1 -c 2
PING web1 (2003:ab11::c000:0:0:10): 48 data bytes
56 bytes from web1.ipv6_bridge: icmp_seq=0 ttl=64 time=0.113 ms
56 bytes from web1.ipv6_bridge: icmp_seq=1 ttl=64 time=0.127 ms
--- web1 ping statistics ---
2 packets transmitted, 2 packets received, 0% packet loss
round-trip min/avg/max/stddev = 0.113/0.120/0.127/0.000 ms
user@docker1:~$
```

11

Troubleshooting Docker Networks

In this chapter, we will cover the following recipes:

- Using tcpdump to verify network paths
- Verifying VETH pairs
- Verifying published ports and outbound masquerading
- Verifying name resolution
- Building a test container
- Resetting the local Docker network database

Introduction

As we've seen in earlier chapters, Docker leverages a combination of relatively well-known Linux networking constructs to deliver container networking. Throughout this book, we've looked at many different ways you can configure, consume, and validate Docker networking configuration. What we haven't done is outline a troubleshooting and validation methodology you can use when you run into issues. When troubleshooting container networking, it is important to understand and be able to troubleshoot each specific networking component used in delivering end-to-end connectivity. The goal of this chapter is to provide specific steps you can take when you need to validate or troubleshoot a Docker networking issue.

Using tcpdump to verify network paths

Although we glanced over its usage in previous chapters, anyone working with networking on a Linux-based system should be comfortable with tcpdump. tcpdump allows you to capture network traffic on one or more interfaces on the host. In this recipe, we'll walk through how we can use tcpdump to verify container network traffic in a couple of different Docker networking scenarios.

Getting ready

In this recipe, we'll be using a single Docker host. It is assumed that Docker is installed and in its default configuration. You'll also need root-level access in order to inspect and change the hosts networking and firewall configuration. You'll also need the tcpdump utility installed. If you don't have it on your system, you can install it with this command:

```
sudo apt-get install tcpdump
```

How to do it...

tcpdump is an amazing troubleshooting tool. When used properly, it can give you a detailed view of packets as they traverse interfaces on a Linux host. To demonstrate, let's start a single container on our Docker host:

```
user@docker1:~$ docker run -dP --name web1 jonlangemak/web_server_1
ea32565ece0c0c22eace935113b6697bebe837f0b5ddf31724f371220792fb15
user@docker1:~$
```

Since we didn't specify any network parameters, this container will run on the docker0 bridge and have any exposed ports published to the hosts interfaces. Traffic generated from the container will also be hidden behind the hosts IP interfaces as the traffic heads toward the outside network. Using tcpdump, we can see this traffic at every stage.

Let's first examine inbound traffic that's coming into the host:

```
user@docker1:~$ docker port web1
80/tcp -> 0.0.0.0:32768
user@docker1:~$
```

In our case, this container was exposing port `80`, which has now been published to the host's interfaces on port `32768`. Let's first ensure that the traffic is coming into the host on the right port. To do this, we can capture on the hosts `eth0` interface for traffic destined to port `32768`:

```
user@docker1:~$ sudo tcpdump -qnn -i eth0 dst port 32768
tcpdump: verbose output suppressed, use -v or -vv for full protocol
decode
listening on eth0, link-type EN10MB (Ethernet), capture size 262144 bytes
15:46:07.629747 IP 10.20.30.41.55939 > 10.10.10.101.32768: tcp 0
15:46:07.629997 IP 10.20.30.41.55940 > 10.10.10.101.32768: tcp 0
15:46:07.630257 IP 10.20.30.41.55939 > 10.10.10.101.32768: tcp 0
```

To use `tcpdump` to capture this inbound traffic, we used a couple of different parameters:

- `q`: This tells `tcpdump` to be quiet, or not generate as much output. Since we really only want to see the layer 3 and layer 4 information this cleans up the output quite nicely
- `nn`: This tells `tcpdump` not to attempt to resolve IPs to DNS names. Again, we want to see the IP address here
- `i`: This specifies the interface we want to capture on, in this case, `eth0`
- `src port`: Tell `tcpdump` to filter on traffic that has a destination port of `32768`

> The `dst` parameter could be removed from this command. Doing so would filter on any traffic with a port of `32768` thus showing you the entire flow including the return traffic.

As shown in the preceding code, we can see the host receiving traffic on its physical interface (`10.10.10.101`) on port `32768` coming from a remote source of `10.20.30.41`. In this case, `10.20.30.41` is a test server that is originating traffic toward the container's published port.

Now that we've seen the traffic get to the host, let's look at it as it traverses the `docker0` bridge:

```
user@docker1:~$ sudo tcpdump -qnn -i docker0
tcpdump: verbose output suppressed, use -v or -vv for full protocol
decode
listening on docker0, link-type EN10MB (Ethernet), capture size 65535
bytes
16:34:54.193822 IP 10.20.30.41.53846 > 172.17.0.2.80: tcp 0
16:34:54.193848 IP 10.20.30.41.53847 > 172.17.0.2.80: tcp 0
16:34:54.193913 IP 172.17.0.2.80 > 10.20.30.41.53846: tcp 0
16:34:54.193940 IP 172.17.0.2.80 > 10.20.30.41.53847: tcp 0
```

In this case, we can see the traffic by just filtering on the docker0 bridge interface. As expected, we see the same traffic, with the same source, but now reflecting the accurate destination IP and port of the service running in the container thanks to the published port functionality.

While this is certainly the easiest means to capture traffic, it's not very effective if you have multiple containers running on the docker0 bridge. The current filtering would provide you all of the traffic traversing the bridge rather than just the specific container you were looking for. In these cases, you can also specify the IP address in the filter like this:

```
user@docker1:~$ sudo tcpdump -qnn -i docker0 dst 172.17.0.2
tcpdump: verbose output suppressed, use -v or -vv for full protocol
decode
listening on docker0, link-type EN10MB (Ethernet), capture size 65535
bytes
16:42:22.332555 IP 10.20.30.41.53878 > 172.17.0.2.80: tcp 0
16:42:22.332940 IP 10.20.30.41.53878 > 172.17.0.2.80: tcp 0
```

We're specifying the destination IP as a filter here. If we wished to see both traffic source and destined to that IP address, we could replace dst with host.

This sort of packet capture is essential to validating that features like port publication are working as expected. Captures can be done on the majority of interface types including those that don't have an IP address associated with them. A good example of such an interface is the host side of a VETH pair used to connect a containers namespace back to the default namespace. When troubleshooting container connectivity, it might be handy to be able to correlate traffic arriving on the docker0 bridge with a specific host-side VETH interface. We can do this by correlating data from multiple places. For instance, assume that we do the following tcpdump:

```
user@docker1:~$ sudo tcpdump -qnne -i docker0 host 172.17.0.2
tcpdump: verbose output suppressed, use -v or -vv for full protocol
decode
listening on docker0, link-type EN10MB (Ethernet), capture size 65535
bytes
16:59:33.334941 02:42:ab:27:0e:3e > 02:42:ac:11:00:02, IPv4, length 66:
10.20.30.41.57260 > 172.17.0.2.80: tcp 0
16:59:33.335012 02:42:ac:11:00:02 > 02:42:ab:27:0e:3e, IPv4, length 66:
172.17.0.2.80 > 10.20.30.41.57260: tcp 0
```

Note that in this case we passed the `e` parameter to `tcpdump`. This tells `tcpdump` to display the source and destination MAC address for each frame. In this case, we can see that we have two MAC addresses. One of these will be the MAC address associated with the `docker0` bridge, and the other will be the MAC address associated with the container. We can look at the `docker0` bridge information to determine what its MAC address is:

```
user@docker1:~$ ip link show dev docker0
4: docker0: <BROADCAST,MULTICAST,UP,LOWER_UP> mtu 1500 qdisc noqueue
state UP mode DEFAULT group default
    link/ether 02:42:ab:27:0e:3e brd ff:ff:ff:ff:ff:ff
user@docker1:~$
```

This leaves the address `02:42:ac:11:00:02`. Using the bridge command that comes as part of the `iproute2` toolset, we can determine on which interface this MAC address lives:

```
user@docker1:~$ bridge fdb show | grep 02:42:ac:11:00:02
02:42:ac:11:00:02 dev vetha431055
user@docker1:~$
```

Here, we can see that the MAC address of the container is accessible through the interface named `vetha431055`. Doing a capture on that interface will confirm that we're looking at the right interface:

```
user@docker1:~$ sudo tcpdump -qnn -i vetha431055
tcpdump: WARNING: vetha431055: no IPv4 address assigned
tcpdump: verbose output suppressed, use -v or -vv for full protocol
decode
listening on vetha431055, link-type EN10MB (Ethernet), capture size 65535
bytes
21:01:24.503939 IP 10.20.30.41.58035 > 172.17.0.2.80: tcp 0
21:01:24.503990 IP 172.17.0.2.80 > 10.20.30.41.58035: tcp 0
```

`tcpdump` can be a vital tool in verifying container communication. It is wise to spend some time understanding the tool and the different ways you can filter on traffic using its different parameters.

Verifying VETH pairs

Of all the Linux network constructs we've reviewed in this book, VETH pairs are likely the most essential. Being namespace aware they allow you to connect a container in a unique namespace to any other namespace including the default. And while Docker handles all of this for you, it is useful to be able to determine where the ends of a VETH pair live and correlate them to determine what purpose a VETH pair is serving. In this recipe, we'll review in depth how to find and correlate the ends of a VETH pair.

Getting ready

In this recipe, we'll be using a single Docker host. It is assumed that Docker is installed and in its default configuration. You'll also need root-level access in order to inspect and change the hosts networking and firewall configuration.

How to do it...

The main use case for VETH pairs in Docker is to connect a containers network namespace back to the default network namespace. It does this by placing one of the VETH pair on the `docker0` bridge and the other end in the container. The container side of the VETH pair gets an IP address assigned to it and then renamed to `eth0`.

When looking to match up ends of a VETH pair for a container, there are two scenarios. The first is when you start with the end in the default namespace, and the second is when you start the end in the container namespace. Let's walk through each case and how to correlate them together.

Let's first start with knowing the host end of the interface. For instance, let's say we're looking for the container end of this interface:

```
user@docker1:~$ ip -d link show
...<Additional output removed for brevity>...
4: docker0: <BROADCAST,MULTICAST,UP,LOWER_UP> mtu 1500 qdisc noqueue
state UP mode DEFAULT group default
    link/ether 02:42:ab:27:0e:3e brd ff:ff:ff:ff:ff:ff promiscuity 0
    bridge
6: vetha431055@if5: <BROADCAST,MULTICAST,UP,LOWER_UP> mtu 1500 qdisc
noqueue master docker0 state UP mode DEFAULT group default
    link/ether 82:69:cb:b6:9a:db brd ff:ff:ff:ff:ff:ff promiscuity 1
    veth
user@docker1:~$
```

There are a couple things to point out here. First, passing the `-d` parameter to the `ip link` subcommand displays extra detail about the interface. In this case, it confirms that the interface is a VETH pair. Second, VETH pair naming generally follows the `<end1>@<end2>` naming convention. In this case, we can see that the end `vetha431055` is the local interface and the `if5` is the other end. `if5` stands for interface 5 or the index ID of the 5th interface on the host. Since VETH interfaces are always created in pairs, it's fair to assume that the end of this VETH pair with index 6 is very likely index 5 or 7. In this case, the naming is indicating that it's 5, but we can confirm that using the `ethtool` command:

```
user@docker1:~$ sudo ethtool -S vetha431055
NIC statistics:
     peer_ifindex: 5
user@docker1:~$
```

As you can see, the other end of this VETH pair has an interface index of 5 as the name indicated. Now finding which container has 5 is the hard part. To do this, we need to inspect each container for a specific interface number. If you're running a lot of containers, this can be a challenge. Instead of inspecting each container manually, you can loop through them using Linux `xargs`. For instance, look at this command:

```
docker ps -q | xargs --verb -I {} docker exec {} ip link | grep ^5:
```

What we're doing here is returning a list of the container IDs for all running containers and then passing that list to `xargs`. In turn, `xargs` is using those container IDs to run a command inside the container with `docker exec`. That command happens to be the `ip link` command, which will return a list of all interfaces and their associated index numbers. If any of that information returned starts with a `5:`, indicating an interface index of 5, we'll print it to the screen. In order to see which container has the interface in question, we have to run the `xargs` command in verbose mode (`--verb`), which will show us each command as it runs. The output will look like this:

```
user@docker1:~$ docker ps -q | xargs --verb -I {} docker exec {} ip link
| grep ^5:
docker exec 4b521df22184 ip link
docker exec 772e12b15c92 ip link
docker exec d8f3e7936690 ip link
docker exec a2e3201278e2 ip link
docker exec f9216233ba56 ip link
docker exec ea32565ece0c ip link
5: eth0@if6: <BROADCAST,MULTICAST,UP,LOWER_UP> mtu 1500 qdisc noqueue
state UP
user@docker1:~$
```

As you can see, there were six containers running on this host. We didn't find the interface ID we were looking for until the last container. Given the container ID, we can tell which container has the other end of the VETH interface.

 You could confirm this by running the `docker exec -it ea32565ece0c ip link` command.

Now, let's try another example of starting with the container end of the VETH pair. This is slightly easier since the naming of the interface tells us the index of the host-side matching interface:

```
user@docker1:~$ docker exec web1 ip -d link show dev eth0
5: eth0@if6: <BROADCAST,MULTICAST,UP,LOWER_UP> mtu 1500 qdisc noqueue
state UP
```

```
    link/ether 02:42:ac:11:00:02 brd ff:ff:ff:ff:ff:ff
    veth
user@docker1:~$
```

We can then validate that the interface on the host with index 6 is a match to the interface with an index 5 in the container by once again using the `ethtool`:

```
user@docker1:~$ ip -d link show | grep ^6:
6: vetha431055@if5: <BROADCAST,MULTICAST,UP,LOWER_UP> mtu 1500 qdisc
noqueue master docker0 state UP mode DEFAULT group default
user@docker1:~$ sudo ethtool -S vetha431055
[sudo] password for user:
NIC statistics:
     peer_ifindex: 5
user@docker1:~$
```

Verifying published ports and outbound masquerading

One of the more difficult pieces involved in Docker networking is `iptables`. The `iptables`/netfilter integration plays a key role in providing functionality like port publication and outbound masquerading. However, `iptables` can be difficult to understand and troubleshoot if you're not already familiar with it. In this recipe, we'll review how to examine the `iptables` configuration in detail and verify that connectivity is working as expected.

Getting ready

In this recipe, we'll be using a single Docker host. It is assumed that Docker is installed and in its default configuration. You'll also need root-level access in order to inspect the `iptables` rule set.

How to do it...

As we've seen in earlier chapters, Docker does an outstanding job of managing host firewall rules on your behalf. There will likely be very few instances in which you need to view or modify the `iptables` rules as they relate to Docker. However, it's always a good idea to be able to validate the configuration to rule out `iptables` as a possible issue when you're troubleshooting container networking.

To demonstrate walking through the `iptables` rule set, we'll examine an example container that's publishing a port. The steps we perform to do this are easily transferable to examining rules for any other Docker-integrated `iptables` use cases. To do this, we'll run a simple container that exposes port `80` for publishing:

```
user@docker1:~$ docker run -dP --name web1 jonlangemak/web_server_1
```

Since we told Docker to publish any exposed ports, we know that this container should have its exposed port of `80` published to the host. To verify that the port is actually being published, we can check the `iptables` rule set. The first thing we'd want to do is to make sure that the destination NAT required for port publication is in place. To examine an `iptables` table, we can use the `iptables` command and pass the following parameters:

- `n`: Tells `iptables` to use numeric information in the output for things such as addresses and ports
- `L`: Tells `iptables` that you want to output a list of rules
- `v`: Tells `iptables` to provide verbose output, so we can see all of the rule information as well as rule counters
- `t`: Tells `iptables` to only show information from a specific table

Putting that all together, we can use the command `sudo iptables -nL -t nat` to view the rules in the NAT table of the host:

```
user@docker1:~$ sudo iptables -vnL -t nat
Chain PREROUTING (policy ACCEPT 0 packets, 0 bytes)
 pkts bytes target     prot opt in     out     source               destination
    4   224 DOCKER     all  --  *      *       0.0.0.0/0            0.0.0.0/0            ADDRTYPE match dst-type LOCAL

Chain INPUT (policy ACCEPT 0 packets, 0 bytes)
 pkts bytes target     prot opt in     out     source               destination

Chain OUTPUT (policy ACCEPT 1 packets, 69 bytes)
 pkts bytes target     prot opt in     out     source               destination
    0     0 DOCKER     all  --  *      *       0.0.0.0/0           !127.0.0.0/8          ADDRTYPE match dst-type LOCAL

Chain POSTROUTING (policy ACCEPT 4 packets, 225 bytes)
 pkts bytes target     prot opt in     out     source               destination
    0     0 MASQUERADE all  --  *      !docker0 172.17.0.0/16        0.0.0.0/0
    0     0 MASQUERADE tcp  --  *      *       172.17.0.2           172.17.0.2           tcp dpt:80

Chain DOCKER (2 references)
 pkts bytes target     prot opt in     out     source               destination
    0     0 RETURN     all  --  docker0 *      0.0.0.0/0            0.0.0.0/0
    3   156 DNAT       tcp  --  !docker0 *     0.0.0.0/0            0.0.0.0/0            tcp dpt:32768 to:172.17.0.2:80
user@docker1:~$
```

Note that all the default table and chain policies we'll examine in this recipe are ACCEPT. If the default chain policy is ACCEPT, it means that even if we don't get a rule match, the flow will still be allowed. Docker will create the rules regardless of what the default policy is set to.

If you're not comfortable with `iptables`, interpreting this output can be a bit daunting. Even though we're looking at the NAT table, we need to know what chain is being processed for inbound communication to the host. In our case, since the traffic is coming into the host, the chain we're interested with is the `PREROUTING` chain. Let's walk through how the table is processed:

- The first line in the `PREROUTING` chain looks for traffic destined for `LOCAL` or the host itself. Since the traffic is destined to an IP address on one of the host's interfaces, we match on this rule and perform the action that references jumping to a new chain named `DOCKER`.

- In the `DOCKER` chain, we hit the first rule that is looking for traffic coming into the `docker0` bridge. Since this traffic isn't coming into the `docker0` bridge, the rule is passed over and we move to the next rule in the chain.

- The second rule in the `DOCKER` chain is looking for traffic that's not coming into the `docker0` bridge and has a destination port of TCP `32768`. We match this rule and perform the action to perform a destination NAT to `172.17.0.2` port `80`.

The processing in the table looks like this:

```
 ┌─────Traffic entering the NAT table (inbound traffic)
 │
 │    user@docker1:~$ sudo iptables -vnL -t nat
 │    Chain PREROUTING (policy ACCEPT 0 packets, 0 bytes)
 │     pkts bytes target     prot opt in     out     source           destination
 └──►   4   224 DOCKER     all  --  *      *       0.0.0.0/0        0.0.0.0/0          ADDRTYPE match dst-type LOCAL
 
      Chain INPUT (policy ACCEPT 0 packets, 0 bytes)
       pkts bytes target     prot opt in     out     source           destination
 
      Chain OUTPUT (policy ACCEPT 1 packets, 69 bytes)
       pkts bytes target     prot opt in     out     source           destination
         0     0 DOCKER     all  --  *      *       0.0.0.0/0        !127.0.0.0/8        ADDRTYPE match dst-type LOCAL
 
      Chain POSTROUTING (policy ACCEPT 4 packets, 225 bytes)
       pkts bytes target     prot opt in     out     source           destination
         0     0 MASQUERADE all  --  *      *       !docker0 172.17.0.0/16   0.0.0.0/0
         0     0 MASQUERADE tcp  --  *      *       172.17.0.2       172.17.0.2         tcp dpt:80
 
      Chain DOCKER (2 references)
       pkts bytes target     prot opt in     out     source           destination
 ──►   0     0 RETURN     all  --  docker0 *       0.0.0.0/0        0.0.0.0/0
 ──►   3   156 DNAT       tcp  --  !docker0 *      0.0.0.0/0        0.0.0.0/0          tcp dpt:32768 to:172.17.0.2:80
      user@docker1:~$
```

The arrows in the preceding image indicate the traffic flow as the traffic traverses the NAT table. In this example, we only have one container running on the host, so it's pretty easy to see which rules are being processed.

 You can couple this sort of output with the `watch` command to get a live output of the counters, for instance:
`sudo watch --interval 0 iptables -vnL -t nat`

Now that we've traversed the NAT table, the next thing we need to worry about is the filter table. We can view the filter table in much the same way that we viewed the NAT table:

```
user@docker1:~$ sudo iptables -vnL -t filter
Chain INPUT (policy ACCEPT 2248 packets, 103K bytes)
 pkts bytes target       prot opt in     out     source               destination
Chain FORWARD (policy ACCEPT 0 packets, 0 bytes)
 pkts bytes target       prot opt in     out     source               destination
   48  8746 DOCKER-ISOLATION  all  --  *      *       0.0.0.0/0            0.0.0.0/0
   25  5016 DOCKER      all  --  *      docker0 0.0.0.0/0            0.0.0.0/0
    0     0 ACCEPT      all  --  *      docker0 0.0.0.0/0            0.0.0.0/0            ctstate RELATED,ESTABLISHED
   23  3730 ACCEPT      all  --  docker0 !docker0 0.0.0.0/0            0.0.0.0/0
    0     0 ACCEPT      all  --  docker0 docker0 0.0.0.0/0            0.0.0.0/0
Chain OUTPUT (policy ACCEPT 3597 packets, 254K bytes)
 pkts bytes target       prot opt in     out     source               destination
Chain DOCKER (1 references)
 pkts bytes target       prot opt in     out     source               destination
   25  5016 ACCEPT      tcp  --  !docker0 docker0 0.0.0.0/0            172.17.0.2           tcp dpt:80
Chain DOCKER-ISOLATION (1 references)
 pkts bytes target       prot opt in     out     source               destination
   48  8746 RETURN      all  --  *      *       0.0.0.0/0            0.0.0.0/0
user@docker1:~$
```

At first glance, we can see that this table is laid out slightly different than the NAT table was. For instance, we have different chains in this table than we did with the NAT table. In our case, the chain we're interested in for inbound published port communication would be the forward chain. This is because the host is forwarding, or routing, the traffic to the container. The traffic will traverse this table as follows:

- The first line in the forward chain sends the traffic directly to the DOCKER-ISOLATION chain.

- In this case, the only rule in the DOCKER-ISOLATION chain is a rule to send the traffic back, so we resume reviewing rules in the FORWARD table.

- The second rule in the forward table says that if the traffic is going out the docker0 bridge to send the traffic to the DOCKER chain. Since our destination (172.17.0.20) lives out the docker0 bridge, we match on this rule and jump to the DOCKER chain.

- In the DOCKER chain, we inspect the first rule and determine that it's looking for traffic that is destined to the container IP address on port TCP 80 and is going out, but not in, the docker0 bridge. We match on this rule and the flow is accepted.

The processing in the table looks like this:

Traffic entering the filter table (inbound traffic)

```
user@docker1:~$ sudo iptables -vnL -t filter
chain INPUT (policy ACCEPT 2248 packets, 103K bytes)
 pkts bytes target       prot opt in     out     source               destination
Chain FORWARD (policy ACCEPT 0 packets, 0 bytes)
 pkts bytes target       prot opt in     out     source               destination
   48  8746 DOCKER-ISOLATION  all  --  *      *       0.0.0.0/0            0.0.0.0/0
   25  5016 DOCKER      all  --  *      docker0 0.0.0.0/0            0.0.0.0/0
    0     0 ACCEPT      all  --  *      docker0 0.0.0.0/0            0.0.0.0/0            ctstate RELATED,ESTABLISHED
   23  3730 ACCEPT      all  --  docker0 !docker0 0.0.0.0/0            0.0.0.0/0
    0     0 ACCEPT      all  --  docker0 docker0 0.0.0.0/0            0.0.0.0/0
chain OUTPUT (policy ACCEPT 3597 packets, 254K bytes)
 pkts bytes target       prot opt in     out     source               destination
Chain DOCKER (1 references)
 pkts bytes target       prot opt in     out     source               destination
   25  5016 ACCEPT      tcp  --  !docker0 docker0 0.0.0.0/0            172.17.0.2           tcp dpt:80
Chain DOCKER-ISOLATION (1 references)
 pkts bytes target       prot opt in     out     source               destination
   48  8746 RETURN      all  --  *      *       0.0.0.0/0            0.0.0.0/0
user@docker1:~$
```

Passing the filter table is the last step published port traffic has to take in order to reach the container. However, we've now only reached the container. We still need to account for the return traffic from the container back to the host talking to the published port. So now, we need to talk about how traffic originated from the container is handled by `iptables`.

The first table we'll encounter with outbound traffic is the filter table. Traffic originating from the container will once again use the forward chain of the filter table. The flow would look something like this:

- The first line in the forward chain sends the traffic directly to the DOCKER-ISOLATION chain.

- In this case, the only rule in the DOCKER-ISOLATION chain is a rule to send the traffic back, so we resume reviewing rules in the FORWARD table.

- The second rule in the forward table says that if the traffic is going from the docker0 bridge, send the traffic to the DOCKER chain. Since our traffic is going into the docker0 bridge rather than out, this rule is passed over and we move to the next rule in the chain.

- The third rule in the forward table says that if the traffic is going out from the docker0 bridge and its connection state is RELATED or ESTABLISHED that the flow should be accepted. This traffic is going into the docker0 bridge, so we won't match this rule either. However, it is worth pointing out that this rule is used to allow return traffic for flows initiated from the container. It's just not hit as part of the initial outbound connection since that represents a new flow.

- The fourth rule in the forward table says that if the traffic is going in the docker0 bridge, but not out the docker0 bridge, to accept it. Because our traffic is going into the docker0 bridge, we match on this rule and the traffic is accepted.

The processing in the table looks like this:

Traffic entering the filter table (outbound traffic)

```
user@docker1:~$ sudo iptables -vnL -t filter
Chain INPUT (policy ACCEPT 2248 packets, 103K bytes)
 pkts bytes target     prot opt in     out     source               destination

Chain FORWARD (policy ACCEPT 0 packets, 0 bytes)
 pkts bytes target          prot opt in     out     source               destination
   48  8746 DOCKER-ISOLATION all  --  *      *       0.0.0.0/0            0.0.0.0/0
   25  5016 DOCKER           all  --  *      docker0 0.0.0.0/0            0.0.0.0/0
    0     0 ACCEPT           all  --  *      docker0 0.0.0.0/0            0.0.0.0/0           ctstate RELATED,ESTABLISHED
   23  3730 ACCEPT           all  --  docker0 !docker0 0.0.0.0/0          0.0.0.0/0
    0     0 ACCEPT           all  --  docker0 docker0 0.0.0.0/0           0.0.0.0/0

Chain OUTPUT (policy ACCEPT 3597 packets, 254K bytes)
 pkts bytes target     prot opt in     out     source               destination

Chain DOCKER (1 references)
 pkts bytes target     prot opt in     out     source               destination
   25  5016 ACCEPT     tcp  --  !docker0 docker0 0.0.0.0/0            172.17.0.2           tcp dpt:80

Chain DOCKER-ISOLATION (1 references)
 pkts bytes target     prot opt in     out     source               destination
   48  8746 RETURN     all  --  *      *       0.0.0.0/0            0.0.0.0/0
user@docker1:~$
```

The next table we'd hit for outbound traffic is the NAT table. This time, we want to look at the POSTROUTING chain. In this case, we match the first rule of the chain which is looking for traffic that is not going out the docker0 bridge and is sourced from the docker0 bridge subnet (172.17.0.0/16):

```
────  Traffic entering the NAT table (outbound traffic)
user@docker1:~$ sudo iptables -nvL -t nat
[sudo] password for user:
Chain PREROUTING (policy ACCEPT 3472 packets, 175K bytes)
 pkts bytes target     prot opt in     out    source               destination
 1583 94964 DOCKER     all  --  *      *      0.0.0.0/0            0.0.0.0/0           ADDRTYPE match dst-type LOCAL

Chain INPUT (policy ACCEPT 1559 packets, 93540 bytes)
 pkts bytes target     prot opt in     out    source               destination

Chain OUTPUT (policy ACCEPT 14 packets, 1048 bytes)
 pkts bytes target     prot opt in     out    source               destination
    0     0 DOCKER     all  --  *      *      0.0.0.0/0            !127.0.0.0/8         ADDRTYPE match dst-type LOCAL

Chain POSTROUTING (policy ACCEPT 14 packets, 1048 bytes)
 pkts bytes target     prot opt in     out      source             destination
→   3   228 MASQUERADE all  --  *      !docker0 172.17.0.0/16      0.0.0.0/0
    0     0 MASQUERADE tcp  --  *      *        172.17.0.2         172.17.0.2          tcp dpt:80

Chain DOCKER (2 references)
 pkts bytes target     prot opt in       out    source             destination
    0     0 RETURN     all  --  docker0  *      0.0.0.0/0          0.0.0.0/0
    0     0 DNAT       tcp  --  !docker0 *      0.0.0.0/0          0.0.0.0/0           tcp dpt:32768 to:172.17.0.2:80
user@docker1:~$
```

The action for this rule is to MASQUERADE, which will hide the traffic behind one of the hosts interfaces based on the hosts routing table.

Taking this same approach, you can easily validate other iptables flows related to Docker. Granted, as the number of containers scale, this becomes a harder task. However, since the majority of rules are written on a per container basis, the hit counters will be unique to each container, making it easier to narrow the scope.

> For more information on the order in which iptables tables and chains are processed, take a look at this iptables web page and the associated flow charts at http://www.iptables.info/en/structure-of-iptables.html.

Verifying name resolution

DNS resolution for containers has always been rather straightforward. The container received the same DNS configuration as the host. However, with the advent of user-defined networks and the embedded DNS server, this has now become a little trickier. A common problem in many of the DNS issues I've seen is not understanding how the embedded DNS server works and how to validate that it's working correctly. In this recipe, we'll step through a container DNS configuration to validate which DNS server it is using to resolve specific namespaces.

Getting ready

In this recipe, we'll be using a single Docker host. It is assumed that Docker is installed and in its default configuration. You'll also need root-level access in order to inspect and change the host's networking and firewall configuration.

How to do it...

The standard DNS configuration for Docker without user-defined networks is to simply copy the DNS configuration from the host into the container. In these cases, the DNS resolution is straightforward:

```
user@docker1:~$ docker run -dP --name web1 jonlangemak/web_server_1
e5735b30ce675d40de8c62fffe28e338a14b03560ce29622f0bb46edf639375f
user@docker1:~$
user@docker1:~$ docker exec web1 more /etc/resolv.conf
# Dynamic resolv.conf(5) file for glibc resolver(3) generated by
resolvconf(8)
#       DO NOT EDIT THIS FILE BY HAND -- YOUR CHANGES WILL BE OVERWRITTEN
nameserver <your local DNS server>
search lab.lab
user@docker1:~$
user@docker1:~$ more /etc/resolv.conf
nameserver <your local DNS server>
search lab.lab
user@docker1:~$
```

In these cases, all DNS requests will go straight to the defined DNS server. This means that our container can resolve any DNS records that our host can:

```
user@docker1:~$ docker exec -it web1 ping docker2.lab.lab -c 2
PING docker2.lab.lab (10.10.10.102): 48 data bytes
56 bytes from 10.10.10.102: icmp_seq=0 ttl=63 time=0.471 ms
56 bytes from 10.10.10.102: icmp_seq=1 ttl=63 time=0.453 ms
--- docker2.lab.lab ping statistics ---
2 packets transmitted, 2 packets received, 0% packet loss
round-trip min/avg/max/stddev = 0.453/0.462/0.471/0.000 ms
user@docker1:~$
```

Coupled with the fact that Docker will masquerade this traffic to the IP address of the host itself makes this a simple and easily maintainable solution.

However, this gets a little trickier when we start using user-defined networks. This is because user-defined networks provide for container name resolution. That is, one container can resolve the name of another container without the use of static or manual host file entries and linking. This is a great feature, but it can cause some confusion if you don't understand how the container receives its DNS configuration. For instance, let's now create a new user-defined network:

```
user@docker1:~$ docker network create -d bridge mybridge1
e8afb0e506298e558baf5408053c64c329b8e605d6ad12efbf10e81f538df7b9
user@docker1:~$
```

Let's now start a new container named web2 on this network:

```
user@docker1:~$ docker run -dP --name web2 --net \
mybridge1 jonlangemak/web_server_2
1b38ad04c3c1be7b0f1af28550bf402dcde1515899234e4b09e482da0a560a0a
user@docker1:~$
```

Now if we connect our existing web1 container to this bridge, we should find that web1 can resolve the container web2 by name:

```
user@docker1:~$ docker network connect mybridge1 web1
user@docker1:~$ docker exec -it web1 ping web2 -c 2
PING web2 (172.18.0.2): 48 data bytes
56 bytes from 172.18.0.2: icmp_seq=0 ttl=64 time=0.100 ms
56 bytes from 172.18.0.2: icmp_seq=1 ttl=64 time=0.086 ms
--- web2 ping statistics ---
2 packets transmitted, 2 packets received, 0% packet loss
round-trip min/avg/max/stddev = 0.086/0.093/0.100/0.000 ms
user@docker1:~$
```

The problem here is that in order to facilitate this, Docker had to change the DNS configuration of the web1 container. In doing so, it injects the embedded DNS server in the middle of a containers DNS request. So before, when we were talking directly to the hosts DNS server, we are now talking to the embedded DNS server:

```
user@docker1:~$ docker exec -t  web1 more /etc/resolv.conf
search lab.lab
nameserver 127.0.0.11
options ndots:0
user@docker1:~$
```

This is required for DNS resolution to containers to work, but it has an interesting side effect. The embedded DNS server reads the host's `/etc/resolv.conf` file and uses any name servers defined in that file as forwarders for the embedded DNS server. The net effect of this is that you don't notice the embedded DNS server since it's still forwarding requests it can't answer to the host's DNS server. However, it only programs these forwarders if they are defined. If they don't exist or are set to `127.0.0.1`, then Docker programs the forwarders to be Google's public DNS server (`8.8.8.8` and `8.4.4.4`).

Although this makes good sense, there are rare circumstances in which your local DNS server happens to be `127.0.0.1`. For instance, you happen to be running some type of local DNS resolver on the same host or using a DNS forwarder application such as **DNSMasq**. In those cases, there are some complications that can be caused by Docker forwarding the container's DNS requests off to the aforementioned external DNS servers instead of the one locally defined. Namely, internal DNS zones will no longer be resolvable:

```
user@docker1:~$ docker exec -it web1 ping docker2.lab.lab
ping: unknown host
user@docker1:~$
```

 This can also cause general resolution issues because it is common to block DNS traffic to external DNS servers preferring instead to force internal endpoints to use internal DNS servers.

In these scenarios, there are a couple of ways to address this. You can either run the container with a specific DNS server by passing the DNS flag at container runtime:

```
user@docker1:~$ docker run -dP --name web2 --net mybridge1 \
--dns <your local DNS server> jonlangemak/web_server_2
```

Otherwise, you can set the DNS server at the Docker service level, which the embedded DNS server will then use as the forwarder:

```
ExecStart=/usr/bin/dockerd --dns=<your local DNS server>
```

In either case, if you're having container resolution issues, always check and see what the container has configured in its `/etc/resolv.conf` file. If it's `127.0.0.11`, that indicates you're using the Docker embedded DNS server. If you are, and you're still having issues, make sure that you validate the host DNS configuration to determine what the embedded DNS server is consuming for a forwarder. If there isn't one defined or it's `127.0.0.1`, then make sure that you tell the Docker service what DNS server it should be passing to containers in one of the two ways defined earlier.

Building a test container

One of the tenants of building Docker containers is to keep them small and lean. In some cases, this can limit your troubleshooting options as the containers won't have many of the common Linux networking tools as part of their image. While not ideal, it is sometimes nice to have a container image that has these tools installed so that you can troubleshoot the network from the container perspective. In this chapter, we'll review how to build a Docker image specifically for this purpose.

Getting ready

In this recipe, we'll be using a single Docker network host. It is assumed that Docker is installed and in its default configuration. You'll also need root-level access in order to inspect and change the hosts networking and firewall configuration.

How to do it...

A Docker image is built by defining a Dockerfile. The Dockerfile defines what base image to use as well as commands to run inside of the container. In my example, I'll define the Dockerfile as follows:

```
FROM ubuntu:16.04
MAINTAINER Jon Langemak jon@interubernet.com
RUN apt-get update && apt-get install -y apache2 net-tools \
inetutils-ping curl dnsutils vim ethtool tcpdump
ADD index.html /var/www/html/index.html
ENV APACHE_RUN_USER www-data
ENV APACHE_RUN_GROUP www-data
ENV APACHE_LOG_DIR /var/log/apache2
ENV APACHE_PID_FILE /var/run/apache2/apache2.pid
ENV APACHE_LOCK_DIR /var/run/apache2
RUN mkdir -p /var/run/apache2
RUN chown www-data:www-data /var/run/apache2
EXPOSE 80
CMD ["/usr/sbin/apache2", "-D", "FOREGROUND"]
```

The goal of this image is twofold. First, I wanted to be able to run the container in detached mode and have it offer a service. This would allow me to define the container and verify that things such as port publishing were working off the host. This container image provides me with a known good container that will publish a service on port 80. For this purpose, we're using Apache to host a simple index page.

The index file is pulled into the image at build time and can be customized by you. I use a simple HTML page, `index.html`, that shows big red font such as this:

```
<body>
   <html>
      <h1><span style="color:#FF0000;font-size:72px;">Test Web Server -
Running on port 80</span>
      </h1>
</body>
   </html>
```

Second, the image has a lot of network tools installed as part of the image. You'll notice that I'm installing the following packages:

- `net-tools`: This provides network utilities to view and configure interfaces
- `inetutils-ping`: This provides ping functionality
- `curl`: This is to pull files from other network endpoints
- `dnsutils`: This is to resolve DNS names and other DNS tracing
- `ethtool`: This is to get information and stats from interfaces
- `tcpdump`: This is to do packet capture from within the container

If you define this Dockerfile, as well as it's required supporting files (an index page), you can build the image as follows:

```
sudo docker build -t <tag name for image> <path files ('.' If local)>
```

 There are a lot of options you can define when building an image. Take a look at `docker build --help` for more information.

Docker will then process the Dockerfile and, if successful, it will generate a `docker image` file, which you can then push to your container registry of choice for consumption on other hosts with `docker pull`.

Once built, you can run it and verify that the tools are working as expected. Having `ethtool` within the container means that we can easily determine the host-side VETH end of the VETH pair:

```
user@docker1:~$ docker run -dP --name nettest jonlangemak/net_tools
user@docker1:~$ docker exec -it nettest /bin/bash
root@2ef59fcc0f60:/# ethtool -S eth0
NIC statistics:
     peer_ifindex: 5
root@2ef59fcc0f60:/#
```

We can also perform local `tcpdump` actions to verify traffic reaching the container:

```
root@2ef59fcc0f60:/# tcpdump -qnn -i eth0
tcpdump: verbose output suppressed, use -v or -vv for full protocol
decode
listening on eth0, link-type EN10MB (Ethernet), capture size 65535 bytes
15:17:43.442243 IP 10.20.30.41.54974 > 172.17.0.3.80: tcp 0
15:17:43.442286 IP 172.17.0.3.80 > 10.20.30.41.54974: tcp 0
```

As your use cases change, you can modify the Dockerfile to make it more specific to your own use cases. Being able to troubleshoot from within the container can be a big help when diagnosing connectivity issues.

 This image is just an example. There are many ways that this can be made more lightweight. I decided to use Ubuntu as the base image just for the sake of familiarity. The image described earlier is fairly heavy because of this.

Resetting the local Docker network database

With the advent of user-defined networks, users are able to define custom network types for their containers. Once defined, these networks persist through system reboots until they are deleted by an administrator. In order for this persistence to work, Docker needs some place to store information related to your user-defined networks. The answer is a database file that's local to the host. In some rare cases, this database can get out of sync with the current state of the containers on the host or become corrupt. This can cause issues related to deleting containers, deleting networks, and starting the Docker service. In this recipe, we'll show you how to remove the database to restore Docker back to its default network configuration.

Getting ready

In this recipe, we'll be using a single Docker network host. It is assumed that Docker is installed and in its default configuration. You'll also need root-level access in order to inspect and change the host's networking and firewall configuration.

How to do it...

Docker stores information related to user-defined networks in a database stored on the local host. This database is written to when networks are defined and read from when the service starts. In the rare case that this database gets out of sync or becomes corrupt, you can delete the database and restart the Docker service in order to reset the Docker user-defined networks and restore the three default network types (bridge, host, and none).

> Warning: Deleting this database deletes any and all Docker user-defined networks on the host. It is wise to only do this as a last resort and if you have the capability of recreating the networks that were previously defined. All other troubleshooting options should be pursued before attempting this and you should create a backup of the file before deleting it.

The database is named `local-kv.db` and is stored in the path `/var/lib/network/files/`. Accessing and or deleting the file requires root-level access. For the purpose of this example, we'll switch to the root user in order to make browsing this protected directory easier:

```
user@docker1:~$ sudo su
[sudo] password for user:
root@docker1:/home/user# cd /var/lib/docker/network/files
root@docker1:/var/lib/docker/network/files# ls -al
total 72
drwxr-x--- 2 root root 32768 Aug  9 21:27 .
drwxr-x--- 3 root root  4096 Apr  3 21:04 ..
-rw-r--r-- 1 root root 65536 Aug  9 21:27 local-kv.db
root@docker1:/var/lib/docker/network/files#
```

To demonstrate what happens when we delete this file, let's first create a new user-defined network and attach a container to it:

```
root@docker1:~# docker network create -d bridge mybridge
c765f1d24345e4652b137383839aabdd3b01b1441d1d81ad4b4e17229ddca7ac
root@docker1:~# docker run -d --name web1 --net mybridge jonlangemak/web_server_1
24a6497e99de9e114b617b65673a8a50492655e9869dbf7f7930dd7f9f930b5e
root@docker1:~#
```

Let's now delete the file `local-db.kv`:

```
root@docker1:/var/lib/docker/network/files# rm local-kv.db
```

While this has no immediate effect on the running container, it does prevent us from adding, removing, or starting new containers associated with this user-defined network:

```
root@docker1:/~# docker run -d --name web2 --net mybridge \
jonlangemak/web_server_2
2ef7e52f44c93412ea7eaa413f523020a65f1a9fa6fd6761ffa6edea157c2623
```
docker: Error response from daemon: failed to update store for object type *libnetwork.endpointCnt: Key not found in store.
```
root@docker1:~#
```

After deleting the `boltdb` database file, `local-kv.db`, you'll need to restart the Docker service in order for Docker to recreate it with the default settings:

```
root@docker1:/var/lib/docker/network/files# cd
root@docker1:~# systemctl restart docker
root@docker1:~# ls /var/lib/docker/network/files
local-kv.db
root@docker1:~# docker network ls
NETWORK ID          NAME                DRIVER
bfd1ba1175a9        none                null
0740840aef37        host                host
97cbc0e116d7        bridge              bridge
root@docker1:/var/lib/docker/network/files#
```

Now that the file is recreated, you'll once again be able to create user-defined networks. However, any containers that were attached to previously configure user-defined network will now fail to start:

```
root@docker1:~# docker start web1
```
Error response from daemon: network mybridge not found
```
Error: failed to start containers: web1
root@docker1:~#
```

This is expected behavior since Docker still believes that the container should have an interface on that network:

```
root@docker1:~# docker inspect web1
…<Additional output removed for brevity>…
        "Networks": {
            "mybridge": {
                "IPAMConfig": null,
                "Links": null,
```

```
            "Aliases": null,

            "NetworkID":
"c765f1d24345e4652b137383839aabdd3b01b1441d1d81ad4b4e17229ddca7ac",

...<Additional output removed for brevity>...
root@docker1:~#
```

To remedy this problem, you have two options. First, you can recreate the user-defined network named `mybridge` using the same configuration options from when it was initially provisioned. If this doesn't work, your only alternative is to delete the container and restart a new instance referencing a newly created or default network.

> There has been some discussion on GitHub of newer versions of Docker supporting a `--force` flag when using the `docker network disconnect` subcommand. In version 1.10, this parameter exists, but still doesn't like that the user-defined network does not exist. If you're running a newer version, this might be worth trying as well.

Index

W

69606279R00209

Made in the USA
Lexington, KY
02 November 2017